HOUSING POLITIC
UNITED KINGI

Power, planning and protest

Brian Lund

First published in Great Britain in 2016 by

Policy Press
University of Bristol
1-9 Old Park Hill
Bristol
BS2 8BB
UK
t: +44 (0)117 954 5940
pp-info@bristol.ac.uk
www.policypress.co.uk

North America office:
Policy Press
c/o The University of Chicago Press
1427 East 60th Street
Chicago, IL 60637, USA
t: +1 773 702 7700
f: +1 773-702-9756
sales@press.uchicago.edu
www.press.uchicago.edu

© Policy Press 2016

British Library Cataloguing in Publication Data
A catalogue record for this book is available from the British Library

Library of Congress Cataloging-in-Publication Data
A catalog record for this book has been requested

ISBN 978-1-4473-2707-3 hardcover
ISBN 978-1-4473-2708-0 paperback
ISBN 978-1-4473-2711-0 ePub
ISBN 978-1-4473-2712-7 Mobi
ISBN 978-1-4473-2710-3 ePdf

Cover design by Hayes Design
Front cover image: Getty
Printed and bound in Great Britain by CPI Group (UK) Ltd, Croydon, CR0 4YY
Policy Press uses environmentally responsible print partners

Contents

Acknowledgements

Thanks are due to a number of people who have contributed to the publication of this book. I am greatly indebted to Policy Press staff for their help. My more personal gratitude is to Sukey, Rachel, Daniel, Carly, Bethany and Max for their continual support and encouragement. Although I would like to, I must not forget Stanley, a ferocious cat.

Preface

Housing has been labeled a 'wicked' problem: complex, territorial, open-ended and intractable. *Housing Politics in the United Kingdom: Power, Planning and Protest* underscores the role of politics in generating this 'wickedness', highlighting the 'actors' involved in the political process and the entrenched territorial electoral politics involved in the 'housing question'. It concentrates on preparing, disputing and implementing policy rather than on policy outcomes and the social and economic determinants of continuity and change.

Its subtitle reflects the book's themes. *Power* is acquired formally through the electoral system but is exercised through a variety of mechanisms, including 'governmentality' – the techniques that regulate and order the people's behaviour. *Planning* draws attention to attempts to modify the role of markets in housing outcomes and includes land-use planning and the influence of alleged 'rational' solutions applied to 'the housing problem'. *Protest* concerns the 'outsiders' in the political system and their attempts to secure a voice and perhaps eventually become the power-holders.

Chapter One sets out the book's principal themes, outlining the major theoretical approaches framing the content of *Housing Politics in the United Kingdom: Power, Planning and Protest*: the 'new institutionalism', social constructionism and public choice theory.

Chapter Two explores political conflicts on the land issue. It charts fluctuations in political focus from ownership to 'betterment' taxation and then to development rights, illustrating the interactions between local and national political concerns. Chapter Three reviews the territorial politics of urban renewal, with its strong connections to campaigns for the preservation of rural Britain.

Chapter Four chronicles private landlordism's fall and rise analysing the role of protest movements and internal and external class conflicts in the demise of private landlordism and the political implications of the recent rapid increase in the number of people joining 'generation rent'.

Chapter Five examines the political salience of the 'property-owning democracy' idea and its support from the financial institutions, whereas, in Chapter Six, the fluctuations in the political base of local authority housing, once the major rival to homeownership as a replacement for private landlordism, are charted.

Chapter Seven is concerned with the changing fortunes of 'housing's third arm' – 'voluntary' housing associations. It highlights the attempts made to shape the sector's hybrid nature for political purposes. Chapter

Eight, on homelessness, has a different theme to the other chapters. It concentrates on how the discourses involved in homelessness definitions are linked to causal notions to construct messages to the public about the problem's extent, with such messages carrying implications for interpreting other social issues. Chapter Nine explores devolution's impact, asking not only 'Where is the difference?', but also 'What political factors have created the differences?'.

Chapters Two to Nine are organised around topics that cut across historical periods. Chapter Ten, organised on the themes of power, planning and protest, reviews the political factors that have shaped housing policy and examines the contemporary politics of housing.

References to Cabinet papers and political biographies feature prominently in the book and there is an abundance of 'actor' names. Ideas are important in both the political communiqués that influence the electorate and interactions between those in power.

Housing Politics in the United Kingdom: Power, Planning and Protest has been written to complement the third edition of *Understanding Housing Policy*, to be published in 2017, which adopts a more conventional approach, concentrating on housing policy outcomes.

ONE

Housing and politics

With rapid population growth, a long-term dearth in new housing construction, 'generation rent', 'greenfield' and green belt controversies, the 'austerity' agenda, and increasing homelessness, housing had a higher political profile in 2015 than at any time since the 1970s. When the 2015 general election hustings began, housing ranked eighth in the issues mentioned by electors 'as the most important facing Britain today' and its importance reached fifth place just before the election (Ipsos Mori, 2015a). The *London Evening Standard* (2015) said 'housing is the big election issue for London', and Shelter claimed that marginal seats nationwide were 'more likely to be worse affected by the housing shortage, especially when it comes to the affordability of home ownership' (Shelter, 2015a, p 1). However, political parties contest general elections in vivid colours, and after the election result declaration, it was clear that 'non-policy' issues, such as leader competence and a perceived threat to England from the Scottish National Party, had a major impact (Ross, 2015; Cowley and Kavanagh, 2016). Housing was not significant in influencing the overall 2015 general election outcome.

In contrast, housing was the overwhelming public concern in the 1945 general election campaign. In a 1945 Gallup poll, 54% of the electorate said the housing shortage was their top priority, well above the second concern, full employment, at only 13% (British Institute of Public Opinion Polls, 1945). A Mass Observation study carried out just before polling day claimed that 'housing was mentioned so often that everything else became by comparison unimportant' (Jones, 2000, p 100). Few houses had been built in the wartime years and the destruction or serious damage to 700,000 homes added to unmet needs in the interwar period. Demobbed soldiers, organised by the Communist Party through a secret committee of ex-servicemen known as the 'Vigilantes', began to squat in empty property and disused army camps. Labour's 1945 manifesto promised to 'proceed with a housing programme with the maximum practical speed until every family in this island has a good standard of accommodation'. New housing would be planned and allocated according to 'need', with the central state controlling building materials and with new powers available to local government 'to acquire land for public purposes wherever the public interest so requires' (Labour Party, 1945). The electorate supported Labour, with twice as many people believing that Labour was more likely to overcome the housing shortage than the Conservatives (Fielding, 1992).

Housing the people

Glasgow's scheme for a planned 'New Jerusalem' represented an extreme of a post-war approach to housing supply adopted in many cities. The plan, *First Planning Report to the Highways and Planning Committee* (Bruce, 1945), produced by Robert Bruce, Glasgow's 'Master of Works and City Engineer', involved demolishing a large part of the city centre and rebuilding Glasgow on Le Corbusier's 'Radiant City' principles (Le Corbusier, 1964 [1933]). Inner-city slum dwellers would be rehoused in flats on Glasgow's outside edge.

Turner (1976, p 62, emphasis in original) states:

> Housing must, therefore, be used as a verb rather than as a noun – as a process that subsumes products. Real values are those that lie in the relationships *between* the elements of housing action – between the actors, their activities and their achievements.

Bruce's plan reflected the term 'housing' used as a verb, that is, 'the act of one who houses or puts under shelter' (Dictionary.com, 2016). Although this political process has been overt in council housing, especially with regard to slum clearance programmes, it has not been restricted to the domain now branded 'social' housing. 'Housing', as a verb, applies 'to the set of actions which (*inter alia*) plans, produces, finances, allocates and maintains dwellings' (Maclennan, 2012, p 9). Land release is salient to housing as a political process, as are the power relations involved in decisions to endorse or stigmatise particular housing tenures, taxation policy, and housing as a mechanism in economic management (see Lund, 2017).

The political dimension

The *Oxford English Dictionary* (2013) defines 'politics' as 'the activities associated with the governance of a country or other area, especially the debate or conflict among individuals or parties having or hoping to achieve power'. Politics entails struggles to secure control, make decisions and implement them, supported by the state's authority, ultimately backed by its monopoly in using force within its territorial area. It is about 'the rules of the game' in establishing the authority to determine 'who gets what, when, how' (Lasswell, 1951, p 1), to which 'why' – how the action is justified – can be added. It involves power, 'the ability to get others to act in a particular way' (Jones et al, 1994, p 6).

In the UK, political institutions have evolved to channel the conflicts involved in control struggles and thereby legitimise decisions. These formal political arenas remain disputed: the United Kingdom's relationship to the European Union (EU), independence for Scotland and the role of local government are contemporary examples. Power contests are also observable outside the particular institutions deemed 'government'. The authority to determine which issues enter the formal political process is important, as is the ability to mould the dominant explanations applied to housing issues that produce policy initiatives.

According to some commentators, political influences on housing outcomes have been underplayed in the 'housing studies' narrative. Lee (2007, p 8) comments:

> This literature has spawned an administrative history of housing concerned largely with policy.... More critically, the tendency to assume that socio-economic shifts were at the root of change means that the ideas, intentions and strategies of politicians have not been explored.

Kemeny (1992) has argued that an 'epistemic drift' towards empiricism and policy relevance in 'housing studies' and away from 'critical' social-scientific approaches embodied in notions of the 'state', 'power' and 'ideology' produced an unhealthy reliance on power-holder definitions of housing problems – a drift intensified by official assessment of academic research output according to its policy relevance (Allen, 2016). Bengtsson (2012, p 206) identified political science as the 'missing link' in 'housing studies', and noted 'its emphasis on outcomes to the relative neglect of politics which is essentially an interaction process with a focus on how decisions are made'. This tendency to underplay political processes in explaining continuity and change in housing policy has arisen not only from a dominant 'policy perspective', but also from the influence of theories focusing on the 'impersonal' social and economic determinants of housing outcomes.

Industrialisation

Organic theory uses the body as a metaphor for society and contains both explanatory and normative dimensions. Its explanatory dimension is reflected in 'structural functionalism', a theoretical framework adopting the notion that society's survival depends on the evolution of structures to meet society's 'functional prerequisites': adaptation; goal attainment; integration; and pattern maintenance (Parsons, 1951). In the 1960s, functionalist explanations received support from an apparent convergence in national housing systems, the consequence, so it was argued, of the 'prerequisites' inherent in the 'logic of industrialisation'. A normative theory, suggesting what *must* be done, developed within organic theory. In the late 19th century, the Fabians and many 'new' Liberals viewed society as evolving to a higher, more coherent, order – towards the 'public good' – with rational social reform going with the grain of organic evolution. As Prideaux (2005, p 30) explains: 'Essentially the structural-functional position rested on the belief that, where there was a lack of subsystem adaptation to change, the appropriate response to any resultant social conflict would be social reform'.

Structural-functionalism idealised the state as an organic entity *above* politics. The perspective begat 'planning', with the Fabians believing an 'intellectual 'samurai' (Wells, 1905) should guide society into a new social order. Planning became locked into the social policy approach to 'housing studies', 'which consisted extensively of empirical, policy-related research, often undertaken for government agencies' (Clapham, 2012, p 163).

Globalisation

Globalisation, with its stress on social and economic determinants rather than politics, is a functionalist scion; as Stephens (2003, p 1011) claims, 'globalisation is only the most recent manifestation of convergence theory'. The perspective views the interchange of finance, products and ideas on a world basis as a severe restriction on the capacity of national politics to alter outcomes (Wachel, 1986), and as a rationale for 'flexible labour markets' and deregulation in a neoliberal agenda (Clapham, 2006). Globalisation has had an effect on housing finance in the UK, with, for example, the movement of international capital, often through offshore investment companies located in tax havens, into housing hotspots such as central London. However, at £32 billion in 2014 (Armstrong, 2016), this accounted for only 7% of

London residential market investment (Savills, 2014a), and housing as a commodity has characteristics – in particular, its immobility – that limits its global impact. Moreover, there are politically embedded norms and pathways in housing transactions. For example, as Aalbers (2012, p 132) points out, 'It is relatively easy for mortgage lenders in the Netherlands and the UK to take possession of the properties of households that default, but very hard or almost impossible in some European countries such as Italy'. Thus, the so-called 'global financial crisis' had dissimilar housing impacts in different countries. Wachter, Cho and Tcha (2014, p 3) note that in East Asia, the global financial crisis 'was in many ways a no show in part because of the macro prudential policies put in place following the 1997 crisis'. In Germany, Lindenthal and Eichholtz (2012, p 69) state: 'the global housing market crisis that started in 2007 largely left Germany untouched, and that also holds for the housing market boom that preceded it. Germany's housing market follows its own path'. In contrast, Ireland and Spain experienced large house price increases followed by major falls. The 'embedded' nature of housing policy was manifest in the UK during the 'credit crunch'. Alistair Darling (2011, p 114), New Labour's Chancellor throughout the 'global financial crisis', said:

> I was always less worried about Britain's housing market. I knew it would fall, that was inevitable, but in the long-run Britain's problem is that the demand for housing exceeds supply.... Ironically, the spectacular failure of successive British governments to deliver increased house-building proved to be a blessing for the housing market, which did not fall anywhere near as much as people feared.

Capitalism

Although many contemporary Marxist thinkers dismiss economic determinism as 'vulgar Marxism', Karl Marx attributed primacy to the economic structure over state politics in his historical development theory. Marxist thinking had an important role in explaining change and continuity in housing policy in the 1970s with the Conference of Socialist Economists claiming that 'in a capitalist society housing is a commodity and shows the characteristics of the commodity under capitalism analysed by Marx' (Clarke and Ginsburg, 1975, p 3). Marxists allege that housing supply and distribution respond to changes in capitalism, with the state helping to maintain capitalist accumulation. The post-2008 'global credit crunch' revived such thinking, with, for example, Bellamy and Magdoff (2009) arguing that the economic crisis was precipitated by capital's capacity to generate a vast surplus by keeping wages down, but in order to continue accumulation, capitalism required the working class to consume. The answer was debt and the eventual inability of the working class to pay this debt produced the crisis. Piketty's (2014) *Capital in the Twenty-First Century* reinforced this approach by demonstrating that, as a general rule, inequality grows faster than economic output; hence, without robust collective intervention, income and wealth will become more concentrated. Since the 1980s, the income share going to the top 1% of UK and US households had doubled, with implications for housing wealth and space distribution (Dorling, 2014a).

Engels (1997 [1872], p 2) was scathing in his condemnation of the state's inability to respond to the 'housing question', declaring that 'the capitalist order of society reproduces again and again the evils which are to be remedied with such inevitable necessity that even in England the remedying of them has hardly advanced a single step'. He attacked Proudhon's notion that working-class housing conditions could be improved by replacing private landlordism with worker cooperatives, claiming 'No matter how much the landlord may overreach the tenant it is still only a transfer of already existing, previously produced value' (Engels, 1997 [1872], p 19).

To Engels, worker exploitation occurred through the appropriation of value created in the production process. The housing crisis was a capitalist crisis in which housing conditions formed 'just one of the innumerable smaller, secondary evils' (Engels, 1997 [1872], p 18). However, other interpretations of the state's role in capitalism, based on Marx's earlier work, have maintained that, in particular circumstances, the state can obtain a degree of autonomy from capitalism (Poulantzas, 1973). This 'relative autonomy' notion contained the promise that worthwhile class politics could be advanced through the state. Indeed, 'dual state' theory made distinctions between the state's 'accumulation', 'control' and 'legitimation' functions. Some state activities, such as investment in worker productivity, helped capitalism to develop, while 'social expenses' – necessary to maintain social control – and 'social consumption' – to keep the workers content – were a drain on capitalist accumulation (Offe, 1984). Working-class social movements could secure concessions via the state's 'control' and 'legitimation' functions and thereby undermine capitalism. However, this emphasis on the 'politics' in Marxist political economy remained subservient to economic determinism. As Jacobs and Manzi (2016, p 5) observe:

A political economy frame generally underestimates the agency accorded to politicians and instead foregrounds the role of ideology as an influence on policy change – evoking Marx's observation in the *Critique of Political Economy* that the 'mode of production of material life conditions the social, political and intellectual life in general'.

With their stress on 'impersonal forces', the theories just outlined tend to undervalue the role of institutionally embedded politics in influencing housing outcomes. Although the political dimension features in the 'housing studies' literature, notably, in the work of Peter Malpass, Alan Murie, Keith Jacobs and Tony Manzi, and also in the political science, urban studies, historical and sociological academic domains, its influence requires highlighting through more systematic consideration. Accordingly, this book's narrative is grounded in explanatory frameworks – the 'new institutionalism', social constructionism and public choice theory – that give more credence to the 'actors' in the political process. Its focus is on 'the process of formulating, implementing and contesting policy' (Bengtsson, 2015, p 3).

The 'new institutionalism'

The 'new institutionalism' places the state at its analytical centre, with political institutions, as 'manifestations of the state' (John, 1998, p 38), regarded as the key to explaining outcomes. 'New institutionalists' claim that 'the organisation of political life makes a difference' (Marsh and Olsen, 1984, p 747). The perspective is a reaction to the deterministic elements in structural approaches and re-emphasises actors' roles in state institutions, even regarding the actions of 'great men and women' as influential in determining outcomes. As Margaret MacMillan (2016, p 92) observes:

> Our understanding and enjoyment of the past would be impoverished without its individuals, even though we know history's currents – its underlying forces and shifts, whether of technology or political structures or social values – must never be ignored'.

The 'new institutionalism' stresses 'purposeful' action, 'path dependency', 'institutional embeddedness' and 'layering' in policy change.

Social constructionism

Social constructionism's objective is to communicate stories on how 'meanings' are socially assembled, and to thereby depict the ways that certain understandings have become privileged and regarded as 'the truth'. It places emphasis on 'practical argumentation, policy judgments, frame analysis, narrative storytelling and rhetorical analysis' (Fircher and Gottweis, 2012, p 1). 'Dominant discourses' frame images and often subjects' self-perception. Foucault (1977, p 194) maintains:

> We must cease once and for all to describe the effects of power in negative terms; it 'excludes', it 'represses', it 'censors', it 'abstracts', it 'marks', it 'conceals'. In fact, power produces reality; it produces domains of objects and rituals of truth.

Social constructionism requires a detailed contextual exploration of *how*, rather than *why*, a situation becomes problematic, including the stages before it becomes taken up – or not taken up – in the formal political process. The approach emphasises 'governability' and 'governmentality' – the mechanisms used to cultivate behaviour appropriate to the regime in power.

Public choice theory

In public choice theory, the actors in the political process are conceptualised as acting rationally to promote their self-interest. There are no 'knights' acting for the public good, only 'knaves' motivated by egotism (Le Grand, 2003), partially a consequence 'of the insuperable information problems involved in knowing the content of the "public interest"' (Pennington, 2000, p 11). Public choice theory is 'politics without romance' (Buchanan, 2003) – the actors in the political process are individuals and there are no such things as 'society' or 'community'. To obtain power, politicians engage in a 'political market', pursuing stratagems aiming at winning more votes than their rivals. Appealing to the median voter in marginal constituencies is one tactic. In 2010, the Conservative Party's marginal seat targeting strategy meant that it won 23 more Labour seats and nine more Liberal Democrat seats than it would have done on a uniform swing (Ashcroft, 2013). Mark Textor, business partner of Lynton Crosby, election strategy advisor to the Conservative Party in the 2015 general election campaign, highlighted the importance of the 'mercenary voter', declaring 'The big lesson from the UK poll was the rise of tactical voting – voters making choices not just on policy or personality … but on understanding and gaming what might happen with a certain poll outcome' (quoted in *Guardian*, 2015a).

Votes in popular elections are only part of the support needed for governance. Within government, trading support is necessary for policy concurrence. In *The Vote Motive*, Tullock (2006) cites UK Cabinet negotiations on expenditure as an example of bartering for backing. Collaboration from interest groups is also necessary in controlling a complex policy domain. Interest groups will adopt tactics to augment their influence over politicians, such as 'log rolling', where interest group combinations – landowners, private landlords, mortgage suppliers, existing homeowners – unite against unorganised groups such as potential first-time buyers to boost house prices. Pennington (2002) has used public choice theory to explain the land release dearth in the UK planning system. He argues that because no single vote has an effect on political outcomes, voters have a disincentive to inform themselves about the overall impact of planning decisions, thereby providing ideal conditions for special interest groups' members to use the political system to benefit themselves at the expense of others.

The state bureaucracy forms a third element in public choice theory. According to Eamonn Butler (2012, p 29), civil servants 'seek the security and status of a large department with a big budget which is why they so often talk legislators into expanding the regulations and laws that they administer'. Bureaucrats, managing central and local government departments, are not public servant 'knights' seeking the common good, but 'knaves' motivated by 'salary, prerequisites of the office, public reputation, power, patronage and the ease of managing the bureau' (Niskanen, 1973, pp 22–3). They often magnify implementation costs, knowing that once committed to a project, politicians will not want the humiliation of failure. The 'new institutionalism', social constructionism and public choice theory identify a range of institutional 'actors' in the political process within which individual politicians operate.

Promotional interest groups

An interest group – often called a 'pressure' group – is an association of people acting together to voice a shared concern or to promote a common economic interest. Shared concern groups, sometimes called 'promotional' groups, cite altruism – apprehension about the welfare of others or the 'common good' – as their motivation. Thus, for example, an early promotional group in the housing domain, the Health of Towns Association, endorsed the public health ideas contained in Edwin Chadwick's (1842) *Report on the Sanitary Conditions of the Labouring Population*, arguing that sanitary reform would benefit everyone by promoting public health, moral improvement and efficient human capital. Contemporary 'promotional' interest groups operating in the housing domain include the following:

- The Town and Country Planning Association was set up in 1899 to advance the ideas in Ebenezer Howard's (1898) *To-morrow: A Peaceful Path to Real Reform*. Howard's basic principles – fair shares in land value uplift for the benefit of all, common ownership of public open space, town and country planned together, and environmental enhancement – remain the contemporary Town and Country Planning Association's core values.
- The Campaign to Protect Rural England (CPRE) was formed in 1926 as the Council for the Preservation of Rural England by Sir Patrick Abercrombie in order to restrict urban sprawl and protect the countryside. Abercrombie was well aware of the interests to be harnessed in preserving rural England via green belts, listing them as:

    the local authorities, the owners, the farmers, the inhabitants; the users of the country, the ramblers, the campers, the motorists; the preservationists of the commons and footpaths, wild flowers, fauna, ancient buildings, trees, etc.; the National Trust; the women's institutes, the rural community councils, the architects, surveyors, engineers and town planners; the garden cities, housing and town-planning propaganda associations. (Abercrombie, 1959, p 228)

    He pointed out that 'the general public creates an outcry if any attempt is made to invade this green belt and that is something we want to get into planning' (Abercrombie, 1948, p 13).
- The National Trust is mainly concerned with looking after historic buildings and the landscape but has joined the CPRE in campaigns to protect green belts.
- Shelter was founded in 1966 by the Reverend Bruce Kenrick, who was concerned about housing conditions in his Notting Hill parish, and it is now a significant lobby in housing politics.
- Crisis provides services for homeless people and campaigns on their behalf.

Economic interest groups

'Socialist'

Economic interest groups have financial advantages to advance or defend. A number of 'socialist' economic interest groups existed at the end of the 19th century. Their aim was to advance working-class living standards, albeit that this objective was often incorporated within the claim that socialism also represented the 'public good'. The Fabian Society, set up in 1884, wanted to promote working-class well-being but was also 'promotional' in that it had a vision that the state could embody the 'common good'. It has had an abiding influence on housing policy.

Other political groups more specifically directed to enhancing working-class interests developed at the end of the 19th century. The Social Democratic Federation, founded by Henry Mayers Hyndman in 1881 to promote Karl Marx's ideas, initially agitated for land nationalisation, whereas William Morris (1885, p 2), the Socialist League's leader, claimed that 'Nationalisation of the land alone, which many earnest and sincere persons are now preaching, would be useless so long as labour was subject to the fleecing of surplus value inevitable under the Capitalist system'.

In 1902, there were 1,454 cooperative societies engaged in not-for-profit retailing and some had started to provide housing for their members, either by building and renting or by supplying mortgages. Initially, building societies also had a collectivist orientation, being set up as working-class organisations intent on mutual aid.

The United Committee for the Taxation of Land Values, the English League for the Taxation of Land Values and the Scottish League for the Taxation of Land Values were all formed in the late 19th and early 20th centuries to promulgate land taxation, as advocated by Henry George (1979 [1879]) in *Progress and Poverty*. Their successor, the Henry George Foundation of Great Britain, was set up in 1929. The Workmen's National Housing Council – representing trade unions and the Independent Labour Party – campaigned on housing issues from its foundation in 1898. It favoured municipal housing and demanded Treasury subsidies and 'fair' rent tribunals to set rents in the private rented sector. It disassociated itself from the National Housing Reform Council with its strong Liberal Party influence and concern about developing housing associations and planning rather than promoting council housing.

'Capitalist'

The 'socialist' agitation over landownership and 'rents' in the late 19th century prompted associations to be formed to defend the 'landed interest', such as the Liberty and Property Defence League – founded in 1882 by Lord Elcho – and the Country Landowners Association, set up in 1907. Local private landlord associations united in the National Federation of Property Owners and Ratepayers.

Today, there are a number of organisations involved in maintaining capitalist relationships in the housing domain. Private landlord associations include the Guild of Residential Landlords and the Residential Landlords Association. The National Landlords Association, formed in 2008 by merging the National Landlords Association with the National Federation of Residential Landlords, claims to be the largest private landlord association, speaking for 60,000 members and associates. The Federation of Master Builders (2016) describes itself as 'acting as the voice of small construction'; the National Federation of Builders looks after the interests of small- and medium-sized builders. The Home Builders Federation (2015), whose membership includes the larger builders, claims to be 'the voice of home building industry', its members delivering '80% of the new homes built each year'. The British Property Federation promotes the interests of property developers, and its membership includes real estate companies, institutional investors, investment banks, housing associations and professional firms. The Country Land and Business Association (2016), successor to the Country Landowners Association, has 33,000 members and claims 'to protect and defend the interests of all landowners in England and Wales'. The Council of Mortgage Lenders represents the financial institutions involved in housing.

Promotional or economic?

The distinction between promotional/altruistic and economic groups is difficult to sustain as almost all pressure groups claim to be acting for the 'public good'. The Campaign to Protect Rural England, despite its 'public good' rhetoric, also safeguards property-owners' economic interests when threatened by new development. The National Housing Federation (2013), representing housing associations, declares that it is 'the voice of affordable housing in England', but it also promotes the economic well-being of those working in the 'social' housing sector. Thus, in response to housing association criticism of the 2015 Conservative manifesto Right to Buy proposal for housing association tenants, the *Daily Mail* (2015) ran the headline 'Housing Fat Cats' Hypocrisy: Furious Backlash at PM's Right-to-Buy Revolution … from Housing Chiefs with Lavish Homes and Six-Figure Salaries'. The numerous professional organisations, such as the Chartered Institute of Housing (representing housing managers) and the Chartered Institute of Environmental Health (acting for environmental health officials), claim 'common good' motivations but are also concerned with their members' economic interests.

Sock puppets?

Shelter and other charitable organisations have had their altruistic motivations questioned. In *Sock Puppets: How the Government Lobbies Itself and Why*, Snowden (2012, p 4) argues that, as part of the 'contract culture', such organisations receive state funding to supply services and:

> In many cases, they call for increased funding for themselves and their associated departments. In public choice terms, they are 'concentrated interests' compelling the taxpayer to meet the costs that come from their policies being implemented, as well as the costs of the lobbying itself.

Some authors accuse charitable homelessness organisations of 'lying for justice', that is, deliberately exaggerating the problem's extent and promoting an image of homeless people as victims of circumstance (White, 1992). 'Sock puppet' suspicion underpinned the Transparency of Lobbying, Non-Party Campaigning and Trade Union Administration Act 2014, which imposed restrictions on campaigning, including expenditure constraints, relating to the 2015 general election. The Commission on Civil Society and Democratic Engagement (2014) described the Act as having a 'chilling effect' on campaigning. It claimed that 'Many non-government organisations are more cautious about campaigning on politically contentious issues because they fear breaking the new law or the reputational risk of vexatious complaints' and that 'the new law makes it almost impossible for charities and campaign groups to work together and speak out on politically contested issues as they did before the Act' (Commission on Civil Society and Democratic Engagement, 2014, pp 6–7). In 2016, the Conservative government announced that charities would not be able to use government grants 'for activity intended to influence – or attempt to influence – Parliament, government or political parties' (Cabinet Office, 2016), thereby restricting charitable engagement in campaigning due to the difficulties involved in separating government grants from other funding sources.

Legal challenge

One avenue open to interest groups is to challenge legislation through the courts. As examples, between the wars, tenants' organisations managed to slow down the introduction of higher rents by contesting the legality of the processes used by private landlords. Several developers have used the legal system to challenge how local authorities have interpreted the 'National Planning Policy Framework' (DCLG, 2012a), and the National Landlords Association has contested local authority decisions to introduce selective licensing schemes. The European Convention on Human Rights was used by tenants – one needing a spare bedroom for a carer and another as a 'panic room' in case of domestic violence – to successfully claim at the Court of Appeal that the 'bedroom tax' unfairly discriminated against them. Judicial review – a procedure in English administrative law by which the courts supervise the exercise of public power – has been a fruitful channel for interest groups, especially in relationship to homelessness legislation. In 2013, Chris Grayling, then Justice Minister, declared:

> One essential part of the campaigner's armoury is the judicial review, through which it is possible for them to challenge decisions of government and public bodies in the courts. As a result, they hire teams of lawyers who have turned such legal challenges into a lucrative industry. (Grayling, quoted in *Daily Mail*, 2013)

Grayling introduced legislation to Parliament to restrict the use of judicial review but this legislation was defeated in the House of Lords.

Consumer groups

Consumer groups exist to promote their members' financial well-being. However, according to the degree that their 'collective consumption' involves 'a collective conscious action aimed at the transformation of the institutionalised urban meaning against the logic, interest and values of the dominant class' (Castells, 1983, p 305), they can become labelled 'urban social movements'. Such movements challenge 'policy from above' via protest, 'primarily outside the normal institutional channels endorsed by authorities' (Jasper, 2014, p 5).

As Castells (1977) has pointed out, 'urban social movements' operating in the 'collective consumption' sphere can cut across class divisions, uniting the working and middle classes on particular issues. Private tenants have tended to unite spasmodically in response to provocation from rent increases, and when the majority of households rented privately, they had a significant impact on private rented sector politics. The decline in private tenant numbers reduced the impact of tenant protest but the rapid emergence of 'generation rent' offers the prospect that 'bottom–up' landlord politics may re-emerge as a political force. There have been recent examples of successful 'bottom-up' campaigns. For example, the residents of the New Era estate in Hackney protested about an increase in rents proposed by its new landlord, the US-based investment fund Westbrook Partners, and after the issue received national publicity, the estate was sold to an affordable housing supplier.

The National Private Tenants Organisation, since 2013 known as 'Generation Rent', attempts to represent private tenants and provides links to the few local organisations that exist. Local authority tenants' associations have been more stable than their private rented equivalents and there is a long history of local and national associations, with the Tenants and Residents Organisations of England (TAROE) now representing residents mainly living in the local authority housing sector. The Scottish Tenants Organisation – born from the 1915 Rent Strike – represents tenants in Scotland, and Welsh Tenants represents those in Wales. Although housing association regulators have stressed tenant participation, national organisations representing housing association tenants have had a very low profile. The Home Owners Alliance claims to speak for owner-occupiers.

'Think tanks'

Although the distinction between interest groups and 'think tanks' is blurred, a 'think tank' is a policy institute that conducts research and is involved in policy advocacy – they are 'idea brokers' (Smith, 1993). Despite their neutrality claims, all have ideological orientations and many have direct connections to political parties. As Schmidt (2003, p 7) points out, they produce 'legitimising discourses', understood 'as encompassing both a set of policy ideas and an interacting process of policy construction and communication'. They can be particularly important when dominant policy paradigms are in crisis (Pautz, 2012), for example, with the Institute of Economic Affairs (IEA) coming to prominence at the time when the so-called 'post-war consensus' was beginning to facture under economic pressures. The 'think tanks' concerned with housing policy can be imprecisely categorised on a right–left continuum.

Right think tanks

The IEA, set up in 1955, proclaims that 'all those associated with the Institute support free markets' (Institute of Economic Affairs, 2013). It has challenged state interventions in the housing market – 'social' housing, rent control and planning controls – as likely to produce more problems than they solve. In 1986, the IEA set up its Health and Welfare Unit, which concentrated on the implications of state welfare on character development. Civitas grew from this Health and Welfare Unit and became independent in January 2000. It has developed a 'One Nation' agenda advocating rent control (Bentley, 2015) and a Right to Buy for private landlord tenants (Saunders, 2016).

The Policy Exchange, established in 2002 by Nicholas Boles, Michael Gove and Francis Maude, describes itself as 'independent' and working 'for better public services, a stronger society and a more dynamic economy' (Policy Exchange, 2013a), but as its founder members indicate, it has strong connections to the Conservative Party. Boles was Planning Minister in 2013/14, and Alex Morton was Head of Housing, Planning & Urban Policy during 2010–13 at the Policy Exchange before joining the Prime Minister's Office. Morton supplied the ideas underpinning the Conservative's 2015 election promise to extend the Right to Buy to housing association tenants and, in *Create Streets* (Boys Smith and Morton, 2013), the foundations of the 2015 Conservative government's proposal to demolish selected council estates. Morton left the Prime Minister's Office in April 2016 to join Field Consulting, which describes itself as 'a consultancy specialising in public affairs, media relations and property and planning communications ... that specialises in helping clients with controversial issues' (Field Consulting, 2016). Also to the right of the political spectrum are the Centre for Policy Studies, set up by Sir Keith Joseph and Margaret Thatcher in 1974 to promote economic liberalism, the rule of law, duty, family and liberty, and the Adam Smith Institute, formed in 1977 to nurture free market solutions to economic and social issues. Iain Duncan Smith created the Centre for Social Justice in 2004 as an 'independent' think tank focused on explaining poverty in 'social breakdown' terms. The Bow Group is an association of Conservative graduates whose original objective was to counter the dominance of left-wing ideas in intellectual circles. Although identified as on the left of the Conservative Party on social issues, it represents a wide range of Conservative opinion. Established in 2001, Reform attempts to demonstrate that institutional reform, as opposed to more spending, is the way to improve public services.

Centre think tanks

The Social Market Foundation can be located in the middle of the political spectrum. Established by David Owen's supporters following the demise of the Social Democratic Party in the late 1980s, it declares its aims as 'exploring ideas that link the state and the market to create a more just, free and prosperous society' (Social Market Foundation, 2016). Demos was founded in 1993 as a 'network of networks' in order to bring together different ideas and expertise to improve public policy, and it was influential in Tony Blair's approach to social policy. The Smith Institute (2016) says that it 'seeks to engage politicians, senior decision makers, practitioners, academia, opinion formers and commentators on promoting policies for a fairer society'. The Strategic Society Centre, founded in 2010, is committed to evidence-based policy, and Centre:Forum has close connections with the Liberal Democrats. The Resolution Foundation (2016) describes its activity as 'analysis and action on living standards'. Although universities are not usually categorised as 'think tanks' because they claim not to have an explicit 'policy advocacy' dimension, they have an important role in research activity that serves to 'frame' housing issues. Many have established 'research centres' with identifiable political orientations. The Institute for Fiscal Studies does not make policy recommendations, but its policy cost and impact assessments have a very high reputation. The Joseph Rowntree Foundation (JRF), founded in 1904, is an independent development and social research charity. It is non-political but the nature of the issues it chooses to research and its policy conclusions have a centre-left flavour.

Left think tanks

Although the Fabian Society retains its association with the Labour Party, it now functions primarily as a think tank. The Institute for Public Policy Research (IPPR) was set up in 1988 and has close connections with the Labour Party. Launched in 2003 by academics and Labour politicians unhappy with the Blair administration's political orientation, Compass has attempted to chart a policy direction for centre-left politics. Shelter, although a provider and campaigning organisation, also conducts research into housing issues and promotes policies from a left-of-centre perspective.

Political parties

Political parties differ from interest groups in that they try to take political office directly and, intent on forming a government, they need to develop a policy programme that appeals to a broad section of the electorate.

Conservative Party

In the early 19th century, political parties were loose MP affiliations known as the 'Tories' and 'Whigs'. The 'Tories' changed their name to the Conservatives in 1834. Aware that as the franchise was extended, it needed mass support, the Conservative Party developed grassroots organisations, notably, the Conservative Registration Association, established to register voters supporting Conservative principles. Although often regarded as cheerleaders for the parliamentary party, keeping the grassroots membership content is important to Conservative Party leaders.

In the 20th century, the Conservative Party became known as the 'pragmatic' party, with Gilmour (1969, p 86) commenting that 'The nearest thing the Tory party has to doctrine is an anti-doctrine: they believe that all political theories are at best inadequate, at worst false.... Scepticism and empiricism are the foundations of Conservatism'. Such pragmatism formed the basis of Conservative participation in the so-called 'post-war consensus' on social policy. Nonetheless, there has been a strong neoliberal undercurrent running through Conservative housing policies, emphasised by Margaret Thatcher from the late 1970s.

Liberal Democratic Party

The Liberal Party was formed in 1859 by a combination of Whigs, Peelites – a faction of the Conservative Party that disagreed with the dominant group, the landed interest, on whether agricultural prices should be kept artificially high by tariffs – and 'Radicals' . It was the major rival to the Conservative Party until the Labour Party's ascent between the wars, and it developed radical plans on land ownership. In the 1970 general election, the Liberals won only six seats in Parliament and later formally adopted 'community politics', a strategy aimed mainly at winning local elections but, in doing so, setting a base to succeed in parliamentary contests. This focus on 'pavement politics', concentrating on local issues, planning applications and local 'information' sheets, was particularly effective in areas with a history of Labour or Conservative dominance. The Liberal Democratic Party was formed in 1988 by a merger between the Liberal Party and the Social Democratic Party, set up in 1981 by Labour Party 'moderates'. Formally, policy is formulated by a party conference held twice a year but, as the Coalition government demonstrated, the party leadership has considerable discretion in accepting or rejecting conference motions.

The Labour Party

Unlike the Conservative and Liberal Democrat Parties, which developed mass organisations in the 19th century to support its parliamentarians, the Labour Party was created to secure representation in Parliament for the working class. A coalition of these movements, including trade unions, the Independent Labour Party, the Fabian Society and the Social Democratic Federation, established the Labour Representation Committee to endorse candidates and offer electoral assistance. When 30 'Labour' members were elected to Parliament in 1906, they formed their own parliamentary organisation under the name 'Labour Party'. In 1918, the Labour Representation Committee adopted a new constitution that allowed individual members, organised in constituencies, to join the 'Labour Party'. The supreme decision-making body was the annual conference, and the party's affairs were organised by the National Executive. Although, in government, the Labour Party leadership was not constitutionally bound by national conference decisions, the 'bottom-up' nature of the Labour Party meant that its 'grassroots', through affiliated organisations, had considerable influence. For example, a Labour Party leadership plan to sell council houses, devised in the late 1970s, was abandoned mainly due to party opposition.

During the transition from Labour to 'New Labour' from the late 1980s, the annual national conference lost its authority and became a stage-managed presentation to support the leadership. Policy formation was through a complex system conducted through a National Policy Forum composed of 186 members representing government, the European and devolved assemblies, local government, affiliated trade unions, socialist societies, and individual Labour Party members, who elected representatives through an all-member ballot. The process allowed the party leadership considerable influence in policy formulation, although the 'one member, one vote' principle gave

Labour Party members the decisive voice in electing their leader. Alongside registered Labour supporters, the party membership elected Jeremy Corbyn as their leader in September 2015 and Corbyn declared that he intended to give more power to the grassroots party.

Parties in Northern Ireland

Birrell (2012, p 272) observes that, 'In a UK context, all of Northern Ireland's political parties fall into the category of non-state-wide parties, and the party system is thus wholly distinctive'. The Democratic Unionist Party (DUP) won 38 seats in the 2016 Northern Ireland Assembly election, whereas the Ulster Unionist Party obtained 16. Sinn Féin, to the left on economic issues, is the major party representing republican interests and won 28 seats The Social Democratic and Labour Party (SDLP) has some links to other European social-democratic parties and obtained 12 seats, whereas the Alliance Party of Northern Ireland, founded in 1970, has moved towards neutrality on the Union, and has come to represent wider liberal and non-sectarian concerns. It acquired eight seats in 2016.

'Single issue' parties

'Single issue' parties initially emphasise a specific issue but, when closer to power, broaden their appeal. The Scottish National Party was founded in 1934 via a merger between the National Party of Scotland and the Scottish National Party. At first, it did not support total independence for Scotland, but full autonomy soon became its raison d'être. In 2007, the Scottish National Party formed a minority government but obtained an overall majority in 2011, winning 69 seats compared to Labour's 37, 15 for the Conservatives and five for the Liberal Democrats. In the 2016 Scottish Parliament election, the Scottish National Party lost its overall majority, obtaining 63 seats. The Conservatives became the second party, with 31 seats, and Scottish Labour won 24. The Greens acquired six seats and the Liberal Democrats won five.

Plaid Cymru, the Party of Wales, was formed in 1925 and advocates the establishment of an independent Welsh state. In the 1974 UK general election, the Scottish National Party secured over one third of votes in Scotland and returned 11 MPs to Westminster, thereby prompting Westminster to promote devolution as an antidote to full independence. Plaid Cymru was not as successful as the Scottish National Party, but in the 1970s, it secured around 11% of the Welsh vote. In 2011, Plaid Cymru, with a 21% vote share, obtained 15 seats in the 60-member National Assembly for Wales. In 2016, by taking a seat from Labour, its representation increased to 12.

The Green Party of England and Wales was created in 1990 when the former UK Green Party devolved into separate parties for England, Scotland and Wales. Although mainly known as an environmentalist party, it supports well-funded, locally controlled public services. The UK Independence Party (UKIP) was set up in 1993, its primary objective being the withdrawal of the UK from the EU. It highlights the implications of free population movement in the EU and its housing policies concentrate on giving priority to social housing applicants whose grandparents or parents were born in the UK and resisting any development on green belts – immigration, not land and housing supply, being the problem. The Land Party is a new party whose platform is based on imposing a land tax similar to that proposed by Henry George (see Chapter Two). In the 2015 general election, UKIP obtained 12.7% of the vote and the Green Party won 3.8%. In Scotland, the Scottish National Party won 50% of the Scottish vote, and in Wales, Plaid Cymru was supported by 12.1% of Welsh voters.

Manifestos are important connections between political parties and the electorate. Communicated through the media, they set out programmes for government and are a mechanism for establishing political accountability. Coalition governments allow parties to discard some of their manifesto commitments but parties with a parliamentary majority can be held to account on commitment delivery. David Cameron described the 2015 Conservative Party manifesto as 'the bible', claiming that his ministers just have to refer to the 'good book' (quoted in *Guardian*, 2015b). Devolution's increasing salience has produced more autonomy for the Scottish and Welsh sections of the major political parties. They produce manifestos related to voter concerns in Scotland and Wales.

The 'media'

The media attempt to reach an audience through a variety of channels. The 'broadcast' media (television, film and radio) transmit their information electronically, whereas print media (newspapers, books, etc) use a physical object as a means to send their information. Internet media forms a third category that is growing in importance as a mechanism for political communication. The media have an important role in 'framing' issues that influence public perceptions of what is important and the causal notions attached to a topic. Newspapers have political affiliations often linked to their owners. In 2015, the *Financial Times* endorsed a 'Conservative-led' government, while the *Guardian/ Observer* and the *Daily Mirror* backed Labour. The *Mail*, *Telegraph* and *Times* and their Sunday versions supported the Conservatives, whereas the *Independent* backed a continuing Conservative–Liberal Democrat Coalition. The *Daily Express* supported UKIP, whereas the *Sun* championed the Conservatives in England but the Scottish National Party in Scotland. Dean (2013, p 355) notes the disappearance of the housing correspondent in the 'quality' press and, apart from an interest in house prices, the green belt and welfare dependency, a lack of reporting on housing issues in the popular press. Indeed, part of the printed media's power resides in its silence on certain issues.

The agreement accompanying the BBC Charter requires the BBC to do all it can to ensure that controversial subjects are treated with due impartiality in its news and other output dealing with public policy matters or political or industrial controversies. Other broadcast media are regulated by Ofcom, which, under the Communications Act 2003 and Article 10 of the European Convention on Human Rights, requires broadcast media to ensure that news, in whatever form, is reported with due accuracy and presented with due impartiality.

Local government

Constitutionally, local government derives its powers from Parliament but local governance developed alongside parliamentary power and has historical, 'embedded' claims to a degree of independence from the central state. From the mid-19th century, the industrial and commercial prowess of the major towns and cities, with their long-established, autonomous financial base – a levy on property values – made them potent actors in urban policy. In the 20th century, local authorities became important accommodation suppliers, land release governors and urban renewal agents. They had significant 'de facto' autonomy in exercising their powers, and as major vehicles for delivering central government policies, they could resist and modify implementation or use power combinations to produce distinct policies. There was considerable 'civic pride' in their activities, in some places reaching 'civic gospel' status (Briggs, 1968). Enterprising local leaders could acquire national prestige: Joseph Chamberlain made his name as Mayor of Birmingham; John Wheatley is as celebrated for his activities as a Glasgow councillor as for his ministerial career; and T. Dan Smith became famous, then infamous, as Newcastle City Council's leader.

In the 1970s, local government's role in providing accommodation, planning and urban regeneration produced speculation about 'local state' power and local government officials as 'urban managers' (Pahl, 1975; Cockburn, 1977). Hostility between Margaret Thatcher's government and some local authorities, controlled by the so-called 'urban left', broke out in the 1980s, resulting in Thatcher curtailing local government's relative independence. However, in the 1990s, local governments acquired a role as urban renewal initiators and managers in partnership with the private sector, sometimes via urban regeneration companies. Both New Labour and the Coalition government encouraged directly elected mayors to boost local executive power, and the 2015 Conservative government promoted elected mayors for the major conurbations as mechanisms to construct 'powerhouses' outside London. The Local Government Association, formed in 1997 as the successor to a range of organisations acting for different local government tiers, now speaks on behalf of local government.

Devolved government

Wales was incorporated within the English legal and constitutional system under the Laws in Wales Acts 1535–42, and the Acts of Union 1706 and 1707 joined England, Wales and Scotland in a single political entity named 'Great Britain'. The Acts of Union 1800 united the Kingdom of Great Britain and the Kingdom of Ireland to create the United Kingdom. During the process leading to the creation of the Irish Free State, the Parliament of Northern Ireland was established under the Government of Ireland Act 1920. Known as Stormont, it controlled housing policy until direct Westminster rule was introduced in 1972. As Paris, Gray and Muir (2003, p 160) note:

> There was no historical tradition (or myth) of nationhood for 'Northern Ireland' as for Wales and Scotland. Rather, Northern Ireland has been divided between 'unionists' who wish to remain 'British' and 'nationalists' who aspire to a united Ireland. This division between two cultural traditions with competing visions of national identity underpins political structures and permeates civil society.

UK devolution has been an ongoing and asymmetrical process, with differences in powers and fiscal autonomy in the four nations. Housing was included in the devolved powers awarded to the Scottish Parliament in 1999. The Scottish Parliament received primary legislative powers and a limited tax-raising capacity but social security, including Housing Benefit, was reserved for Westminster, and the main fiscal and economic levers, so important to housing outcomes, remained with the UK 'core executive'. The National Assembly for Wales, established in 1999, was granted neither the right to vary taxation nor primary legislative powers, but it could change secondary legislation. Under direct rule by Westminster, housing in Northern Ireland was administered by an appointed Northern Ireland Housing Executive. However, as part of the Belfast Agreement, a Northern Ireland Assembly were set up in 1999 and the Assembly gained legislative competence in housing. The Assembly was suspended three times when its powers reverted to the Secretary of State for Northern Ireland. The Northern Ireland Executive, the administrative branch of the Northern Ireland Assembly, embodies a 'mandatory coalition' with all the major political parties entitled to representation.

In the years immediately following devolution, it was difficult to detect significant divergence between English housing policy and the policies adopted in the devolved administrations. However, under the Conservative-led Coalition government, promoting a neoliberal, 'austerity' agenda, marked policy differences emerged between Westminster and the devolved governments, particularly in Scotland.

Devolution is a process rather than an event, with changes made post-1999, such as powers for Wales to introduce primary legislation and powers to adjust taxation that varied between the devolved governments (see Stephens, 2016). More changes are in the pipeline (see Birrell and Gray, 2016). The promise of additional devolved powers for Scotland made in the referendum campaign resurrected the so-called 'West Lothian Question' – the arrangement whereby English MPs cannot vote on matters devolved to other parts of the UK, but Scottish, Welsh and Northern Ireland MPs can vote on the same matters in the UK Parliament when legislating only for England. In October 2015, the UK Parliament voted to change its Standing Orders to allow members from England or England and Wales to give their consent to legislation that affected only England, or only England and Wales. The 2016 Housing and Planning Act was the first piece of legislation to pass through Parliament under this procedure, with the Speaker of the House of Commons designating the sections of the Bill affecting only England, or only England and Wales.

The voters

Although the Reform Act 1832 has attracted the most attention, only a small proportion of the total adult population was entitled to vote after the Act was passed. The Second Reform Act of 1867 more than doubled the electorate by including urban working-class householders, although working-class householders in rural areas remained excluded. The Act meant that about 16% of the adult population (those who had reached the age of 21) could register to vote. Under the Third Reform Act of 1884, residents in the counties became entitled to vote on the same terms as those in the boroughs – mainly benefiting agricultural workers – and the proportion of the adult population able to vote in parliamentary elections reached almost 29%. The Representation of the People Act 1918 introduced universal male suffrage, adding 4.5 million men to the franchise who were previously excluded under the householder qualification. Women could register only if they were 30 years old. Universal suffrage at the age of 21 was granted to women in 1928 following the passing of the Representation of the People (Equal Franchise) Act. Voting in elections was extended to 18 year olds in 1969. In Scotland, 16 and 17 year olds were allowed to vote in the independence referendum and in subsequent ballots for local government and the Scottish Parliament.

The UK Parliament

The United Kingdom of Great Britain and Northern Ireland Parliament is the supreme legislative body in the UK. It possesses legislative supremacy and hence ultimate power over all other political bodies. The Prime Minister must be someone who can command a majority in a confidence vote in the House of Commons. All legislation, other than in domains specifically delegated under devolution, must be approved by Parliament to become law, and the Commons controls most taxation powers and the supply of resources to the Westminster government. Government ministers must regularly answer questions in the House of Commons and select committees scrutinise particular policy domains.

Some political commentators regard the House of Commons as having little 'de facto' power (Hulne, 2009; Mount, 2012). However, whereas government defeats in the Commons are infrequent, influence has come through what Friedrich (1937) called the 'rule of anticipated reactions', whereby actors shape their behaviour to conform to what they believe are the desires of others. Governments are reluctant to risk defeat and ministers, sometimes with leadership ambitions, adjust their proposals to minimise the danger. Moreover, the Commons – with its official opposition – often becomes a source of alternative approaches, and governments attempt to 'shoot opposition foxes' by modifying policies, a recent example being the additional discretionary payments made to mitigate the 'bedroom tax' impact.

Ministers and shadow ministers meet their party's backbenchers on a regular basis, with the Conservative Party's 1922 Committee – an association of Conservative MPs with a formal organisation – regarded as particularly important. Various groupings of like-minded MPs attempt to influence policy. The Conservative Party, for example, contains the One Nation Group, formed in 1950 to promote the approach adopted by Benjamin Disraeli in the 19th century, and in the Labour Party, the Tribune Group was set up in 1964 to assist the *Tribune* newspaper in offering advice to Labour governments from a left-wing perspective.

Under the Salisbury Convention, the House of Lords does not frustrate measures included in party manifestos but it can hold up non-money Bills and the delays, inconvenience and the publicity generated by reverses sometimes results in governments accepting House of Lords amendments (Russell and Sciara, 2008). For example, a Right to Buy for charitable housing association tenants contained in the 1980 Housing Bill was removed in the House of Lords and the government reluctantly accepted this amendment (see Chapter Seven). Indeed, perhaps due to 'noblesse oblige' and, more recently, the absence of a Conservative majority, the Lords has supported the voluntary housing movement. Anticipated House of Lords opposition to the Conservative's 2015 Right to Buy proposal for housing association tenants was a factor in the voluntary agreement on sales between the government and housing associations (see Chapter Seven), and members of the Lords tabled amendments to the 2015 Housing Bill that forced many concessions from the government, such as increasing the income thresholds on 'Pay to Stay' and reducing the 'taper' rate (see Chapter Six).

The European Union

Although housing is not a specific EU mandate, other dimensions of the EU's remit have implications for UK housing politics. The EU's regulations on credit agreements affect mortgages in the UK, and the European System of Accounts rules affect debt division between public and private, which influenced the 2015 Office for National

Statistics decision to move housing association debt into the public sector (Stothart, 2015). The European Investment Bank invests in social housing, and in 2016, a deal to lend £1 billion for affordable housing in the UK, supported by a UK government guarantee, was signed, but the Bank warned that leaving the EU would put its activities at risk (*Financial Times*, 2016). The EU requirement to remove barriers to the free movement of persons has been controversial, with UKIP alleging that EU immigration has been a major contributor to the housing problem. Restricting Housing Benefit for working migrants from the EU was a significant element in the Conservative government's renegotiation of the UK's relationship to the EU. The 'leave' vote in the 2016 European Union referendum revealed some of the wider economic implications of EU membership. Before the ballot, George Osborne, then Chancellor of the Exchequer, predicted a 'leave' vote would produce a 18% house price reduction by 1918 (BBC News, 2016). Immediately after the vote, Moodys, the credit ratings agency, downgraded the ratings of many banks and the share value of most building firms fell, leading to predictions of 'turmoil in the housing market' (*Inside Housing*, 2016). However, within a month of the 'Brexit' vote, PricewaterhouseCoopers (2016) predicted slower UK house price growth but no major house price crash.

Quasi-autonomous non-governmental organisations

As the name suggests, 'quasi-autonomous non-governmental organisations' (quangos) allow governments to influence a policy domain at arm's length and to deploy expertise from outside the civil service. As such, they contribute to 'policy networks'. The Housing Corporation, responsible for nurturing and distributing resources to housing associations, was the most significant housing 'quango'. It was abolished in 2008 and the Homes and Communities Agency assumed its functions, including social housing provider regulation after the Coalition government axed the Tenant Services Authority. The 2015 Conservative government established the National Infrastructure Commission to 'set out a clear picture of the future infrastructure we need, producing an in-depth assessment of the UK's major infrastructure needs on a 30-year time horizon' (HM Treasury, 2016, p 3). Its remit covers energy, transport, water and sewage, waste, and flood defences. The Treasury declared:

> The government has removed top-down housing targets, and will continue to ensure that homes are delivered

through Local Plans, in consultation with local people. However, infrastructure can affect the viability of housing projects both large and small. As such, the commission will consider the potential impact of infrastructure decisions on housing supply. (HM Treasury, 2016, p 60)

Government departments

In the 19th century, housing was regarded as a dimension of health and land policy. Administrative responsibility for health was placed in a General Board of Health from 1848 to 1858 and then with the Local Government Board. Land policy, with its salience to Irish politics, was 'high' politics and mainly dealt with at prime ministerial level.

Post-1919, the Ministry of Health became responsible for housing policy, reflecting the perception of housing as a dimension of public health. This continued until 1951 when the Ministry of Town and Country Planning, set up in 1943, was merged with housing from the Ministry of Health to form the Ministry of Housing and Local Government. In June 1955, Duncan Sandys, Minister of Housing and Local Government, told the Cabinet:

> There would be some advantage in altering the present name of his Department to 'Ministry of Local Government'. Its present name was cumbersome and was often abbreviated to 'Ministry of Housing'; and this title was becoming increasingly inappropriate as the emphasis in house building came to be transferred to building by private enterprise with which the Department had little concern. (Cabinet, 1955, p 111)

The Cabinet rejected Sandys' proposal. Subsequently, housing became the domain of other departments, such as the Department for the Environment and later the Department of Transport, Local Government and the Regions. The Office of the Deputy Prime Minister (ODPM) was created in 2002 from the portfolio of the former Department of Transport, Local Government and the Regions – its title reflecting the political rank of the then Deputy Prime Minister, John Prescott. The Department for Communities and Local Government (DCLG) was established in 2006 as successor to the ODPM. Despite name and responsibility changes, the DCLG's core functions have continuity with the Ministry of Housing and Local Government. A housing policy 'departmental view' can be identified at various points in time. In the 1960s and 1970s, for example, the Ministry of Housing and Local Government promoted higher rents, with rent rebates and housing allowances targeted at lower-income households. Margaret Thatcher thought that the Department of the Environment had a particular 'departmental view', being 'in collusion with local government' (Thatcher, 1993, p 605) and reluctant to engage in radical ideas to end local government's involvement in housing supply.

Housing policy has historical and contemporary associations with the income maintenance system. Today, cash assistance is the responsibility of the Department for Work and Pensions, with Housing Benefit (in the process of being absorbed into Universal Credit) being an important part of its remit.

Policy networks and policy communities

Rhodes (2006, p 426) has defined policy networks as 'sets of formal institutional and informal linkages between governmental and other actors structured around shared if endlessly negotiated beliefs and interests in public policymaking and implementation. These actors are interdependent and policy emerges from the interactions between them'. When established and able to exclude 'outsiders', they are often called 'policy communities'. The 'policy network' idea has been linked to the 'governance' notion, it being claimed that rather than 'governing' to achieve a specified end via direct state power, those with formal political power have had to steer a course through unstable global forces, fostering cooperation from external and internal agencies. Informal partnerships have been established wherein resources of various types are exchanged in the pursuit of agreed objectives.

The utility of concepts such as 'governance', 'policy networks' and 'policy communities' to housing policy analysis depends on the governing regime's nature. Margaret Thatcher's 'one of us' attitude – 'suspicious of the embedded policy communities around Whitehall' (Richardson, 2000, p 1010) – meant that 'governance', 'policy networks' and 'policy communities' had restricted relevance to policy construction, whereas the Blair administrations – being less ideological and more interested in 'what works is what counts' – placed greater reliance on 'policy networks' and 'policy communities'.

The 'core executive'

The Prime Minister appoints ministers to the Cabinet, with Cabinet membership regarded as symbolic that the policy domain represented by a departmental minister has high priority in the government's objectives. The Cabinet is served by the Cabinet Office, which portrays its role as 'the corporate headquarters for government, in partnership with HM Treasury, and we take the lead in certain critical policy areas' (Cabinet Office, 2013). However, reality is more complex, with the Prime Minister's access to policy initiatives coming from outside the Cabinet via, for example, the Prime Minister's Office and his/her close advisory team – often called the 'kitchen cabinet'. Most decisions are made via networks of ministers and advisors (see, for example, Powell, 2010; Moore, 2013, 2015) with the Prime Minister at the centre, and, in recent years, the Cabinet mainly ratifies decisions made elsewhere. Cabinet committees carry out most of the Cabinet's routine implementation work, with, for example, the Housing Implementation Taskforce Committee responsible for managing housing policy in the 2015 Conservative government.

Prime ministerial influence varies according to the office-holder's interests. Harold Macmillan, Harold Wilson and Margaret Thatcher gave close attention to housing policy, whereas Tony Blair left most initiatives to his Chancellor. When the Coalition government was in office, the so-called 'quad' – David Cameron, George Osborne, Nick Clegg and Danny Alexander – had a role in decision-making, with Clegg and Alexander able to veto proposals. Liberal Democrat influence negated some Conservative proposals. For example, Laws (2016, p 198) claims that in a 2012 policy review meeting:

> David Cameron then said that the Tories had a radical idea for the mid-term review, which he was personally very keen on. This turned out to be giving social tenants the right to sell their properties and receive all the money from the sale. In exchange, they would agree never to claim any more housing benefit. 'Its our big idea', he said, 'Setting the people free'. A number of us expressed scepticism.

The idea did not enter the public domain but, overall, Liberal Democrat sway on housing policy appears to have been limited. They had only one third-tier representative in the Department of Communities and Local Government's ministerial team. Clegg maintains that he constantly tried to obtain more resources for social housing but the Tories rejected his appeals on the argument that 'all it does is to produce more Labour voters' (Clegg, quoted in *Independent*, 2016).

The Treasury has great authority in housing policy via its roles in determining public expenditure and economic management. As housing supply has become more neoliberal, Treasury influence on policy has increased. Departments regard negotiations with the Treasury on public spending as a touchstone of departmental influence, with ministers expected to fight their corners in 'expenditure rounds'. For example, in 1984, Ian Gow, Minister for Housing and a close ally of Margaret Thatcher, threatened to resign if his budget was cut, and, at least in the short term, he received significant concessions.

Conclusion

Economic and social change – whether labelled 'industrialisation', 'urbanisation', 'capitalism' or 'globalisation' – prompt reactions from governments moulded by ideology and concerns about gaining and holding political power. These responses have the capacity to shape the impact of 'industrialisation', 'urbanisation', 'capitalism' and 'globalisation'. Non-response to these allegedly 'impersonal' forces with the cry that 'there is no alternative' is a political act. The remaining chapters in this book chart political encounters with change determinants, recording how the 'actors' in the political process have responded to the problems generated by social and economic transformations and, in turn, shaped their forms.

Further reading

Bengtsson, B. (2015) 'Between Structure and Thatcher: Towards a Research Agenda for Theory-Informed Actor-Related Analysis of Housing Politics', *Housing Studies*, vol 30, no 5 pp 677–93.

Birrell, D. and Gray, A.M. (2016) 'Social Policy, the Devolved Administrations in the UK Coalition Government', in H. Bochel and M. Powell (eds) *The Coalition Government and Social Policy: Restructuring the Welfare State*, Bristol: The Policy Press, pp 325–46.

Butler, E. (2012) *Public Choice: A Primer*, London: Institute of Economic Affairs.

Clapham, D.F., Clark W.A.V. and Gibb, K. (eds) (2012) *The Sage Handbook of Housing Studies*, London: Sage.

Hay, C., Lister, M. and Marsh, D. (eds) (2006) *The State: Theories and Issues*, Basingstoke: Palgrave Macmillan.

King, A. (2015) *Who Governs Britain?*, London: Pelican.

Mishra, R. (1981) *Society and Social Policy: Theory and Practice of Welfare*, London: Palgrave Macmillan.

Pautz, H. (2012) *Think-Tanks, Social Democracy and Social Policy*, Basingstoke: Palgrave.

TWO

Land politics

A natural limited resource – Mark Twain advised 'Buy land: they're not making it anymore' – planning controls have made housing land scarcer. Although general rules prescribed by central government and appeals to central authority regulate the process, land supply is managed within the local political process. Development plans do not confer development rights. Each development requires specific permission, although the 2015 Conservative government announced that certain sites could be designated as having 'planning permission in principle'.

In the 1930s, land contributed less than 5% to house costs; in the 1960s, around 10%; in the 1970s, about 20%; and in the late 1990s, about 40%. Up-to-date information on the percentage that land captures in house prices is sparse because the Coalition government cancelled the annual publication of residential land price statistics, alongside new development densities – indeed, residential land prices with planning permission statistics terminate in 2010 in the authoritative *UK Housing Review* (Wilcox et al, 2016, p 172). Belatedly, the Department for Communities and Local government (DCLG) produced figures on land values, applying different assumptions to those used in earlier publications. The values were based on 'valuing the proposed development and deducting the development costs, including allowances for base build cost, developer's profit, marketing costs, fees, and finance to leave a "residual" for the site value' (DCLG, 2015a, p 4). The average land cost was £6,017,000 per hectare in England. Assuming a density of 43 houses per hectare (the average density in 2013), the payment to the landowner would be £139,930 per house.

The Policy Exchange (2013b), using information on construction costs per dwelling and total residential property value, estimated land price contribution to total house cost at 55% in 2013. Thus, as Morton (2012, p 1) claims, 'House prices are really about land prices. Higher house prices simply mean land with residential planning permission has increased in value, including the land crystallised in existing homes'.

In 2014, UK house prices per square metre were the second highest in the world, with London the expensive epicentre. In 2015, prices in the capital were 50% above their pre-2007 peak compared to 7% in the UK (Nationwide, 2015), with a £200,000 price gap between

London and the rest of the UK. New York house prices were 63.9% of London prices and Paris prices were 47.2% (Hilber, 2015).

Land taxation

A common economic interest in land bonded the Whigs and the Tories. Cannadine (1990, p 16) comments that 'Land was wealth: the most secure, reliable and permanent asset. Land was status: its ownership conferred unique and unrivalled celebrity. And land was power: over the locality, the county and the nation'.

Socialist ideas on land formed the basis for agitation in the 1840s and the 'land question' returned to the political agenda towards the end of the 19th century as the Liberal Party started to advocate taxing the 'unearned increments' generated by community-created land values. Following the Liberal Party's demise after the First World War, the Labour Party pushed the land question but more as a taxation than an ownership issue. It attempted to tax the 'betterment' arising from community infrastructure investment. The Conservatives repealed all Labour's 'betterment tax' initiatives.

Henry George

The land issue dominated UK domestic politics from the 1880s until the outbreak of the First World War. In 1886, unwilling to tolerate the 'landed interest' becoming subject to an Irish Parliament in Dublin, as proposed by Gladstone, many Liberal landowners defected to the Conservative Party, leaving the remaining Liberals free to harass the landowning class. John Bright demanded the repeal of primogeniture legislation – the firstborn male child right to inherit the entire family estate – to break up the landed property fortunes. He alleged that less than 150 men owned half of England, a figure refuted by Lord Derby, who sanctioned an inquiry into land ownership to confirm his view. The inquiry result was a Lord Derby 'own goal', giving far more support to Bright's calculations.

There were three main opinion groupings on land reform. Some wanted site value rating, arguing that landowners escaped the local property tax – the rates – and that site value rating would force unused land sat on by landlords hoping for price increases to be brought into use. The Land Nationalisation Society, claiming support from 130 MPs, wanted to nationalise all land. Henry George's acolytes promoted a new universal land tax to replace the rates and all other taxes. In *Progress and Poverty*, George (1979 [1879], p 66) defined 'rent' as 'consideration for the use of land'. 'Rent' increased with an expanding population and the consequent inflation in land values, to which the landowner made no contribution, reducing the social product accruing to capital and labour. The remedy was to take 'rent' by land taxation on the value above the unimproved 'site' value. Such a tax would represent 'the taking by the community, for the use of the community, of the value that is the creation of the community' and would be easy to collect 'for land cannot be hidden or carried off' (George, 1979 [1879], p 139).

George's ideas were extremely influential, with *Poverty and Progress* selling over three million copies worldwide and George Bernard Shaw commenting that 'When I was thus swept into the great Socialist revival of 1883, I found that five-sixths of those who were swept in with me had been converted by Henry George' (quoted Blaug, 1992, p 360). The Liberty and Property Defence League, with almost all of its members having a title, strongly opposed land taxation. Its most prolific pamphleteer, W.H. Mallock, declared:

> If they [the 'labouring classes'] are poor, squalid and dependent it is because they have no desire to be anything else. The magnificence of the castle does not come from the plunder of the alley, but it is the cause of the alley existing, where otherwise there would be no shelter at all. (Mallock, 1882, p 195)

The landed aristocracy launched fierce attacks on George's work. Lord Herbert had *Progress and Poverty* withdrawn as a textbook at the City of London College, describing it as 'immoral', and the Duke of Argyll declared that 'the world has never seen such a preacher of unrighteousness as Mr. Henry George' (quotations from Lawrence, 1951, pp 235, 237).

Lloyd George and land politics

David Lloyd-George and Winston Churchill, the most prominent 'new' liberals at the time, needed revenue to pay for battleships and state pensions, and they promoted Henry George's ideas with gusto. The existing land tax – Estate Duty, introduced in 1894 – was modest. It imposed a levy of 1% on an estate between £100 and £500 in value, to a maximum of 8% on an estate valued at over £1,000,000.

Churchill (1909) claimed:

Roads are made, streets are made, services are improved, electric light turns night into day, water is brought from reservoirs a hundred miles off in the mountains, and all the while the landlord sits still.... To not one of those improvements does the land monopolist contribute. He renders no service to the community, he contributes nothing to the general welfare, he contributes nothing to the process from which his own enrichment is derived.

Lloyd George (1909) added:

Not far from here, not so many years ago, between the Lea and the Thames you had hundreds of acres of land.... In the main it was a sodden marsh. The commerce and the trade of London increased.... All that land became valuable building land, and land which used to be rented at £2 or £3 an acre has been selling within the last few years at £2,000 an acre, £3,000 an acre, £6,000 an acre, £8,000 an acre. Who created that increment? It was purely the combined efforts of all the people engaged in the trade and commerce of the Port of London – trader, merchant, ship-owner, dock labourer, workman, everybody except the landlord.

These speeches were aimed at defending the 1909 'Peoples' Budget – introducing land taxation at 20% on the 'unearned increments' from land sales and an annual tax on the capital value of undeveloped land – from hostile opposition in the House of Lords. The Lords eventually passed the Budget after the Liberals' democratic mandate was confirmed in the 1910 general election.

Land campaigns

Lloyd George despised the aristocracy and refused to modify Estate Duty rates in response to the death of aristocrats' sons in the First World War. Buoyed by his success on the land issue, he set up a land enquiry, directed by Seebohm Rowntree. On rural land, the enquiry, published in 1913, focused on setting a minimum wage for agricultural workers and establishing 'Land Commissioners' to supervise tenancy agreements, rents and land acquisition. There would be state-built cottages for workers. The Urban Land Enquiry recommendations, published in April 1914, contained proposals to allow local authorities to purchase land for housing at its 'true' market price, that is, minus its development value, to sell on to developers, and legal protection against eviction. In 1913, Lloyd George mounted a rural land campaign, promoting the rural policies, and later started an urban campaign, although the outbreak of the First World War limited its impact. He anticipated that his rural land campaign would raise 'savage passions' (quoted in Crosby, 2014, p 134) and, indeed, the prospect of losing its rural vote 'filled the Tory party with alarm and some horror' (Packer, 1996, p 45). Lloyd George's campaigns were not put to an electoral test but, despite Tory apprehension, they had a limited impact, with the failure to commit to subsidised housing for the rural and urban working class – whereas Labour endorsed subsidies – being significant (Packer, 2001). Not only were the land campaigns ineffective, but Lloyd George's land tax, introduced in 1910, encountered problems. Difficulties with land valuation, despite recruiting a 4,000-strong land valuer army, plus adverse court judgements, meant that by 1914, only £612,787 had been collected. The Conservative-dominated post-war Coalition government removed all land taxation traces from the statute book. According to Masterman (quoted in Morgan, 1971, pp 208–9), 'They stamped down the ground over the grave.... And finally – so that there should be no doubt at all to their triumph – they ... returned two millions of the money'.

Labour and land

The Labour Party fluctuated between supporting land nationalisation and endorsing Henry George's single land tax. The Labour minority government's 1924 Budget proposed that the Land Valuation Office, a relic of Lloyd George's land tax schemes, should be reinvigorated to plan for a new land tax. Civil servants prepared reports on the land tax and Vaughan (2009, p 100) concludes that 'the reports exude scepticism, though they are clear that the tax would be technically possible'. Philip Snowden, Labour's Chancellor in the 1924 Labour minority government, was committed to introducing the new tax but work on the levy ended when Labour lost office. The 1931 Labour minority government's Budget included a modest land value tax at one penny per pound of value but the Conservative-dominated National Government repealed the legislation.

'Betterment' taxation

In the late 1930s, land ownership had a lower political profile than earlier in the century. Increases in Estate Duty and agricultural recession had undermined the aristocracy's wealth: in 1938, land as an asset proportion in private hands was only a third of its 1920 share. According to Tichelar (2003, p 202), 'Labour had come to recognise that land nationalisation was an irrelevance to the immediate problem of post-war food shortages which might compromise its relationship with the farmers in the drive for increased productivity'. Rather than nationalise land, Labour concentrated on taxing 'betterment'. Its 1945 manifesto declared:

> Labour believes in land nationalisation and will work towards it, but as a first step the State and the local authorities must have wider and speedier powers to acquire land for public purposes ... we will also provide revenue for public funds from 'betterment'. (Labour Party, 1945)

To meet this promise, Labour's Town and Country Planning Act 1947, following the Uthwatt Committee recommendations (Uthwatt, 1942), allowed local authorities to acquire land by compulsion at 1947 values. It also imposed a tax at 100% on the 'betterment' value of privately transacted development land, collected by a Central Land Board. A £300 million fund was set up to compensate landowners for losing their development rights.

The Conservatives and land

The National Federation of Property Owners called the betterment tax 'the greatest ever deterrent to the development of building and industry' (quoted in Conservative Party Archives, 1949). The 1949 Conservative Party Conference demanded its repeal but the party leadership was divided on the issue. Richard Austen Butler, Chancellor of the Exchequer in the 1951–55 Conservative government, was influenced by information from the Central Land Board that, after teething problems, the system was producing a good return, and he argued that repeal would put 'the Conservative Party on the side of landowners and against the public interest' (quoted in Weiler, 2000, p 125). He wanted to retain betterment tax with a lower rate, whereas Harold Macmillan, the Minister for Housing and Local Government, argued that the tax restricted land availability. Macmillan's view prevailed in Cabinet and the betterment tax was abolished for private transactions, although local authorities were allowed to continue compulsorily purchasing land at 1947 values. Later, following the publicity surrounding the suicide of Edward Pilgrim, who had his land compulsorily purchased at a value far less than the mortgage he was paying, the Conservatives ended compulsory purchase by local authorities at 1947 land values.

After a hike in land prices in the early 1960s, the land issue returned to the political agenda. Green belt release was considered as a solution but the outcome was only a limited rule relaxation on infilling and future designation (Bridgen and Lowe, 1998). As Minister of Housing in 1963, Keith Joseph expressed his concerns about the mounting public anger surrounding property and land speculation and the Cabinet set up a committee on land values. It declared that 'we have felt bound to conclude that there is no action open to the Government that will have the effect of reducing the price of land in the short term' (quoted in Weiler, 2000, p 122). Joseph, although hesitant on land taxation (Bridgen and Lowe, 1998), persisted, stating in a memorandum to the Cabinet:

> If we say nothing [on land taxation] it will be generally supposed ... that we – who were responsible for getting rid of development charge – are indifferent to the fact that the public has no share in the profits being made out of land, largely as a result of public action and expense. (Joseph, 1964)

Joseph was crushed by a combination of Cabinet members who thought the state's role in housing should be limited and a group arguing that Joseph's proposal was electoral suicide – it would be presented by Labour as endorsing a 'socialist' approach to land values and be seen as 'naked electioneering' (Cox, 1984, p 124). Sir Alex Douglas-Home, who had renounced his Earldom when he became Prime Minister in 1963, but wanted to preserve property rights, also opposed Joseph.

The Land Commission

Labour governments revisited taxing 'betterment' in the 1960s and 1970s. The Land Commission Act 1967 made provision for a Land Commission to acquire and manage land and a 40% 'betterment levy' when planning permission was awarded. Although Prime Minister Harold Wilson supported establishing the Land Commission, it and its new sponsor, the Ministry of Land and Natural Resources, met with internal opposition from Richard Crossman and his Permanent Secretary, Dame Evelyn Sharp, both determined not to erode their control over the planning system. The compromise was that the Land Commission would not have the authority to grant planning permission. The Conservative opposition team, including Margaret Thatcher, mounted a vigorous attack on the legislation, claiming that it infringed individual rights and was a levy on house-building (Thatcher, 1966). Some local authorities, fearing development in their areas, obstructed the Commission's work and, as had occurred after the 1947 Act, landowners held on to land anticipating that the Conservatives would return to government. When, in 1970, the Conservatives abolished the Land Commission, it had raised only £46 million – less than its running costs – although it was beginning to promote land release.

The Community Land Act 1975

On its return to power, Labour passed the Community Land Act 1975, with local authorities enabled to buy development land at its existing use value and develop the land itself or lease it to other public bodies or private agencies. The Development Land Tax Act 1976 introduced a tax at up to 80% on development increase, with a slice from the gain exempt from the tax. Local authorities acquiring land would not pay the tax. However, local authorities lacked the resources to purchase land and owners often avoided the tax via fragmenting landownership to utilise annual exemptions and converting land sale receipts from capital to income. The Conservatives repealed the Act in 1980 and reduced the Development Land Tax to 60% with higher exemptions, before abolishing it in 1985.

The entrenched relationship between the Conservative Party and 'the landed interest' meant that it could be expected that the Conservatives would repeal all Labour's attempts to tax 'betterment'. However, given the huge gains to landowners accruing from planning permission, the Conservatives found it expedient to ensure that some financial rewards from development benefited the community. Land transactions continued to be subject to Capital Gains taxation introduced by Labour in 1965 and to Stamp Duty. Section 106 of the Town and Country Planning Act 1990 allowed local planning authorities and persons interested in land development to agree contributions to infrastructure and other activities, such as providing 'social' housing.

The Community Infrastructure Levy

New Labour did not attempt to tax betterment gain when it came to power in 1997 but Stamp Duty rates – renamed Stamp Duty Land Tax in 2003 – on property transactions, including land, were increased, pushing the Treasury yield on land and property from £3.5 billion in 2001/02 to £9.0 billion in 2007/08 (HM Revenue and Customs, 2014). Following the Barker Report (Barker, 2004), New Labour announced a proposal to introduce a Planning-gain Supplement (PGS), similar to Labour's earlier attempts to tax 'betterment' but set at a lower 25% rate. This proposal provoked hostility from developers. The British Property Federation, the Home Builders Federation and the Major Developers Association lobbied hard against PGS. The government compromised (Barker, 2014) and the PGS was replaced by the Community Infrastructure Levy (CIL) − to be charged on granting planning permission. Local authorities could choose the levy rate for their areas, rather than there being one central tariff, as proposed for PGS. An authority was permitted to negotiate a Section 106 agreement but it would be restricted to site-specific measures and providing affordable housing. Although not openly opposed by the Coalition government, the roll-out of CIL was painfully slow. Up to April 2014, only 52 local authorities had implemented a charging schedule and were actively collecting the levy; £57 million had been raised, 94% by the London Mayoral CIL (Savills, 2014b).

Planning

Demand for a planned built environment started at the end of the 19th century. Ebenezer Howard's (1902) *Garden Cities of Tomorrow* outlined town and country living 'magnets'. Town positives included 'social opportunity', 'places of amusement', 'high money wages' and 'chances of employment', whereas the negatives were 'closing out of nature', 'high rents', 'fogs' and 'distance from work'. Country living attractions included 'beauty of nature', 'low rents', 'sunshine' and the 'abundance of water'; its negatives were 'lack of society', 'long hours', 'lack of drainage' and 'hands out of work'. Howard claimed the 'magnets' of living in the town or the country could be combined by residence in a planned garden city surrounded by a rural 'green belt'.

Although not a part of Howard's vision − he wanted to contain urban growth − 'town plus country' generated the garden suburb idea, influential in the passing of the Housing and Planning Act 1909. Between 1893 and 1908, cheap public transport had allowed half-a-million acres to be used for suburban building. The 1909 Act was a watered-down version of an attempt, promoted by the National Housing Reform Council, to allow local government to acquire land by compulsory purchase and control suburban development. Rather than grant such a power, the Act gave local government the authority to prepare plans for development land. It also allowed a tax on gains, set at 50% of value increase, resulting from planning permissions where a town planning scheme was in place. The Town and Country Planning Act 1932 extended the local government power to all land, not only that currently 'in course of development', but plan preparation remained permissive. If local authorities produced a plan, they could levy a 75% tax on the increase in land value obtained from building in permitted areas. Ravetz (1986, p 30) comments that betterment tax was 'scarcely ever paid'. Very few plans were prepared and they were usually pro-development; this was because when planning permission was refused, compensation was payable.

An 'octopus strangling England'

During the 1930s, there was extensive development along the major roads radiating out from cities – houses, petrol stations, cafes and so on. This 'ribbon' development attracted vociferous criticism. Described in 1928 by architect Clough Williams-Ellis (1996 [1928], p 3) as an 'octopus strangling England', suburban development was opposed by motoring organisations as hindering free traffic flow and by the Council for the Preservation of Rural England as destroying the countryside. Many architects and planners denounced suburban housing 'as shabby, shoddy, romantic nature-worship' (Sharp, 1932, p 11). The brouhaha was such that Neville Chamberlain proposed granting powers to local authorities to compulsorily purchase land around the major arterial roads without compensation. In the event, the Restriction of Ribbon Development Act 1935 made new building within 220 feet of classified roads subject to planning control. This suburban development restriction, guided through Parliament by Health Minister Edward Hilton Young, coincided with attempts to contain the urban working class in city centres (see Chapter Three). Despite restrictions on ribbon development, the countryside protection campaigners remained concerned. William-Ellis followed up his 'octopus' allegations by editing *Britain and the Beast* (William-Ellis, 1937), urging resistance to the urban 'beast' devouring the countryside, praising landowners for the stability they provided in rural areas and condemning suburbia as 'selfish and anti-social' (quoted in Lewis, 2014, p 219). Special revulsion was directed at the 'plotlanders', people living in cities who bought land in rural and coastal areas, sometimes for as little as £8 a plot, and self-built bungalows and shacks on the land.

Planning and the Second World War

Three reports published in the war years helped to advance the idea that the built environment had to be planned. The Barlow Committee (Barlow, 1940) raised the congested city and town problem, concluding that 'planned decentralisation' was necessary. It also emphasised food production, stating:

> Since 1900 urbanisation has been so rapid that it is stated to have covered with bricks and mortar an area equal in size to the counties of Buckingham and Bedford combined ... regard must be had to the agricultural needs of the country. (Barlow, 1940, para 36)

The Scott Report (Scott, 1942), *Land Utilisation in Rural Areas*, also concentrated on agricultural land loss. Both reports urged government to take action to control development location on a national basis, recommending setting up a central planning authority, immediate planning control nationwide and a national plan for locating industry and population. The Expert Committee on Compensation and Betterment (Uthwatt, 1942) advised on the compensation issue.

The wartime Coalition government did little to implement the proposals in the Barlow, Uttwatt and Scott reports, but in the Distribution of Industry Act 1945, passed at the insistence of Hugh Dalton, then Minister for Trade, introduced a system of 'industrial development certificates' aimed at directing industry to the 1930s' depressed areas. Industrial development certificates, widely applied in the 1960s but falling out of favour in the 1970s, were abolished in 1986.

Post-war planning

The planning ideals formed in the 20th century culminated in legislation passed by the 1945–51 Labour government.

The Town and Country Planning Act 1947

Development rights were nationalised under the Town and Country Planning Act 1947. Henceforth, land development would require permission from planning authorities, subject to appeal to the relevant minister, and planning decisions had to conform to local plans. Ravetz (1986, p 87) notes that for the public 'to "participate" in planning on the terms laid down was quite daunting, if not impossible'. Local authorities advertised planning applications on notices attached to lampposts, and the public hearings to examine plans took a quasi-judicial form. The Skeffington Committee (Skeffington, 1969) was set up to examine ways to extend public participation in planning and some of Skeffington's recommendations for greater public involvement were included in the Town and Country Planning Act 1971 – more publicity for planning applications and procedures for participation in the early stages of plan preparation. Labour was ambivalent on public participation in planning; according to Shapely (2014, p viii), 'Many including Wilson, felt that only a few interfering members of the middle class, who were hostile to Labour, really wanted participation'. Perhaps Harold Wilson was right. The Town and Country Planning Act 1971 coincided with homeownership becoming the majority UK tenure. Planning – 'essentially a ruthless bargaining process ... concerned with conflicts of interest and the distribution of limited resources' (Bruton and Nicholson, 1986, p 7) and not a rational process seeking the 'common good' – now had the home-owning middle class at the table, initiating what Ortalo-Magné and Prat (2007, p 4) called a 'vicious circle between homeownership and housing supply'. Commenting on contemporary planning and its impact on working farmers in the Lake District, Rebanks (2015, p 123) says:

> Sheep to the 'incomers' were things that held them up on the road.... At worst, some of these people had such a strong sense of 'ownership' of our landscape as a kind of public commodity that they believed they should have a powerful voice in its future. If anyone threatened to build anything new they would launch vociferous letter-writing campaigns and scare the wits out of planning officers.

Local opposition was particularly vociferous when 'social' housing was proposed. Legacy et al (2016, p 2) comment:

> Urban strategies will frame affordable and social housing as integral to achieving liveable, inclusive and diverse urban environments. Yet the discussions about the role social housing plays often cease when social housing proposals are being considered. Instead, these discussions are usually forced by affected residents in a haze of emotion reacting to social housing proposals, often in the form of fierce opposition to proposals.

New towns

Labour entrusted the new town establishment to 'Development Corporations' with powers to acquire sites and financed by public loans plus the housing subsidies normally paid to local authorities. The Conservatives regarded New Towns as useful mechanisms to avoid 'urban sprawl' and there was little opposition to the New Towns Act 1946 as it progressed through Parliament. However, local objectors strenuously contested the first new towns. When Lewis Silkin, the responsible minister, attended a packed public meeting in Stevenage, the site for the first proposed new town, he met with an angry reaction. Silkin stood firm, telling his audience 'It's no good your jeering, it's going to be done' (quoted in Kynaston, 2007, p 163). Silkin's car was damaged and fake railway station signs were erected renaming Stevenage as 'Silkingrad'.

Fourteen new towns, mainly aimed at relieving London's population 'overspill', were designated in the first wave, and the second and third waves – targeted more at provincial areas – authorised 18 more. Long public enquiries and court challenges delayed new town starts, but by the mid-1960s, new towns housed 1.5 million people. The houses supplied were mainly terraced and semi-detached and the schemes attracted scathing attacks from factions in the architectural profession. Labelling the new towns 'prairie planning' with houses 'marooned in a desert of grass verges', Richards (1953, p 33) concluded that 'the Englishman today goes on building suburbs which he dignifies by the name of towns' – a critique chiming with the developing Conservative notion that state housing must be contained. Macmillan, faced with Treasury demands for programme cutbacks and calls from his party to increase owner-occupation, endorsed selling houses in new towns and encouraged private developers to build homes.

The Town Development Act 1952 was an attempt to add a further outlet for 'overspill' and reduce the need for more new town designations. It granted Exchequer subsidies to encourage 'orderly and friendly arrangements' between 'receiving' and 'exporting' local authorities (Macmillan, 1952). By the early 1960s, London County Council had entered into agreements to construct 60,000 rented houses in 20 areas, Birmingham had a dozen agreements for 17,000 homes and there were other contracts in Manchester, Liverpool and Newcastle. However, this was insufficient to meet the major city slum clearance programmes and Sir Keith Joseph, when Minister for Housing and Local Government, pressed the Cabinet to designate more new towns.

New town demise

Despite increasing concern about their social impact – the term 'new town blues' was becoming popular – those around London were a 'profitable venture' (Macmillan, 1969, p 418), producing development gains more than sufficient to compensate for the struggling northern new towns. The New Towns Act 1946 envisaged that as the new towns reached maturity, the Development Corporations would transfer their assets to the appropriate local authority, but the maturing new town economic success prompted the Conservatives to set up a government-controlled body – the New Towns Commission – to take central control over the industrial and commercial assets. Under the Thatcher/Major governments, all the Development Corporations were dissolved, their commercial assets and many freehold sites were sold to private companies, and much of their housing stock was passed to housing associations. Alexander (2009, pp 4–5) reports that 'The last of the loans were repaid in 1999 with the final sum estimated at £4.75 billion.... Since then surplus land assets in the New Towns have generated a further £600 million profit for the government'.

Another dimension to new town politics was revealed in 1983 when Consortium Developments Ltd wanted to develop up to 15 privately financed new country towns around London, hoping that Thatcher's government would respond to a private sector initiative. Four proposals went to the planning stage but they were rejected by the Secretary of State for the Environment.

Eco-towns

Eco-towns formed part of New Labour's belated response to the housing supply issue. They would have between 5,000 and 20,000 homes with a variety of tenures and house sizes and, as 'an exemplar of ... environmental technology', would 'achieve zero carbon' (DCLG, 2007, p 4). There was considerable interest in eco-towns, and by April 2008, 57 – largely private developer-led – bids had been made. In 2009, New Labour announced a second wave of eco-towns to produce 10 in total by 2020, with £70 million of state funding. However, if New Labour expected its eco-town idea would nullify opposition to development from the rural protection lobby, it was to be disappointed. Strong local opposition to eco-towns developed, supported by Grant Shapps, then shadow housing minister. In April 2011, the Coalition government announced that only one eco-town, Northwest Bicester in Oxfordshire, would be built to the originally proposed standards, and in 2015, the programme, except for Northwest Bicester, was abandoned. Brandon Lewis, Minister for Housing and Planning, said:

> the eco-towns programme built nothing but resentment. The initiative was a total shambles, with developers abandoning the process, application for judicial review, the timetable being extended over and over, and local opposition growing to the then government's unsustainable and environmentally damaging proposals. (Lewis, 2015)

Green belts

Herbert Morrison, London County Council Leader in the late 1930s, devised the first operative green belt. The (London and Home Counties) Green Belt Act 1938 empowered local authorities to buy land in order to keep it undeveloped and made provision for landowners to enter into covenants for their land to become green belt in return for compensatory payments. The Greater London Plan of 1944 prepared by Sir Patrick Abercrombie incorporated a 'green belt ring'.

Containing urban Britain

When agricultural land loss to housing development was raised in 1952, Harold Macmillan 'went into battle' with the Minister of Agriculture to ensure that land was available for housing (Glendinning and Mulhesius, 1994). However, with progress made in easing the housing shortage, urban containment became more important in Conservative circles.

In the early 1950s, some large boroughs, anxious to acquire sites to house residents displaced by slum clearance, came into conflict with their surrounding county councils. Sheffield, for example, sponsored a private Bill in Parliament annexing part of the West Riding to meet its predicted 49,000 new homes requirement, and Staffordshire persuaded the House of Lords to reject a Bill promoted by Wolverhampton to extend its boundaries. Manchester continued its interwar resistance to inner-city flats, with a Manchester councillor telling a House of Lords committee that Manchester must 'expand or die' (*The Times* 1954, quoted in Shapely, 2007a, p 102). It put forward proposals for a new development in either Mobberley or Lymm to accommodate a projected 87,000 housing shortfall arising from slum clearance. These proposals were opposed by Cheshire – 'resenting any notion of Manchester extending its power' (Shapely, 2007a, p 100) – with some of its residents worried about 'immigration' by Mancunians (*The*

Times, 1954, quoted in Shapely, 2007a, p 111). The minister called in Manchester's applications and rejected them because the land had agricultural value and due to 'their position in a natural green belt around the conurbation, a formal green belt not then having been designated' (quoted in Hall et al, 1973, p 588). Manchester councillors, claiming that they would 'never give up in their claims to the "green areas of Cheshire"' (*Manchester Evening News*, 1957), persisted in their demand for a site in Lymm and the issue was discussed by the Cabinet several times in the 1950s, with Manchester plan rejection the recurring outcome.

Mindful of its rural vote, the Conservative government responded to lobbying from the Council for the Protection of Rural England. The Minister for Housing, Duncan Sandys, prompted local government into action by declaring:

> I am convinced that for the well-being of our people and for the preservation of our countryside the unrestricted sprawl of the great cities must be contained.... But I regret that nowhere [outside London] has any formal green belt as yet been posed. (Quoted in Elson, 1986, pp 13–14)

Circular 42/55 (MHLG, 1955) stated '[The Minister] is satisfied that the only really effective way to achieve [checking the unrestricted sprawl of built-up areas] is by the formal designation of clearly defined Green Belts around the areas concerned', and recommended that 'wherever practicable a Green Belt should be several miles wide'. Despite objections from large boroughs, protesting that they had no say in green belt designation and were being 'fenced in', green belts were rapidly designated. Land prices escalated and the Conservatives devised plans to house inner-city residents in high-density accommodation (see Chapter Three).

Fencing the cities continued into the 1970s. Despite a Royal Commission, chaired by Lord Redcliffe-Maud (1969), recommending extending metropolitan boundaries, the eventual reform undertaken by the Conservatives in the early 1970s drew narrow borders around most conurbations. In Greater Manchester, for example, the Redcliffe-Maud Report included land from Cheshire (including Macclesfield, Warrington, Alderley Edge, Northwich, Middlewich, Wilmslow and Lymm) and Derbyshire (the towns of New Mills, Whaley Bridge, Glossop and Chapel-en-le-Frith). The Local Government Act 1972 incorporated none of this territory into Greater Manchester.

Margaret Thatcher and green belts

Despite prompting from neoliberal think tanks, Margaret Thatcher's government made only limited attempts to loosen planning's grip on the land market. Patrick Jenkin attempted to modify green belt designation when Secretary of State for the Environment between 1983 and 1985. He told Parliament that 'If green belt policy is to be successful, however, it is important that local planning authorities should, when drawing detailed green belt boundaries, make provision for necessary future development' (Jenkin, 1983). This announcement was met with hostility from the Council for the Protection of Rural England and many Conservative MPs. Jenkin dropped the idea but his political career was damaged (Ward, 2004). William Waldegrave, a junior Environment Minister in the mid-1980s, expressed the political reality, stating:

> there is actually a lot of derelict land in the Green Belt, so why do we not try and create something attractive instead of, for instance, these terrible old gravel pits. The trouble is everyone believes that this would be seized upon as a wonderfully convenient opening by the developers.... So it has become almost impossible to change it. (Quoted in Porritt and Winner, 1988, pp 83–4)

Nicholas Ridley, Secretary of State for the Environment from 1987 to 1989, also expressed concerns about development land scarcity. He declared:

> The fact is that it is simply not possible to accommodate all demand in towns or force all development into towns and cities.... They need parks and green spaces and gardens too, and resent the implication that all development can be dumped in their back yard. (Quoted in Conservative Party, 1989)

Soon after these views became public, Ridley was identified as the principal objector to a low-cost housing development near his own property!

John Major's government responded to the land availability issue by trying to restrict household formation and encouraging building on brownfield sites. *Household Growth: Where Shall We Live?* (Secretary of State for the Environment, 1996) explicitly ruled out meeting housing demand in areas where requirements were highest because such a policy was 'environmentally unsustainable'. The paper contained proposals on how household formation might be restricted, such as: encouraging more students to remain at home; persuading more elderly people to live with their children; measures to reduce the incidence of divorce and separation; and 'taking action to ensure that benefits do not encourage household formation unnecessarily' (Secretary of State for the Environment, 1996, p 16). The commitment to green belt policy by the Thatcher/Major governments meant that between 1979 and 1997, the total size of the UK green belt increased from 721,500 hectares to 1,649,640 hectares.

Planning and New Labour

To the extent that New Labour had a land release strategy, it was confined to extending brownfield site use and bolstering the regional government dimension, hoping that a regional outlook would counterbalance local authority resistance to development. Under the Regional Development Agencies Act 1998, Regional Development Agencies were set up with a Chair from the business community and representatives from business, local government, trade unions and voluntary organisations. 'Regional Assemblies' were also established to channel regional opinion to the Development Agencies. New Labour endorsed the Conservatives' brownfield policy and dwellings built on brownfield sites increased from 56% in 1997 to 77% in 2007. Over the same period, density soared from 25 to 44 per hectare.

Post-2003, the planning system moved into Treasury control. Gordon Brown started to try to boost overall land release by setting targets for local authorities through 'regional spatial strategies' prepared by Regional Assemblies and Regional Development Agencies, and influencing the 'planning culture' by emphasising planning's impact on economic growth. Brown appointed Kate Barker, a Bank of England Monetary Policy Committee member, to explore ways to deliver stability in the housing market. She recommended setting national and regional affordability targets that, if unmet, would trigger land release (Barker, 2004). The Green Paper 'Homes for the Future: More Affordable, More Sustainable' (DCLG, 2007) announced an increase in housing supply to 240,000 per year by 2016. Local authorities would be required to allocate enough land to meet their target share, with a threat that if a local authority did not allocate ample land for a rolling five-year house-building programme, then developers would find it easy to obtain planning permission. The 'credit crunch' derailed New

Labour's housing target but continued pressure was applied to the planning system in the hope that this would stimulate supply. Regional Assemblies were gradually abolished from 2008 because local council representation had proved troublesome in adopting regional planning strategies. New Labour viewed the unelected Regional Assemblies as a prelude to directly elected Regional Assemblies but abandoned this idea after a referendum in North-East England overwhelmingly rejected an assembly. Regional Development Agencies prepared Regional Spatial Strategies and a Planning Delivery Grant was introduced to encourage local authorities to deliver new homes.

The Coalition government

Localism

Soon after he became Conservative Party leader, David Cameron claimed that the failure to provide an adequate number of new homes in Britain had contributed to the affordability problem. He said that 'This situation is bananas. I say it's bananas because one of the problems we've faced is a system that encourages people to believe we should Build Absolutely Nothing Anywhere Near Anyone' (Cameron, 2006). However, as the strength of 'Middle England' opposition to development became evident, the Conservatives started to advocate local housing requirement determination. Prior to the 2010 election campaign, many Tory MPs, including Greg Clark, Grant Shapps and Eric Pickles, backed local battles against development in their constituencies and the Conservative Party campaigned against New Labour's 'top-down' planning targets. The Liberal Democrats adopted a similar position, with their 2010 manifesto declaring that the party would 'return decision making, including housing targets, to local people' (Liberal Democrats, 2010, p 81). The Coalition government agreement announced the abolition of Regional Spatial Strategies and that decision-making powers on housing and planning would return to local councils. It stated:

> in the longer term, we will radically reform the planning system to give neighbourhoods far more ability to determine the shape of the places in which their inhabitants live, based on the principles set out in the Conservative Party publication Open Source Planning. (HM Government, 2010, p 11)

In 2010, Eric Pickles declared that he would axe New Labour's 'soviet tractor style' regional planning (Gov.uk, 2010) and replace it with a 'New Homes Bonus'. Local authorities would receive a 100% addition to the council tax raised for six years, with extra resources for delivering 'affordable' homes. However, the declaration on abolishing Regional Housing Strategies produced a planning vacuum that, according to a joint report by the Chartered Institute of Housing, the National Housing Federation and Shelter (2011, p 11), 'may already be having an effect on potential development. Independent research by Tetlow King Planning ... demonstrated that local authorities reduced planning targets by 221,000 dwellings by not adhering to RSS [Regional Spatial Strategies] figures'. Moreover, the potential house-building hiatus meant that the Coalition government did little to enhance construction industry capacity, badly damaged in the credit crunch, thus limiting the industry's ability to respond to future demand.

Planning and economic growth

The planning vacuum started alarm bells ringing in the Treasury. In early 2011, Cabinet member Oliver Letwin reviewed housing policy relating to the private housing market, and in his 2011 Budget speech, Chancellor George Osborne stated that planning was a 'chronic obstacle' to economic growth. He announced that there would be 'a new presumption in favour of sustainable development' (Osborne, 2011).

'The Draft Planning Policy Framework' (DCLG, 2011a) was a victory for the Treasury in its ambition to make the planning system an economic growth mechanism. It asserted that 'Planning must operate to encourage growth and not act as an impediment' (DCLG, 2011a, p 3). Although the framework re-emphasised local plan importance, it announced that local authorities should 'grant permission where the plan is absent, silent, indeterminate or where relevant policies are out of date ... there should be "a presumption in favour of sustainable development"' (DCLG, 2011a, p 4). No emphasis was placed on using brownfield sites. Reflecting New Labour's approach to setting regional targets, it claimed that 'planning policies and decisions should take into account local circumstances and market signals such as land prices, commercial rents and housing affordability' (DCLG, 2011a, p 5). Each local plan would be examined by an independent examiner, whose role was to assess if the plan was 'sound', that is, objectively ascertained need and identified and maintained a 'rolling supply of specific deliverable sites sufficient to provide five years' worth of housing against their housing requirements' (DCLG, 2011a, p 30). The supply had to include 'an additional allowance set at a minimum of 20% to ensure choice and competition in the market for land' (DCLG, 2011a, p 30).

'Middle England' revolt

'The Draft Planning Policy Framework' provoked a forceful reaction from the Campaign to Protect Rural England and the National Trust. The Campaign to Protect Rural England (2011, p 1) claimed that the document 'will place the countryside under increasing threat. Many elements of the Framework are deeply worrying. In particular, Ministers have failed to commit to the principle that the countryside should be protected for its own intrinsic character, beauty and heritage'. The National Trust Chair and journalist Simon Jenkins claimed:

> It's a recipe for civil war.... There is simply no evidence, beyond the howls of lobbyists, that land-use planning impedes growth.... Rural England will start to look like the south of Ireland, Spain or New Jersey, its inhabitants ever more reliant on cars, and cities ever more impoverished. (Jenkins, 2011)

The National Trust's Director General wrote to the Trust's four million members asking them to protest against key proposals in 'The Draft Planning Policy Framework', and the *Telegraph* mounted a campaign against the policy under the banner 'Hands Off Our Land', running articles such as 'The Horrors Hidden in the Draft National Planning Policy Framework' (*Telegraph*, 2011).

At first, this 'Middle England' revolt had only a limited impact. The final 'National Planning Policy Framework' (DCLG, 2012a) was less strident in tone and contained warm words, such as preserving the 'intrinsic character and beauty of the countryside'. It made a few concessions, such as a reference to the first use of brownfield land, but the framework retained the main draft document proposals. Moreover, the 'localism' agenda was diluted. Neighbourhood development plans, part of 'localism' and the related 'Big Society' agenda, were not compulsory and became subject to an independent examination by the local planning authority. Plans had to conform to the National Planning Policy Framework. In Cameron's government reshuffle in September 2012, Nick Boles replaced Greg Clark as Planning Minister. Boles, a founding Director of the pro-market Policy Exchange, made a number of vigorous pro-development speeches. In one lecture, he asserted:

> I think everyone has the right to live somewhere that is not
> just affordable but that is beautiful and has some green space
> nearby … a basic moral right, like healthcare and education.
> There's a right to a home with a little bit of ground around
> it to bring your family up in. (Quoted in Wintour, 2012)

Land release: the developer's role

Construction industry representatives often portray land release as a clash between new housing construction and rural protectionism but developers have an interest in 'land banking'. In order to ensure production flow, developers need a stock of land with and without planning permission. Their 'current' land bank is land with planning permission, whereas they buy their 'strategic' land on 'option', hoping for future planning permission. Hence, because developers purchase land well before they start on site, a significant part of their profit comes from land price increases. Developers time their building to secure the maximum value for their land, hence the accusation of 'land hoarding' made against them. Indeed, the Institute for Public Policy Research has stated that 'For decades our developers have focused more on playing the land market and the planning system than on building homes: we must break this link' (Griffith, 2012, p 3). Concern about land banking led Nick Boles, Coalition Planning Minister, to announce that he would no longer allow developers to rollover planning permissions (*Inside Housing*, 2013) and Labour declared that developers with planning permission must 'use it or lose it'. However, in 2015, the nine major house-builders held more than 600,000 housing plots but sold only 66,881 homes (Ruddick, 2015). In 2016, planning approval had been granted for 475,627 houses, and although planning approvals had increased by 60% since 2010, there had only been a 48% increase in the number of homes built (Wright, 2016).

Mansion Tax

Contemporary land and property taxation is complicated, involving Council Tax, Stamp Duty Land Tax, Inheritance Tax, Capital Gains Tax, the CIL and planning obligations. The Policy Exchange (2013b) has estimated that these taxes – including levies on buildings as well as land – are worth 4.1% of gross domestic product (GDP), indicating that current land taxes produce low revenues. The Liberal Democrats put forward a Mansion Tax, capturing land and buildings value, in their 2010 manifesto. Initially with a threshold at £1 million, recognition of its electoral implications for London produced a £2 million threshold (Liberal Democrats, 2010). In 2014, the Labour Party endorsed the idea, with progressive rates starting at £2 million and with the facility for households with modest incomes to pay the tax on the sale of the property. The Mansion Tax did not form part of the Coalition agreement but the Liberal Democrats continued to promote it, claiming that it would not require any general revaluation of property. Cameron resisted the tax, stating 'With Ed Balls and Vince Cable banging on about mansion taxes every day, the Conservative election coffers are going to be full in no time at all. They really, really, really hate this' (quoted in Laws, 2016, p 197).

The 2015 general election

Both the parties forming the Coalition government relied on anti-development stances to garner votes in the 2010 general election. Post-2012, the stagnant economy prompted the Coalition to adopt a more pro-development stance, but as the 2015 general election approached and threatened by United Kingdom Independence Party's (UKIP's) strong pro-green belt stance, the Conservative Party's attitude to land release started to change. Oakeshott and Henry (2013) claim that David Cameron was 'facing a revolt in more than 30 Conservative constituencies as his relaxation of planning laws backfires', and *Inside Housing* (2014) reported that Nick Boles had been told to tone down his tough talk on promoting house-building. Although enthusiastic about new garden cities and towns in 2012, an article in the *Financial Times* (2013) alleged that Cameron's interest had started to wilt by late 2013, and fearful of a 'NIMBY' backlash, he had forbidden ministers from identifying new town sites. According to the *Telegraph* (2014), a report advocating two new garden cities in Buckinghamshire, Warwickshire or Oxfordshire, was suppressed. Nick Clegg demanded that the Conservatives announce where the new garden cities should be built, prompting a response from Boris Johnson (2014) accusing Clegg of planning to 'plonk colossal new Cleggograds and Cleggopolises' in Buckinghamshire, Oxfordshire and Berkshire.

In his March 2014 Budget, George Osborne announced only one new town at Ebbsfleet in Kent, already the subject of an agreement between three Kent councils and a developer for 22,600 new homes to be built over 20 years. The government published a prospectus 'Locally-led Garden Cities' (DCLG, 2014) inviting expressions of interest from local authorities in developing garden cities. Only limited government support was promised in the form of 'brokerage', help from an advisory team, capacity funding to contribute to planning and assistance in identifying private sector funding. The amount of direct capital assistance from central government was unspecified but there would be access to a Large Sites Fund, a Custom Build Fund and a Builders Finance Fund. This lukewarm approach to development was reflected in Nick Boles' removal from the post of Planning Minister, having been asked to apologise for losing Tory seats (*Telegraph*, 2014). His replacement, Brandon Lewis, expressed disapproval of any extra new towns (Lewis, 2014). Pickles and Lewis (2014) published additional guidance reaffirming the government's belief in green belt protection, stating that, once established, green belt boundaries should only be altered in exceptional cases and housing need did not justify the harm done to the green belt.

The final 'National Planning Policy Framework' had retained the notion that in the absence of an adopted local plan, there would be a presumption in favour of sustainable development. An investigation by Savills found that 76% of local authorities did not have an adopted post-National Planning Policy Framework plan and many adopted plans were based on out-of-date housing requirement assessments. The investigation claimed:

> Our analysis shows that the number of homes planned by local authorities in England is likely to result in a shortfall of around 36,000 homes a year, unless local planning authorities take greater account of housing need both within and beyond their boundaries. (Savills, 2015, p 4)

A survey by *Inside Housing* (Maier, 2014) found that local authorities without an approved plan had a higher rate of new build than those with a plan. They were more likely to lose appeals against planning permission refusals but did win some of them. Indeed, having left the Prime Minister's Office, where he was advisor on housing, Alex Morton claimed:

> But when I was in Number 10 and dug out the figures (which officials were not keen to share) fewer than ten councils (out of 326) turned out to have an up to date local plan and deliver their housing needs. A similar number do so without an up to date local plan.

Later, *Inside Housing* (2015) reported that 'Eric Pickles blocked the development of 9,200 homes in the run up to the General Election, refusing all applications he considered in Conservative-controlled councils'. The presumption that in the absence of an approved local plan, 'sustainable' development would be approved had been modified through 'planning by appeal'.

Manifestos

The 2015 Conservative Party manifesto pledged to protect the green belt and concentrate new housing on brownfield sites. It stated:

> We will ensure that brownfield land is used as much as possible for new development ... and ensure that 90 per cent of suitable brownfield sites have planning permission for housing by 2020. To meet the capital's housing needs, we will create a new London Land Commission, with a mandate to identify and release all surplus brownfield land owned by the public sector. We will fund Housing Zones to transform brownfield sites into new housing, which will create 95,000 new homes. (Conservative Party, 2015, pp 52–3)

Other than claiming that it had 'unblocked the planning system' (Conservative Party, 2015, p 50), the manifesto ignored the Conservative role in the planning reform contained in the 'National Planning Policy Framework' (DCLG, 2012a). In contrast, the 2015 Liberal Democrat manifesto was far more enthusiastic about releasing land than its 2010 manifesto. It set a 300,000 new homes per annum target and contained robust proposals to stimulate housing supply, including at least 10 new garden cities in England and new garden villages or suburbs. It claimed 'We have liberalised the planning system' (Liberal Democrats, 2015, p 94) and went beyond the National Planning Policy Framework by proposing that local authorities would have to plan to meet housing requirements for 15 years. Future green belt protection was absent from the manifesto, although the importance of 'green spaces' was highlighted.

Apart from giving local authorities new 'use it or lose it' powers to encourage developers to build and alluding to the Lyons Committee recommendations that had proposed 'Housing Growth Areas' and endorsed new towns (Lyons, 2014), the Labour Party manifesto was silent on the mechanisms to release land, although, significantly, it did not mention protecting existing green belts. Given UKIP's belief that the housing shortage was due to immigration, it was not surprising that the party set no target for new house construction. UKIP's manifesto declared:

> UKIP will not allow new housing to strip our nation of prime agricultural land. This must be kept for its primary purpose, creating a secure food supply for Britain and for export. Neither will we allow the countryside to be swamped by over-development: we believe strongly that our countryside must be preserved so it can be enjoyed by future generations. (UKIP, 2015, p 35)

The Green Party's manifesto, despite a commitment to building 500,000 new social rented homes, declared its intention to 'minimize encroachment onto undeveloped greenfield sites' (Green Party, 2015, p 41). It did not endorse garden cities.

Conclusion

Land politics changed significantly during the 20th century. The landowning 'aristocracy' waned as a political force as Estate Duty and declining agricultural profitability eroded its wealth and the 'meritocracy' idea diminished its prestige. Nonetheless, reflecting the notion that some issues remain aloof from the political agenda, landownership in the UK remains obscure. KPMG (2014, p 8) noted 'the lack of transparency or published data on the land market', and the Lyons Committee (Lyons, 2014, p 63) claimed that 'greater transparency about ownership, options and transactions would deliver a number of important benefits that would result in better operation of the land market'.

In the 1930s, influenced by the growing salience of homeownership, Conservative land politics started to switch to restraining urban Britain, with ribbon development restriction accompanied by high-density flats in inner cities, a policy revisited in the 1950s with green belt designation complemented by building tower blocks in the major cities. Commenting on planning's impact, Simmie (1993, p 3) said:

> It has created a residential form of apartheid. Existing rural county property owners and the new service class have used Green Belts and other restrictive practices to raise the cost of access to their sub-urban environments. This has confined groups not able to meet these inflated costs ... to the older urban cores.

Containing urban Britain took a different form in the 2000s. Rather than fencing in slum dwellers, the 'brownfield first' policy was aimed at households without children. The policy produced small flats, mainly occupied by 'new', childless households and located in urban centres.

The sudden change in Coalition government policy on land release – from outright opposition to central government involvement in local planning decisions to centrally promoting development via planning guidance – reflected concerns about the moribund economy. The residential construction industry was particularly depressed: new housing starts in England – 167,068 in 2007 – were only 110,740 in 2011. However, by 2014, the economic upturn and the electoral politics involved in development control, emphasised by public choice theory, had combined to modify Conservative enthusiasm for house-building. A KPMG report noted:

> Planning reform is extremely tough politically. The coalition government's planning reforms faced strong opposition from conservation groups and rural local authorities. Further planning liberalisation would face equally tough opposition and may not be politically possible, especially if it involves major changes to green belt policies. (KPMG, 2014, p 40)

Kate Barker (2014, p 85) echoed this view, declaring that 'The opposition to new development in the South East ... makes it questionable that the rate of new dwelling supply will keep up with unconstrained demand in this and other parts of southern England'. The Lyons Committee was careful to place local government at the forefront of its proposals to boost housing production via land release.

New Labour made only a lukewarm attempt to reduce London's influence in generating economic growth. Between 1997 and 2010, London accounted for 43% of all extra full-time jobs created in the UK. The potential ballot box consequences of promoting housing development in the South focused the Coalition government's attention on stimulating economic growth in other regions, culminating in the 'Northern Powerhouse' idea (see Chapter Three). However, from 2010 to 2014, London saw the fastest economic growth at 24.0% – not adjusted for inflation – followed by the South-East at 16.6%, whereas the growth in the North-East was 12.1%, the North-West was 11.1% and Yorkshire and Humberside was 10.7% (Harari, 2015), indicating that redirecting southern growth and its associated housing requirements will be difficult. Meanwhile, the London green belt remained intact and seemingly politically sacrosanct, with Sadiq Khan (2016, p 66) declaring in his London mayoral manifesto that he would 'oppose building on the Green Belt, which is even more important today than it was when it was created'. The Conservative candidate announced that 'London's green spaces are safer with me, not Sadiq Khan' (Goldsmith, 2016a). The full London green belt, extending into the South-East of England, envelops four times as much land as the built-up area of London, and within the Greater London border, 22% of all land is green belt. Fourteen London boroughs have more land assigned as green belt than with houses (Quod and London First, 2015). A 2016 poll by the *Observer* found that although 69% agreed with the statement 'Britain is in the throes of a housing crisis', only 9% agreed that building homes in the green belt was a solution (*Observer*, 2016). The 2015 general election outcome did not settle the land question. It is unlikely that brownfield sites can accommodate future housing requirements and land release for housing will remain a major political issue (see Chapter Ten).

Further reading

Alexander, A. (2009) *Britain's New Towns: Garden Cities to Sustainable Communities*, London: Routledge.

Amati, M. (ed) (2008) *Urban Green Belts in the Twenty-first Century*, Aldershot: Ashgate.

Cannadine, D. (1990) *The Decline and Fall of the British Aristocracy*, Yale: Yale University Press.

Cox, A. (1984) *Adversary Politics and Land: The Conflict Over Land and Property Policy in Post-War Britain*, Cambridge: Cambridge University Press.

Elson, M.J. (1986) *Green Belts: Conflict Mediation in the Urban Fringe*, London: Heinemann.

George, H. (1979 [1879]) *Progress and Poverty*, London: Hogarth Press.

Hall, P., Gracey, H., Drewett, R. and Thomas, R. (1973) *The Containment of Urban England, Volume One: Urban and Metropolitan Growth Processes or Megalopolis Denied*, London: George Allen and Unwin.

Howard, E. (1902) *Garden Cities of Tomorrow*, London: Faber.

THREE

Urban renewal:
fencing the cities

Urban renewal policies in the 19th century and most of the 20th century focused on the 'slum', identified as the locale of disease, crime, mob violence and moral degeneration – the social evil epicentre. Although many Victorian politicians regarded slum eradication as necessary for public health and public morality, unfit, densely packed and internally overcrowded dwellings were a lucrative profit source, well defended by vested interests. Urban redevelopment produced intermittent but significant progress in the 20th century, with 'reconditioning' versus 'clearance' and urban containment being recurring themes. By the late 1970s, political attention started to shift away from the housing stock's physical condition towards the economic drivers of inner-city decline, producing economic and 'property-led' initiatives accompanied by 'gentrification'. New Labour reintroduced area selective schemes mainly focused on upgrading 'human' and 'social' capital to reduce social exclusion. The Coalition government abandoned this approach, concentrating on market-led growth, 'whole city' approaches and workforce 'activation' via changes in the social security system – a policy intensified by the 2015 Conservative government.

Nineteenth-century public health politics

The rapid urbanisation in the 19th century could be sensed, with noses particularly sensitive in London. The stench from cesspits, rivers, 'fat-boilers, glue-renderers, fell-mongers, tripe-scrapers [and] dog-skinners' (Chesney, 1970, p 16) eventually became the 'Great Stink' as the Thames failed to absorb London's waste. There was 'Fog everywhere…. The raw afternoon is rawest, the dense fog is densest, and the muddy streets are muddiest near that leaden-headed old obstruction … Temple Bar' (Dickens, 1993 [1852], p 1). The 'labyrinths' and 'rookeries' were visited and their sensations reported but attempts to understand urbanisation's impact 'objectively' relied on 'evangelical bureaucrats': experts in medicine, engineering and statistics with a 'public good' vision.

The evangelistic bureaucrat

Edwin Chadwick was the prototype 'evangelical bureaucrat'. His *Report on the Sanitary Condition of the Labouring Population of Great Britain* (Chadwick, 1842) assembled statistics on urbanisation's effects. Areas with the highest death rates were characterised by deficient fresh water supplies and inadequate waste removal. He then set out what economists now call 'externalities': the side impacts of a condition that affect other parties without being reflected in the price of the good or service involved. These 'externalities' included the poor relief costs for orphans and widows, that 'the younger population … is inferior in physical organization and general health', and the adult population was 'short-lived, improvident, reckless, and intemperate', with 'habitual avidity for sensual gratifications' (Chadwick, 1842, pp 369–72).

Chadwick's report demonstrates how a particular 'social problem' explanation can become dominant. His statistics showed a strong relationship between social class and health but other interpretations of this association, developed by Scottish investigators, were available – hard labour and lack of proper food – known as 'privation' at the time (Hamlin, 1995). Although aware of these explanations, Chadwick ignored them because they were politically unacceptable. Heffer (2013) identifies three years in the 19th century when revolution was a threat. One such year was 1842, and with Chartism still a force, ill-health explanations located in economic structures might have sparked further unrest. The Home Secretary, Lord John Russell, had vetoed an earlier inquiry into 'the discontents the working classes in populous districts' because it might lead to 'suggestion of political remedies' (quoted in Brundage, 1988, p 81).

Despite the report's emphasis on the economic benefits to be obtained from sanitary reform – apart from improved human capital, Chadwick thought that nitrogen-rich 'sewer manure' would be valuable – Sir Robert Peel's Conservative government, mindful of sanitation's upfront costs, insisted on a further investigation by a Royal Commission. Chadwick and his followers were determined to press the issue. They launched the Health of Towns Association to promote action, and by the time the Royal Commission's report was published verifying Chadwick's account, another cholera epidemic had pushed the public health issue up the political agenda. The Whigs, in power from 1846 to 1852, were more receptive than the Tories to 'scientific enquiry' findings, and in 1848, they passed the Public Health Act, making provision to establish local Boards of Health, except in London, which was already under the Metropolitan Commission of Sewers' control. The Act created a General Board of Health as a central authority to administer the Act. Strong economic interests were involved in opposing the General Board of Health's actions. The water companies had profits to defend and the 'vestries' – with powers to regulate insanitary properties but representing those with property interests – resisted action.

'Sanitas sanitatum, omnia sanitas'

Chadwick's hectoring, authoritarian style – he was called 'England's Prussian Minister' (Brundage, 1988) – was unhelpful to his cause. Hostility, based on infringing local government and property rights, mounted, and in 1858, the Board was abolished, with its duties taken over by the Privy Council. Not all local authorities were antagonistic to public health measures, and to improve conditions, some used special legislation applying only to their areas. For example, at a time when a third of Mancunians had one 'privy' per 78 people, Manchester acquired powers to require all new properties to have a lavatory – effectively outlawing 'back to backs' – and existing properties had to have at least one 'privy' for every three households (Hylton, 2010).

Following more cholera outbreaks, by the 1870s, the case for public health was so well established that Disraeli – pushing his concern about 'Two Nations' after the 1867 franchise extension – could declare that he had no desire 'to plunder landlords' but *'Sanitas sanitatum, omnia sanitas'* – 'health, everyone's health, all is health' (Disraeli, 1872, p 1). Firmly linking public health to national efficiency, he added:

> After all, the first consideration of a minister should be the
> health of the people … the country may be even famous in
> the annals and action of the world, but, gentlemen, if the
> population every ten years decreases, and the stature of the
> race every ten years diminishes, the history of that country
> will soon be the history of the past. (Disraeli, 1872, pp 1–2)

The rookery and the slum

The term 'rookery', applied to overcrowded areas, was derived from the numerous rooks nesting in a single tree. With its 'to rook', meaning to cheat, undertone, it neatly encapsulated prevailing attitudes to 'the poorest of the poor' – often new migrants struggling for existence in hopelessly overcrowded dwellings. 'Slum', perhaps derived from 'slumber' – 'a sleepy back alley' (Wohl, 1977, p 5) – appeared a little later.

Slums were a dimension of the public health problem – another label applied to the slum was 'plague spot' – but public physical health was only part of the problem. Overcrowded dwellings were regarded as a threat to national decency. Overcrowding was at its worst in Common Lodging Houses, seen as a special threat, with Henry Mayhew, writing in the *Morning Chronicle*, proclaiming:

> Prisons, tread-mills, penal settlements, gallows are all in vain and ragged schools and city missions are of no avail as preventives of crime, as long as these wretched dens of infamy, brutality and vice continue their daily and nightly work of demoralization. (Quoted in O'Neill, 2014, p 49)

Many witnesses giving evidence to Chadwick's enquiry did not mention overcrowding's health implications. They concentrated on its moral consequences, noting that 'young men and women are promiscuously sleeping in the same apartment' (Chadwick, 1842, p 191). Chadwick emphasised that overcrowding was 'destructive to the morality as well as the health of large classes of both sexes' (Chadwick, 1842, p 192). Entire areas were viewed as so teeming with people that 'respectable' society was excluded – often physically by railway embankments (Fishman, 1988) – with 'alien' cultures ascendant. Yet another name for the slum was 'labyrinth', referring to the maze of courts and criss-crossing alleyways in the slum districts. Fogs, more frequent in the marshy districts where slums were often built – Lambeth Marsh was renamed Waterloo in 1848 – enhanced the slum's impenetrable reputation. Slums were 'terra incognito' (Wohl, 1983, p 2) and 'slumming' – visiting the 'rookeries' to report to the mainstream – became a media obsession. Victorian versions of *Benefits Street*, the book titles, often newspaper article compilations, were melodramatic: *The Bitter Cry of Outcast London: An Inquiry into the Condition of the Abject Poor* (Mearns, 1883), *The Paupers, the Thief and the Convict: Sketches of Some of Their Homes, Haunts and Habits* (Archer, 1865) and *The Dens of London Exposed* (Duncombe, 1835). As Gaskell (1990, p 3) remarks, the slums – 'rookeries', 'feverdens', 'little hells', 'devils acres' – were 'a sensation'. Thus, although conditions were real and brutal, 'slum' identity was, in part, 'imagined' (Mayne, 1993) and aimed at provoking particular forms of political action.

Religious conviction had a role in 19th-century housing politics. Evangelical Christians presented the moral case for housing reform, well expressed in Parliament by Lord Shaftesbury, 'for whom social reform was a species of moral reform and moral reform the instrument of spiritual redemption' (Himmelfarb,1984, p 140). Shaftesbury was a member of the Health of Towns Association and influential in establishing the first voluntary organisation aimed at improving working-class housing conditions – the Society for the Improvement of the Condition of the Labouring Classes – formed in 1844 and based on 'Christian principles and Christian ends' (Finlayson, 1994, p 250).

The 'slum' was not only seen as the locale of crime, vice and disease, but also believed to supply a disproportionate share of 'the mob', prone to rebellion and rampage. In 1855, for example, a Sunday Trading Bill was introduced to Parliament with the objective of closing shops, beer houses and public transport to protect the Sabbath. In Hyde Park, 150,000 people gathered to protest against the Bill and the demonstration ended in a riot. In 1886, there was 'rampage' when unemployed workers made their way home to the East End from a central London demonstration. Brodie (2001, p 1) records:

> The *Daily News* said the rioters were 'loafers from the docks, and habitual criminals from the East- End'. Most of those involved, said the *Daily Telegraph*, 'were not genuine industrious working men, but members of the "rough" class, largely recruited from the East-end'.

Dispersal, regulation, ventilation and improvement

The initial political answers to the slum were regulation, dispersal, ventilation and improvement. Many believed that the poor caused overcrowding because they preferred to spend their incomes on drink rather than better accommodation, so local action consisted of regulations allowing the police and sanitary authorities to set standards and control the number of people occupying a Commons Lodging House. Although largely ignored in the growing Northern industrial towns, allegedly because the police feared to enter the premises (O'Neil, 2014), the Act was enforced in London, where, to discourage prostitution, women were not allowed to use Common Lodging Houses.

The Artisans' and Labourers' Dwellings Act 1868 gave stronger powers to local authorities to require owners to demolish unfit houses. The Act was concerned with widening alleys and courts to enhance ventilation and surveillance. If such action forced people to leave congested areas, then, to some, as Dewsnup (1907, p 223) said later, 'it is to the public benefit that they should be driven out of their warrens into the light of day'. Others argued that displacement by improvement schemes led to overcrowding in nearby areas, with Sir Sydney Waterlow advocating rehousing displaced people on the cleared area. Waterlow's view prevailed and led to the Artisans' and Labourers' Dwellings Improvement Act 1875. This Act placed a duty on local authorities to arrange for new dwellings to be built on or near the cleared site, sufficient to rehouse all the displaced persons – later reduced to 50% – but placed severe restrictions on building by local authorities. The land, cleared at public expense, had to be sold to philanthropic, 'model dwelling' housing associations (see Chapter Seven). However, compensation to slum landlords was at full market value and some owners packed their houses with temporary lodgers to claim maximum compensation. The land cost, when passed on to the associations, meant that building on the cleared sites was expensive, so rehousing obligations were often ignored. Joseph Chamberlain's famous central Birmingham 'grand improvement' scheme, started in 1875, eventually led to building Corporation Street but not one new house was built on or near the site. Clearance, when undertaken, simply restricted the availability of low-cost housing to poor families, and when added to the loss of homes in railway construction, it augmented the housing shortage. Gauldie (1974, p 267) notes:

> The first and most sweeping improvement schemes were deliberately driven through the most criminal areas, with the dispersal of criminals from their haunts and the suppression of crime as the first motive.... The frequency with which the emotive phrase 'dens of vice' crops up is some indication of this attitude.

State socialism?

In the 1880s, as clearance legislation consequences became apparent and agitation mounted, housing the working classes became a major political issue. Radical solutions, including land taxation and subsidised state housing, were on offer (see Chapters Two and Six). Such solutions alarmed the property-owning class and the Liberty and Property Defence League vigorously defended property rights in the name of liberty, adding that subsidies to local government to supply houses was the thin edge of a wedge that would lead to putting 'fire in the grate' and 'food in the cupboard' for all families (Wemyss, 1884). New housing was unnecessary because slum dwellers were used to 'foul air and evil smells' (Robertson, 1884, p 46). In an article published in 1883, Lord Salisbury justified cheap Treasury loans on the externalities argument. He warned that 'The overcrowded centres of population are also the centres of disease. The successive discoveries of biologists tell us more clearly that there is in this matter an indissoluble partnership among all human beings breathing in the same vicinity' (Salisbury, quoted in Roberts, 1999, p 282).

Lord Salisbury's modest proposal to improve working-class housing was condemned as entering 'the turbid waters of State Socialism' (*Pall Mall Gazette*, 1884, quoted in Roberts, 1999, p 283). Nonetheless, local government intervention in the housing market continued using 'improvement' powers, consolidated and extended in Part Two of the Housing of the Working Classes Act 1890. Briggs records that, using the 1890 Act, Birmingham 'carried out a large programme of private sector improvement, compelling or persuading owners to thoroughly repair or improve their property.... By 1913 over 28,000 houses had been 'completely repaired' in this way' (Briggs, 1952, p 86).

Filtering

From the 1890s, on the only available national housing condition measure – overcrowding – there was progress. The 1901 census revealed that 8.2% of the population was overcrowded in England and Wales, on the more than two people per room standard adopted by the Registrar General – down from 11.2% in 1891. 'Filtering' was the dominant explanation. Sir Sydney Waterlow – changing his earlier position about rehousing displaced persons on site – conceded that the dwellings companies did not house the very poor. He claimed:

> It would not have been right to build down to the lower class, because you must have built a class of tenement which I hope none of them would be satisfied with at the end of fifty years. We have rather built for the first class, and by lifting them up leave more room for the second and third who are below them. (Quoted in Gauldie, 1974, p 234)

Unfortunately, the model dwelling companies built too few homes to have a significant filtering impact but suburban development eased the 'cramming' problem. Overcrowded slums were, in part, an outcome of the worker's need to be near his workplace and the Cheap Trains Act 1883, requiring railway companies to operate inexpensive workman's trains, although often ignored, helped to disperse the population. More important was the growing middle-class movement into suburbia, leaving behind dwellings that facilitated filtering via renting rooms in subdivided large houses, hence the evocative phrase 'ragged urchins play on marquetry floors' (Harris, 2012).

The 'Residuum'

Harris (1993, p 67) has identified the 'Residuum' idea as 'one of the key concepts in Victorian social science'. The 'Residuum' lived in slums – as Bosanquet (1902, p 3) stated: 'We call it the Residuum, the Poor, the Submerged, the Proletariat, the Abyss and we call its homes Slums and Ghettos and Mean Streets'. 'Over-parent' became a popular phrase to describe the relationship between the middle class and the 'Residuum': the middle class had a duty to guide and, if necessary, coerce the 'submerged' into the mainstream. The 'science' of eugenics was the most coercive element in this 'over-parenting' approach. The Eugenics Education Society, founded in 1907, 'spoke on behalf of the educated middle class who wanted to work with "better human material".... The "unfit" must be discouraged (and perhaps ultimately prevented) from propagating' (Mazumder, 1992, pp 8, 27). Fabians, such as Sydney and Beatrice Webb, George Bernard Shaw and H.G. Wells, supported eugenics, as did many 'new' Liberals – Winston Churchill, William Beveridge and John Atkinson Hobson being the most prominent.

Eugenics and slums

Eugenicists concentrated on the 'feeble-minded' but there was a tendency to generalise the theory's application to other groups. Masterman (1909, p 8) identified a new 'urban type' as 'stunted, narrow-chested, easily wearied; yet voluble, excitable, with little ballast, stamina or endurance – seeking stimulus in drink, in betting, in any unaccustomed conflicts at home or abroad'. Charles Booth graded the London population into eight 'classes', carefully mapping their locations, with Class A being 'the lowest class of occasional labourers, loafers and semi-criminals' (Booth, 1969 [1902], p 33). In evidence to the Inter-departmental Committee on Physical Deterioration, set up to examine why 31% of potential armed forces recruits were rejected due to physical unfitness, Charles Booth replied 'Yes' to the question: 'The undesirable class, which you describe as a dead loss to the State, is composed of the wastrels and ineffectives of society? (quoted in FitzRoy, 1904, p 48). The Inter-departmental Committee concluded that overcrowding in slum areas was a principal cause of physical deterioration, stating that 'The evil is of course greatest in one-roomed tenements, the overcrowding there being among persons usually of the lowest type, steeped in every kind of degradation and cynically indifferent to the vile surroundings engendered by their filthy habits' (FitzRoy, 1904, p 17). It recommended 'that local attacks, "without hesitation or sentimentality", should be launched upon over-crowded areas, without re-housing in order to create dispersion' (quoted in Stedman Jones, 1992, p 331). Garden city advocates also made the connection between slums and poor-quality human stock (Voigt, 1989; Currell, 2010). Ebenezer Howard commented on the 'city eugenic impact', quoting Farrar's belief:

> if it be true that great cites tend more and more to become
> the graves of the physique of our race, can we wonder at it
> when we see the houses so foul, so squalid, so ill-drained,
> so vitiated by neglect and dirt. (Howard, 1902, p 43)

Eugenic influence continued into the interwar period. In 1923, the Secretary of the Eugenics Education Society reminded public health officials that 'plagues in poultry yards have been banished by the prompt destruction of every seedy chick' (Hodson, 1923). Having started its research venture – the Pauper Pedigree Project focused on Liverpool – the Eugenics Education Society continued to make connections between the 'feeble-minded' and the 'slum'. In *The Slum Problem*, Bernard Townroe (1928, p 4), at one time a senior official at the Ministry of Health and Chair of Hampstead's Housing Committee, declared:

> there is unfortunately a type of tenant who always makes
> a 'slum' and can only be prevented from wrecking a house
> by discipline. The same man who as a private soldier was
> compelled to keep himself clean and pay respect to the
> laws of sanitation in the trenches, has since gone back to
> his former undesirable ways.

In a letter to the *Spectator*, Townroe examined 'the Dutch System', commenting:

> They have faced up to it boldly by forming Training
> Colonies. These consist at Amsterdam of large bare halls,
> surrounded by small cubicles. In each there are some

forty families, who live and feed in the central room, and sleep in the cubicles. They are under strict discipline and supervision.... Judging from information received this experiment is not an entire success. Some British housing reformers, who entered one of the buildings recently, were greeted with missiles and oaths. One Communist admitted among the forty families can infect all with his revolutionary doctrines, and the political consequences of herding together these unfortunate people with a slum mentality may be more serious than is foreseen. (Townroe, 1927)

In a review of *The Slum Problem* for the *Eugenics Review*, J.C. Pringle attacked the environmental explanation of slum behaviour as 'putting the cart before the horse'. He went on to state that 'Mr. Townroe emphasises – though not, we think, unduly – the difficulties that arise from tenants who carry the slum mind and the slum habit wherever they go' (Pringle, 1929, pp 173–4). The Report of the Departmental Committee on Sterilisation, chaired by L.G. Brock, declared 'defectives drift to the slums', where 'like marries like ... and the chances of two carriers [of defective genes] mating is many times greater than it is in any other section of the population' (Brock, 1933, pp 41–2).

A 'sewage' policy

In its 1929 manifesto, the Labour Party promised 'to deal drastically with the Slum disgrace', alongside boosting overall housing production for rent. Labour's Housing Act 1930 introduced a local authority subsidy specifically directed at clearing slums and intended to run in parallel with other Acts aimed at building for 'general' needs. Indeed, Greenwood, Labour's Health Minister, wanted to increase such subsidies but met with civil servant resistance on the argument that 'general needs' subsidies lowered rents rather than increased production. The Housing Act 1930 included provisions for local authorities to declare 'improvement areas', where local authorities could use the clearance subsidy to improve an area by measures such as converting houses from multiple occupation. Labour also attempted to allow local authorities more extensive powers to use planning controls in slum areas but the legislation was 'butchered in Parliament' (Garside, 1988, p 40).

In 1932, Conservative Minister for Health Hilton Young called the slums 'a public health problem ... not a first line problem of housing; it is a problem of ridding our social organism of radiating centres of depravity and disease'. Subsidies were 'appropriate in this region as a measure for the protection and preservation of the public health'. Ending the 'abnormal and artificial machinery' of the 'general needs' subsidy meant a return to the market in renting and owner-occupation – forms of provision that were 'normal and natural to the economic life of the country' (all quotes from Yelling, 1992, pp 88–91). In 1933, the government abolished general needs subsidies, leaving only houses built to accommodate people from slums eligible for central assistance. Circular 1331 (Ministry of Health, 1933) left no doubt about where local authority efforts should be directed:

> The slum … is a strictly limited problem; and it is measurable both as to the cost and the time required for its solution. Conditions are now exceptionally favourable for the work. With low building costs and cheap money, houses built with the subsidy payable under the Housing Act, 1930, can be let at rents well within the capacity of the poorest of the working classes.

To Hilton Young, concentrating on slums meant a residual role for the state: later, Iain Macleod (1973 [1954]), when contemplating a return to the 1930s' Conservative housing policy, called Hilton Young's approach 'a policy of sewage'.

'Slum' is a nebulous concept (see Lund, 2017) and Hilton Young thought that clearing 'slums' at 12,000 per year would end the problem by 1938, implying that there were only 60,000 'slums' in the UK. Final slum eradication meant that the state's role in housing had ended. However, Hilton Young's slum clearance drive met with opposition. Landlords, infuriated by the low compensation payable under the Housing and Town Planning Act 1919, argued that many so-called slums could be 'reconditioned', and this view received support from many Conservative MPs. Even Hilton Young's 'residual' local authority housing function created anxiety among leading Conservatives about, what Austen Chamberlain said was, 'the trend of recent events which turn our local authorities into owners and still more managers of small house properties' (quoted in Yelling, 1992, p 90).

Overcrowding

Overcrowding started to re-emerge as a social issue in the 1920s, with some commentators identifying a 'new overcrowding'. London County Councillor Major Barnes (1926, p 10) stated:

> Overcrowding in London is developing a new and sinister aspect. No longer is it confined to areas where poverty and squalor have been notorious for years. Hard-working, self-respecting people who have had good homes in their time ... are now living in hidden dens that are not fit to house the most degraded human beings.

In 1933, a Departmental Committee on Housing was set up to 'consider and report what, if any, further steps are necessary or desirable to secure the maintenance of a proper standard of fitness for human habitation' (Moyne, 1933). Its report stated that 'overcrowding is a more serious problem to health than deficiencies which can be met by reconditioning' (Moyne, 1933, p 7).

Moyne's focus on overcrowding presented a dilemma for the Conservative Party, anxious to contain local authority housing intrusion into the private developer's suburban domain but aware that the housing shortage had growing political salience, with Labour making major gains in local elections between 1932 and 1934. The political answer was to associate overcrowding with the sanitary idea. Hilton Young (1934) stated that 'where people are improperly crowded together, especially at night, their disease flourishes'. Thus, if a tight statutory overcrowding definition could be applied, then local government's role in housing supply could be capped by limiting action to inner cities, where overcrowding could be overcome by 'direct action' – building 'near the central sites by means of blocks of flats' (Hilton Young, 1934). Ministry of Health civil servants viewed the Conservative's Housing Act 1935 as a potential mechanism for comprehensive city centre redevelopment but Hilton Young did not share this vision. His overcrowding definition was stringent, with, for example, living rooms and kitchens counted as bedrooms, the test being whether such rooms were normally used in a locality for sleeping purposes – a yardstick that neatly reduced the overcrowding problem by defining it in terms of its existence!

This severe overcrowding definition was set to minimise the condition's extent, thereby limiting the salience of Labour's 'suburban solution' and ensuring that the identified problem could be dealt with within the resources made available by abolishing 'general needs' subsidies. The Act offered subsidies to assist new building but they were restricted to building flats on expensive central sites. Despite representations from local government calling for subsidies for small houses, the Cabinet (1934, p 154) specifically stated that no such subsidies would be offered. Thus, in the early 1930s, the Conservatives reconstructed state involvement in housing back towards the 19th-century 'sanitary' idea. In so doing, they attempted to curtail city expansion ambitions using 'general needs' subsidies. Build quality under local government's 'public health' role declined significantly when compared to those constructed under local government's 'general needs' role (see Chapter Six).

The Labour Party attacked the Conservatives' housing policy as 're-crowding' people in inner areas. *Up with the Houses! Down with the Slums* located the housing problem in the overall shortage of new houses at low rents that should be built with 'tree-lined streets, houses well set back, varied groupings of houses, quadrangles and open spaces' (Labour Party, 1934, p 6). However, the 1935 general election result demonstrated that the Conservatives had managed to neutralise housing as a political issue. They emphasised their house-building record and were able to point to the overcrowding reduction drive to counter Labour's claim that most new houses were for middle-class homeowners (Stannage, 1980).

Rehabilitation

Neville Chamberlain, Minister for Health in the 1920s, attempted to construct a 'slum prevention' strategy for the inner cities but this met with Cabinet resistance, mainly from Winston Churchill, who opposed all subsidies to private landlords. Grants to landlords were made available only in rural areas under the Housing (Rural Workers Act) 1926. Eventually, Chamberlain produced a scheme, not implemented at the time, allowing local authorities to buy dilapidated properties in urban areas, refurbish them and then transfer their management to special commissioners. However, despite the absence of grants for rehabilitation in urban areas, many local authorities continued to use the Housing of the Working Classes Act 1890 to induce landlords to improve their properties. According to Moore (1980), 123,000 dwellings were made fit by statutory measures between 1930 and 1936 and 332,000 made fit by other action.

'Sewage' again

Fée (2008) identifies a residual view of local authority housing in 1940s' Conservative Party policy, citing the Conservative Party Research Department's 1949 recommendation that council housing should be restricted to slum clearance and Anthony Eden's disapproval of

Bevan's removal of the phrase 'for the working classes' in the legislation specifying the purpose of council housing.

Post-1954, the Conservative Party pursued a dual policy on urban renewal: expanding improvement grants and directing local government towards slum clearance. Conditions on awarding improvement grants were relaxed, with only a 15-year rather than a 30-year life required, and in 1959, grants for basic amenities became mandatory. Mandatory improvement grants were accompanied by central government loans to building societies in order to encourage them to lend on pre-1919 property. The policy had an impact as homeowners bought privately rented property and used mandatory grants to improve them. Indeed, in some local authorities, there was significant improvement activity – regarded as an alternative to clearance – throughout the 1960s. Crossman (1975, p 124) records that in 1965:

> From Oldham I drove across to Salford ... and saw how they were trying ... to compel landlords to improve their property. It is far better to give thirty years' more life to some of the existing property then let it become a slum....
> In Salford, I found that for £200 they were making people happy.

The White Paper *Houses: The Next Step* (MHLG, 1953) announced that subsidies to local authorities would be concentrated on slums. Macmillan declared that he looked forward to 'a second scoreboard to run alongside "houses built", called "slum houses demolished"' (quoted in *Estates Gazette*, 1953, p 389). The Housing Subsidies Act 1956 abolished 'general needs' subsidies, providing assistance only for dwellings built to replace slums and for old people. The new subsidies encouraged high-rise housing: the higher the block, the greater the subsidy. Although the Conservatives restored 'general needs' subsidies in 1961, they were set at a lower rate than in the 1950s and yet higher subsidies for multi-storey flats were introduced. In 1964, Edward Heath, to become Prime Minister in 1970, said that he wanted 'to see the guts torn out of our older cities' (quoted in Campbell, 1993, p 162).

In the mid-1960s, the Labour government increased clearance and high-rise subsidies, and by the late 1960s, local authorities were demolishing over 70,000 houses each year. As 'the guts [were] torn out of our older cities', the people who lived in the slums were offered little choice on where they were rehoused. Dunleavy (1981, p 31) comments:

Re-housing was largely determined by the new houses under construction and in many cities this was dominated by high-rise by the mid-1960s. Frequently also it would be concentrated in a particular area so that locational choice would be limited. Finally, most large urban local authorities imposed stringent limits on the number of offers of accommodation made to the clearance residents.

Improving property

Most dwellings bulldozed in the 1950s and early 1960s were seriously unfit and, as 'non-owners', their inhabitants were barred from formal appeal mechanisms against a clearance order. By the late 1960s, local authorities were beginning to deal with different neighbourhoods, classified as 'grey' rather than 'red' areas, where not all the dwellings were grossly unfit and with more owner-occupiers – former private landlord tenants. Owner-occupiers were not entitled to full market value for their unfit houses until 1969, and it is not surprising that in Dennis's study of clearance from 1965 to 1970, 64% of homeowners were against demolition compared with only 29% of private landlord tenants (Dennis, 1972). Objections to compulsory purchase orders became more frequent and residents began to organise protests against clearance. Community activists started to assist local people to devise rehabilitation schemes as alternatives to clearance. As examples, Ray Gosling, later to become a documentary maker for the BBC, led a group of local people opposed to clearing the St Ann's area in Nottingham, and Geoff Green, a postgraduate student at Sheffield University, helped to organise local residents to fight a clearance scheme in Sheffield (Cao, 2014). Activist skirmishes were complemented by social research starting to reveal a loss of community and the imbalances in power between officials and residents (Dennis, 1972; Gower Davies, 1972; Shelter, 1973). Other studies pointed out the 'wastelands' generated by clearance as the derelict sites awaited redevelopment (Shelter, 1973) and the loss of cheap rented accommodation (McKie, 1971).

Labour's demolition zeal receded towards the end of the 1960s and the Housing Act 1969 made provision for local authorities to declare 'general improvement areas', where resources would be available to improve the environment as well as the houses. Labour declared that 'within a total of public investment at about the level it has now reached, a greater share should go to the improvement of older houses' (MHLG, 1968, p 4). Using the 1969 Act and the Housing Act 1974 – allowing 'Housing Action Areas' to be designated – many local authorities started to switch to improvement schemes, not least because more owner-occupiers were involved in clearance operations and they were now entitled to full market value, making clearance much more costly. Birmingham, for example, pioneered the use of 'enveloping', whereby the external fabric of terraced houses was renewed largely free to the owner. Some authors have detected a sinister politics in this switch from demolition/local authority provision to 'in situ' improvement. Smith (1987, p 29) notes that 'an additional pressure, though, was perceived social resistance to the re-housing of black people onto new council estates'. 'Gentrification' – demographic change as the poor residents in a neighbourhood are displaced by the middle class – started in the late 1950s as landlords started to 'winkle out' tenants to sell properties to owner-occupiers. Nineteenth-century middle-class houses, sublet to several families as the original occupants had departed to suburbia, started to return to middle-class occupation, with renovation grants and area renewal schemes facilitating the process. Once started, 'gentrification' gathered momentum. As middle-class people settled in an area, others followed, thereby boosting property prices. Ragged urchins no longer played on marquetry floors.

Area selectivity

Specific post-war urban initiatives, other than clearance, started in 1966 as racial tensions simmered in the inner cities. Patrick Gordon Walker, Labour's shadow Foreign Secretary, lost his Smethwick seat in the 1964 general election to Peter Griffith, a Conservative whose campaign had been anti-immigration and racist. The Urban Programme, introduced under the Local Government Act 1966, was an attempt to direct resources to areas where immigration levels were creating anxiety. Significantly, the Home Office, responsible for immigration and law and order, administered the Urban Programme. 'Area selectivity' featured in other government initiatives, such as Educational Priority Areas and the Community Development Projects.

The 1977 White Paper *Policy for the Inner Cities* (DoE, 1977a) and the subsequent Inner Urban Areas Act 1978 marked a step change in urban policy towards economic regeneration. Influenced by a series of 'inner area studies' commissioned by the DOE in London, Birmingham and Liverpool (DOE, 1977b), the White Paper directed attention to job losses in inner cities that had lost population on a significant scale. In future, manufacturing employment was to be boosted by the relaxation of Industrial Development Certificate control, encouraging planning authorities to modify their 'zoning' of industrial and residential land and new powers awarded to local authorities to assist industry. The Inner Urban Areas Act 1978 also gave the Secretary of State wide-ranging powers to approve 'partnership schemes' between local authorities and central departments in order to identify problems and produce action programmes. Local residents would be included in these partnerships to enable public authorities 'to draw on the ideas of local residents to discover their priorities and enable them to play a practical part in reviving their areas' (DoE, 1977b, para 34). Labour's emphasis on inner cities created a political problem: what of the peripheral council estates inhabited mainly by the white working class? The civil servants in the DoE had an answer. In 1974, they had identified 62,000 'difficult to let' council houses and reached the conclusion that they were 'difficult to let' because local authority administrative structures were inflexible and insensitive to the physical decay on some estates. In 1978, the Secretary of State for the Environment set out proposals to tackle the problem by creating a new housing category – 'management priority estates' – on which capital expenditure and management resources would be concentrated.

'It took a riot'

The 1979 Conservative government placed emphasis on cutting public expenditure but Michael Heseltine, then Secretary of State for the Environment, appeared to be in a strong political position to enhance his department's spending following the 1981 urban riots in Brixton, Bristol, Manchester and Liverpool. However, his Cabinet colleagues were in parsimonious mood. In a Cabinet paper with the title *It Took a Riot*, Heseltine demanded £200 million extra resources for Liverpool alone to tackle its problems. The offer was only £15 million – not much change after financing a Garden Festival. Chancellor Geoffrey Howe thought that offering money to Liverpool was like 'pumping water uphill' and 'managed decline' would be a better option' (Beckett, 2015, p 198). Although Lord Scarman's report (Scarman, 1981) pointed to underlying issues such as unemployment, urban deprivation, racial disadvantage and political representation, the Conservatives branded the 1981 riots a 'law and order' issue. This approach was reaffirmed after the 1985 urban disturbances when Oliver Letwin and Hartley Booth advised Margaret Thatcher that 'Riots, criminality and social disintegration are caused solely by individual characters and attitudes' and that help to black communities would end up in 'the disco and drugs trade' (*Guardian*, 2015c). Thatcher never deviated from her 'stark message … which put the blame for riots squarely on the shoulders of the rioters and not the police, and still less on society' (Kwarteng, 2015, p 133).

Property before people

Of necessity, then, urban regeneration had to become more reliant on property-led initiatives, primed by public finance such as Derelict Land Grant but mainly dependent on private sector investment stimulated by tax breaks. Enterprise Boards – with 100% corporation and income tax allowances for capital expenditure, exemption from business rates and Development Land Tax, and reduced planning constraints – supplied one conduit for extra investment. In addition, Development Corporations, based on the new towns model and without local government involvement, were set up as statutory bodies appointed and funded by central government. They had planning powers and could buy and sell land. As examples, the revival of Salford Docks, closed in 1982 with the loss of 3,000 jobs, as Salford Quays was kick-started by Enterprise Zone status, although a partnership led by Salford City Council undertook later redevelopment. The London Docklands Development Corporation led the London docks redevelopment, creating Canary Wharf. Urban Task Forces and City Action Teams, consisting of Whitehall civil servants and appointees from local government and business, were set up to coordinate local initiatives.

Private sector improvement

There was a significant increase in private sector housing rehabilitation financed from public funds in Margaret Thatcher's first government. Improving the private housing stock was a way to keep some receipts from selling council houses within the housing domain and forestall the need for future council housing by preventing houses becoming unfit. Despite Treasury opposition, Thatcher backed Michael Heseltine in allowing councils to keep 50% of Right to Buy receipts as an incentive to sell (Moore, 2013). Renovations using public funds increased from 80,197 in 1979 to 319,746 in 1984. However, post-1983, as the Treasury secured control of Right to Buy receipts, the use of public funds to improve the private housing stock became increasingly selective and the resources allocated diminished significantly. A Green Paper, *Home Improvement – A New Approach* (DoE, 1985), heralded a more concentrated selectivity policy. It attacked the notion that minimum housing standards should be relative, stating that, in future, there would be a fixed unfitness definition. Grants to remedy unfitness would be means-tested. The Local Government and Housing Act 1989 implemented the principles set out in the 1989 Green Paper. By 1992, only 29,993 private sector improvement grants were made (Newton, 1994). Later, the Housing Grants, Construction and Regeneration Act 1996 made all grants discretionary, except for the Disabled Facilities Grant.

Challenging cities

Michael Heseltine's return to the Department of the Environment (DoE) in 1990 produced a re-emphasis on regeneration, this time involving local government via the City Challenge, which allocated £37.5 million to authorities submitting successful bids based on establishing cross-sector partnerships and conformity to government policies. Heseltine used competitive bidding for resources to bend local government to his will, declaring that 'one of the charms of local government is that in the end it has a simple understanding of the financial imperative' (Heseltine, 2000, p 395). In 1994, competitive bidding for resources based on partnerships and economic outputs was extended by creating the Single Regeneration Budget (SRB), combining 20 previously separate programmes into a single programme.

Council houses

The Conservatives' 'property before people' mantra was reflected in its approach to refurbishing council estates. Labour's 'management priority estates' programme survived the public sector housing investment retrenchment in the 1980s. The approach was absorbed into the Estate Action Initiative, introduced in 1986, whereby local authorities made bids to central government for funds to renew rundown estates. Decentralised housing management was an essential element for the submission to be deemed 'fit for purpose' and tenure diversification was increasingly required but a successful bid brought the resources necessary to upgrade the internal amenities and exteriors of the chosen estates. Estate Action was one of the few DoE initiatives approved by Thatcher. Its emphasis on poor local authority management and the mistakes of socialist utopian planners fitted well with her ideology. She commented:

> Many of these schemes were good and imaginative. Indeed, I went further than the DoE in believing that the design of estates was crucial to their success and to reducing the

amount of crime. I was a great admirer of the work of Professor Alice Coleman and I had made her an adviser to the DoE, to their dismay. But what I did not believe was that local authorities should be the main agents for improvement. (Thatcher, 1993, p 605)

Reluctantly, the DoE introduced the Design Improvement Controlled Experiment, based on Oscar Newman's 'defensible space' concept promoted by Alice Coleman (Newman, 1973; Coleman, 1986). Under the scheme, the number of flats with a common entrance was reduced, walkways were demolished and cul-de-sacs became roads. When John Major replaced Margaret Thatcher as Prime Minister, the DoE ended the Design Improvement Controlled Experiment, putting the resources into Estate Action.

New Labour

Discussing the 2001 general election, Paris and Muir (2002, p 154, emphasis in original) comment that 'the parties were more interested in *restricting* housing construction, especially on "greenbelt" sites, than in seeking to boost housing production'.

Brownfield development

New Labour's policy reflected its concern to protect 'greenfield' sites. Central planning policy guidance promoted the first use of brownfield sites, that is, land or premises that was previously used but had subsequently become vacant, derelict or contaminated. Brownfield development, in the so-called 'compact city', was linked to sustainability and promoted urban inner-city regeneration but also protected suburbia and rural England, where New Labour had generated support. Space standards fell and the term 'hobbit houses' began to be used to describe the new developments.

'Decent' homes

A 'decent' homes standard was set out in 2001 as an aspirational yardstick to be applied to 'social' and private housing. In addition to meeting the statutory unfitness standard, for a house to be 'decent', it had to be in a reasonable state of repair, have reasonably modern facilities such as a bathroom of 30 years old or less, and a reasonable degree of thermal comfort. However, state aid to promote 'decent' homes was concentrated on 'social' housing, with private housing regarded as primarily the owner's responsibility. A target was set for all houses to meet the decent homes threshold in the 'social' housing sector, but for the private sector, the target was for 70% of 'vulnerable' households to have a 'decent' home by 2010. Later, this target was downgraded to 'dormant' status.

Improving people

Within weeks of coming to power in 1997, Tony Blair set up a Social Exclusion Unit inside the Cabinet Office. This was a response to a debate unleashed in the UK by the publication of Charles Murray's (1992) *The Emerging British Underclass*, promoted by Andrew Neil, then Editor of the *Sunday Times*. Murray identified similar trends in Britain to the US, that is, rising illegitimacy, increased crime and a growing tendency to avoid work (Murray, 1992). In his first speech as Prime Minister, Blair identified 'an underclass of people cut off from society's mainstream, without any sense of shared purpose', adding that 'there is a case not just in moral terms but in enlightened self interest to deal with the problem' (Blair, 1997a). He launched a series of initiatives under the 'social exclusion' agenda. The Social Exclusion Unit's (1998a, para 1.2) *Bringing Britain Together: A National Strategy for Neighbourhood Renewal* made the point that 'Poor neighbourhoods are not a pure housing problem. They are not all the same kind of design, they don't all consist of rented or council housing, and they are not all in towns and cities'.

In its deprived neighbourhood analysis, the report, alongside income measures, included deficient human and social capital indicators such as lone parenthood, poor numeracy and literacy, and the lack of educational qualifications. Future policy guiding principles would be: 'investing in people, not just buildings; involving communities, not parachuting in solutions; developing integrated approaches with clear leadership and making a long-term commitment with sustained political priority' (Social Exclusion Unit, 1998a, para 2.2). The emphasis was on social and human, not financial, capital. Under the New Deal for Communities (NDC) programme, partnerships were set up in 39 chosen areas with substantial community participation to ensure that change was community-led. By 2008, the NDC partnerships had spent a total of £1.71 billion on some 6,900 projects, with a third of the spending on housing and environmental projects. NDC was augmented by the Neighbourhood Renewal Fund (NRF) targeted at the 88 most deprived local authorities (rather than the 44 targeted by NDC). Its aim was to 'bend' mainstream provision to achieve 'floor' (absolute) and 'convergence' (relative) targets via 'joined-up' thinking. Up to 2007/08, the NRF spent £2,925 million on crime and community safety projects, education, health, housing, and work promotion schemes. Although New Labour's *Bringing Britain Together: A National Strategy for Neighbourhood Renewal* (Social Exclusion Unit, 1998a) had identified 'too many initiatives' as a reason why previous area-based policies had failed, government departments scrambled to add area dimensions to their policies. Sure Start and Health, Employment and Education 'Action' Zones were set up.

The overall impact of New Labour's area initiatives is difficult to evaluate (see Lund, 2017) but Lupton (2013) concluded that they had achieved some success. Having examined 400 evaluation reports, Crisp et al (2015, p 179) conclude:

> Broadly, therefore, place-based interventions that have addressed housing, community safety and environmental issues have generated positive change, particularly in terms of higher levels of satisfaction with the area and the local environment as well as reductions in fear or experiences of crime.... By contrast, people-based interventions around health, education and community participation reach fewer people, require longer time-scales to bring about change than most time-limited programmes allow, and lend themselves less readily to influencing, or 'bending the spend', of mainstream providers.

A report tracking neighbourhood deprivation since 1999 showed that the 10% most deprived neighbourhoods in England became less deprived from 1999 to 2008 but deprivation in such neighbourhoods increased sharply post-2009 as the recession began to bite (DCLG, 2012b), indicating the importance of economic growth relative to special initiatives in reducing deprivation.

Perhaps the real value of New Labour's numerous area policies was political. They allowed the injection of substantial extra resources into Labour's political heartlands, outside the established mechanisms for distributing central assistance to local government. Their emphasis on improving human and social capital and their self-help aura appealed to the right-wing press.

Low demand

Rising property prices encouraged private sector involvement in refurbishing older properties but not all parts of the country experienced a property boom, and in the early 2000s, 'low demand' was identified in some areas, particularly along the M62 corridor. The Housing Market Renewal Initiative – closely identified with Gordon Brown, who appears to have wanted to emphasise material capital compared to Blair's emphasis on social and human capital – was New Labour's response. Its aim was to restore housing *markets*, as well as the housing stock, in the parts of the North where housing demand was relatively fragile. By 2010, £2 billion had been allocated to the task. The initiative was controversial from the start, with tension between the ambitions of existing communities and schemes aimed at attracting new residents into decaying areas. Many 'pathfinders' initially concentrated on demolishing older property to create space for new housing, thereby 'uplifting' an area. This provoked accusations of 'gentrification' (Lees and Leys, 2008), destroying the Victorian heritage (Save Britain's Heritage, 2011), uprooting communities and replacing cheap homes simply in need of an upgrade with more expensive housing. Allen argued that the Housing Market Renewal Initiative represented the imposition of middle-class cultural values – a concern for housing as a commodity signified by price increases – on the working class, who were essentially concerned with 'houses and "community" as lived space' (Allen, 2008, p 178).

As the 'pathfinders' started their work, house prices in low-demand areas started to increase, a consequence of the house price boom squeezing people into what had been 'low-demand' areas. Residents in the 'low-demand' areas were concerned that their compensation would be insufficient to afford alternative accommodation. In many areas, resistance produced a rethink towards greater emphasis on retaining and upgrading properties. The Housing Market Renewal Initiative was strongly criticised by the Conservative opposition, and when he became Housing Minister in the Coalition government, Grant Shapps, justifying axing the scheme, likened it to a 'Luftwaffe attack' (quoted in *Inside Housing*, 2012).

Mixed communities

An underlying theme in New Labour's housing policy was to create more balanced, 'mixed' communities. Introducing a 'consumer' element to social housing via choice-based lettings, the Housing

Market Renewal Initiative and the use of Section 106 agreements to include social housing in new, predominantly homeownership, developments were elements in the approach (see Lund, 2017). As Chancellor of the Exchequer in 2005, Gordon Brown introduced a new scheme, the Mixed Communities Demonstration Initiative, aimed at creating balanced communities in existing council estates. He declared that 'overcoming ... "area" effects will require the transformation of neighbourhoods from mono-tenure social housing estates into communities containing a much broader socio-economic mix of households' (HM Treasury, 2005, p 147).

The Coalition government

The Coalition government ended New Labour's area initiatives, and as the Work Foundation (2012, p 1) pointed out, 'for the first time in over forty years there are no area based initiatives targeted at the most deprived parts of England'. Moreover, as Lupton and Fitzgerald (2015, p 15) note, 'The Coalition has also been silent on another area of policy, which had enjoyed considerable popularity under Labour since the mid-2000s: the desirability of socially mixed communities'. Under the Growth and Infrastructure Act 2013, the use of Section 106 agreements to generate mixed communities was diluted, and as council estates were being 'regenerated', especially in London, an accelerating gentrification process was identified (Just Space, 2014).

The Housing Market Renewal Initiative was the principal victim of the cuts, with its long-term separate funding ended and a meagre 'transition fund' established to 'help families trapped in abandoned streets resulting from the pathfinder demolition schemes' (Shapps, 2011). Other work would depend on how local authorities allocated their mainstream funding and successful bids for resources from a small central fund. However, the local politics continued in some areas, with, for example, Eric Pickles calling in and refusing a planning application to demolish the 'Welsh Streets' in Liverpool after sustained local campaigning against demolition (Brownfield Briefing, 2015). Ending specific schemes aimed at deprived communities and low-demand housing areas contributed to the significant reduction in central resources allocated to the most deprived local authorities. All the local authorities included in the Housing Market Renewal Pathfinder programme lost more than £200 per head of population under the 2010–15 cuts in local government expenditure (Butler, 2014).

It was difficult to detect an 'urban policy' in the first two years of the Coalition government's term in office. *Local Growth: Realising Every*

Place's Potential (Secretary of State for Business, Innovation & Skills, 2010, p 7) stated:

> A further feature of earlier approaches was the belief that planning could both determine where growth should happen and stimulate that growth. This approach failed as it went against the grain of markets. Regional and other strategies stifled natural and healthy competition between places and inhibited growth as a consequence.

The document supported the 'agglomeration economics' manifest in London, suggesting that 'such agglomeration effects may also help drive further growth in other areas' (Secretary of State for Business, Innovation & Skills, 2010, p 9). The strategy was to 'follow the market', supplemented by the revival of Enterprise Zones, Local Enterprise Partnerships between business and local government and a modest — when compared to the resources devoted to New Labour's Regional Development Agencies — Regional Growth Fund. Incentives such as the New Homes Bonus and allowing local authorities to spend part of the business rates enhancement resulting from economic growth were added.

Broken Britain

In August 2011, thousands of people rioted in London and in cities and towns across England. The Coalition government's immediate reaction was to label the riots as a 'law and order' issue. 'This is criminality pure and simple', said Cameron 'and it has to be confronted and defeated' (Cameron, 2011a). However, he also placed the issue in the context of a broader 'Broken Britain' narrative, stating:

> Perhaps they [the rioters] come from one of the neighbourhoods where it's standard for children to have a mum and not a dad ... where it's normal for young men to grow up without a male role model, looking to the streets for their father figures, filled up with rage and anger. (Cameron, 2011b)

Later, the 'Government Response to the Riots, Communities and Victims Panel's Final Report' (DCLG, 2013a) commented that 'many of the recommendations chime with our ambition to strengthen socially responsible attitudes' and referred extensively to the government's

Troubled Families Programme, aimed at tackling the multiple problems of 120,000 'troubled' families. Hancock and Mooney (2013) have explored the consistent attempts of the Conservative Party to apply territorial stigma to the 'problem area', especially council estates – 'and by extension the people resident in that area' (Mooney et al, 2015, p 913) – representing them as 'places of blemish' (Wacquant, 2007 p 67) and symbolic spaces of 'Broken Britain'.

Powerhouses

In his report *No Stone Unturned: In Pursuit of Growth*, Lord Heseltine (2012) recommended greater devolution of power to the regions. According to Laws (2016, pp 226–7), Cameron and Osborne were not impressed:

> At a meeting, he [Osborne] described the Heseltine Report 'as a very personal report, and a bid to steal every department's capital budget'. David Cameron joked that the whole thing sounded like a 'fourth-term priority'. The ever-sharp George Osborne added 'Yes, a fourth-term priority – but for a different government'.... Even in early 2013, when the Chancellor first started to advocate the devolving of money from central government to local areas, one seasoned government adviser told me, George's view was that the money will either be wasted by central government or local government. He thinks the only advantage of devolution is that you can slice 10 per cent off the money as you devolve it, so the Treasury has to pay less.

However, led by Nick Clegg, the Coalition government started to promote devolution but highlighted cities rather than regions. 'City Deals' allowed cities more discretion in allocating resources in return for plans to stimulate economic growth and extra resources according to the growth achieved. Initially, City Deals were tied to elected mayors, but although most cities rejected elected mayors, the initiative continued.

The idea of greater resource autonomy for cities received a boost from the fallout from the Scottish referendum campaign (see Chapter Nine). When public opinion polls predicted a close outcome in the independence referendum, the major UK political parties all promised greater devolution to Scotland in the event of a 'no' vote. These promises raised the issue of greater powers to Wales and Northern Ireland, plus devolution *to* and *in* England. One response to this issue, now promoted by Osborne, was a step change in city devolution motivated by a concern to find new magnets for economic growth and a desire to boost support for the Conservatives in the North. In November 2014, the 'Greater Manchester Agreement' was announced between the 10 local authorities in Greater Manchester and the government. Greater Manchester would obtain more control of budgets, including the resources allocated to housing and the National Health Service (NHS), currently directed by central government, in return for an elected mayor for Greater Manchester and an executive composed of the leaders of the 10 local authorities that constitute Greater Manchester (HM Treasury and Greater Manchester Combined Authority, 2014). This agreement reflected the flexibility of the 'localism' mantra: local authority leaders and the government could decide on a new local governance structure, with or without public consultation.

The 2015 Conservative government

After the 2015 general election, Osborne announced proposals to reinvigorate 'City Deals' – this time in the form of 'Super-city' conurbations and local authority combinations, based on the Manchester model (see Chapter Ten). Many areas expressed interest, some outside the 'North', and 38 local authority combinations eventually declared their intention to sign up. Their interest in participation was stimulated by ongoing changes in local government finance. After 1990, local authorities has to pass on the business rates they collected to the Treasury, but in 2013, they were allowed to retain up to 50% of the business rates, with, of course, associated reductions in central grants. In October 2015, further business rate retention by local government was announced, so that by 2020, councils would retain all the business rates and would be able to lower the business rate to attract development. Moreover, combined authorities with mayors would be able to increase rates up to 2% to fund infrastructure investment (*Financial Times*, 2015). These changes meant that with central grants diminishing, local economic growth, including housing development, would have enhanced salience in raising resources for service delivery.

In January 2016, David Cameron, returning to the theme of *Breakthrough Britain: Housing Poverty, from Social Breakdown to Social Mobility* (Centre for Social Justice, 2008), declared his intention to 'really get to grips with the deep social problems – the blocked opportunity, poor parenting, addiction and mental health problems – that mean so many are unable to fulfil their potential'. He added:

> There's one issue that brings together many of these social problems – and for me, epitomises both the scale of the challenge we face and the nature of state failure over decades. It's our housing estates. Some of them, especially those built just after the war, are actually entrenching poverty in Britain – isolating and entrapping many of our families and communities. (Cameron, 2016, p 1)

Cameron's remedy was a programme to regenerate selected council estates pump-primed by a £140 million fund and guided by an Advisory Panel that would 'establish a set of binding guarantees for tenants and homeowners so that they are protected' (Cameron, 2016, p 2). The regeneration would be based on creating streets to replace high-rises, it being argued that street patterns could house more people than tower blocks. An investigation by the London Assembly Housing Committee (2015) into 50 estates regenerated in London from 2004 to 2014 revealed that the number of social rented homes on the estates had dropped by almost a third and, with an increase in overall density, market sale homes had increased tenfold.

Conclusion

So far, only half the clearance story has been told. The remainder – the type of accommodation provided for 'decanted' slum inhabitants – follows in Chapter Six. The slum clearance process is a good example of 'housing' used as a verb: slum inhabitants, often stigmatised, were 'taken or put' into what those with power regarded as better accommodation. The process had two dimensions; slum dwellers' alleged inability to appreciate their existing condition and the alleged 'professional' knowledge claimed by those planning the new environments. As Scott (1998, p 346) has commented:

> What is striking ... is that such subjects – like the 'unmarked citizens' of liberal theory – have, for the purpose of the planning exercise, no gender, no tastes, no history, no values, no opinions or original ideas, no traditions, and no distinctive personalities to contribute to the enterprise. They have none of the particular, situated, and contextual

attributes that one would expect of any population and that we, as a matter of course, always attribute to elites.

Moreover, as Foucault's 'governmentality' idea highlights, some clearance 'subjects' seem to have absorbed the dominant discourses on their condition, there being very little bottom-up resistance to clearance and its associated rehousing forms. Thus, it is hardly surprising that in the 1930s' 'clearance drive', the slum inhabitants in clearance areas were never asked directly about their aspirations and were often placed in flats, although public opinion surveys always clearly demonstrated a clear distaste for such accommodation. This paternalistic approach continued throughout the 1950s and 1960s and into the 1970s, augmented by the professional, technical planners – the 'evangelist bureaucrats' – who, like Edwin Chadwick in the 19th century, claimed an expertise in the public good unknown to the ordinary man and woman. Resistance developed when clearance areas started to incorporate growing numbers of homeowners.

As political attention switched from unfit property to economic regeneration, Michael Heseltine's Enterprise Zones and Urban Development Corporations were set up to evade local involvement in decision-making, and the new approach, together with the 'brownfields first' policy, had some success in kick-starting property-led regeneration. Blair's New Deal for Communities and the Neighbourhood Renewal Fund had a strong emphasis on community involvement but a large proportion of the resources available to neighbourhoods were allocated outside the programmes, controlled by officials working in the education, health and employment sectors.

Urban renewal has been dominated by the politics involved in the 'containment of urban England' (Hall et al, 1973): building flats in inner cities, although contributing to urban renaissance in the 2000s, has also reflected an attempt to restrain suburban expansion and safeguard 'rural England'. The 'rural England' preservers have been well organised, whereas those who had to endure the consequences of conservation have had a muted and dishonoured voice. Middle-class 'sharp elbows' and electoral concerns – the quest for the median voter (see Chapters One and Ten) – favoured urban containment.

Further reading

Allen, C. (2008) *Housing Market Renewal and Social Class*, London: Routledge.

Edwards, C. and Imrie, R. (2015) *The Short Guide to Urban Policy*, Bristol: Policy Press.

Hancock, L. and Mooney, G. (2013) '"Welfare ghettos" and the "Broken Society": Territorial Stigmatization in the Contemporary UK', *Housing, Theory and Society*, vol 30, no 1, pp 46–64.

Searle, G.R. (1976) *Eugenics and Politics in Britain*, Leyden, Netherlands: Noordhoff International.

Tallon, A. (2013) *Urban Regeneration in the UK*, second edition, Abingdon: Routledge.

Yelling, J.A. (1992) *Slums and Redevelopment: Policy and Practice in England, 1918–45, with Particular Reference to London*, London: UCL Press.

FOUR

Private landlords: 'Rachmans' or 'Residential property-owners'?

Between 80% and 90% of households rented from a private landlord in the early 20th century. The Labour movement was antagonist to the sector, and rent control, introduced in 1915 as a wartime 'interim' measure in response to tenant agitation, was difficult for the Conservatives to roll back. The electoral arithmetic – 54% of households were still renting from private landlords in the early 1950s – meant that 'creeping decontrol', launched in 1923 and again in 1957, had to be modified in response to its ballot box consequences. Under rent control, many landlords sold their properties to sitting tenants or on vacant possession, and with the growth of council housing plus new-builds for owner-occupation, by 1987, the private landlord's market share had declined to 8%. The Housing Act 1988, mortgage lender support via 'Buy-to-Let' (BTL) and New Labour's enthusiasm for private landlordism as a 'flexible' tenure revived the sector. Its renaissance continued under the Coalition government. In 2015, 19.6% of households in England were privately renting, and on current trends, by 2032, 35% of households will rent from a private landlord (Bentley, 2015).

Slum landlords

In the 19th century, builders wanted to sell their houses as quickly as possible to acquire capital for new developments. Residential landlords bought the dwellings and 'realised' their assets over time through renting. Most landlords owned only a few properties, although there were some large-scale property-owners – Stedman Jones (1992) records Thomas Flight as owning 18,000 houses in London. The typical landlord had savings from a business (eg traders, shopkeepers and publicans) that they augmented by borrowing. Local solicitors supplied an important financial source via organising people interested in passive urban investment through 'building clubs'. Offer (1981, p 143) comments:

> A large number of investors of purely local horizons were glad to place their money in the hands of those like the

Forsytes, who had a 'talent for bricks and mortar' and 'no dread in life like that of a 3 per cent for their money'.

In poorer areas, there was constant conflict between property-owners and tenants, with tenants often unable, and sometimes unwilling, to pay the rent. Landlords responded by eviction and tenants retaliated with violent protest. Chadwick (1842, p 100) reported:

> I was informed by the superintendent of police of that town [Manchester] that one of the most dangerous services for a small force was attending to enforce ejectments. This they often had to do, cutlass in hand, and were frequently driven off by showers of bricks from the mobs.

'House farming'

'House farmers' shouldered part of the blame for the alleged moral consequences of slum living (see Chapter Three). Freeholders, mostly large landowners, rented land on short leases, with the land and the buildings thereon reverting to the freeholder when the lease ended. 'Rogue' landlords bought lease fag-ends and 'sweated' the rundown properties by placing families in single rooms. Tenants often sublet parts of a dwelling and even single room sections. Shoddy building, poor locations (swamps were not a good choice), high occupancy and landlord unwillingness to repair – why bother, the land and buildings would soon revert back to the freeholder – created slums. Society's elite shunned direct renting. Although it could be highly profitable – a 36% annual return in Stepney in 1912 – renting was a tough business, with high management costs (Kemp, 1982). According to one estate agent, addressing the Surveyors Institution, 'larger capitalists had better leave it alone' (Griffin, 1893, p 364). In *Little Dorrit*, Charles Dickens (1996 [1857]) portrayed Christopher Casby, landlord of Bleeding Heart Yard, as interested only in 'squeezing' his tenants, a view shared by Octavia Hill, well connected in 'high' society, who often quoted a slum landlord and undertaker who said he was in the private landlord business for 'the bodies it produced'! Hill believed that such owners and their agents had to be replaced by 'fit and proper', female housing managers, interested in improving their tenants' moral fibre, not just in collecting rents.

The aristocracy and the slum

In part, 19th-century housing politics involved revelations that the upper and middle classes had a role in slum creation. The Duchy of Cornwall and the Ecclesiastical Commission owned slums but Lord Salisbury, Tory Prime Minister, attracted the most press interest. He held the freehold to Cecil Court, a slum off St Martin's Lane, and the Liberal newspaper *The Star* ran an article headlined 'The Premier's Rookeries Fall', stating:

> The houses in Cecil-court, which were long since ordered
> to be closed by the parish authorities, are now giving way
> all round ... the public have to pay two policemen to keep
> people away from the property of the Prime Minister of
> England in case it should fall on their heads. (*The Star*, 1888)

Bernard Shaw's (1892) 'Widowers' Houses', first performed in 1892, exposed the landed interest in unfit property and the ways in which the middle class obtained returns from slum assets. Shaw's play emphasised the owner's immunity from 'rent farming' reality. Lickcheese, the agent, did the dirty work, Sartorius, the leaseholder, received the rents, whereas Dr Trench, Sartorius's sanctimonious prospective son-in-law, derived his income from slum investments.

By the 1880s, a literature on working-class exploitation via the housing system – pointing out the various layers of profiteers (landowners, developers, lawyers, landlords and their agents) involved in the rental process – was available (Engels, 1997 [1872]), and organised opposition to the private landlords and their agents, the identifiable persons in the exploitation chain, was growing. 'Tenant mutual protection associations' were formed in some areas, with, for example, the Hackney association organising a rally against rent increases that attracted 2,000 tenants and the Salford Tenants' Association demanding a right to buy! In the 1880s, the Social Democratic Federation declared itself in favour of 'fair rents' and attempted to organise rent strikes.

The rates issue

'From high values and large sales to low values and low sales – that was the dominant trend of the property market between 1902 and 1912' (Offer, 1981, p 217). Values declined by 20% and new investment in residential property plummeted. The reasons for this property slump are obscure but can be attributed, in part, to a correction to the rapidly increasing rents in the late 19th century. However, rising local government rates – they increased by up to 50% in London between 1891 and 1906 – were depicted as falling disproportionately on 'property' and restricting investment. The 'Progressives', in control of the London County Council (LCC), were regarded as the main culprits. Their plan was to build houses for the working class in a zone around London and bring the workers to the centre by trams. House-building would be financed by acquiring utilities, especially water, and using the surplus from these utilities to finance a housing programme. The Conservative government 'clearly understood that to control the flow of water was to control the flow of power' (Broich, 2013, p 121) and obstructed the LCC's attempts to acquire the private water companies. Deprived of finance from municipal water, the LCC put up the rates.

In granting male householders a right to vote, the Representation of the People Act 1867 ended the compounding system whereby rates were paid directly by the landlord. This produced large-scale agitation because landlords did not reduce the amount charged to the tenant and was quickly changed back to the compounding system (Grayson, 1996). With landlords responsible for collecting rates and, by the late 1890s, rates forming 20% of working-class housing costs, there were allegations that soaring rates were reducing returns from letting as there was a limit to the rent and rates that tenants could afford. Ratepayer Associations, with private landlords playing a major role, were established throughout the country. They campaigned against rate increases, claiming, for example, that paupers in workhouses were fed on rump steaks (Offer, 1981). In arguments reminiscent of Margaret Thatcher's case for the Poll Tax, the associations demanded an end to 'compounding' – landlords collecting rent and rates – to make tenants aware of the 'rate burden'. They also advocated higher central government grants to spread the load across a broader taxpayer base. Landlords used rate rises in local election campaigns, with, for example, a West Ham landlord writing to his tenants about a large rent increase, stating:

> If you wish, as you surely must, to stop this constant raising of your rent your remedy is to remove from office those who, by their extravagance in dealing with *your* money compel *you* as the very natural result to 'pay the piper'. (Quoted in Englander, 1983, p 62, emphasis in original)

The 1907 LCC election was mainly fought on the rates issue, with the Conservatives, under the banners of 'Moderates' and 'Municipal Reformers', successfully challenging the Progressives on their 'eighteen wasteful years' with 'Vans parading the streets bearing tableaux of tumbledown "Progressive" houses and "Progressive" steamers foundering in the Thames' (Gibbon and Bell, 1939, p 103).

Rent control

House-building declined dramatically on the outbreak of the First World War and worker migration to the munitions factories produced large rent increases. Agitation against these rises erupted across the UK in places such as Northampton, Newcastle, Birmingham, Dudley, Birkenhead, Poplar, Coventry and Weymouth. There was an unsuccessful rent strike in Leeds in 1914 prompted by a sudden rent hike imposed by the local landlord association. In contrast, the Glasgow rent strike was a triumph. In certain parts of Glasgow, rents increased by between 11.7% and 23.1% when the war started, and this sparked a rent strike in which women played a prominent role, marking a partial shift towards 'consumption' politics (Melling, 1983). Local employers supported the strikes, with the Managing Director of Harland and Wolff's shipyard stating that 'We are very pleased to hear that the tenants of Govan propose refusing to pay these increased rents and we sympathise entirely with them' (quoted in *Forward*, 1915, p 1).

Evictions for not paying rent were met with turbulent resistance organised by Mary Barbour and the South Govan Women's Housing Association. The strike had considerable press support because evicting women was linked to their husbands' service in the armed forces. When the unions in Glasgow threatened industrial strike action – indicating the critical importance of class-based production politics – and other rent strikes started in England, the government announced the introduction of rent control. Whereas agitation on rent increases in other parts of the UK was often impulsive, as Castells (1983) has pointed out, the rent strike in 'Red Clydeside' was planned and linked to a demand for municipal housing. The Increase of Rent and Mortgage Interest (War Restrictions) Act 1915 imposed a rent freeze on existing rented properties and granted tenure security. It also restricted interest on mortgages. Many Conservatives were opposed to the 1915 Act but Lloyd George, Minister for Munitions, would not tolerate any disruption to his armaments programme.

Creeping decontrol

Although a 'temporary expedient', intended to last only 'for the duration of hostilities', rent regulation was difficult to dismantle. The Conservative strategy between the wars was to remove controls gradually, each move preceded by advice from an 'expert' committee that usually classified houses by value and scarcity. Even this 'slow but sure' decontrol encountered tenant resistance. Following the 1920 Salisbury Committee report into the continuing deterioration in housing supply, the Increase of Rent and Mortgage Interest (Restrictions) Act 1920 allowed a 40% rent increase, much to the satisfaction of the building societies who benefited from the associated higher 6.5% mortgage interest rate. In response, rent strikes resurfaced along the Clyde, and by 1924, rent arrears amounted to 60% in Clydebank. However, by 1926, the strikes had petered out, perhaps because, unlike in 1915, they were not fully supported by the trade unions. The Rent and Mortgage Interest Restriction Act 1923 introduced 'creeping decontrol', whereby premises came out of protection when tenants died or moved away. Although this stealthier process produced less direct tenant resistance, rent was a political issue nationwide and not just on the Clyde. It was conventional at the time for newly appointed Cabinet ministers to stand down from Parliament and face re-election, and in 1923, Mr Griffith-Boscawen, Conservative Minister for Health, lost Mitcham, normally a safe Conservative seat, to Labour in a by-election fought almost entirely on the rent issue. Unrest over rent levels and landlord behaviour continued throughout the 1920s. With Labour making strong local election gains in the early 1930s, the Cabinet accepted a memorandum from the Minister of Health. It claimed that it was necessary to hasten the decontrol of the better class of houses, and 'that decontrol of the class of the smallest and cheapest houses should be stopped until the acute shortage therein is over' (Cabinet, 1931, p 50). The Housing Act 1933 divided dwellings into three categories. The largest houses became decontrolled, the 'middle band' remained subject to 'creeping' decontrol but the smallest houses could not become decontrolled piecemeal and some, already decontrolled, were returned to regulation.

The building societies, awash with funds, approached the government in 1932 about a scheme for the state to guarantee 20% of a mortgage loan – enabling advances of 90% to be made to landlords wanting to provide accommodation for the working class. The Housing (Financial Provisions) Act 1933 allowed local authorities to guarantee loans made by building societies for building rented accommodation. At least 350,000 new dwellings were built for private letting in the five-and-a-half years from September 1933 to March 1939. The Increase of Rent and Mortgage Interest (Restrictions) Act 1938 automatically decontrolled houses in the 'middle-value' band. However, in London, with its higher rateable values, this Act decontrolled many working-class houses and provoked agitation and rent strikes.

The Rent Act 1957

When the Second World War started, rent control was reintroduced for all unfurnished rented accommodation except those with very high values, with new property included. Viscount Ridley produced a report on rent control recommending that control should continue after the war but new property should be exempt and Rent Tribunals should be established to set 'fair rents' (Ridley, 1945). The Labour Party ignored these recommendations but the Furnished Houses (Rent Control) Act 1946 made furnished accommodation – never controlled between the wars – subject to Rent Tribunals with powers to limit rent increases.

In the early 1950s, Harold Macmillan was under pressure from a section of his party, fronted by Enoch Powell, to relax rent control and Macmillan's housing drive was motivated, in part, by an attempt to increase supply to make rent decontrol easier. In 1952, Macmillan said that 'It is all right to put up houses. The next job is to put up rents' (quoted in Raison, 1990, p 38). The National Federation of Property Owners (NFPO) placed articles in *The Times* spotlighting the need for reform. Macmillan was well aware that, with nine million private landlord tenants, rent control was a politically sensitive issue, and in 1952, he warned the Cabinet that the 'increase of rents is a bold and hazardous undertaking.... Everything will depend on the scheme not merely being fair, but seeming to be fair' (quoted in Weiler, 2000, p 127). Moreover, he was unconvinced by the propaganda coming from the private landlord associations, stating:

> I am rather sceptical about the 'widows and orphans' who are said to own these houses. There are some in Lancashire and the northern industrial towns. But the 'widows and orphans' in my political life have owned the brewers, the coalmines, the pubs and the railways. (Quoted in Yelling, 1995, p 57)

Macmillan tied the initial venture in rent rises to repairs. The Housing Repairs and Rents Act 1954 allowed a 'repairs increase' for improved houses. It also excluded from control all dwellings built after 30 August 1954 and all self-contained accommodation produced by conversion, except when they had attracted improvement grants. The Conservative Cabinet agreed to further legislation in 1955, with the policy shift promoted by Geoffrey Howe and Colin Jones (1956) in a pamphlet entitled *Houses to Let*. They argued that the 1954 Act had failed: controlled rents were heavily subsidising tenants and there was a need for a general rent increase up to 285%. According to Barnett (1969), the Bill on rent decontrol had the full support of the civil servants in the ministry, including the Under-Secretary for Local Government, who immediately resigned to become chief executive of a landlord pressure group! Civil servants presented a long list of reasons why rent control had to end. Piecemeal control had produced 'anomalies', with similar dwellings let at different rents, and landlords received insufficient income to keep their properties in good repair, leading to future slums and new council housing. Moreover, low rents produced under-occupation and reduced labour mobility. Added to this list was the low percentage of working-class income taken in rent compared to a high percentage spent on 'immoral' expenditures such as drink and tobacco, and, a Treasury idea, rent increases would have a deflationary impact, taking from those who spend to give to those who invest. At first, Henry Brooke, the Minister for Housing, was cautious, not wanting to 'block' the decontrol of higher-value properties, but Enoch Powell and Iain Macleod argued for radical action and Brooke accepted their case.

Rachmanism

The Rent Act 1957 decontrolled all dwelling houses with rateable values above the value for houses that might reasonably be considered 'slums' ('block' control), made provision to increase rents in the remaining controlled sector and decontrolled all houses on vacant possession. The Act generated political problems from the start, with tenants in 'block' decontrolled properties, often middle-class Conservative voters, complaining about higher rents and the loss of tenure security. This middle-class reaction caused anxiety in the Cabinet. The 'block' decontrol transition period was extended and the Landlord and Tenant Act 1958 restored tenure security for three years. In its 1959 election manifesto, Labour promised to repeal the Rent Act 1957 but the Conservatives were returned to power with an increased majority. Sir Keith Joseph, then a junior minister at the Department of Housing and Local Government and in a 'dry', free market mood, claimed that following a long period of rent control, tenants needed 'training' in market rents (Denham and Garnett, 2001, p 92).

For a time, rent decontrol had a low political profile but, illustrating media power in identifying issues, the 'slum landlord' returned to the political agenda in the early 1960s. The catalyst was the 'Profumo Affair'. John Profumo, the British Secretary of State for War, had an affair with Christine Keeler, the reputed mistress of Yevgeny Ivanov, a naval attaché at the Soviet Union embassy. After lying to the House of Commons when questioned about the matter, Profumo resigned. Keeler was a friend of Mandy Rice-Davies, Perec Rachman's mistress, and Rachman set up Rice-Davies in a flat in which he had previously allowed Keeler to stay. Rachman's connections to the 'Profumo Affair' led to his property empire being investigated, culminating in a *Panorama* programme with the opening words: 'We start with the story of a man: a sordid story that some of you may not want the younger children to hear'. The programme claimed Rachman used 'strong arm' tactics to evict tenants to secure the higher rents allowed by the Rent Act 1957. The Rachman scandal added a new word to the English language, with the *Oxford English Dictionary* (Oxford Dictionaries, 2016) defining 'Rachmanism' as 'the exploitation and intimidation of tenants by unscrupulous landlords'. 'Rachmanism' put the Conservatives on the defensive and Sir Keith Joseph set out plans to compel owners to improve their property or face local authority acquisition. This proposal was strongly opposed in Cabinet by Enoch Powell, who, in response to Joseph's argument that many landlords did not demonstrate 'responsible management', replied that 'we are asked to use compulsion to make private owners do what it is not worthwhile to do' (quoted in Weiler, 2000, p 139). Ian Macleod wrote to Macmillan in 1963, telling him that landlord controls and other proposed housing interventions were socialist. It was 'dangerous to follow socialist policy in this way', he said, and the party would respond with 'horror' to these 'Fabian proposals' – 'revolutionary' and 'objectionable to a Tory' (quoted in Weiler, 2000, p 138) – but Harold Macmillan supported Joseph. They were included in the White Paper *Housing* (MHLG, 1963).

In its 1964 general election campaign, Labour promised to 'Repeal the notorious Rent Act' and provide machinery for settling rents on a fair basis (Labour Party, 1964). The Conservative Party was now in retreat. Its 1964 manifesto stated that 'In the next Parliament we shall take no further steps to remove rent control. Additional safeguards for tenants will be provided if shown to be necessary by the inquiry into rented housing in London' (Conservative Party, 1964).

'Fair' rents

In power, Labour took immediate action to mitigate the impact of the Rent Act 1957 by making it a criminal offence to evict a tenant without a court order. Further action followed the Milner Holland (1965) Commission on Housing in Greater London – an investigation set up by the Conservatives in 1963. The Milner Holland Commission found that, despite rogue landlords, tenant–landlord relationships were generally satisfactory but there was an acute shortage of rented accommodation in London and it was necessary for rents to be regulated.

The Rent Act 1965 introduced the 'fair rent' concept. Rent officers would be appointed to determine a rent for a regulated property having disregarded the improvements and repairs attributable to the tenant. It was to be assumed that the number of persons seeking to become tenants of similar dwelling houses in a locality was not substantially greater than the number of such dwelling houses in that locality available for letting, that is, so-called 'scarcity value' was to be ignored. Appeal could be made to a Rent Assessment Committee. Under the Act, most houses decontrolled by the 1957 Act became 'regulated'.

Some economists believed the 'fair rent' notion – ignoring 'scarcity value' – was economic nonsense. However, at the time, the scarcity concept was well established, with, for example, the Marley Committee (Ministry of Health, 1931) categorising rented properties according to the balance of supply and demand. This 'expert fix' – relying on 'impartial' rent officers, backed up by Rent Assessment Committees, to arbitrate between landlord and tenant – seemed to be a judicious way to resolve the rent issue. Nevertheless, the presumption was in favour of market rents. As David Donnison (1967, p 226), one of the architects of the 1965 Act, commented:

> Unlike rent control ... rent regulation is designed to recreate
> a market in which the overall pattern of prices responds
> to changes in supply and demand, while the local impact
> of severe and abnormal scarcities is kept within bounds.

'Fair' rents had all-party support, with Margaret Thatcher stating in Parliament: 'I hope the major objective of achieving fair rents will be well and speedily achieved' (Thatcher, 1965).

Withering on the vine

Between 1965 and 1987, private landlord politics marked time. Some owners made good use of the 'fair' rents legislation to ensure that the initial rents set, being precedents for future adjudications, were as high as possible, with the Freshwater Group, the largest private landlord in the UK, reportedly sending expensive presents to rent officers (*Sunday Times*, 8th November, 1970 quoted in Barnes, 1971, p 1388). Between 1966 and 1970, 30.2% of rents were reduced, 61% were increased and the remainder stayed the same (Francis, 1971). Although the National Association of Property Owners complained that 'fair' rents were too low, William Stern, head of the property company Wilstar Securities, managed to develop a 25,000-property portfolio in London. Under the Rent Act 1965, property with a low rateable value remained controlled but there was always the option to convert to furnished accommodation and such conversion increased rapidly. Furnished accommodation remained regulated under the Furnished Houses (Rent Control) Act 1946 but tenants used the legislation infrequently because they had very limited security of tenure.

The Francis Committee (Francis, 1971), set up by the Conservative government to examine the impact of the Rent Act 1965, believed that the Act was working quite well. A study by Doling and Davies (1984) concluded that owners could make a reasonable investment return and were selling to owner-occupation because the substantial tax concessions to homeowners made a property more valuable when sold for owner-occupation. The Labour leadership was content to allow the private landlord sector to 'wither on the vine', and in the mid-1970s, it attempted to hasten its decline by allowing local authorities to purchase privately let property in stress areas – a modest attempt at 'municipalisation', a long-held ambition of the party's grass roots. Birmingham had pioneered 'municipalisation' in the 1950s, and in 1956, the Labour Party Conference had endorsed a National Executive policy document for wholesale private rented sector municipalisation. This so alarmed the building societies that a 'Rented Homes Campaign' was set up to resist the idea. A pamphlet, commissioned by the campaign, warned that owner-occupiers in streets with private tenants would soon have council tenants as neighbours and that, although in Tory areas, there would not be pressure to 'put families of teddy boys into quiet, bank-clerk Acacia Avenue', 'one could not be sure in Labour areas' (MacCrae, 1958, p 14).

The Conservatives attempted to stimulate private landlordism in 1972 by introducing rent allowances for low-income private tenants.

However, by 1974, even the Conservatives appeared to have given up on the sector, with the Conservative Political Centre stating that 'the private landlord, as he exists now and has existed, will, within a generation, be as extinct as the dinosaur. There is nothing that can be done about it' (quoted in Rugg and Rhodes, 2008, p 3). In 1974, the Conservative government abolished the distinction between furnished and unfurnished accommodation, replacing it by a 'resident'/non-resident division, which brought most private landlord accommodation into the 'fair' rent, security of tenure, regime. In the early 1980s, the remaining controlled tenancies were brought into the regulated sector and landlords were allowed to let property as 'shorthold' tenancies subject to 'fair' rents but with the landlord able to repossess after a fixed term. In an attempt to bring institutional investment into the rented sector, 'assured' tenancies were introduced, allowing approved landlords to let at market rents. None of these measures halted the decline in private renting, squeezed between homeownership and council housing.

A market in rented accommodation?

By the 1980s, private renting had become a niche market with a low political profile, and the rent control legislation was widely ignored (Marsh and Riseborough, 1998). The Housing Act 1988 reintroduced the 'creeping decontrol' familiar in the 1933 and 1957 Rent Acts. By default, a new tenant would become an assured shorthold tenant with six months tenure security and would pay a market rent, with Housing Benefit 'taking the strain'. In 1985, Ian Gow, then Housing Minister, had put a similar scheme to the Cabinet but Thatcher rejected it, arguing that there was no limit to rent increases and hence no control on Housing Benefit costs.

Nicholas Ridley, Secretary of State for the Environment, had a plan that went well beyond abolishing rent control. As he later explained:

> I saw the solution as being to provide housing benefit on a sufficiently generous scale to enable all tenants to be in a position to pay their rents, and at the same time to bring rents up towards market levels. This would put all three classes of landlord – councils, housing associations and private landlords – into the same competitive position, giving tenants a choice. (Ridley, 1992, p 88)

Margaret Thatcher was aware that Ridley's scheme had implications for 'the dependency culture' but eventually accepted it as a means to reduce local authority subsidies and encourage Right to Buy take-up. In her memoirs, she said:

> More people on housing benefit means more welfare dependency; on the other hand, it seems better to provide help with housing costs through benefit rather than through subsidising the rents of local authority tenants indiscriminately. Moreover, the higher rents paid by those not on benefit, would provide an added incentive for them to buy their homes and escape the net altogether. (Thatcher, 1993, pp 600–1)

Housing Benefit

The Housing Act 1988 was facilitated by earlier changes in the Housing Benefit system making it more generous to those with the lowest incomes but with a steep 65% withdrawal rate, and by extending the Business Expansion Scheme (BES) to private letting. BES allowed individual investors income tax relief up to £40,000 each tax year for five years and exemption from capital gains tax on any gains from selling shares after five years. However, most of the 'BES landlord companies' were small, only 20% of 80,000 dwellings acquired were newly constructed, and at the end of the five years, many companies were wound up and the properties sold to owner-occupiers. Moreover, the scheme was extremely costly in 'tax expenditure' terms – £20,874 per dwelling (Crook and Kemp, 2011).

Margaret Thatcher was correct in her assessment of Ridley's scheme. New private tenants faced market rents and existing tenants, allegedly protected from large rent increases, found their rents rising at twice the inflation rate. Landlords referred more existing 'fair rents' to Rent Assessment Committees, successfully arguing that private rented supply growth meant that there was no scarcity and fair rents should be set in line with market rents (Wilson, 2014). Total Housing Benefit expenditure soared, from £4.6 billion in 1985/86 to £12.3 billion in 1994/95. As Housing Benefit costs increased, John Major's government tried to stem the flow by stratagems including 'reference rents', involving setting a maximum rent on which Housing Benefit would be paid set increasingly on area boundaries – known as 'Broad Market Rental Areas' – which restricted the ability of low-income households to move 'upmarket'.

Buy-to-Let (BTL)

The most important initiative promoting private landlordism came not from the government but from mortgage lenders under BTL. Post-1988, the growth in the private landlord sector was slow, but in 1996, prompted by the Association of Residential Letting Agents, some mortgage lenders agreed to offer loans to private landlords on terms close to those available to owner-occupiers. Kemp (2015, p 7) comments that 'the arrival of BTL lending transformed mortgage finance for investors in private rental housing'. Its growth was rapid: by 2007, there were 991,600 BTL mortgages, valued at over £116 billion, compared to only 7,713, valued at £575 million, in 1997.

New Labour

The Labour Party's metamorphosis into 'New Labour' under Tony Blair's leadership was reflected in attitudes to the private rented sector. New Labour's 1997 manifesto stated:

> We value a revived private rented sector. We will provide protection where most needed: for tenants in houses in multiple occupation. There will be a proper system of licensing by local authorities which will benefit tenants and responsible landlords alike. (Labour Party, 1997)

Even this limited intervention into the private landlord sector was not implemented in New Labour's first term in office, the only significant measure being the Rent Acts (Maximum Fair Rents) Order 1999, limiting fair rent increases to the retail price index plus 7.5%! The promise to introduce a compulsory licensing scheme for houses in multiple occupation (HMOs), implemented by local authorities, was redeemed in the Housing Act 2004. Local government also gained powers to license all landlords in 'low-demand' areas.

Responsible private landlords

New Labour's Housing Green Paper (DETR, 2000a, ss 5:1, 5:2) was enthusiastic about private landlordism, declaring: 'Landlords can be assured that we intend no change in the present structure of assured and assured shorthold tenancies, which is working well. Nor is there any question of our re-introducing rent controls in the deregulated market'. The private landlord sector's 'flexibility' helped to supply accommodation to immigrants. According to the 2011 census:

> The population of England and Wales grew by 3.7 million in the 10 years since the last census, rising from 52.4 million in 2001, an increase of 7.1 per cent. This was the largest growth in the population in England and Wales in any 10-year period since census taking began, in 1801. (Office for National Statistics, 2012, p 1)

More than half of this population growth was driven by immigration, with two thirds of immigrants coming from non-European Union (EU) countries. In London, 61% of private renters were born outside the UK, compared to 37% of Londoners as a whole (Mayor of London, 2012).

Private landlordism's 'flexibility' might have been undermined by tighter regulation and New Labour only proposed mandatory registration of all private landlords towards the end of its third term. However, before this initiative entered the legislative process, New Labour was replaced by the Coalition government, which announced that there would be no compulsory landlord or private sector letting and management agent registration.

The Right to Buy and private landlordism

One reason for the growth in private landlordism was the purchase of former council houses bought under the Right to Buy, which were relatively cheap because flats in multi-storey blocks were difficult to sell to homeowners (Jones, 2010). New Labour found evidence that, in some areas, private companies were using cash incentives to encourage tenants to buy their homes (ODPM, 2003). In return for a payment, residents agreed to buy their council houses and then sell them to a company to let at market rents. The *Daily Mirror* (2013) used the Freedom of Information Act to ask city councils how many of their ex-flats, where they still owned the freehold, were being sublet by the leaseholder. Of the 13 that responded, an average 32% of former flats had a leaseholder with an address different to the tenant – according to the *Daily Mirror*, a clear sign the flat was rented. At 46%, the Royal Borough of Kingston had the highest proportions of former council houses rented out. A later investigation by *Inside Housing* (Apps, 2015b) found that private landlords now owned 40% of all council flats sold under the Right to Buy in England, the highest percentage (69.6%) being in Milton Keynes.

The Coalition government and 'generation rent'?

The increase in private lettings was accompanied by a decline in homeownership, which started to fall in 2005, and in England, was 400,000 down on its 2005 zenith by 2014. Moreover, there was a shift in the private renters' demographic profile. In 2014, 49.2% of private renters were aged over 35, 31% of single lone parents were private renters (15% in 1997), as were 17.2% of couples with children (7% in 1997). The number of privately rented households containing children increased from 500,000 to 1.5 million between 2003/04 and 2013/14. In 2015, 2.2 million children were growing up in a privately rented home and 26% of the poorest fifth of the UK population lived in privately rented accommodation compared to 9% in 1995 (Belfield et al, 2016). Moreover, as the New Policy Institute (2015, p 10) noted:

> one in three privately rented properties (30 per cent) fall short of the decent home standard, a far higher proportion than other tenures.... Half a million (510,000) children live in privately rented homes that are unsafe. 180,000 disabled people and 120,000 people living in poverty also live in unsafe privately rented homes.

Private landlords and tax exemptions

Small-scale investors putting their savings into property due to low returns elsewhere explain part of private landlordism's growth but private landlords have had tax advantages compared to first-time buyers and those wanting to move up the housing market. Phasing out mortgage interest tax relief for owner–occupiers removed private landlordism's major tax disadvantage and left landlords with significant tax concessions. As 'businesses', landlords were able to offset mortgage payments against tax liability – wealthier landlords received tax relief at 40% or 45%. Landlords also benefited from a tax allowance worth 10% of their annual net rental income covering 'wear and tear' on furniture and fixtures. Other expenses, such as buildings and contents insurance, letting agents' fees and cleaning or gardening, could be set against taxable income. In 2010/11, £13 billion was claimed by landlords in tax relief (Kingman, 2013). In addition, although liable to pay Capital Gains Tax (CGT), a loophole enabled landlords, provided that they had occupied a property as their main residence at some point, to be exempt from CGT on any gain that accrued during the final 36 months of ownership – a get-out exposed during the MPs' expenses scandal. There also appears to have been substantial tax avoidance in the sector, with at least £550 million tax liability being evaded in 2010/11 (*Independent*, 2013a). In 2014, the *Daily Mail* reported that '900,000 landlords face buy-to-let tax probe' (*Daily Mail*, 2014), claiming that of an estimated 1.4 million landlords, only 500,000 had declared profits from private renting on their tax returns.

Private landlords had other advantages over first-time buyers. An analysis of private landlord characteristics by Lloyd (2013) demonstrated that landlords were financially comfortable, most having a full-time job with pension rights and a median £333,999 total net property wealth and a mean of £479,598. This put them in a stronger position than first-time buyers to obtain mortgage finance. Private landlords made good use of the Coalition government's 'Funding for Lending' scheme, which reduced mortgage costs. The Bank of England (2015, p 5) noted:

> The outstanding stock of buy-to-let mortgage lending has increased by over 40% since 2008. Over the same period, the stock of owner-occupier mortgage lending rose by only 2%. The share of buy-to-let in the stock of outstanding mortgage lending has risen to 16% from 12% in 2008.

BTL was unaffected by the restrictions on mortgage lending applied to owner-occupiers in 2014 (see Chapter Five). However, worried about the potential impact of BTL on housing market stability, the Bank of England (2016) proposed new regulations on lending to landlords, including testing a borrower's ability to pay a 5.5% interest rate.

Private landlord politics now focuses around five issues: how to stimulate institutional investment into new-build private renting; voluntary versus statutory regulation; rent control; Housing Benefit expenditure; and the role of private landlordism in reducing homeownership.

Institutional investment in private landlordism

The estate agent's advice that 'larger capitalists had better leave it alone' (Griffin, 1893, p 364) was heeded and private landlords have historically mainly been 'small-scale' investors. Under New Labour, as private renting came to regarded as an important, 'flexible' tenure, the 'holy grail' was to discover ways to bring institutional investors into the *new* house-building market, that is, *build* to let rather than *buy* to let. New Labour tried but failed to find ways to access this institutional investor fund. In 2011, the Coalition government set up a committee led by Sir Adrian Montague 'to review the barriers to institutional investment in private rented homes' (DCLG, 2012c). The Montague Report (DCLG, 2012c), when examining the 'potential for investors', identified a number of positives, including the high demand for rented accommodation and that 'returns on residential property have totalled 9.6% on average over the last 10 years, significantly above comparable figures for commercial property that ranged from 7.3% to 5.7%' (DCLG, 2012c, para 20). However, there were barriers to institutional investment, including the higher yields necessary to attract institutional investment in this 'novel' area, high management costs and aspects of the planning system (DCLG, 2012c, para 33).

Montague's recommendations amounted to a call on government to encourage institutional investment in new private landlord accommodation, mainly by preferential access to public sector land and abandoning 'affordable' housing provision in the planning system in favour of a simple division between houses built for homeownership and houses built for rent, with land values based on rental not owner-occupied use. In its statement 'Plan to Boost House-Building, Jobs and the Economy' (DCLG, 2012d, p 1), the government announced that 'Developers who can prove that council's costly affordable housing requirements make the project unviable will see them removed' but made no distinction between houses built for homeownership and houses built for rent. Later, a £200-million Build-to-Rent fund was set up to finance the construction of homes until they are built, let out and managed, and to create new 'demonstration' projects to showcase larger-scale rental developments in action. The 2013 Budget announced that the fund would be increased to £1 billion and a £10-billion Private Rented Sector Guarantee scheme would be established to underwrite 20% of the finance needed for new private rented homes.

Regulation

In England, local government has powers to regulate the private landlord sector in low-demand areas and when houses are multi-occupied but such regulation has had a low priority in most local authorities. Sir Robin Wales, elected Mayor of Newham, the first authority to adopt borough-wide regulation, in his evidence to the House of Commons Select Committee on Communities and Local Government (Wales, 2013), stated:

> Before we went to do borough-wide licensing, we did a pilot in Little Ilford, which is an area in Newham.... One-third were very good; one-third were okay and dragged a wee bit doing it; and about 25% were cash-in-hand criminal landlords ... we are discovering quite a lot of what we think is fraud.... It is much bigger than we thought. We thought we had 5,000 landlords; we now know we have 15,000 and those are just the ones who have registered early. It is amazing.

The *Guardian* (2013) uncovered a new form of 'rent to rent' landlords; renting property from an existing landlord and then converting the living room into sleeping space to cram in more paying tenants. 'Beds in sheds' – renting garages and sheds as living accommodation – was another dimension of the 'rogue landlord' issue.

The Coalition government introduced tentative steps to encourage more responsible landlord and lettings agency practices. It amended the Enterprise and Regulatory Reform Act 2013 to enable the government to require agents to sign up to a redress scheme and required letting agents to publish a full tariff of their fees. However, Eric Pickles, Secretary of State for Communities and Local Government, was responsive to the private landlord lobby. When Cameron demanded that private landlords should be compelled to check immigration papers:

> Eric Pickles pushed back hard: Prime Minister, can I be blunt with you? I think this is a seriously bad idea. Checking immigration papers is hard. Many of them, you will be shocked to know, Prime Minister, are frankly forged. What are you asking private landlords to do – act as an arm of the immigration service? (Laws, 2016, p 354)

In response to growing local authority interest in borough-wide licensing schemes and lobbying from the National Landlords Association, Pickles announced that there would be a threshold limiting licensing to covering 'more than 20% of their geographical area or that would affect more than 20% of privately rented homes in the local authority area' (DCLG, 2015b, para 1). Labour favoured compulsory nationwide registration and banning letting agencies from charging fees to tenants. The 2015 Conservative government – with Eric Pickles replaced by Greg Clark as Secretary of State for Communities and Local Government – gave more attention to the 'rogue landlord' problem, proposing a list of rascal landlords and letting agents, higher fines, extending the housing offence catalogue, and extending mandatory licensing of HMOs (DCLG, 2015c, 2015d). The 2016 Housing and Planning Act introduced 'banning orders' to prevent a person from letting or managing a house if they had a housing offence record.

Rent control

When he advocated rent control in his 2012 London Mayor campaign, Ken Livingstone received little support from the Labour Party leadership, and an all-party Select Committee declared in 2013:

> We do not, however, support rent control which would serve only to reduce investment in the sector at a time when it is most needed. We agree that the most effective way to make rents more affordable would be to increase supply, particularly in those areas where demand is highest. (House of Commons Communities and Local Government Committee, 2013, para 109)

That private landlord tenant associations lack a voice equivalent to those representing their landlords was revealed in the oral evidence given to the House of Commons Communities and Local Government Committee inquiry into the private landlord sector. The Committee took oral evidence from nine landlord interest groups but only one interest group representing private landlord tenants. The most cynical public choice theorists might attribute this to the economic interests of MPs, with 200-plus MPs owning rented property (Cadwalladr, 2013), and in 2013, five of the 11 members of the House of Commons Communities and Local Government Committee derived income from private renting. Political apathy to private renting tenants also reflected private tenants' voting behaviour. Research by the Electoral Commission (2011) revealed that 89% of outright owners and 87% buying with a mortgage were registered to vote in 2010, compared to 58% of private renters and only 26% of people who had moved within the private rented sector in the last year. Even when registered, tenant inclination to vote is lower than in other tenures: in 2011, 80% of owners, 72% of mortgage-holders, 65% of social renters and 60% of private renters said that they were likely to vote in the next general election (Ipsos Mori, 2013). Moreover, although in the absence of compulsory registration in England, the number of private landlords is unknown, it has been estimated as being as high as 2.1 million (Ronald,

2015). This represents a sizeable vote more easily activated than private landlord tenants. Labour leader Jeremy Corbyn has expressed concern about the landlord vote:

> you're looking at several million people letting out one or two flats. And they can become a politically significant group. Particularly in marginal constituencies. So you will find all parties trimming towards them: landlords tend to be people who vote. (Corbyn, quoted in Walker and Jeraj, 2016, p 79)

Before the 2015 general election, the National Landlords Association (2015) declared that 'Landlord support for Labour and the Liberal Democrat Party has halved since the 2010 General Election because of their interventionist policies for the private rented sector'.

By 2015, private landlordism had moved up the political agenda, especially in London, where the percentage of households privately renting has increased from 15% in 2001 to 27% in 2015. One in three households renting from private landlords had children. In 2015, the median rent for a privately rented home in London was £1,500 per month, a 7.7% increase from 2014 (Homelet, 2015). This produced media headlines that, in London, housing cost as a percentage of household income was 59% for private renters (Londonist, 2016).

In January 2014, Emma Reynolds, then shadow Housing Minister, stated that 'it is not Labour party policy to introduce rent controls' (quoted in Redbrick, 2014). Nonetheless, buoyed by the success of its pledge to freeze energy prices, Labour gradually moved towards adopting rent regulation. Its 2015 manifesto stated:

> For the 11 million people who rent privately, we will legislate to make three-year tenancies the norm, with a ceiling on excessive rent rises. A ban on unfair letting agent fees will save renters over £600. We will drive standards up by creating a national register of private landlords. (Labour Party, 2015 p 46)

Labour's proposals were based on a distinction between 'first-' and 'second-' generation rent control. 'First' referred to rent freezes and 'fair' rents set by rent tribunals, characteristic of the 1945–88 period, and 'second' referred to the 'rent-dampening' regime applied in Germany, where, once freely negotiated, rent increases are limited to inflation and landlords have limited grounds for terminating the tenancy.

Labour's plan attracted criticism, mainly on the argument that it would produce a decline in the availability of private sector lets, but it also attracted unexpected backers. Civitas, an offshoot of the right-wing Institute for Economic Affairs, supported rent control on the arguments that:

> In London, moreover, it is quite conceivable that supply will never match demand, such are the space limitations and the seemingly limitless allure of the capital to newcomers and investors from around the world.... Despite the claims of some landlords, the private rented sector has not supported the building of new homes. In fact, mainly owner-occupiers purchase new-build homes. Private landlords tend to buy existing homes, meaning their investments merely change the tenure profile of what is already there. (Bentley, 2015, pp 5, 16).

Housing Benefit expenditure

Spending on Housing Benefit in the private landlord sector flatlined in the early 2000s but expenditure increased from £3.4 billion in 2005/06 to £9 billion in 2014, the outcome of lower real earnings, higher rents and the rise in the number of private landlord tenants as homeownership declined. According to the English Housing Survey (DCLG, 2013b), housing costs for private renters absorbed 41% of their gross weekly income (*after* Housing Benefit); among owner-occupiers, the figure was 19%, and for social renters, it was 30%. The average eligible private sector rent for Housing Benefit increased by 45% in real terms between 2000/01 and 2010/11. An estimated £2.9 billion (33%) of private sector Housing Benefit expenditure in 2010/11 was attributable to real rent increases over the previous 10 years (DWP, 2013a), and in 2013, 25% of private renters relied on Housing Benefit. Some commentators have argued that Housing Benefit actually increases rents, with Bentley (2015, p 7), on the basis that the 'reference' rents used to restrict Housing Benefit cover broad areas that disguise sub-markets, claiming:

> private sector rents are already distorted – upwards – by a system of subsidies that places a floor under prices, at least at the lower end of the price spectrum. This, in turn, increases the numbers of lower-income households forced to rely on it, further inflating rents.

The Coalition government's reaction to the mounting Housing Benefit cost was to impose entitlement restrictions. Housing Benefit was limited to the 30th percentile of rent in an area rather than the 50th percentile, a 'bedroom tax' was introduced and an overall cap on 'welfare' entitlements – operative through Housing Benefit – was set at £26,000 per year for workless, 'working-age' people. In contrast to earlier recessions, which had been accompanied by greater public sympathy for people dependent on social security payments, the post-2008 recession produced a marked hardening of attitudes, with, for example, 62% of respondents to the British Social Attitudes Survey agreeing that unemployment benefits were too high and discouraged work in 2011, compared to 25% in 2005. Although the percentage agreeing that unemployment benefits were too high and discouraged work had declined to 51% in 2012 (British Social Attitudes, 2013), the contrast with earlier recessions was significant. Hills (2014, p 23) notes that the number of people agreeing with the statement that 'the government should spend more on welfare benefits for the poor if it leads to higher taxes' declined from 60% in 1990 to 33% in 2012.

Initially opposed by Labour, the 'welfare cap' was very popular with the public. According to an Ipsos Mori survey commissioned by the Department for Work and Pensions (DWP, 2013b), 70% were in support and 13% against. Buoyed by the public response to the 'welfare cap', the Conservatives promised to reduce the cap should they be elected to government in 2015, a promise subsequently redeemed together with other reductions in Housing Benefit entitlements, although sweetened by reductions in 'social' rents (see Chapter Ten).

Private landlordism versus homeownership

Private landlordism and homeownership are two sides of the same coin. As private landlordism waned, owner-occupation increased: from the 1920s to the 1980s, 4.5 million dwellings were transferred from private landlords to homeowners. Post-2005, private landlordism's advance was accompanied by a decline in homeownership. Aware that private landlordism was a barrier to the Conservatives' 'property-owning democracy' vision, and sensitive to the 2016 London Mayoral election, in his 2015 Summer Budget, Chancellor George Osborne said:

> First, we will create a more level playing field between those buying a home to let, and those who are buying a home to live in. Buy-to-let landlords have a huge advantage in the market as they can offset their mortgage interest

payments against their income, whereas homebuyers cannot. (Osborne, 2015a)

He announced that offsetting mortgage payments against rental income for tax purposes would be reduced in phases to the standard income tax rate by 2020. Moreover, rather than receive an automatic 'wear and tear allowance', landlords would have to demonstrate that they had replaced furniture and fixtures. Pressure on private landlords was ratcheted up in the 2015 Autumn Statement and Spending Review. Osborne said:

> Frankly, people buying a home to let should not be squeezing out families who can't afford a home to buy. So I am introducing new rates of Stamp Duty that will be 3 per cent higher on the purchase of additional properties like buy-to-lets and second homes. (Osborne, 2015b)

The extra Stamp Duty levy applied above the existing rates, this meant that there would be a tax of 3% (previously zero) on homes worth up to £125,000, 5% (instead of 2%) on homes that cost between £125,001 and £250,000, and 8% (currently 5%) on homes worth between £250,001 and £925,000. Houses worth up to £1.5 million would be subject to 13% rate and those above this amount would incur a 15% charge.

Commenting on the Chancellor's announcement, Richard Lambert, Chief Executive Officer at the National Landlords Association, said:

> The Chancellor's political intention is crystal clear; he wants to choke off future investment in private properties to rent. The exemption for corporate investment makes this effectively an attack on the small private landlords who responded to the housing crisis by putting their own money into providing homes by the party that they put their faith in at the election. If it's the Chancellor's intention to completely eradicate buy to let in the UK then it's a mystery to us why he doesn't just come out and say so. (Lambert, 2015)

Conclusion

In the 19th century, private landlordism was a 'cottage industry', albeit a very large one. Landlords were mainly 'petit bourgeoisie' and it is possible to view private landlordism's demise as a capitalist class sacrifice of the 'petit bourgeoisie' in its 20th-century conflict with the working class. Clarke and Ginsburg (1975, p 5) quote Thomas Cubitt, owner of a large building firm building middle-class housing, as stating in 1840 that working-class houses 'belong to a little shop-keeping class of persons, who have saved a little money in business…. I think very few persons of great capital have anything to do with them at all'. Daunton (1983) agrees with this explanation, pointing out that in the 19th century, landlords could influence the housing system via engagement in local government politics, but in the 20th century, as the issues became national, the sway of private landlords diminished. However, this explanation underplays the role of other factors involved in the demise of private landlordism, not least increasing homeownership and council tenancy availability. The homeownership ideology made owner-occupation increasingly attractive to the working and middle class, and this homeownership 'premium' produced selling into the tenure of both controlled and decontrolled private rented properties. Moreover, as Merrett (1982, p 10) points out, 'the development of the capital market, including the building societies, now offered rentiers a much greater range of placements which, in comparison with "widowers' houses", were less risky, more liquid, less lumpy and simpler to administer'. In addition, landlordism's political sway has been underestimated. Landlord lobbying was influential in the passing of the Rent Act 1957 and local landlord pressure, backed by national building society influence, were factors in impeding the growth of local authority housing.

By the late 1980s, private landlordism had become a 'niche' market providing for young professionals, especially in London, a declining elderly cohort with security of tenure and still protected by 'fair' rents, and students and other transitory groups often living in multi-occupied houses, so the 'creeping decontrol' in the Housing Act 1988 initially had a low electoral impact. The sector remains a 'cottage industry' – in 2010, only 8% of landlords stated that they were full-time landlords (DCLG, 2010a) – but its clientele is now much larger – more students, more people aged 25 to 44, more recent immigrants and far more families with children. Moreover, some 'cottages' are becoming 'mansions' as accumulated assets have enabled more landlords to become major property investors, financing their purchases from cash rather than mortgages. A study by the Intermediary Mortgage Lenders Association (IMLA, 2014, p 1) found that 'Only 420,000 of the additional 1,310,000 properties in the private rented sector between 2007 and 2012 were financed by BTL loans'. This trend is predicted to accelerate as 13 million savers aged over 55 take their pension pots as lump sums with a quarter tax-free and the rest taxed at marginal rates rather than 55%. The growth in private landlordism has contributed to its political influence. The National Landlords Association has a staff of over 60 – compared to Generation Rent, the principal tenant campaign group, with a staff of two to five (Walker and Jeraj, 2016).

The private landlord sector was once described as a 'waiting room' for other tenures, especially owner-occupation (Kemp, 2009). It still is, but waiting time has increased. In 1969, the average age of first-time buyers was 25, by 2010, it was 30, and in 2014, it was 36. Despite private landlordism's impact in eroding 'a property-owning democracy', Conservative Party support for private landlordism was high before the 2015 general election but the rising political salience of 'generation rent' has eroded Conservative backing.

Further reading

Barnett, M.J. (1969) *The Politics of Legislation: The Rent Act of 1957*, London: Weidenfeld and Nicolson.

Bentley, D. (2015) *The Future of Private Renting: Shaping a Fairer Market for Tenants and Taxpayers*, London: Civitas.

Offer, A. (1981) *Property and Politics 1870–1914: Landownership, Law, Ideology and Urban Development in England*, Cambridge: Cambridge University Press.

Simmonds, A.G.V. (2002) 'Raising Rachman: The Origins of the Rent Act, 1957', *The Historical Journal*, vol 45, no 4, pp 843–68.

FIVE

A property-owning democracy?

Land tenure complexities in the early 20th century make it difficult to assess how many people owned their homes. Although usually assessed at between 10% and 15% in 1914 (Pawley, 1978), local studies (Daunton, 1983) demonstrate considerable variations around this approximation. Holmans (2005) estimated owner-occupation at 23% in 1918 and a 2013 Census Report (Office for National Statistics, 2013) gave a 20% figure. Owner-occupation increased from around 750,000 after the First World War to 3,250,000 by 1938, when the homeowner proportion was 34%. The Conservative Party and the building societies nurtured progression towards a 'property-owning democracy'. The catchphrase was coined by Noel Skelton, a Conservative Scottish Unionist MP and informal leader of a Conservative Parliamentary group, the 'Young Men's Christian Association', whose membership included Anthony Eden and Harold Macmillan. Sir Alec Douglas Home, Skelton's Parliamentary Private Secretary from 1931 to 1935, was also influenced by Skelton.

In *Constructive Conservatism*, Skelton (1924, pp 10–12) argued that because Britain had become an educated democracy, its citizens were susceptible to 'fundamental principles' embodying a 'social conscience', an ideology coming from 'the Socialist disguised as an educator and a teacher'. He claimed that the Conservatives had to occupy the moral uplands, territory located in the 'property-owning democracy' idea. Skelton turned the 18th-century notion – only 'the man of property' could be trusted to vote responsibly – on its head. The franchise could no longer be denied to those without assets, so those without property had to be supplied with enhanced opportunities to acquire individual assets and develop the 'character' coming from ownership responsibilities. Although Skelton had a broad view of property, including share-ownership, homeownership came to dominate the Conservatives' property-ownership notion. The Right to Buy was motivated, in part, by the desire to break the relationship between living in a local authority house and voting Labour. Promoting homeownership had other potential advantages for the Conservatives, with Ansell (2013) arguing that 'stored' homeowner wealth undermines support for redistributive social protection policies.

Between 1945 and 1954, the owner-occupied market share declined. However, post-1955, sustained growth was promoted by: tax relief on mortgage interest; homeownership endorsement by the Labour Party leadership; erratic but overall positive price increases; selling from the private landlord sector; low-cost homeownership schemes; and council house sales. From 2005, high house prices, market competition from private landlords, larger deposits after the 'credit crunch' and a steep decline in council house sales produced a decline in homeownership. This continued into the Coalition government's term of office, and faced with the prospect that he might become the first Conservative Prime Minister to leave office with a homeownership rate below his inheritance, David Cameron introduced schemes to boost owner-occupation. The 2015 Conservative government made promoting homeownership its principal housing objective.

Suburban politics

Suburban development started to gain momentum in the late 19th century as the rail, tram, bus and underground networks expanded. Although suburbia is usually associated with middle-class 'bourgeois utopias' (Fishman, 1989), working-class rented suburbs with a few working-class homeowners also started to develop, especially in Greater London, where their growth was facilitated by cheap, early morning 'workman's trains'. In 1909, Masterman was so impressed by suburban growth that he divided England into three categories – a ruling 'Conqueror' class, the 'Multitude' and the 'Suburbans' – a 'homogeneous civilisation, detached, self-centred, unostentatious' (Masterman, 1909, p 57). He was concerned that suburbia was producing insularity, 'a vision of life in which there is no adequate test or judgment, which are the heroic, which the trivial.... a noticeable absence of vision' (Masterman, 1909, p 99). Others shared Masterman's disquiet, with H.G. Wells referring to suburbia as a 'dull useless boiling up of human activities, an immense clustering of futilities ... going at an unprecedented pace nowhere in particular' (quoted in Hunt, 2004, p 410). Despite these reservations, in the interwar period, suburbia expanded as a physical space and a mindset.

Building societies

Most early societies were 'terminating': working-class people agreed to pay into a fund to build houses, and having raised sufficient finance to acquire a property, members drew lots to determine who would move into a new dwelling. Payments continued until all subscribers were able to own a house, whereupon the society terminated. To hasten the housing process, some societies allowed people not requiring homes to join the association and paid interest on the investment. The society then became 'permanent', and in the late 19th century, many associations were first established as 'permanent'. The Liberals and Conservatives boosted building societies by sponsoring Freehold Land Societies, aimed at encouraging franchise extension by enabling freehold ownership worth at least 40 shillings (the franchise threshold under the Reform Act 1832). Over a hundred Freehold Land Societies were formed between 1847 and 1857. Building Clubs were similar to the terminating building societies but differed in that they raised wholesale finance from potential investors, often through local solicitors and accountants who were invited to join the management boards.

The Chief Registrar of Friendly Societies regulated societies under the Building Societies Act 1874. The Registrar's powers were strengthened in 1894 after the largest society, the *Liberator*, collapsed. The Liberal politician Jabez Spencer Balfour, MP for Burnley, had set up the society to lend money to purchase the high-priced property he owned. By the start of the 20th century, 'permanent' societies dominated the sector and were lending extensively to private landlords. The societies created an aura of decorum and status. They emphasised their mutuality – societies had no shareholders and claimed that they were working for the mutual advantage of investors and borrowers – and the esteem to be acquired from investing in a society and, in return, eventually becoming a homeowner. In 1906, William Brabrook, Registrar of Building Societies, said: 'if a man joined a building society, he would become more highly esteemed by his neighbours as a man of substance and as a landowner and may interest himself in every public movement' (Brabrook, 2009 [1906], p 14).

After the First World War, the societies started to change. Regional and locally based organisations began to be dominated by larger societies with national ambitions focused on moving savings to areas where mortgage demand was the highest. Despite the occasional failure, after the 1929 crash in stocks and shares, societies attracted investment on such a scale that the National Building Society's leader observed that they were 'in some danger of being overwhelmed by a huge increase of capital which it was quite impossible to utilise' (quoted in Yelling, 1992, p 88). By the mid-1930s, the societies were well-heeled and in an ebullient mood, asking Hilton Young, the Health Minister, to assist in transferring local authority mortgages to the societies, claiming they had been approached by entrepreneurs interested in buying council estates (Townroe, 1936). The minister agreed to pursue these initiatives but no schemes entered the public domain, mainly because local authorities refused to provide the mortgage guarantees demanded by the societies.

Live in Kent and be content

Mass house production required a selling strategy. The new houses, mainly semi-detached, were marketed as a lifestyle, with advertising slogans such as 'Live in Surrey without a worry' and 'Live in Kent and be content'. Moving to suburbia meant family harmony, a husband, wife and children choosing to spend their leisure time together in a new house with a garden. 'Mod-con' labour-saving devices, powered by 'clean electricity', allowed the 'housewife' to spend more time with her family. It meant establishing roots in a semi-rural, safe environment, an ideal reflected in 'avenue' names – 'Acadia', 'Brook', 'Oak' – and the names posted on the homes, 'Dunroamin', 'Chez-nous' and Samantha and Dennis's abode, 'Samanden'. Newspapers promoted this homeownership ideal, in particular, the *Daily Mail*, which sponsored the Ideal Home Exhibition, attracting 700,000 visitors in the 1930s.

Homeownership needed sustenance by extension down the housing chain. Both Speight (2000) and Scott (2013) argue that although the growth in homeownership in the 1920s was middle-class, more and more manual and lower-paid non-manual workers became homeowners in the 1930s, accounting for up 50% of the new owners. Under the Small Dwellings Acquisition Act 1899, local authorities could grant loans for house purchase, and by 1939, 150,000 loans had been advanced. Low interest rates, introduced in 1932, helped the process and building societies reduced deposit sizes – sometimes to as low as 5% – lengthened repayment periods from 20 years to up to 27 years and relaxed restrictions on loan-to-income ratios. This was facilitated by the 'builders' pool', an arrangement through which builders agreed to take responsibility for properties coming into repossession by setting aside a 'fund pool' for building society use if a loss was made. The 'builders' pool' supported over half the new houses built in the 1930s and, at times, the relationship between builders and the building societies seemed too close. There were accusations that collusion was involved in inflating sale prices and complications developed over respective liabilities if properties were defective (Craig, 1986).

'Homeownership ideology'

State subsidy support for homeownership between the wars was moderate in comparison to the tax incentives offered from the early 1960s, but if financial support was limited, encouragement in moral terms was plentiful as the Conservatives, in power for most of the interwar years, promoted the 'property-owning democracy' idea. 'When working men become men of substance they naturally vote Conservative', said the National Union of Conservative and Unionist Associations in 1933 (quoted in Fée, 2008, p 49). The Conservatives pitched their appeal to the working-class elite – called the 'good class artisan' in Cabinet minutes – in the hope that their views would filter down. As Roberts (1973, p 183) states:

> the top-class natural leaders of the workers – the good, intelligent talkers – acted above all else as assessors, arbiters and makers of the common conscience.... The pressure of their beliefs ... seeped slowly into the social layers of working-class life and conditioned the minds of all.

Housing was identified as a principal cause of social instability. The problem was twofold. In 1910, the electorate size had been about 8 million, at the December 1918 election, it was over 21 million, raising the spectre of mass democracy's political impact. In addition, there was the potential for extra parliamentary action if grievances were not assuaged. Morgan (2002, p 59) states 'The Conservative mind teemed with images of single young-men, ex-soldiers or unemployed, driven into the streets and the clutches of the agitator', and he quotes Winston Churchill as recommending plural votes for householders to negate the influence of the country's 'more dependent and more volatile elements ... the lodgers of all kinds of both sexes'. Skelton's 'property-owning democracy' idea had an immediate impact on Conservative housing policy. Merrett (1982, p 5) argues that the Housing Act 1923 'was the most important legislative measure specifically concerned with home-ownership before the Second World War'. It extended local authority mortgages, allowed local authorities to guarantee building society loans and gave lump sum subsidies to builders for the construction of low-cost houses.

Stanley Baldwin and a property-owning democracy

After the 1923 general election, Baldwin's leadership was under threat. At a meeting of the Conservative Party Executive in early 1924, he delivered a speech heralded as the birth of a 'New Conservatism', claiming that the Conservatives could no longer depend on the Liberals and therefore 'we must rely upon ourselves and our own efforts'. The Labour Party, with a 2 million increase in its vote between 1919 and 1923, was now the chief opponent and:

> The great source of strength of Labour in this country at present is that ... they have the type of men ... who will give the whole of his strength and the whole of his time to bring about, as he believes he can, a better condition for his fellow-men. (Quoted in Ramsden, 1978, p 190)

In terms of public choice theory, political competition meant that the Conservatives required an appeal to the new electorate created in 1918. Baldwin found this lure in Skelton's 'property-owning democracy' idea. He declared that the Conservatives 'differ profoundly from the Socialists [in wanting] the people to own their own homes' and linked this aspiration to the promotion of 'self-respect and independence' (Baldwin, 1924, quoted in Williamson, 1999, p 182). He constantly evoked suburban/rural Britain's stability in his speeches, dress and demeanour. As Morgan (2002, p 59) comments:

> In the ethos of Conservatism it was not the house but the home – with its richer and sometimes suffocating connotations – which had a powerful symbolic value resting on a gendered familial ideology and the threatened integrity of the private sphere. 'Socialism stands for class war, chaos and disruption, the break-up of family and religion' ran Mrs Baldwin's message to women voters in 1929.

Status

Status was a key element in selling suburbia, with some developers taking potential customers to their sites in chauffeur-driven cars. The suburban owner-occupier's full citizenship status was contrasted to the 'slum dweller', to be rehoused in inner-city council flats. The Conservative Health Minister in 1922 said the 'slum problem' was that 'slum dwellers unfortunately often love their slums' (Griffith-

Boscawen, 1925, p 141). The Minister for Health in the 1930s, Hilton Young, denounced inner-city areas as 'radiating centres of depravity and disease'. In contrast, owner-occupation was 'normal and natural to the economic life of the country' (quoted in Yelling, 1992, p 92). This homeowner–former slum dweller/council house tenant dichotomy had physical manifestations. In 1926, a barrier was erected to stop the working classes from a council estate in Bromley entering the streets of the adjoining middle-class area and a wall was put up to prevent council tenants in Lewisham using a path through a private estate. Homeowners in Oxford erected the notorious Cutteslowe Wall, topped by barbed wire, to separate their territory from a council estate. Walls were built after the Second World War in Cardiff, Newcastle-upon-Tyne, County Durham and Gillingham (Tucker, 1966).

Anthony Eden placed 'a property-owning democracy' at the centre of post-war Conservative Party policy, stating that 'of all forms of property suitable for such distribution, house property is one of the best' (Eden, 1946, quoted in Evans, 2009, p 109). Some Conservative politicians continued to denigrate council house tenants after the Second World War; Lady Treedmuir remarked in 1949 that 'a man who has his own doorstep and his own garden is a far better and more valuable citizen in this country than the man who is a thriftless council tenant' (quoted in Labour Party, 1951).

Suburban censure

Although the norm between the wars was to extol suburbia, dissenting voices echoed the disquiet expressed by Masterman and Wells before the First World War. In *England and the Octopus*, Williams-Ellis (1996 [1928]) decried urban and rural loss through their suburban fusion. D.H. Lawrence complained that suburbia stifled 'the real urban side of man, the civic side' (quoted in Hunt, 2004, p 50). Architects condemned 'embellishment' on suburban houses, especially the mock-Tudor style. In *The House: A Machine for Living In*, the architect Anthony Bertram declared that 'The man who builds a bogus Tudoresque villa or castellates his suburban home is committing a crime against truth and tradition' (1935, quoted in Sharp and Rendel, 2008, p 122). This 'high-minded' distaste for suburbia was to have an impact on Britain's reconstruction after the Second World War (see Chapter Six).

Tax relief on mortgage interest

In the early 1950s, Macmillan was under pressure from his party to deliver more homes for owner-occupation. Herbert Brabin, Local Government Officer at the Conservative Party Central Office, published an article in *Tory Challenge* in which he claimed that 'it was party policy to promote building for sale by small firms [and] to enable the purchase of houses by the lower income groups through the sale of council houses to sitting tenants' (Jones, 2000, pp 103–4). Brabin was supported by the Conservative Party Chair, Lord Woolton, who urged Macmillan to do more to bring a 'property-owning democracy' into effect, arguing that 'it would remove in some measure the herding of more people into these huge County Council housing areas, which become predominantly Socialist in political outlook' (Woolton, 1952, p 2). Having achieved his 300,000 houses target, Macmillan set in motion policies designed to promote homeownership, principally by restricting council subsidies to clearance schemes (see Chapters Three and Six) and allowing local authorities to grant larger mortgages. The Treasury, reflecting its future position on homeownership subsidies, vetoed Lord Woolton's suggestion to award direct subsidies to homeowners (Bridgen and Lowe, 1998).

Between 1955 and 1964, new houses for owner-occupation exceeded new council house construction. Homeownership was boosted by schemes similar to the 2013 'Help to Buy' programme. In 1955, local authorities were allowed to guarantee mortgages so that building societies could offer 90–95% mortgages, and the House Purchase and Housing Act 1959 set up a loan fund to underpin 75%-plus mortgages on pre-1919 houses. However, tohese measures were modest compared to the future impact of tax relief on mortgage interest, justified as compensation to homeowners for having to pay Schedule A tax on imputed rental income. Schedule A tax was based on 1936 values and its impact had gradually declined. When abolished in 1963, it was yielding only about £25–30 million per year (Whitehead, 1980).

The economic rationale of tax relief on mortgage interest without Schedule A tax is opaque. Perhaps it had none and the announcement in 1962 that Schedule A tax would be abolished was a desperate, if unsuccessful, attempt to win the Orpington by-election (Hills, 1991). Margaret Thatcher, in her battles with her Chancellors to preserve the relief, said that it was a 'well deserved' reward to households with mortgages – 'our people' (quoted in Campbell, 1993, p 175). Schedule A tax abolition for homeowners, together with the introduction of mandatory home improvement grants in 1959, helped to accelerate sales to owner-occupiers from the private landlord sector.

Labour and homeownership

The Labour leadership, aware that homeownership was becoming popular, backed the tenure. In his diaries, Richard Crossman, Labour Housing Minister from 1964 to 1966, referring to the 1964 general election, said 'Of course we wooed the owner-occupier during the general election', adding that his plan was 'primarily concerned to increase the production of owner-occupied houses [and] ... make owner-occupation a possibility for a whole group of average and below-average workers at present excluded because they can't afford the current mortgage rates' (Crossman, 1975, pp 383, 377).

Crossman records negotiations with building societies and builders to try to reach agreement on mortgage finance availability to match planned new building for homeownership. The negotiations failed because the building societies were suspicious that the government wanted to control interest rates. Later government–building society relationships were more productive. In the 1970s, both the Conservatives and Labour granted loans to building societies to lower interest rates. Labour introduced the Option Mortgage Scheme in 1967, making low-income house-buyers eligible for subsidies equivalent to tax relief on mortgage interest payments. In 1974, Labour imposed a £25,000 cap on the mortgage interest that could be set against tax but this was a modest gesture to the grass-roots party – still faithful to council housing – given that the average house price was then £10,000.

Selling council houses

The 'crisis' nature of the Housing, Town Planning etc Act 1919 was reflected in its provisions for allowing council houses to be sold. The *First Interim Report of the Committee on National Expenditure* recommended a 'vigorous policy of sale' (Geddes, 1922, p 131). However, although some local authorities – notably, Birmingham – built for direct sale, selling existing council houses at 'best price', as set out in central regulations, was very limited.

After the Second World War, Bevan refused the occasional requests from local councils to sell council houses and this prompted an unsuccessful attempt by a Conservative backbencher, David Gammons, MP for London Hornsey, to commit his party to a tenant Right to Buy. In 1952, Macmillan, under pressure from the Conservative Party to promote homeownership, gave a general consent for local authorities to sell council houses at below market value (Bridgen and Lowe, 1998), but this had little impact. Some Labour Party policy advisors promoted council house sales. In 1948, Michael Young perceived electoral advantages in selling council homes to tenants after the housing shortage had been overcome and claimed that the occupant would have 'security of tenure, pride in possession and encouragement to improve the property' (quoted in Francis, 1997, p 122). James Meade, Director the Cabinet Economic Section from 1946 to 1947 and a Labour Party advisor in the 1950s, 'repeatedly argued that the government "should enable the occupiers of municipal homes to acquire the properties for themselves by saving and paying a weekly sum in addition to the rent"' (Francis, 2012, p 431). Although Labour's 1959 manifesto announced that 'Every tenant will have a chance first to buy from the Council the house he lives in' (Labour Party, 1959), no detail on the mechanisms involved or the sale terms were included.

Local democracy and council house sales

Housing tenure has a long history as a local political battleground. Dunleavy (1991, p 120) notes that 'In the 1930s the Labour leader of the London County Council pledged to "build the Tories out of London" launching an extensive public housing programme to boost the number of pro-Labour tenants'.

The Conservatives won some major urban local authorities in the late 1960s, including Manchester and Birmingham, and started to sell council houses. In response, the Labour government restricted sales by a quota system in the major conurbations and set minimum prices, but made no general sale prohibition. Respect for local democracy was the reason given by ministers. On their return to power in 1970, the Conservatives revoked Labour's restrictions and some Conservative-controlled authorities – notably, the Greater London Council – showed enthusiasm for selling houses at discounted prices to tenants. Other Conservative authorities did not, with the Conservative Party Housing Minister saying that he had 'a little list of Tory authorities which refuse to sell council houses' (quoted in Forrest and Murie, 1988, p 52). The Conservative Party retained power in many 'big city' councils in the early 1970s and more than 45,000 houses were sold in 1972, perhaps because tenants showed a greater willingness to buy given that the Housing Finance Act 1972 contained a higher rent threat (see Chapter Six). Council house sales declined as the Conservative Party gradually lost control of local councils. Although some Conservative

Party members expressed concern that Labour councils would not sell their council houses, Conservative ministers did not compel sales, once again using the local democracy argument.

A Right to Buy

The Conservative Party manifesto for the February 1974 general election revealed a policy change. It stated:

> The number of new homeowners would have been still larger had certain Councils not opposed the sale of Council houses … we shall ensure that, in future, established Council tenants are able, as of right, to buy on reasonable terms the house or flat in which they live. (Conservative Party, 1974a)

As shadow Environment Minister, Margaret Thatcher was opposed to council house sales on generous terms because:

> I was wary of alienating the already hard-pressed families who had scrimped to buy a house on one of the new private estates at the market price…. They would, I feared, strongly object to council house tenants who had made none of these sacrifices suddenly receiving what was in effect a large capital sum from the Government. We might end up losing more support than we gained. (Thatcher, 1995, p 246)

According to Young (1989), Thatcher argued vigorously with Edward Heath before accepting sales. The October 1974 Conservative Party manifesto stated:

> Our third proposal for extending home ownership is to give a new deal to every council tenant who has been in his home for three years or more. These tenants will have the right to purchase their homes at a price one-third below market value. (Conservative Party, 1974b)

In 1975, Peter Walker unveiled a more radical plan to transfer the ownership of all council houses to their tenants, with those who had inhabited a house for 30 years receiving it free and the others paying a mortgage based on generous discounts. He claimed to have received 7,000 letters, with 5,000, almost all from council tenants, in support and 2,000, mainly from existing homeowners, against. Walker argued that those against his proposal had failed to appreciate the substantial gains to taxpayers accruing from ending state support for management and repairs and the gains to society from 'the liberation of the permanent tenantry' (Walker, 1977, p 163).

Labour's plan

Meanwhile, Harold Wilson's No 10 Policy Unit, headed by Bernard Donoughue, started work on a scheme to sell council houses. Sandbrook (2012) comments that in the 1974 elections, Labour's canvassers reported that tenants often raised the issue on the doorstep and that polls showed three in 10 council tenants interested in buying. Donoughue had a brother working as a carpenter for Manchester's direct-labour organisation who confided that he did little work – direct or otherwise – and Donoughue wanted to promote freedom for the working class to move in pursuit of employment. His plan involved tenants buying their homes at historic cost minus the amount already paid by local authorities on the loan, with receipts from sales reinvested in local authority accommodation. Local authorities would not be forced to sell their houses (Lipsey, 2013). However, when Labour published *Housing Policy: A Consultative Document* (Secretary of State for the Environment and Secretary of State for Wales, 1977), selling council houses was omitted.

According to Sandbrook (2012, p 423), Donoughue 'got Wilson to almost launch the policy', and Peter Shore, the minister responsible for housing, made a speech to the Housing Centre Conference welcoming increased council sales and looking forward to a time when 70% of households were owner-occupiers (Brand, 1992, p 166). However, Labour's membership disliked council house sales and a resolution to the September 1976 Conference, demanding a law to forbid such sales, was 'heavily carried amid applause' (Sandbook, 2012, p 697). Jim Callaghan, who succeeded Harold Wilson as Prime Minister, finally killed the idea.

The Housing Act 1980

The Conservative Party's 1979 election manifesto stated:

> We shall therefore give council and new town tenants the legal right to buy their homes.... Our discounts will range from 33 per cent after three years, rising with length of tenancy to a maximum of 50 per cent after twenty years....

As far as possible, we will extend these rights to housing association tenants. (Conservative Party, 1979)

Michael Heseltine, the minister responsible for the Housing Act 1980 – in Scotland, the Tenants' Rights, Etc (Scotland) Act 1980 – was aware that the scheme would generate resistance in Labour-controlled authorities and was determined to make the legislation as tight as possible. Although a remark by one Labour Housing Committee Chair – 'you can choose to buy your council house but you cannot choose who lives next door to you' (quoted in Hoath, 1981) – may have surprised Heseltine, he had thought through almost every other contingency:

> we briefed a barrister from outside government to assume that he had been retained by a dedicated Marxist council, committed at any lawful price to frustrate the right to buy. It was a valuable exercise. Loopholes were found and closed. (Heseltine, 1990, p 79)

The masterstroke was to make council house sales an individual right vested in a 'secure tenant' – a new tenancy status for the council tenant – rather than an obligation on local authorities to sell to tenants. This right cut out legal challenges based on resource constraints that may have hindered local authorities from discharging their obligations. One tactic open to local authorities opposed to the Right to Buy – delay – was successfully challenged through the courts. Norwich, one of a number of authorities tardy in implementing the Right to Buy, argued that it was not refusing to sell houses, but that due process, for example, councillors being present at all valuations, and resource constraints led to a slow process. After unsuccessful negotiations with Heseltine, the issue went to court and, on appeal, Norwich lost. Lord Denning, who adjudicated in the Norwich case, had a low opinion of council house tenants. In *Liverpool City Council vs Irwin*, involving a tenant's claim that the council had failed to maintain its properties, he commented:

> It is to be remembered, too, that these tower blocks are occupied by council tenants at very low rents.... If they were to recover damages for the discomfort and inconvenience they have suffered, the amount of such damages could be offset against their rents: and they would be able to stay in the flats for years without paying anything. That does not seem to me to be right, especially when they are all,

in a sense, responsible for the deplorable state of affairs. (Denning, 1976)

Heseltine had carefully framed the legislation to place its interpretation in the hands of the Secretary of State for the Environment. Included in the numerous references to the Secretary of State's powers was that 'The Secretary of State may do all such things as appear to him necessary or expedient to enable secure tenants of the landlord or landlords ... to exercise the right to buy and the right to a mortgage' (Housing Act 1980, section 23(2)).

The Labour Party opposed the Right to Buy, arguing that it infringed local democracy and depleted the rented housing supply in high-demand areas. Labour's 1983 manifesto stated that, in power, it would 'End enforced council house sales, empower public landlords to repurchase homes sold under the Tories on first resale and provide that future voluntary agreed sales will be at market value' (Labour Party, 1983).

Margaret Thatcher believed that the Right to Buy made a substantial contribution to her 1979 election victory, claiming in the 1979 Queen's Speech debate that 'thousands of people in council houses and new towns came out to support us for the first time because they wanted to buy their homes' (quoted in Forrest and Murie, 1988, p 54). Whether the Right to Buy made a significant impact on the 1979 and subsequent general elections is difficult to access. Williams, Sewel and Twine (1987) found that in the 1983 general election, purchasers were more likely to vote Conservative than non-purchasers but this might have been a reflection of purchasers' political orientations and their different socio-economic profile – purchasers had higher incomes than non-purchasers. Johnston (1987) noted the material benefits of homeownership in high-price districts were sufficient to erode class identity to Labour, with potential marginal seat advantages for the Conservatives. By 1987, fearful about the electoral consequences of Right to Buy opposition, Labour had endorsed the policy, with the caveat that receipts should be used to build new council homes. Even so, there is evidence that Conservative association with the Right to Buy produced electoral dividends for the Conservatives in the 1992 general election (Field, 1997).

Gerrymandering?

The District Auditor's 1994 investigation into Westminster City Council revealed a blatant abuse involving council home sales for political purposes. Homeless families were rehoused outside the borough or in asbestos-ridden hostels in safe Labour wards, whereas designated vacant council properties were sold to owner-occupiers in marginal wards. The Conservatives had won the borough in 1986 by a narrow majority, but in 1990, they won convincingly, with the gains concentrated in the eight wards subject to the so-called 'building stable communities' policy. Touche Ross (1994, para 22e), the auditors, stated that 'both the decision to increase the number of designated sales and the selection of properties for designated sale were influenced by an irrelevant consideration, namely the electoral advantage of the majority party'. Lady Porter, leader of Westminster Council, and five councillors and officers, were surcharged £27 million, a surcharge subsequently upheld on appeal to the House of Lords. Eventually, the debt was settled by a £12.3 million payment.

New Labour and the Right to Buy

The Labour Party commitment to using the capital receipts from council house sales for new housing was a reaction to Conservative receipt diversion to other purposes. Initially, councils could use half of receipts from council house sales. These receipts might have contributed to a council house building programme especially as mortgage lenders, rather than local authorities, financed more Right to Buy sales. Michael Heseltine anticipated an annual 60,000 council houses programme (Murie, 2016). In 1984, the Treasury wanted to cut £310 million from the housing budget. Faced with Ian Gow, Minister for Housing, threatening to resign, the cut was reduced to £65 million. This stratagem prevented Gow's resignation but at the cost of a long-term restriction in the local resources available for housing purposes. The Treasury reduced the percentage of housing capital receipts from the Right to Buy available to spend by local authorities in any year to 20% – a real reduction of about 1 billion.

Initially, New Labour did not modify the Right to Buy, but under rising homelessness pressure and fewer 'social' housing lettings, it substantially reduced maximum discounts and extended both the qualifying period and the time after the sale when local authorities could require owners to repay some of the discount. This initiative had a dramatic impact: by 2008/09, only 2,880 homes were sold to tenants in England.

Lending competition

By the late 1970s, building societies had become major financial institutions responsible for 79% of net mortgage lending. Believers in free market economics noted the lack of competition in the market. Banks were restricted in granting mortgages for residential purposes and the societies operated a cartel, the Recommended Rate System (RRS), thereby preventing interest rate competition and perpetuating a mortgage dearth. According to Boyle (2013), Geoffrey Howe and Nigel Lawson were determined to end credit market regulation by reducing constraints on credit availability. Margaret Thatcher was unconvinced, suspecting that such deregulation would lead, at least in the short term, to higher mortgage rates. She sent a note to Howe saying: 'I am very worried about reports in today's press that mortgage rates may have to go up within days. This *must NOT* happen. If necessary, there must be a temporary subsidy' (Thatcher, 1979a, emphasis in original). Boyle (2013, p 63) comments: 'Political mythology suggests that it was Lawson who persuaded Thatcher that a "property-owning democracy" required people to go into debt – which definitely meant changes to the mortgage market.... What we do know is that she was persuaded'.

In 1980, the Conservative government removed the so-called 'corset' on lending by banks, effectively allowing banks, specialist mortgage companies and other financial institutions into the residential mortgage lending market and breaking the building societies' cartel. The subsequent changes in mortgage availability produced a rapid increase in house prices and economic growth, as homeowners, feeling confident that their wealth was increasing and able to finance expenditure by equity withdrawal – increasing from 6% of after-tax income in 1981 to 13% in 1988 (Early, 2001) – had a spending spree. The building societies' market share started to decline rapidly – to 58% in 1982 – as the banks, with their access to wholesale funds, had an advantage in securing capital. The aggrieved societies argued for the freedom to diversify and become banks. The Building Societies Act 1986 enabled building societies to: raise more funds from wholesale markets; purchase land; act as developers; set up estate agencies; and offer cheque-clearing facilities. Many building societies abandoned their mutual status, offering dividends to shareholders.

Despite rollercoaster fluctuations, the tendency for house prices to exceed general inflation, making houses an investment as well as consumption good, was a post-war homeownership attraction. In 1984, at Thatcher's insistence, the cap on the mortgage eligible for tax relief was increased to £30,000, the average house price at the time, and in the mid-1980s, there was a large real house price increase. Chancellor Nigel Lawson's Budget announcement to remove multiple tax relief on mortgage interest – £30,000 per person – restricting it to £30,000 per dwelling, produced a stampede of couples and friends to buy a house before the new rules were applied. The price boom that this provoked was followed by a slump: between 1990 and 1994, prices dropped in cash as well as real terms. Builders were left with unsold houses, and in an attempt to stabilise the market, the government negotiated with mortgage providers to reduce repossessions and brought forward funds earmarked for housing associations to allow them to purchase unsold properties.

Ending tax relief on mortgage interest

There was a near consensus among economists that tax relief on mortgage interest was unjustifiable: it was highly regressive, bolstered inflation in house prices and cost the Exchequer millions in lost revenue. Margaret Thatcher's Chancellors, Geoffrey Howe and Nigel Lawson, shared this consensus, with Howe saying that it was 'a glaring anomaly, distorting the housing market almost as much as rent control and unjustly favouring the better off' (Howe, 1994, p 280). He wanted it reduced but Thatcher demanded an increase. She had a similar dispute with Nigel Lawson, declaring: 'We had some differences – not least about mortgage tax relief which he would probably have liked to abolish and whose threshold I would certainly have liked to raise' (Thatcher, 1993, p 672). Much to Thatcher's annoyance when she had left office (Thatcher, 2002), the Major government took advantage of the lower post-1994 interest rates to start the phasing out of tax relief on mortgage interest. New Labour continued this process and ended the tax concession in 2000.

Boom

Under New Labour, there was a 10-year house price boom before the bust. Four factors underpinned the sustained growth in house prices from 1997 to 2007: credit availability; a house-building dearth; New Labour's homeownership promotion as 'asset-based' welfare in a 'stakeholder' society; and the lure of easy wealth. New Labour passed the power to set interest rates to the Bank of England, charging it with maintaining inflation at less than 3%. The index used to measure inflation was the consumer price index, which excluded mortgage interest and other housing costs. Between 1997 and 2007, the Bank of England base rate was modest relative to preceding years, reaching a low of 3.5% in July 2003. Extra credit became available partially from 'securitisation', and as prices increased, more people wanted to become homeowners, move to a higher-value house and/or join the growing private landlord cohort. In contrast to the 1930s, cheaper, more accessible, finance did not produce more houses; rather, it increased the price of the existing stock.

Securitisation

'Securitisation' involves packaging existing mortgages and then selling the parcels on the global financial market. The technique had a long history in the US but a new dimension was added in the 2000s – the 'sub-prime mortgage'. Encouraged by the US government, anxious to promote the homeownership 'American Dream', mortgages were offered to households finding it difficult to afford to buy a home, often involving a 'teaser' introductory interest rate, usually 2%, followed by a sharp hike up to 10%. Some borrowers were allowed to estimate their incomes on the mortgage application form – so-called 'liar' loans. Mortgage brokers sold these mortgages to banks who then resold them in packages, sometimes bundled with 'prime' mortgages. The credit-rating agencies often gave these packages AAA status. The full extent of 'securitisation' in the UK is unknown but the mortgage lenders that later ran into difficulties used it extensively, and by 2006, 18% of new mortgages were four times annual income and 1% were set at six times; 100% mortgages, sometimes more, were received by 10% of first-time buyers. Income self-certification was commonplace.

Other countries experiencing a house price boom from 1997 to 2007 substantially increased their new housing construction. This was not the case in the UK. In 2004, for example, new housing construction was 3.2 per 1,000 population in the UK, 19 in Ireland, 12.6 in Spain and 7.1 in the US. Moreover, the percentage of houses (compared to flats) built in England dropped from 71 to 34, and three-bedroomed homes (flats or houses) declined from 33% to 18%. New construction density climbed from 25 to 44 per hectare and dwellings became smaller. A Royal Institute of British Architects (RIBA) survey found that the average new one-bedroomed-home size was four square metres below the minimum standard adopted by the Mayor of London in 2011. The average three-bedroomed home was eight square metres below the standard – 'It's the space that could take the kitchen out of the lounge and the sound and smells that go with it' (RIBA, 2011, p 1). Of the

15 European countries examined by Morgan and Cruickshank (2014), the UK had the smallest new homes.

A boom in extensions to existing properties mitigated this new housing dearth. Nonetheless, overall housing space in the UK, when measured by floor space rather than the number of rooms, ranked tenth of the 15 countries scrutinised by Morgan and Cruickshank (2014) – a consequence of extensive house subdivision. According to Dorling (2014b), the existing housing space distribution was more unequal in 2011 than in 1921. Research by Liverpool Victoria Insurance (2014) found that the average family home had shrunk by two square metres over the past 10 years and an estimated that 150,000 children had seen their bedrooms partitioned in an attempt to create extra bedrooms.

Asset-based welfare

As the house price rollercoaster ascended, New Labour started to promote homeownership as 'asset-based' welfare on the notion that 'when individuals own homes they can get by on smaller pensions' (Castles, 1998, p 13). Watson (2008) claimed that New Labour attempted to generate an ever-growing number of homeowners to sustain house prices. This housing wealth 'super-portfolio' would promote 'asset-based' welfare and opportunities to reduce other forms of welfare spending. In evidence, Watson cited the neglected opportunities to introduce fiscal measures that could have quelled the house price surge, inflation measurement in a way that reduced housing cost impact on the Bank of England's interest rate decisions and the structured incentives facilitating individuals' attempts to ride on the back of the housing bubble. Locking in house price growth facilitated asset-based welfare promotion.

In his autobiography, Tony Blair makes only two references to housing – one to his first speech as Prime Minister made at the Aylesbury Estate and the other to his personal housing situation. As he contemplated resigning as Prime Minister – seemingly oblivious to his government's role in house price inflation – Blair (2010, p 5) commented: 'Meanwhile, I prepared for the likely departure. Cherie and I had been out of the London housing market since 1997, during which time prices had rocketed'. Homeownership growth seemed 'win, win, win': 'win' for the government, with Land Stamp Duty tax raising £6.5 billion in 2006/07, compared to £625 million in 1996/97; 'win' for existing homeowners as rising demand pushed house prices upwards; 'win' for the mortgage lenders; 'win' for the 'exchange professionals', such as solicitors and surveyors; and 'win' for the MPs, whose tax-financed second homes were increasing in value. The jilted losers were potential first-time buyers forced out of the market by rising prices and those who bought at the boom's height before the inevitable crash.

Bust

The US housing market started to crumple in 2007, and as mortgage foreclosures mounted, the extent of the sub-prime sector started to be exposed. In the UK, Northern Rock was the first mortgage lender to feel the US heat. It was heavily involved in 'securitisation' and derived a large proportion of its mortgage funds from short-term loans raised on the financial markets. It attracted new mortgage business by deals such as its 'Together' loan, offering up to 125% of house values and up to six times annual incomes. Other mortgage lenders – Bradford and Bingley, Abbey, HBOS and Clydesdale – were involved in 'securitisation' and were exposed to high loan-to-value ratios. For example, by the end of 2008, around one third of HBOS's mortgage book had loan-to-value ratios of over 90%. As 'securitisation' suspicion grew in the US, Northern Rock, unable to finance its operation by selling on its mortgages and with other banks unwilling to supply loans, faced a liquidity crisis. When its submission for a loan from the Bank of England became public knowledge, there was a run on the bank and it was nationalised in early 2008. As the bank confidence crisis spread, inter-bank lending froze, and having reached a peak in the third quarter of 2007, UK houses started to decline. In 2008, other banks, including Lloyds/TSB, HBOS and Bradford and Bingley, were rescued by the state. UK repossessions increased from 25,900 in 2007 to 40,000 in 2008 but New Labour had learnt lessons from the US housing market collapse, where repossessions and 'fire sales' had further depressed the market, so that in cities like Detroit, house prices had collapsed and thousands of dwellings were vacant. New Labour's Homeowner Mortgage Support Scheme involved a government guarantee against losses higher than 20% incurred on a mortgage by the lender. Under the Mortgage Rescue Scheme, a local authority could assess if a household was in mortgage default danger and likely to be covered by the homelessness legislation, and could then involve a housing association in providing an equity loan or purchasing the home, with the former owner remaining in the house as a tenant. In addition, Income Support changes were made for workless homeowners, with 'waiting time' reduced to 13 weeks and the mortgage ceiling eligibility raised to £200,000.

Bank mergers, state guarantees for savers, nationalisation, state support to the financial sector on a massive scale, mortgage rescue, a reduction in the base interest rate to 0.5%, bringing forward resources for social housing allocated for later years and injecting cash into the economy had some success in bolstering the housing market. Indeed, in 2010, house prices started to increase. The UK avoided the substantial reductions in house prices over the period 2008 to 2011 common in other countries – Spain, the US and Ireland – that had experienced a house price explosion from 2000 to 2007. However, new housing construction in the UK plummeted from 226,420 in 2007 to 137,270 in 2010 and the loss of capacity in the residential construction sector made it difficult to boost new house-building as the economy recovered post–2013.

The Coalition government

New Labour's bank bailouts and the boosts to public expenditure thought necessary to mitigate the recession produced a sharp increase in government debt, from 36.4% of gross domestic product (GDP) in 2007 to 62% in 2010 (Keep, 2015). Reducing the national debt was the dominant 2010 general election theme. The Conservatives wanted big reductions phased in over a relatively short period (Conservative Party, 2010), whereas the Liberal Democrats favoured lower cuts implemented over a longer period (Liberal Democrats, 2010). The Coalition Agreement reflected the Conservative approach. It stated 'We will significantly accelerate the reduction in the structural deficit over the course of a Parliament, with the main burden of deficit reduction borne by reducing spending rather than increasing taxes' (HM Government, 2010, p 15).

Austerity and homeownership

This 'austerity' agenda reduced the scope for stimulating owner-occupation by measures contributing to public expenditure. Initially, government action was limited to the Department for Communities and Local Government (DCLG) devoting a proportion of its much-reduced budget to kick-starting stalled building sites via its 'Get Britain Building' and 'Growing Places' programmes. Labour's Housing and Planning Delivery Grant to local authorities, awarded for delivering more houses, was replaced with the New Homes Bonus scheme, matching the Council Tax raised on each new home built for a period of 6 years but with no obligation on local government to spend the resources on housing.

The drift away from homeownership continued under the Coalition government. Three main drivers influenced this trend. First, despite the 2007–09 dip, house prices remained high relative to incomes: the ratio of lower-quartile house prices to lower-quartile incomes increased from 3.6 in 1997 to 6.5 in 2011, and from 4.6 to 9 in London. Second, the deposit required to obtain a mortgage increased during the 'credit crunch': 100% mortgages disappeared, 90% became rare and the typical first-time buyer paid a 20% deposit. The Council of Mortgage Lenders (2013) estimated that 65% of first-time buyers had financial assistance from 'the Bank of Mum and Dad' in mid-2012, compared to 31% seven years earlier. Third, Buy-to-Let landlords were competing on favourable terms with first-time buyers (see Chapter Four).

Help to Buy

As the economy stagnated and new housing starts remained very low, the Coalition government attempted to revive homeownership. 'Quantitative easing' – essentially 'printing money' – was one response, as was 'Funding for Lending', offering banks and other mortgage lending agencies funding from the Bank of England at low interest rates on condition that they were passed on to households and businesses.

New Labour had introduced a variety of Homebuy schemes that, in its 2010 manifesto, the Liberal Democrat Party said it would scale back. However, this commitment was not included in the Coalition government agreement (Somerville, 2016). Indeed, the Coalition government extended support for homeownership. Its flagship 'Help to Buy' was introduced in two phases. The first phase started in England in April 2013. The government offered a 20% equity loan to buyers of newly built properties up to the value of 600,000 who had a 5% deposit. The second phase began in October 2013. Under this system, borrowers put down a deposit of 5% of the property price and the lender offered a mortgage covering the other 95%. Lenders paid a fee to the government that provided a seven-year taxpayer guarantee covering 15% of the loan value. The maximum property price eligible was £600,000 (existing or new-build) and there was no cap on the maximum household income eligible for inclusion. Help to Buy did not count as public expenditure – the equity share element was expected to produce a return and the mortgage guarantee element, although it carried risk, involved no upfront state payment (National Audit Office, 2014). The scheme met with almost unanimous disapproval from economists as likely to stimulate a house price bubble (*Independent*, 2013b). They were right. Data from the Office for National Statistics (2015) showed that a typical first-time buyer would have paid £179,000 for their home in April 2013 when Help to Buy was launched, but this price tag had reached £213,000 by June 2015, a 19% increase. Perhaps a house price bubble is what the Chancellor wanted. Despite a rapid house price increase in London and a few other housing hotspots, house prices elsewhere were stagnant, and given a recent history of house prices and electoral advantage, the feel-good factor for homeowners associated with rising house prices and the linked consumer spending promised electoral gains. Moreover, tax receipts from Land Stamp Duty were predicted to increase from £6.9 million in 2012/13 to £12.7 billion in 2014/15 (Office for Budget Responsibility, 2015).

A new bubble?

Seemingly worried about a 'bubble' danger, and with house prices in London rising rapidly, the Bank of England acted to mitigate the boom. It withdrew its mortgage support under the 'Funding for Lending' scheme and the Financial Conduct Authority announced new rules on mortgage lending to come into force on 26 April 2014. Interest-only mortgages were prohibited except in special circumstances, borrowing would be based on how much applicants would have left after regular expenditure, rather than on their income, and lenders would have to check that people could still afford repayments should interest rates rise (Financial Conduct Authority, 2015).

In his 2014 Autumn Budget Statement, Chancellor George Osborne announced a radical change to Land Stamp Duty Tax. The previous 'slab' system, whereby a percentage of the house price was levied on the whole purchase cost depending on price bands, was replaced by a more progressive system. Only those purchasing properties above £937,000 would be worse off. Shooting the Labour and the Liberal Democrat Mansion Tax fox, the Chancellor claimed that his scheme would be a more effective way to tax housing wealth than a Mansion Tax (see Chapter Two). He said:

> It increases the taxes on the most expensive 2% of homes, but only asks people to pay that tax when they buy the house and they have the money and it does not involve a revaluation of hundreds of thousands of homes in this country. (Osborne, 2014, p 10)

In response to Labour's promise to build 200,000 houses per year by 2020 and allow local people first choice on a proportion of the new homes, David Cameron announced that if his party was in power after the 2015 general election, 200,000 'Starter' homes would be built for first-time buyers – a commitment included in the 2015 Conservative Party manifesto. They would be priced at 20% less than the market price, a discount made possible, according to Cameron, by building on brownfield sites, reducing the cost of planning permissions and exempting developers from affordable housing requirements, community infrastructure levies and the zero-carbon homes standard. 'Starter' houses would only be available to first-time buyers under the age of 40 and there would be a cap on the price set at £250,000 outside London and £450,000 in London. It would not be possible for anyone to sell the discounted homes at full market price for the first five years of ownership due to a special levy to claw back the discount. In addition, a boost was given to 'self-build' homes by requiring local authorities to maintain a register of people wanting to build their own homes and to allocate sufficient land to meet the demand. In another attempt to bolster Conservative Party fortunes before the 2015 general election, Osborne announced a Help to Buy ISA. First-time buyers purchasing a house up to £450,000 in London or £250,000 elsewhere would be eligible to receive a government bonus of 25% up to the maximum monthly saving of £200, with a government contribution capped at £3,000.

The Right to Buy 'reinvigorated'

Under a 'reinvigorated' Right to Buy, introduced in April 2012, the Coalition government imposed a uniform 60% maximum discount on market value, with a £75,000 cap in England. This more than quadrupled the discount available in most parts of London, and trebled it in large areas of England. In the 2013 Budget, the Chancellor of the Exchequer announced that in London, the maximum discount would be raised to £100,000, and in early 2014, the maximum discount was raised to 70% of market value (already available on flats), with a promise that the cap would be raised in line with inflation. In contrast to Margaret Thatcher's scheme, Cameron's initiative was accompanied by the promise of a 'one for one' replacement financed by the sales receipts.

Green housing

New Labour was committed to a substantial reduction in carbon emissions through its acceptance of the Kyoto Protocol (United Nations, 1997), which set binding obligations on industrialised countries to reduce greenhouse gas emissions. Combating global warming was added to the reasons why new housing should be concentrated on 'brownfield' sites, it being argued that the 'compact city' would reduce carbon emissions (Urban Task Force, 1999). The Green Paper 'Homes for the Future: More Affordable, More Sustainable' (DCLG, 2007) proposed to phase in enhanced building regulations so that, by 2016, all new homes would be 'zero-carbon', defined as 'over a year, the net carbon emissions from all energy use in the home would be zero'. Blair's government set a target of 60% carbon emissions reduction by 2050 and, boosted by David Cameron's green agenda adoption as a way of repositioning the Conservative Party, under the Carbon Act 2008, the reduction target was increased to 80%.

New Labour tried to improve energy efficiency in existing homes through: requirements to upgrade energy efficiency when a house was extended; special deals to owners for micro-energy generation such as solar panels; Home Information Packs requiring an energy efficiency declaration; and assistance to low-income households via the Warm Front programme. In 2008, the Carbon Emissions Reduction Target (CERT) came into effect, obliging electricity and gas suppliers in Great Britain to help reduce carbon dioxide emissions from homes and including an obligation to offer subsidised or free insulation to groups likely to experience fuel poverty.

Coalition disagreements

The building industry resisted the new home zero-carbon target, claiming that its cost made it more difficult to sell new homes in a recession. There were disputes between the Liberal Democrats and the Conservatives about energy policy. The Liberal Democrats, in charge of the Department for Energy and Climate Change, favoured higher standards to eliminate carbon emissions but the Conservatives, now supporting house-builders, were concerned that higher standards would add to new house prices. A *Guardian* report claimed that when asked about the delay in establishing new standards, a DCLG spokesperson said: 'We want to see greener homes, but we need to avoid excessive regulation which will simply reduce house-building and push up the cost of buying a new home' (Harvey, 2013).

The Coalition compromise was that the commitment to delivering zero-carbon homes from 2016 would be retained but zero-carbon homes could be achieved off-site via 'allowable solutions'. 'Allowable solutions' included measures such as investment in the retrofitting of low-carbon technologies to communal buildings and investment in district heating pipework, allowing developers to pay into a fund to offset carbon emissions and exempting 'small sites' from a zero-carbon obligation (Cabinet Office, 2014). However, builder's lobby continued to claim that the extra costs involved in delivering low- or zero-carbon homes were not captured in the development process as added value (Payne, 2015), and free from Liberal Democrat influence, the 2015 Conservative government announced there would be no zero-carbon obligations imposed on developers.

Retrofit

With regard to existing homes, New Labour's Home Information Pack requirement for property sales was axed by the Coalition government but the Energy Performance Certificate – rating homes on a scale of A–G, with A being the most efficient – was retained. The Coalition government's Energy Act 2011 had all-party support and made provision for the 'Green Deal', which started to operate in early 2013. If owners installed new green technology via an approved installer, they would pay nothing upfront but pay back the costs through their energy bills over a period of time, with an interest rate set at just below 7%. The 'Green Deal' replaced 'Warm Front', which had been targeted on low-income households, but the Energy Company Obligation (ECO) placed a requirement on the energy companies to help people with low incomes and/or hard-to-treat homes. However, following a brouhaha about large increases in energy prices in 2013, the Coalition government reduced energy companies' obligations to free resources for an overall energy price reduction. The Green Deal had a very low take-up, with only 10,000 plans complete in 2015 (Department of Energy and Climate Change, 2015), and it was terminated by the 2015 Conservative government.

Homeownership and the 2015 Conservative government

In its 2015 general election manifesto, Labour promised 200,000 new homes per annum by 2020, with a proportion reserved for first-time buyers, and to invest the Help to Buy ISA in new homes, but during the election campaign, it added the demand-side proposal that properties priced at up to £300,000 would be exempt from Stamp Duty Tax. The Liberal Democrats promised 300,000 houses per annum by an unspecified date and concentrated on land release to achieve this objective. It made only one cautious demand-side proposal: to help young people to obtain a deposit for renting accommodation. The Green Party (2015) blamed past demand-side policies for having created a house price boom and promised to scrap most of them.

Given the rapid decline in homeownership under the Conservative-led Coalition government, the Conservative Party thought it necessary to reaffirm its commitment to 'a property-owning democracy'. Its manifesto declared: 'Conservatives believe passionately in home ownership. We understand how good it feels when you have worked long hours, saved money for years, and finally take possession of the keys to your first home' (Conservative Party, 2015, p 51). Existing commitments to Help to Buy, 'Starter homes' on brownfield sites and a Help to Buy ISA were reaffirmed but the flagship of the Conservative programme was extending the council house 'Right to Buy' to 1.3 million housing association tenancies (see Chapter Seven). After the general election, the Conservative government embraced a 1 million new house target by 2020 and injected public funds into building 'Starter' homes on brownfield sites. It also introduced a 'London Help to Buy' scheme, allowing Londoners to borrow up to 40% of the home's value as an equity loan. An agreement with the National Housing Federation on a 'voluntary' Right to Buy for housing association tenants was made and a 'Lifetime ISA' was announced. This would enable people aged under 40 to receive a £1,000 bonus on every £4,000 per annum saved but with exit penalties if the ISA is not used to fund a first home or retirement, making it likely that the ISA would be used for home purchases. Housing associations were directed towards shared ownership schemes (see Chapter Seven).

Conclusion

The 'property-owning democracy' idea has had a major impact on UK housing policy; indeed, it was exported to 'new' commonwealth countries, with some commentators referring to an 'Anglo-Saxon' category in their housing system taxonomies (Doling and Elsinga, 2006; Ronald, 2008). Saunders (1990, p 70) has directed attention to intrinsic homeownership attractions – the 'possessive instinct', the desire the mark out territory and the feelings of autonomy, security and personal identity Nonetheless, homeownership's virtues have been heavily promoted by the financial institutions, the Conservative

Party and, to a lesser extent, Labour and the Liberal Democrats. This praise has been accompanied by the denigration of its principal rival: cost-renting by local government. Moreover, *homeowner* – not *house-ownership* – appeal has been bolstered by political action to boost house prices. In the 'longue durée', house prices have increased at a faster rate than inflation, with state aid – mortgage guarantees, supplying funds to mortgage lenders, tax relief on mortgage interest, Help to Buy and so on – having an important impact on house prices. Electors react badly to housing wealth erosion. Hobson (1999, p 172) claims that 'Middle England' has a 'natural expectation that [housing wealth] should pass, undiminished and unencumbered to their children'. In 2007, when Labour, with Gordon Brown as the new Prime Minister, was ahead in the public opinion polls and contemplating a snap general election, the Conservatives declared that they were in favour of increasing the Inheritance Tax threshold from £300,000 to £1 million. Conservative popularity increased, especially in marginal constituencies (Seely, 2013). Brown did not call a general election.

The electoral appeal of stored housing wealth has other housing consequences. Public choice theorists make connections between the growth in homeownership and resistance to new development. Commenting on the planning process, Pennington (2000, p 75) states:

> On the one hand, the number of individuals within the locality is likely to be relatively small, so the per capita benefit for individuals to engage in collective action to protect their own 'back yard' is likely to be fairly high. This may be particularly important where homeownership coalitions seeking to protect property values are concerned … the equity investment in homeownership may represent a substantial fraction of their personal wealth.

Taylor (2013) found that objections to planning applications were most likely where existing housing values were higher, and that communities with greater economic interests in, and resources to engage with, the planning system make disproportionate use of opposition channels.

Ronald (2015) has directed attention to the link between accumulated homeownership wealth and the growth in private landlordism, with homeowners using their wealth to help purchase dwellings to let. He notes that the ratio of private sector landlords comprised of private individuals increased from 61% in 1998 to 89% in 2010, and that the overwhelming majority of private landlords own only one property. He states 'Assuming that nearly all landlords are also owner-occupiers, the data suggests that one in seven home owning households in Britain also let out at least one residential property for rent' (Ronald, 2015, p 4). Thus, there is a connection between homeownership and private landlord interests, concentrated in the age groups where the Conservatives gained the most support in the 2015 general election.

Given these powerful homeownership ballot box attractions, it is a bold politician that neglects its salience in winning elections. Cameron has announced that his 2015 Conservative government will transform 'generation rent' into 'generation buy' (Cameron, 2015a).

Further reading

Daunton, M.J. (1987) *A Property Owning Democracy? Housing in Britain*, London: Faber and Faber.

Davies, A. (2013) '"Right to Buy": The Development of a Conservative Housing Policy, 1950–1980', *Contemporary British History*, vol 27, no 4, pp 421–44.

Francis, M. (2012) '"A Crusade to Enfranchise the Many": Thatcherism and the "Property-Owning Democracy"', *Twentieth Century British History*, vol 23, no 2, pp 275–97.

Ronald, R. (2008) *The Ideology of Home Ownership: Homeowner Societies and the Role of Housing*, London: AIAA.

Skelton, N. (1924) *Constructive Conservatism*, London: William Blackwood and Sons.

Somerville, P. (2016) 'Coalition Housing Policy in England', in H. Bochel and M. Powell (eds) *The Coalition Government and Social Policy: Restructuring the Welfare State*, Bristol: Policy Press, pp 151–78.

SIX

Eclipsing council housing

State houses, supplied by local government, presented a fundamental challenge to capitalist relationships. Rather than pay a 'market' rent as a private renter or a 'market' price and a 'market' mortgage interest rate to become a homeowner, council tenants would pay only their accommodation's 'historic cost' plus management and maintenance charges and possibly a small surplus for new investment. John Wheatley encapsulated the idea in his 1914 '£8 cottage' scheme. Cottages – not tenements – would be built on Glasgow's fringes from the surplus produced by Glasgow's municipal trams. Peripheral land was cheap and there would be no loan interest so the rent would be less than a quarter charged by private landlords (Wheatley, 1914). Bevan repeated the socialist case for council housing in 1949, saying: 'I believe that one of the reasons why modern nations have not been able to solve their housing problems is that they have looked upon houses as commodities to be bought and sold and not as a social service (quoted in Howarth, 1985, p 103).

Influenced by the Workmen's National Housing Council, which campaigned for Treasury subsidies to local authorities and, as second best, hundred-year Treasury loans at 2%, the Labour Party supported subsidised council housing. In contrast, the Liberal Party, pitching its appeal to the better-paid 'artisan', favoured higher wages to enable workers to afford 'independent' accommodation and not-for-profit, non-state providers. The Conservative Party was willing to tolerate central state-subsidised council housing as a 'necessary expedient' when housing was scarce, as a solution to the sanitary problem radiating from the slums and as a way to reduce the 'rate burden', but it promoted market solutions as the norm. Post-1964, the enthusiasm for council housing among the Labour Party leadership waned, and under Margaret Thatcher, antagonism to the sector, always a strong current in Conservative thinking, blossomed. Local authority housing reached its zenith in 1978, when 31.6% of UK households rented from their local council. By 1997, local authority housing was 'residualised'. Its stock share in England had declined to 16.4% and the sector accommodated an increasing proportion of people fluctuating between worklessness and low-paid employment – called the 'Precariat' by Standing (2014). New Labour attempted to blur the distinction between housing provided by housing associations and local government, increasingly referring to 'social' housing, and encouraged stock transfer from local authorities to housing associations. Local authority housing's stock share in England declined to 8% while New Labour was in government, and to 7.0% under the Coalition government. The 2015 Conservative government introduced measures to accelerate council house 'residualisation' in England.

Pauperising the working class and undermining private enterprise?

Mainstream political opinion in the 19th century was opposed to local government involvement in housing supply. Very few council houses were built under legislation directed at slum clearance. Against a background of new revelations on 'the condition of the working class' and agitation on the housing issue, the Housing of the Working Classes Act 1890 made it clear that local authorities in London had the power to erect buildings suitable for the working class, including 'separate houses or cottages' and not just in clearance areas. This was extended nationwide in the Housing of the Working Classes Act 1900. Such powers provoked hostility – the Liberty and Property Defence League called it 'class legislation' likely to destroy 'the moral fibre of our race in the anaconda coils of state socialism' (quoted in Roberts, 1999, p 286).

Subsidies?

If allowing local government to build houses was contentious, Conservatives and most Liberals thought that direct subsidies were abhorrent. Octavia Hill expressed the entrenched objection in stating 'never let them [the working class] accept a rate in aid of wages whether in the form of houses or anything else' (Hill, 1883, p 925). Lord Shaftesbury (1883) added: 'If the state is to be summoned not only to provide housing for the labouring class but supply such dwellings at nominal rent it will … utterly destroy their moral energies'. Thus, when permitted, local authority housing schemes under the 1890 Act had to be 'self-financing', albeit that 'self-financing' was a flexible concept. As George Bernard Shaw (1908, p 72) pointed out, some local authorities, having had to buy land at market value, 'charged it to its housing schemes at its value for working class dwellings (a pure figment) the ratepayer making up the difference between this and the real market value'.

Only Liverpool, Sheffield and London made significant use of the 1890 Act, with political attention focusing on London. When the London County Council (LCC) was formed in 1889, Annie Besant (1889, pp 12–3), a Fabian socialist, declared: 'In perfect unconsciousness of the nature of his act, Mr Richie [Tory President of the Local Government Board] has established the Commune. He has ... created the machinery without which Socialism was impracticable'. The 'Progressives' – Fabians and 'new' Liberals – gained control of the LCC. They wanted to build houses but struggled to balance costs and sanitary standards with the rent levels required to break even. Spartan schemes were the outcome. George Bernard Shaw (1908, p 12) commented:

> These places seem at first so enormously superior to the filthy rookeries they replace that their revolting ugliness, their asphalted yards with the sunlight shut out by huge cliffs of brick and mortar, their flights upon flights of stony steps between the street and the unfortunate women and children on the upper floors. Their quaint plan of relieving a crowd on the floor by stacking the people on shelves are overlooked for the moment; but long before they become uninhabitable from decay they will become as repugnant as the warrens they have supplanted. In short, the municipalities of the future will be almost as active in knocking our towns down as in building them up.

Despite such austerity, slum dwellers could not afford the rents charged and there were voices urging 'building down'. Professor Sharp of Glasgow University claimed that, 'given the destructive habits of this class', new dwellings should be 'indestructible cells' made of concrete with only basic amenities and no removable facilities (quoted in Fraser, 1993, pp 274–5).

A 'housing famine'

The Labour Party, claiming slums to be part of a larger 'housing famine', advocated a suburban solution, with new council housing concentrated on city fringes. Filtering theory was part of Labour's answer to the housing question, with Keir Hardie using filtering to justify local government provision for artisans, with 'housing vacancies created right down to the lowest slums' (quoted in Ball and Sunderland, 2006, p 381).

Post-1902, there was a major reduction in new private sector house-building and the number of empty properties available to the working class was insufficient to allow for the 'ordinary shifting of population from one tenement to another' (Spensley, 1918, p 167). This housing dearth prompted more local authorities to consider building but private landlords, often well represented on local councils, resisted council houses, arguing that subsidised municipal housing was unfair competition (North Tyneside Community Development Project, 1978). A potential answer to the unreasonable competition charge was to restrict local authorities to building in inner areas, where private enterprise was less willing to venture. This idea was taken up by Sir Arthur Griffith-Boscawen, who, following the ratepayer revolt against the 'Progressives' on the LCC, had become Chair of the LCC housing committee. This move was resisted by many Labour politicians, with Keir Hardie urging local authorities to 'cater for the better class of artisans ... instead of playing the part of the scavenger to the private house builder and taking charge of the refuse out of which they could not make a profit' (quoted in Yelling, 1992, p 20).

As a Conservative backbencher, Sir Arthur Griffith-Boscawen introduced two Bills to Parliament in 1912 aimed at providing limited central grants to local authorities to enable them to supply houses in inner areas. His aim was to 'spread the burden over the broader shoulders of the taxpayers' (quoted in Daunton, 1987, p 56). There was little enthusiasm for the Bills among Conservative leaders, and the Liberals opposed the measures on the 'subsidies' equals 'doles' argument. W.J. Nettleford, Liberal Unionist and Chair of Birmingham's Housing Committee, asserted that subsidised council housing undermined private enterprise, and argued that 'wages follow rents, and therefore [subsidies] would only result in providing capitalists with cheap labour at the expense of the general body of ratepayers' (quoted in Daunton, 1983, p 290).

The Housing and Town Planning etc Act 1919

Working-class agitation against private landlord rent increases was the major factor in transforming local government's role in housing supply (see Chapter Three). Post-1915, the government took care to ensure that housing provision matched job creation in the munitions industry. The Ministry of Munitions subsidised dwellings, and by 1918, it had built 10,284 homes, with showcase schemes at Gretna and Woolwich Arsenal. In an attempt to attract and retain armament workers, the housing estates contained public houses, canteens and community centres. Marr (2009, p 165) detects 'the real origins of the modern welfare state' in Lloyd George's munitions estates.

A wave of industrial strikes erupted in 1917, many unofficial, involving miners, engineers and munitions workers. The government established regional committees to investigate the unrest and housing featured as a major grievance. Widespread resentment of landlord 'profiteering' dented the prospects that private landlordism could be trusted with the post-war task of building houses for the working class. Support for subsidised council housing came from the Tudor Walters Committee report, mainly written by Raymond Unwin, a Fabian socialist. The report associated municipal housing with planned estate layout, recommending that new estates should have a 12 per acre density. It made the point that the new houses would need to meet the requirements of future generations, hence its recommendations that a bath in a separate bathroom should be a standard fixture, each house should have a garden and some should have a 'parlour'. It also claimed that, although subsidies may be necessary in the short term, 'ultimate economy in the provision of dwellings will depend on the relation between the average rental secured over a long period' (Tudor Walters, 1918, para 27) and the initial dwelling cost.

'A land fit for heroes to live in'

Treasury reluctance to guarantee a cap on local authority losses from any housing scheme hindered negotiations with local government on post-war house-building. The Treasury's best offer was 75% of a scheme's cost but with no commitment to fund a specified programme. To counter Treasury resistance, Lloyd George raised the Bolshevik spectre. He put the issue to a Cabinet meeting in 1919. In an exchange with Austen Chamberlain, the Conservative Chancellor of the Exchequer, Lloyd George asserted:

> Russia had gone almost completely over to Bolshevism ... and in a short time we might have three-quarters of Europe converted to Bolshevism. None would be left but France and Great Britain. Great Britain would hold out, but only if the people were given a sense of confidence – only if they were made to believe that things were being done for them.... We must give them the conviction this time that we mean it, and we must give them that conviction quickly.... We were 300,000 houses below our normal level, and that level was itself far below what it should

be…. Even if we could do all we wished to do during the coming year, it would cost us £71,000,000. Even if it cost £100,000,000, what was that compared with the stability of the State? (Lloyd George, 1919, p 529)

Cabinet opposition disintegrated, and as an incentive to build, local authorities were protected against all costs above a penny on the rate.

Did Lloyd George believe that revolution was imminent or was his Bolshevism rhetoric calculated to intimidate the Conservatives into supporting his reforms? Beatrice Webb claimed that Lloyd George exaggerated the 'Bolshevik threat' for political reasons (MacKenzie and MacKenzie, 1984, p 349). He had a monopoly on the information coming from intelligence services – data he used 'in the same way that he approached everything else, with a keen eye for politics' (Larsen, no date, p 2) – to produce a 'dodgy dossier'. Intelligence reports at the time, subsequently published, do not reveal Bolshevik revolutionary movements outside Glasgow and the trade union leaders were intent on disassociating themselves from the shop stewards promoting unofficial strike action.

Implementation

The Housing and Town Planning etc Act 1919 met with almost unanimous approval from Parliament. Nonetheless, in Conservative and Liberal circles, there were strong undertones that state support for housing was necessary only for a very short post-war 'reconstruction' period and a few Conservative MPs wanted the government to provide loans directly to builders as an alternative to state housing. The Liberals favoured 'time-limited' subsidies and Addison (1919, quoted in Orbach, 1977, p 78), indicating that subsidies would last seven years and then rents would be 'economic', said 'we cannot undertake under any circumstances to subsidise a rent that is lower than what ought properly to be charged'.

Addison had considerable difficulty in starting his 'housing drive'. The Treasury – under Austen Chamberlain – was reluctant to endorse local authority bonds at an interest rate necessary to attract capital. The initial slow progress produced criticism from the Liberals excluded from Lloyd George's Coalition government, with Asquith claiming the Housing Act 1919 was 'an admirable piece of paper but with little practical value' (quoted in Morgan and Morgan, 1980, p 112). Other problems emerged as housing production gained momentum. The attempt to ramp up housing supply, with the Housing (Additional

Powers) Act 1919 adding to demand by providing a fixed grant to private builders to construct working-class houses, led to high demand chasing limited building industry capacity. Licensing building materials ended in 1918 and the trade unions resisted 'dilution' via training more building workers. Costs escalated – £1,000 per house compared to £400 in 1913. It is possible that, in time, supply would have caught up with demand as the building industry returned to its pre-war capacity and the post-war boom, which had absorbed many workers into building factories, warehouses, offices, cinemas and so on, evaporated. Indeed, prices had started to decline but the Cabinet, faced with rising interest rates, local authority problems in raising capital and an 'anti-waste' campaign in the popular press, did not wait to discover if the trend would continue. Subsidies were reduced and, in January 1921, abolished. Swenarton (1981, 2009) claims that subsidised local authority housing was a response to a social revolution threat that could be ended when rising unemployment was beginning to erode working-class power but, according to Gilbert (1970, p 148), the 'open ended' subsidies in the 1919 Act were a recipe for house price inflation and deserved the axe. He points out that the £208.5 million pounds spent by the British government on housing subsidies in England and Wales between the wars produced 1.5 million houses, but £131 million – £625 per house – was spent on the 208,000 houses built under the Addison Act.

Subsidies and standards

With subsidies eliminated, Griffith-Boscawen, now the Conservative Health Minister, declared that he hoped 'the building industry will return to its pre-war economic basis' (quoted in Burnett, 1978, p 226). However, faced with growing Labour Party popularity, local authority subsidies were restored, albeit in a 'residual' role. The Housing Act 1923 offered a fixed, limited central subsidy for 20 years to both local authority and private enterprise supplying houses for the working class and thereby avoided the pitfalls of Addison's deficit subsidy (Malpass, 1992). Local authorities were allowed to build only after demonstrating that private enterprise could not meet identified need. Moreover, local authority Direct Labour Organisations, introduced in 1892 by the LCC and spreading to other local authorities, were curtailed (Langford, 1982). In Cabinet, the 1923 Act was linked to rent control, demonstrating that the Conservatives had recognised that more working-class houses were necessary before full decontrol could be implemented.

The contrast between the Conservatives' 'residual' view of council housing and Labour's 'institutional' approach was illustrated in the Housing (Financial Provisions) Act 1924, passed by a short-lived minority Labour government. John Wheatley – in 1915, a 'Red Clydesider', and in 1924, the minister responsible for housing – had radical intentions. His approach was corporatist. The committee he appointed to advise on the legislation 'comprised fifteen union representatives and nineteen representatives from the employers; there was nobody from the government' (Morgan, 2005, p 241). Wheatley offered the unions 'fair wages' in housing contracts and promised secure employment via a 15-year rolling house-building programme in return for 'dilution' in entry terms to the building trades. He promised the housing industry full order books and told the builders that he wanted the houses erected 'at a fair and reasonable price, and we want you to meet us in that spirit' (quoted in Vaughan, 2009, p 58). In his diaries, the Assistant Secretary to the Cabinet, records:

> He harangued the [Cabinet] Standing Committee for a couple of days, advocating a ten years' programme of 200,000 per annum, each to cost exactly £500 and to be let at exactly 7s per week. How this sum was to be raised and how prices and rents are to be kept static regardless of all market changes, he had no idea. (Jones, 1969, p 270)

Officials quickly diluted Wheatley's radicalism. The 1924 Act increased government subsidies paid to local authorities and extended the time over which the subsidy was paid from 20 to 40 years. Although there was a statutory rate contribution and restrictions on local authority house-building were removed, rents were well above Wheatley's initial intention.

'Rough houses for rough people'

The 1923 and 1924 subsidies continued in parallel until the early 1930s and helped to produce hundreds of 'corporation suburbs' (Crookston, 2004) but new home quality deteriorated. Chamberlain was under pressure from the National Federation of Master Builders to get local authorities out of housing supply. At a Cabinet meeting in February 1926, he gave assurances that 'it is his desire and intention to bring the Wheatley Scheme to an end as soon as practicable and also to proceed actively with the policy of the sale of Addison Houses' (Cabinet, 1926, p 306). Subsidies were reduced in 1926 and new home quality deteriorated. 'Parlour' houses became rare and a fixed bath in the kitchen often replaced a bathroom.

The May Committee on national expenditure recommended the ending of 'general needs' housing subsidies, stating:

> We view with deep concern the steadily growing charge upon the Exchequer ... for the housing of the working classes. There is a serious danger of the nation ... finding itself committed to the principle that a man's wages are not normally intended to enable him to pay fully for his housing. (May, 1931, p 220)

'General needs' subsidies were abolished in 1933 in England and Wales and severely reduced in Scotland, leaving only the Greenwood Act's slum clearance subsidy, to which, in 1935, the Conservatives added subsidies for overcrowding relief (see Chapter Three). Moreover, Hilton Young received Cabinet authorisation to begin negotiations with the building societies and local authorities about selling houses built under the Addison Act to building societies (Cabinet, 1932, p 108). Abolishing general needs subsidies to local government supplied a clear run for builders and building societies to construct homes in suburbia.

The switch to subsidies for slum clearance and overcrowding relief produced a striking change in the type of houses built. Hilton Young, the Health Minister, was enthusiastic about flats as a mechanism to contain urban growth. His zeal was shared by the growing number of architects attracted to the 'modernist' movement, who made frequent visits to the Continent to study the 'splendid structures' and 'sweetness and light' of new flats (Gardiner, 2010, p 290). The higher grants on offer to construct flats on 'expensive' sites produced a very large proportion of four- and six-storey walk-up flats, sometimes in large blocks surrounding a central courtyard. Their austere exterior 'seemed to emphasise that they were rough places for rough people' (Branson and Heinemann, 1973, p 211). Hobhouse (1994, p 3) describes Birchfield House in Poplar as:

> intended to re-house people from clearance areas and one of the LCC's euphemistically named 'simplified' five-storey blocks of flats. It had a communal washroom/bathroom shared between every two or three flats.... Although all tenants had their own WC and scullery (with a sink), these were not usually within the flat but situated adjacent to the

bathrooms and, like them, were reached across a common passage or landing.

The 'rough' houses built for former slum inhabitants served to highlight the contrast between homeownership and renting. By 1937, estate agents were advising prospective homeowners how much a council estate in the area devalued property (Crookston, 2004).

Differential rents

Each local authority housing development had a separate account setting the rent for each scheme but the Housing Act 1930 allowed these accounts to be pooled and 'differential' rents, based on a means test, charged. Differential rent policy was promoted by the Conservatives throughout the 1930s. A variant was to charge 'compulsory' tenants – those displaced by clearance – a lower rent than 'voluntary' tenants – those rehoused from the waiting list. Differential rents were not only a Conservative policy. 'Red Clydesider' John Wheatley expressed sympathy for differential rents (Vaughan, 2009) and Labour-controlled Leeds, with the committed socialist the Reverend Charles Jenkinson as Housing Committee Chair, introduced a differential rent scheme in 1934. Jenkinson had plans to rehouse 30,000 households from clearance areas and was aware that the new tenants would not be able to afford the rents necessary to make the plan viable, let alone the cost of a new housing management department 'with estate management officers, home inspections, and gardeners to teach people how to maintain their lawns' (Tenant's History, 2013). Jenkinson proposed to charge 'economic rents' but with reduced rents, possibly zero, for those with low incomes. This provoked a rent strike, with T.H. Gilberthorpe, President of the Leeds Federation of Municipal Tenants Associations, declaring: 'One has sympathy with people who have fallen on hard times but why should the burden of their rent fall only on other municipal tenants? Why not ratepayers?' (quoted in Tenant's History, 2013). The strike was defeated but Labour's proposal was a major issue in the subsequent local election when the Conservatives gained control of Leeds City Council. In 1938, Birmingham, under Conservative control and contemplating a large slum clearance initiative, attempted to introduce 'economic' rents for its tenants, accompanied by a rent rebate scheme. This met with well-organised tenant resistance: between 6,000 to 8,000 tenants stayed on a rent strike for 13 weeks and the Birmingham scheme was abandoned (Schifferes, 1976). Given these demonstrations of differential rent unpopularity, it is hardly surprising that, despite constant exhortations from the central government, only a minority of local authorities introduced such schemes. However, the Leeds rent strike starkly exposed a working-class division between those council tenants in regular work with reasonable pay and those without.

Local governance

Between the wars, there were large variations among local authorities in the number of council houses built. For example, under Wheatley's 1924 Act, Carlisle built 45.5 per 1,000 population, Walsall built 40.8, whereas in Salford, Grimsby, Blackpool, Croydon and Southend, less than 1.3 were built (Jennings, 1971). Labour-controlled councils were usually enthusiastic but Labour controlled few councils and other authorities held varying views about the need to build houses. Some embraced the idea but others, often with a high proportion of private landlords as councillors, were reluctant to build – demonstrating the salience of 'civic culture' and local political factors in explaining local variations in national policy (Shapely, 2007b; Smyth and Robertson, 2013). Despite the variations in council housing standards between the wars, in 1943, Mass Observation found that 80% of people living in council houses were satisfied with their homes. People liked the modern amenities but only 5% said that they preferred a flat to a house. What most people wanted was a house with a garden on the town's 'outskirts' (Tsubaki, 1993). Nonetheless, Orwell (1937, pp 61–2) noted that 'they don't really feel at home ... in a Corporation estate there is an uncomfortable, almost prison-like atmosphere, and the people who live there are perfectly aware of it'.

The war years

During the Second World War, the Coalition government split its housing plan into 'immediate' measures – linked to the need to absorb manpower when the war was over – and a long-term programme. Extensive local authority involvement in the 'immediate' measures met with broad support from the Coalition partners. An ambitious long-term programme was set – 3–4 million houses in 10 years – but the assumption among civil servants was that after 'immediate' measures were complete, private enterprise would be the main delivery mechanism. However, there was little integration between the housing plans and the planning proposals contained in the Uthwatt, Scott and Barlow Reports (see Chapter Three). There was some support for setting up a national Housing Corporation (see Chapter Seven), both to provide mortgages at cheap rates and to build houses (Malpass, 2003a).

Despite the housing issue's high political profile, there was no comprehensive housing policy review similar to the Beveridge Report on social security. Beveridge failed to find a solution to the 'rent problem' in establishing a universal national minimum income (Beveridge, 1942). Later, in *Pillars of Security* (Beveridge, 1943, p 111), he said that 'squalor' – his term for the housing problem – was 'a formidable giant – far harder than the attack on Want – a true Goliath'. Nonetheless, there was optimism that the housing problem could be overcome by organising housing production in similar ways to munitions output. Peaceful military apparatus use was demonstrated by a project to build 500,000 temporary 'pre-fabs' using airfield construction plant for site preparation and aircraft factories for component production.

Universal

Malpass (2003b, p 646) notes that 'as far as housing is concerned there is little evidence of a distinctively Labour flavour to the policies that were to emerge before the end of the war'. The appointment of Aneurin Bevan as Minister for Health, with housing part of his responsibilities, changed the outlook. Bevan wanted most new houses to be rented from a local authority. Although not opposed to homeownership in principle, he argued that 'it has not dawned on some people that the vast majority of people cannot afford to buy' (Bevan, 1946), and in times of shortage, housing, like health care, required distribution according to need. Bevan also believed that 'we shall be judged in a year or two by the number of houses we build but we will be judged in ten years time by the type of houses we build' (quoted in Foot, 1975, p 82), so he wanted to produce high-quality homes. New housing schemes would also promote mixed communities not the past 'castrated communities', with their spatial division between council tenants and homeowners. In 1945, Bevan urged local authorities to 'make provision for building some houses also for higher income groups at higher rents' (Bevan, 1945), and in 1949, he removed the phrase 'for the working class' from the legislation governing local authority housing.

To attain his objectives, Bevan introduced a strict licensing system to control building by private enterprise and tripled the pre-war subsidy levels to local authorities. In 1948, 171,000 permanent houses plus 11,000 temporary 'pre-fabs' were built by local authorities in England and Wales, but in 1950, local authority housing construction had declined to 139,000 per year. Perhaps Bevan's mistake, in 'numbers game' terms, was to run down the temporary prefabricated housing programme. He labelled the 'pre-fabs' as 'rabbit hutches', but although more expensive than traditional houses and costly to heat, they could be constructed quickly and were very popular. The 1950 housing hiatus supplied the opportunity for the Conservative Party and Tory press to attack Bevan's record. A young Margaret Thatcher joined in, declaring in a leaflet to her Dartford constituents: 'In spite of the special preparations made by the Conservatives when they were in office, houses are only being built half as fast as under the Tories in the late thirties and this is not fast enough' (Thatcher, 1950).

Bevan's divided responsibilities between health and housing attracted comment, the joke being that housing received only 'half a Nye'. Bureaucracy was implicated, it being pointed out that seven ministries were involved in the housing production process. Bevan's insistence on high standards – he had accepted the Dudley Committee's recommendation that the size of council houses should increase, and that for five persons or more, there should be two WCs (Dudley, 1944) – was questioned both inside and outside the Cabinet (Thomas Symonds, 2014). A Gallup poll in January 1949 showed that 61% were dissatisfied with Labour's housing record (Howarth, 1985, p 106), and in the 1950 general election campaign, Conservative activists noted widespread disillusionment with Labour's housing progress. This prompted a resolution to the Party Conference, according to Davis (2008, p 129), 'engineered by a group of free marketers with Enoch Powell at the helm' – indicating that private enterprise would deliver – demanding a target of 300,000 houses per year. Many leading Conservatives had doubts about the pledge's wisdom. When asked 'Could we build 300,000?', Shadow Chancellor 'Rab' Butler replied, 'The question is should we' (Butler, 1971, p 155). Nonetheless, the target was included in the 1951 Conservative Party manifesto.

The 'People's House'

The 300,000 target in the Conservatives' 1951 election manifesto came with the caveat that 'there should be no reduction in the number of houses and flats built to let but more freedom must be given to the private builder' (Conservative Party, 1951, p 15). The statement implied that in attempting to meet its target, the Conservatives could restrict council and new town building to the level inherited from Labour and supply the remainder through the private sector. This appears to be the strategy adopted by Macmillan when he first became Minister of

Housing. In his memoirs, he states: 'I introduced, in answer to several arranged questions, my new policy, on [the] ratio between council and private building, 1 for 1 instead of 1 for 5; sale of council houses to tenants; thirdly, the simpler house' (Macmillan, 2004, p 119).

However, when Macmillan hit his 300,000 target in 1954, the public sector supplied 221,000 houses. Macmillan was fearful that Labour would win the next general election with a substantial majority and Bevan might be Prime Minister: electoral arithmetic meant that the working class had to benefit quickly from Conservative measures. Moreover, Labour had developed a strong local authority housing delivery mechanism. Assisted by Percy Mills, an industrialist who had directed wartime production, Macmillan boosted local authority building. He had accepted Bevan's notion that local authority housing was a 'plannable instrument' – it delivered. The keys to success were restricting house size – Macmillan's 'People's House' was smaller than those built under Labour, saving 10% on materials – and his 'boneless wonder', a 'timberless' house to overcome the wood shortage, plus supply chain management via Regional Housing Boards and local authorities. Thus, for instance, when the 300,000 target was threatened by supply shortages, Macmillan was able to direct available materials to completing houses already under construction rather than to new starts, thereby avoiding a large number of houses under construction but few completions.

Jones (2000, p 109) reports that 'Macmillan told his Permanent Secretary, Sir Thomas Sheepshanks, shortly after taking office that "I lunched with him [Churchill] on Saturday. He will support us in everything"'. Churchill's backing was vital to Macmillan in his many battles with the Treasury to maintain the housing programme. Addison (2013, p 418) comments:

> The Treasury argued, with much justice, that capital investment in housing diverted resources from industrial investment and the export trade. At a critical cabinet meeting on 24th July, Churchill ruled that it would be wrong to accept a reduction in the programme for 1953.

Macmillan was under constant pressure from his party to increase homeownership and he started work on a 'grand design' for housing, incorporating promoting owner-occupation, modifying rent control and ending 'general needs' subsidies. He also considered a national differential rents scheme, informing the Cabinet that 'I am therefore considering whether it would be possible to have regard to the value of the house, granting a rebate to those in need but only to those in need', but he noted that 'it has great political danger' (Cabinet, 1953, p 69). Willetts (1992) refers to wet–dry cycles in Conservative social policy: 1955 to 1960 was a dry period in housing policy. Alongside the Rent Act 1957, council housing declined as a proportion of new houses built, with 'general needs' subsidies reduced and then abolished.

Sir Keith Joseph and the housing issue

Housing reignited as a political issue in the early 1960s. On becoming responsible for housing, Sir Keith Joseph prepared a demand list for his Cabinet colleagues: restoring 'general needs' subsidies; local authority development corporations to acquire land; green belt relaxations; and a land tax. He was cajoled into action by Prime Minister Harold Macmillan, who wrote to Joseph ordering: 'you must (and will) recreate the spirit of 1951–54' (quoted in Denham and Garnett, 2001, p 101). General needs subsidies were restored but Sir Alex Douglas Home, who became Prime Minister in October 1963, not only wanted to preserve the 'landed interest', but was also firmly committed to Skelton's 'property-owning democracy' (Young, 1970). Butler and Maudling were unleashed in the Cabinet and Joseph's more radical proposals were squashed (Cox, 1984).

Residual high-rise

The politics involved in the Conservatives' switch from 'general needs' to supporting only slum clearance subsidies have been explained in Chapters Three and Five. Here, the complementary high-rise and other 'modernist' housing story is told. Between 1945 and 1950, 10.5% of the accommodation constructed by local authorities was in flats, by 1966–70, it was 50.6%, rising to 90% in inner cities. Exploring this change, Dunleavy refers to 'the Public Housing Apparatus' – central government, the design professions and the construction industry – 'unified at a national level by an extensive network of advisory bodies which influence central government policy' (Dunleavy, 1981, p 10), augmented by informal contacts.

The government introduced extra grants for flats – the higher the tower the greater the subsidy – concentrated on 39 'priority areas'. These measures, plus the city 'land trap' embodied in green belts (see Chapter Two), encouraged authorities to build tower blocks. As Frederic Osborn, an advocate of new towns, noted:

> The architects want to go up in the air.... They are
> supported by the lucky people in country houses and parks
> who don't want their Arcadia invaded. They have succeeded
> to some extent, owing to the structure of our democracy.
> But they are overriding the inarticulate yet vast majority.
> (Osborn, 1959, quoted in Kynaston, 2014, p 6)

High-rise encountered opposition; for example, in 1957 Poplar
Borough Council rejected a LCC 19-storey housing scheme, arguing
'we are convinced that this sort of dwelling is not conducive to a full
family life, apart from the many social evils which can be traced to
this form of housing of the working classes' (Poplar Borough Council
quoted in Hobhouse, 1994, p 10). The Housing Minister overruled
Poplar's objection.

Labour's leadership also embraced building flats: Harold Wilson
was enthusiastic about a large house-building programme and
'industrialised' building meant hitting housing targets faster. Richard
Crossman (1965) justified building flats, claiming that 'The great
metropolis needs people who are electricians, needs charladies who
will do the cleaning ... and we have to build houses for them'. It is
a tribute to the volume building industry's influence that population
density near to or above those obtained by high-rise were achievable
by building terraced properties. This was known at the time (MHLG,
1958), and according to Boys Smith and Morton (2013, p 11, emphasis
in original), 'One study quoted by the 1999 Urban Task Force showed
that terraced houses *at least* match the housing densities (about 75
units/hectare) of most high-rise'.

Having launched a promotional agency, set up a grant structure and
established 'yardsticks' to contain costs, central government adopted
a 'laissez-faire' attitude to local government, meaning that 'it leaves
local authorities to decide what is their local need and how far (if at
all) it is to be met' (Griffiths, 1966, p 591). The formidable Dame
Evelyn Sharp, Permanent Secretary to the Ministry of Housing and
Local Government, was a staunch local government defender as a
housing provider, albeit regarding them 'as children worthy of constant
rebuke' (Theakston, 1993, p 57). This reliance on local government
placed considerable power with local politicians, who were by no
means pawns in national politics. Many city authorities enthusiastically
embraced high density to maintain rateable value and enhance 'civic
status'. T. Dan Smith, for example, leader of Newcastle City Council
from 1960 to 1965, but later jailed for corruption, had a vision for
Newcastle as 'The Brasilia of the North'. In Liverpool, Jack Braddock,

Labour council leader, supported high-rises to promote redevelopment 'without disturbing existing religious-political groupings' (Glendinning and Muthesius, 1994, p 164). Other authorities such as Manchester and Sheffield resisted 'town cramming' until fenced in by the green belt.

Modernism

A new architectural movement known as 'modernism' started to gain influence in the 1930s. According to Le Corbusier (1964 [1933]), houses should be 'machines for living in', incorporating 'modern' materials such as glass, steel and concrete and located in well-spaced tower blocks ('unités') providing equal access to daylight. 'Unités' should be linked by overhead motorways creating a 'Radiant City', with the space below used as recreational parkland. As Glendinning and Muthesius (1994, p 105) point out, 'Bearing in mind that other forms of architectural commissions were scarce in the early post-war years, one might say, with considerable truth, that Modern Council Housing was Modern Architecture'.

There was infighting within the architectural profession for the kudos garnering contracts. As Le Corbusier's 'vertical garden city' notion gained influence, the 'suburban solution' became passé, despite the attempts by Sir Frederic Osborn, Chair of the Town and Country Planning Association throughout the 1950s and 1960s, to promote planned dispersal in new and expanding towns.

Tower blocks have received the most attention in the post-mortems on the 'mass housing' era but there were other, equally unsuccessful, experiments in urban design. Peter and Alison Smithson, having declared gardens as unnecessary and that 'Folk-build is dead in England' (quoted in Kynaston, 2009, p 280), attacked high-rises as being too obsessed by light, greenery and air. They designed Robin Hood Gardens in Poplar, London, to replicate the 'terraced house community', but stacked in storeys and linked by 'streets in the sky' – a design repeated in Sheffield's Park Hill flats. Later, Peter Smithson blamed his scheme's inhabitants for its problems, saying that he had 'imagined council tenants to be people with similar backgrounds to his own – the optimistic, ambitious, skilled working class' (quoted in Harwood and Powers, 2008, p 11). Some estates were designed on 'Radburn' principles, keeping vehicle access separate from the houses and including garage blocks remotely located from the accommodation. 'Low-rise', 'deck access', 'slab' flat blocks and maisonettes become common despite yet more survey evidence revealing that people did not want flats, high or low.

High-rise demise is usually associated with the collapse of Ronan Point in 1968 but doubts had been circulating in the Ministry of Housing and Local Government for many years. Towers were expensive – 55% more costly than conventional housing – and research was beginning to reveal their limitations as family dwellings. A high-rise study of Leeds, Liverpool and London concluded that 'high rise is better avoided' (quoted in Dunleavy, 1981, p 171). *Family and Kinship in East London* (Young and Willmott, 1957), an examination of how tight-knit working-class communities were being eroded by clearance and peripheral estate development, became more influential. Even Joseph had concerns. In 1962, when talking to borough officials, he said:

> I'd roll up a piece of paper stand it on the table and I'd say 'This is what you want to do – build a high block – but when you've allowed for panning, sun lighting and so on, why don't you do this ?' – and I'd lay it out horizontally'. But it was high-rise blocks they wanted. (Quoted in Glendinning and Muthesius, 1994, p 186)

In 1967, high-rise subsidies were cut and changes in cost yardsticks made tower blocks difficult to build. Nevertheless, although high-rise fell out of fashion, flat-building in inner cities by local government continued well into the 1970s. Tenant satisfaction in flat living followed a pattern. Initial enthusiasm – the cleanliness, amenities and space were so much better than the slums – followed by disillusionment as the problems of high-density living and design faults became manifest.

'Fair' rents?

In 1968, council rents were 7.5% of average earnings and rents paid for 74% of council house costs in England but only 38% in Scotland, where rate funds contributed 35% to total council house costs (Crouch and Wolf, 1970). Local attempts to push up rents and introduce rent rebate schemes provoked rent strikes in Sheffield, Walsall and Tower Hamlets.

The 1970 Conservative Party manifesto declared:

> all too often those receiving subsidies are better off than those who pay for them through rates and taxes. We will change the system so that subsidies are used for adequate rent rebates for those tenants who cannot afford to pay fair rents, and also for slum clearance and other essential programmes. (Conservative Party, 1970)

The Housing Finance Act 1972 made provision for all local authority rents to rise to the 'fair' rents charged in the private landlord sector, underpinned by rent rebates (for council tenants) and rent allowances (for private landlord tenants) to help lower-income households pay the rent. The change was justified in the White Paper *Fair Deal for Housing* (DoE, 1971, p 3) as rationalising the historic central subsidy pattern that gave 'too little to authorities with the worst problems of slum clearance and overcrowding'.

The 1972 scheme was the Leeds 1934 differential rents applied nationally; indeed, Peter Walker, Secretary of State for the Environment, claimed that the measure would make Britain the first capitalist country in which no one would be evicted for not paying the rent (Walker, 1991, p 88). Conservative-controlled councils welcomed 'fair' rents, sometimes asserting that higher rents would eliminate the 'unfair' rate fund contribution to council housing (Passmore, 2015). However, many Labour-controlled authorities, with a good local authority stock built at low cost from the 1930s to the 1960s, could see no reason why their tenants should be charged 'fair' rents and any surplus given to the Treasury. Most tenants agreed; to them, 'fair' rents meant higher rents and there was considerable resistance to the Act via rent strikes, with 45 local authorities initially refusing to implement the legislation. Eventually, this opposition faded, except in Clay Cross, Derbyshire, where a Housing Commissioner was appointed to enforce the Act and local councillors – including Dennis Skinner – were surcharged and debarred from office.

The strategic housing authority

On its return to power in 1974, Labour retained rent rebates and allowances but instructed local authorities to charge only 'reasonable' rents. The Treasury, pushing its long-term ambition to means-test housing subsidies, pressed for rent increases mitigated by an enhanced rent rebate scheme. Labour MPs resisted the move. The Chief Secretary to the Treasury at the time complained: 'Talk of increasing council house rents, and it was as if you were planning to snatch children from mothers and put them to work down a mine' (Barnett, 1982, p 70). An internal review of housing policy was set up that included the consideration and rejection of a scheme, devised by civil servants, for market rents across all tenures (Lipsey, 2013), similar to that put forward by Nicholas Ridley in the 1980s. The review produced little change in the financial regime, its only lasting outcome being the notion there was no longer a national housing shortage, but a series of local problems

(Secretary of State for the Environment and Secretary of State for Wales, 1977). Accordingly, a new mechanism for distributing resources to councils was set up, whereby local authorities had to produce a housing strategy and make bids for resources via a Housing Investment Programme based on their identified priorities. After the 1976 sterling crisis, Labour cut capital expenditure on housing, reducing new local authority output. Labour's 1979 White Paper on public expenditure (Treasury, 1979, p 94) declared that 'The government's objectives are: to provide a decent home for every family, at a price within their means, that implies a more selective and discriminating approach to housing policy; it means a more efficient method of tackling need'.

Goodbye council housing 1: Conservative policy

Labour started the eclipse of council housing but the full-bodied assault was mounted by the Conservatives. Sir Keith Joseph, now thoroughly dehydrated following his damp period, announced that 'It was only in April 1974 that I was converted to Conservatism. I had thought I was a Conservative but I now see that I was not really one at all' (quoted in Halcrow, 1989, p 56). He denounced council housing because it had destroyed the market and 'wrought hard to the social fabric' (Joseph, 1976, p 31). On his road to Damascus, Joseph looked back with horror over his time as Housing Minister, saying: 'I suppose that I was genuinely convinced I had a new answer. It was prefabrication and Heaven help me, high blocks' (quoted in *Guardian*, 1973).

By the mid-1970s, council housing had become an easier target for the Conservatives to attack. As the problems generated by the late 1950s' and 1960s' modernist architecture became apparent, trust between councils and tenants started to erode and 'new slums and the rising tenant anger' (Shapely, 2007b, p 157) framed the council house debate. Public opinion surveys in the late 1970s revealed less than 20% of council tenants under 55 stating that their ideal tenure in two years' time was a council house and 59% of tenants gave negative reasons for living in their current accommodation (Coles, 1989). Tenants were finding some estates difficult to live in and councils were finding them difficult to manage. Moreover, due to mounting interest rates, national contributions to council housing almost doubled between 1973/74 and 1976/77. Local rate payments to the Housing Revenue Account – usually favoured by Labour councils but not by the Conservatives and becoming a feature of local election campaigns – also increased. Rents remained low – 7.1% of male manual workers' average earnings – and the Labour Party became vulnerable to the charge of 'featherbedding' council tenants.

Margaret Thatcher disliked council housing. Jenkins (2006, pp 125–6) records 'When Thatcher was briefly an Opposition housing spokesman in 1974 I offered to show her examples of London's good and bad council estates. She cut me short, "No, there are only bad ones"'. She also had a low opinion on council tenants, regarding them, at best, as 'flawed consumers' (Flint, 2000, p 901). Her attitude was revealed in a letter sent in 1979 to a council tenant who had written complaining about the condition of her house:

> I hope you will not think me too blunt if I say that it may well be that your council accommodation is unsatisfactory but considering the fact you have been unable to buy your own accommodation you are lucky to have been given something which the rest of us are paying for out of our taxes. (Quoted in Butler and Kavanagh, 1980, p 191)

In the 1980s, central housing subsidies to local government were gradually withdrawn. Despite attempts by some Labour-controlled councils to keep rents low by extra rate contributions (Midwinter, 1985), rents were forced upwards, thereby reminding tenants of the Right to Buy's virtues. When there were no more central subsidies to withdraw, Housing Benefit costs were added to the Housing Revenue Account – the account that determined rents – pushing most accounts into deficit, and in 1989, the Housing Revenue Account was 'ring-fenced', preventing any subsidy from the local authority's General Fund. Capital expenditure was substantially reduced: by 1989, 16,492 local authority houses were completed in the UK, compared to 96,196 in 1978.

'Tenant's Choice' and Housing Action Trusts

Nicholas Ridley, Secretary of State for the Environment in Margaret Thatcher's third government, regarded local government as 'enabling' other agencies to supply services. In the housing domain, the mechanisms for promoting the 'enabling' role were 'Tenant's Choice' – allowing a tenant ballot to change landlord – and Housing Action Trusts (HATs). Implementing these initiatives met with tenant resistance. Despite the central government appointing consultants to promote 'Tenant's Choice', tenants were suspicious that 'alternative' landlords were private landlords and only 1,470 homes were transferred, mostly to Walterton and Elgin Community Homes Ltd, set up by a tenant's action group to liberate their homes from Conservative-controlled Westminster Council. The Conservatives formally abandoned 'Tenants Choice' in 1996.

Tiesdell (2001, p 358) states 'HATs were initially perceived as an exit mechanism for local authority housing and – more controversially – as a means for private developers to asset strip that housing'. In the initial HATs scheme, a local authority could be required to transfer its housing stock to a HAT, its members appointed by the government. The HAT would refurbish the properties and then pass them to an unspecified receiving agency, perhaps a private landlord. In the Bill making provision for HATs, there was no provision for a tenant ballot, with Nicholas Ridley (1988) arguing that tenants would be 'misinformed by Labour-controlled councils', so there would be 'no chance of balanced and informed opinion among tenants'. However, following a tenants' lobby, the House of Lords amended the legislation to include a right for tenants to decide for or against a HAT on a majority vote. Tenants – fearful of transfer to a private landlord – resisted HATs, and the first two going to ballot were rejected by large majorities.

The government had miscalculated badly – it had expected gratitude for the £20,000–£25,000 spending per house. In her memoirs, Thatcher (1993, p 601) expressed her frustration, saying that 'one would never have guessed that we were offering huge sums of taxpayer's money – it would probably have worked out at £100 million a HAT – to improve the conditions of some of the worst housing in the country'.

Faced with the ignominy associated with large amounts of allocated yet unspent cash, the Department for the Environment became less aggressive and started to work with local authorities and tenants to ensure that HATs became acceptable. Eventually, after assurances to tenants about returning to their local authority following improvements, six HATs were established. Thatcher declared she 'had expected more from "tenants' choice" and from HATS' (Thatcher, 1993, p 601) and called in her housing ministerial team to discuss 'Community Housing Trusts' – similar to HATs but with an equity stake for tenants. Later, she wrote to Chris Patten, then Secretary of State for the Environment, reaffirming:

> I wanted to get local authorities out of managing and owning housing.... It was clear to me that we must now get back to the kind of fundamental policy thinking which Nick Ridley – now no longer a member of the Government – had once supplied. (Thatcher, 1993, p 606)

John Major's government tried to advance Thatcher's agenda. Local government's 'enabling' role was promoted via the Housing Investment Programme machinery. Under Labour, the housing investment requirements in different local authorities were based mainly on an objective formula – the General Needs Index – but the Conservatives gradually replaced this by ministers assessing the 'quality' of a local authority's bid for resources. 'Quality' meant following the government's priorities.

Rents were increased well above inflation until the mounting Housing Benefit cost prompted a rethink, with more emphasis placed on upfront production subsidies than Housing Benefit 'consumer' spending. Rather the bracket housing associations with private landlords as part of the 'independent' rented sector, the terms 'social housing' and 'social rent' started to be applied to housing association and local authority houses. In a section headed 'Creating a new framework for social renting', a 1995 White Paper said 'We will ensure that rents in the social sector remain affordable for tenants in low paid work' (DoE and the Welsh Office, 1995, p 10).

Goodbye council housing 2: New Labour

New Labour inherited a local authority housing repairs deficit estimated at £19 billion and its Decent Homes programme was an attempt to reduce this backlog. The Green Paper *Quality and Choice: A Decent Home for All* (DETR, 2000a, p 12) stated: 'We aim for a step change in the quality of the stock and the performance of social landlords and are committed to ensuring that all social housing is of a decent standard within 10 years'. A Major Repairs Allowance was introduced into Housing Revenue Accounts to help meet the decent home standard but stock transfer was the main mechanism for achieving decent homes. However, in response to opposition to stock transfer organised within the Labour Party by 'Defend Council Housing' (see Chapter Seven), a 'half-way' house was offered in the form of an Arms Length Management Organisation (ALMO). Local authorities could access additional central resources if they set up a not-for-profit organisation run by an unpaid board of directors, including councillors and tenant representatives but with no faction having a controlling majority. The council continued to own the homes and determine allocation policy but the ALMO was responsible for stock management. By 2010, 70 ALMOs were managing more than a million council homes. Between 2000 and 2010, 770,340 local authority houses were transferred to housing associations in England, enabling the associations, free from public sector borrowing constraints, to upgrade the signed-over stock (see Chapter Seven).

Exit, Voice and Loyalty

In *Exit, Voice, and Loyalty*, Hirschman (1970) makes distinctions between 'exit', 'voice', and 'loyalty'. 'Loyalty' refers to a feeling of attachment, and to be loyal means that one believes that, over time, the right actions will more than balance the wrong ones. Loyalty was expected from council tenants. As the tenants' landlord was a democratically elected local authority, and because local authorities were expected to act for the 'public', not only for the tenants' good, direct tenant participation in decision-making was unavailable.

Demands for a 'tenant voice' in policy and management came from tenants' organisations. The Association of London Housing Estates, for example, published a tenant's charter in 1970 and the Sheffield Federation of Tenants Associations managed to secure a degree of tenant involvement via representation on a Housing Advisory Committee (Bradley, 2014). Nonetheless, throughout the 1970s, council tenants remained local authority housing's passive recipients. In response to the Conservatives promoting 'exit' politics via the Right to Buy, the Labour Party started to show more interest in 'voice' politics, and provisions for increasing tenant participation were included in a Bill introduced to Parliament in 1978. The Conservatives adopted elements of this Bill in the Housing Act 1980. In defining a 'secure tenant' with a Right to Buy, tenants gained other rights, such as greater protection from eviction, and a provision was included placing an obligation on local authorities to foster tenant participation, an obligation developed in the 1990s as part of John Major's citizen's charter initiative. A 'right to manage' was introduced in 1994 to encourage tenant management boards and tenant management cooperatives and promote the dissolution of local authority dominance in rented accommodation supply.

Under New Labour, local councils had to begin a process of agreeing a framework for tenant involvement via Tenant Participation Compacts, aimed at 'best value' in housing services delivery. The objective of the compacts was to 'help to bring the quality of participation across all councils up to the best and to ensure that all tenants have equal opportunity to participate' (DETR, 2000b, p 6). However, as New Labour adopted a 'consumer' orientation via schemes such as 'choice-based lettings', tenant participation was directed towards assisting local government to evaluate 'best value' performance and even to facilitate stock transfer. Tenant management boards and tenant management cooperatives marked time under New Labour (see Lund, 2011) and the Tenant Participation Compacts idea gradually faded away. However, towards the end of its term in office, New Labour established 'National Tenant Voice' to ensure that social housing tenants had a say in shaping national policy on housing issues.

Welcome home?

New Labour's 2007 Green Paper 'Homes for the Future: More Affordable, More Sustainable' (DCLG, 2007) was guarded in expanding local government's provider role, but as the 2008/09 recession cast a chill over new private building, central government resources were allocated to stimulate local authority provision. A Local Authority New Build Programme produced 1,390 new house starts in 2010, more than twice the number produced in the best production year since 1997. In addition, New Labour entered into discussions with local government on ways to reform local authority housing finance to allow local authorities to use any surplus arising from renting the existing stock and Right to Buy receipts. In its 2010 manifesto, New Labour claimed these new freedoms meant that 'councils would build up to 10,000 council houses a year by the end of the next Parliament' (Labour Party, 2010, para 2.5).

The Coalition government: 'welfare' housing

As local authority housing supply diminished, it moved on the same trajectory as public housing in the US, towards a 'residual', 'welfare' model catering for people with very low incomes. A feature of US 'welfare housing' is the notion that people living in 'the projects' have behavioural problems requiring attention from public sector housing managers. Thus, for example, President Clinton signed the Quality Housing and Work Responsibility Act 1998, specifying that public housing residents must participate for at least eight hours a month in community service or economic self-sufficiency training. Failure to participate meant that their one-year tenancy would end.

'Breakdown Britain'

In 2006, David Cameron set up the Centre for Social Justice, with Iain Duncan Smith as its Chair. An early report identified five interrelated 'pathways to poverty': 'family breakdown, educational failure, economic dependence, indebtedness and addiction' (Centre for Social

Justice, 2006, p 15). Low pay was not included. It followed that 'social' housing tenants living in areas where poverty was concentrated must be experiencing 'pathways to poverty', and given their spatial proximity, the interrelatedness of these characteristics would compound the problem. Later, *Breakthrough Britain: Housing Poverty* declared that 'the level of dependency among social housing renters is quite staggering' and that 'this is not a situation that will resolve itself. How can we expect different from people who never see anything different?' (Centre for Social Justice, 2008, p 5). It recommended 'Housing Managers should be actively involved in the improvement of service delivery, becoming specialists in meeting people's support needs and acting as advocates for social and economic mobility; enabling people to realise their aspirations' (Centre for Social Justice, 2008, p 110).

However, Cameron was under pressure to mitigate his party's 'nasty' image and the 2010 Conservative Party manifesto did not include specific behaviour controls. Indeed, it included the promise to 'respect the tenures and rents of social housing tenants' (Conservative Party, 2010, p 76). The manifesto also included pledges to give equity stakes to 'good' social tenants, and to create a 'Right to Move'.

Despite the promise to 'respect the tenures and rents of social housing tenants' included in the 2010 Conservative Party manifesto, the Coalition government continued to push the 'residual' model of local authority housing. *Laying the Foundations: A Housing Strategy for England* (HM Government, 2011, p ix) stated that 'Social housing must both provide the support that people need, when they need it, and be a springboard for social mobility, rather than trapping people into patterns of worklessness and benefit dependency'.

Axing financial support for 'Tenant's Voice' marked a step away from regarding tenants as 'citizen-consumers', and, reported in *The Sun* (2012) as 'Council House Boot for the Rich', Grant Shapps, then Minister for Housing, announced that council tenants with a household income of £60,000 would have to pay the full market rent for their accommodation or face eviction. Perhaps due to Liberal Democrat influence, this requirement was not made mandatory. From April 2012, local authorities were allowed to offer 'flexible' tenancies lasting from two to five years, indicating that should a tenant's economic circumstances improve or behaviour become problematic during the tenancy, renewal would not be offered. Although primarily a cost-cutting measure, changes to the Housing Benefit system under new 'underoccupancy' rules – the 'bedroom tax' – can also be seen as an attempt to push tenants away from local authority housing. There was 14% benefit cut if tenants had one extra bedroom and a 25%

reduction for two or more extra bedrooms. A study commissioned by the government found that only 4.5% of the 570,000 households affected by the 'spare room subsidy' cuts were able to move to a smaller property and 59% of those hit by the tax – 300,000 tenants – were in rent arrears and hence in danger of eviction (DWP, 2014). These findings produced a U-turn from the Liberal Democrats, who had fully supported the 'bedroom tax', with Danny Alexander, Chief Secretary to the Treasury, suggesting that the only people in the 'social' rented sector who should suffer a cut were those who had turned down a suitable smaller home offer. Moreover, disabled adults should be 'permanently exempt' from the tax (BBC News, 2014).

The 'residual' social housing model was accompanied by an attempt to redefine poverty as a behavioural issue on the lines suggested by the Centre for Social Justice in 2006. One proposed new measure – 'lives in poor housing or a troubled area' – was prefaced by the remark: 'The young kids are always outside, even in the snow and the rain, their house is not their sanctuary, it's something to escape' (Secretary of State for Work and Pensions, 2012, p 30).

Local authority new-build: Coalition controversy

New housing construction remained in the doldrums under the Coalition government and the need to boost housing supply encouraged the Liberal Democrats in the Coalition to enlist local government as a partner in a housing drive. The Liberal Democrat Party's 2010 manifesto stated that the party would 'Investigate reforming public sector borrowing requirements to free councils to borrow money against their assets in order to build a new generation of council homes, and allow them to keep all the revenue from these new homes' (Liberal Democrats, 2010, p 78).

The 2010 Conservative manifesto was silent on the matter, but although the Conservatives rejected relaxing central constraints on borrowing, the idea of revising Housing Revenue Accounts to provide more local government autonomy was included in the Coalition's 'Our Programme for Government' (HM Government, 2010, p 12). The 2010 Spending Review confirmed that the government would reform the Housing Revenue Account on the principles set out by New Labour, but for four years, the Treasury would retain a proportion of Right to Buy receipts. The new system started in 2012. Previously, via a complicated mechanism, any surplus on a particular local authority housing revenue account was taken by the Treasury to redistribute to those local authorities with a deficit, with any remainder retained by the Treasury. Under the new scheme, the housing debt owed by local authorities was pooled and redistributed according to a negotiated formula. It was argued that local authorities, having paid interest on the redistributed debt, would be able to retain their rental income and use their asset base to build new homes. Much depended on the pooled debt share attributed to a specific authority and any Treasury caps on borrowing. Reflecting Conservative resistance to new local authority building, the borrowing caps were stringent. Rifts between Liberal Democrats and Conservatives became public when Vince Cable, Business Secretary in the Coalition government, declared that 'Tory dogma' was preventing councils from building thousands of homes (Apps, 2013). Local authority housing starts in England marked time under the Coalition government, declining slightly from 1,640 in 2010/11 to 1,550 in 2012/13. However, the Chancellor's 'Autumn Statement' (HM Treasury, 2014a) revealed a compromise between the Liberal Democrats and the Conservatives. Borrowing caps on local authorities would be lifted by enough to allow 10,000 new homes to be built but, reflecting Conservative antagonism, impediments were put in place: the resources would be released via competitive bidding; partnerships with housing associations had to be formed; high-value council homes had to be sold; a £100-million fund would be set up to help council tenants access mortgage finance; and Right to Buy agents would be appointed to facilitate Right to Buy take-up.

Although local authority new house-building in England was higher under the Coalition government than under New Labour, very few local authority homes were built and the promise that there would be one-to-one replacement of council houses sold under the 'revitalised' Right to Buy was not kept. By mid-2015, 30,000 council homes had been sold in the three years since Right to Buy discounts increased, but only an estimated 3,337 replacements, financed by sales, had started (Apps, 2015a).

The 2015 Conservative government

All political parties now merge local authority and housing association housing into the category 'social housing', making it difficult to identify specific manifesto commitments on the local authority sector. However, the Conservatives' core attitude to council housing was evident in its 2015 manifesto commitment to granting a Right to Buy to housing association tenants financed by forcing local authorities to sell their high-value properties. Free from Liberal Democrat constraint, the Conservative government introduced a mandatory 'Pay to Stay' scheme.

Tenants with a threshold household income of £40,000 and above in London, and £30,000 and above in the rest of England, would be required to pay a market or near-market rent for their accommodation. Rents would be tapered towards the market level by tenants paying an extra 20 pence (reduced to 15 pence through amendments in the House of Lords) for every pound of extra income above the threshold.

Conclusion

Historically, mainstream Conservative Party opinion, buttressed by the financial institutions, has regarded local authorities as the residual element in the housing system – useful to boost production in times of severe housing stress and to advance the sanitary agenda, but ripe for eclipse in 'normal' times. However, not all Conservative opinion has been opposed to council housing. Harold Macmillan, under pressure from his party, reluctantly switched local authorities away from 'general needs' housing provision, and as Prime Minister, he exhorted Sir Keith Joseph to return to the '1951–54' spirit. Some Conservative-controlled local authorities have supported council housing, as revealed in their reluctance to sell their housing and in the way they pioneered voluntary stock transfer to specially created housing associations, usually their former Housing Department, in an attempt to retain low-cost housing in their areas (see Chapters Five and Seven).

Labour Party members, not always supported by the leadership, have championed council housing. Nationwide, council housing has often made a surplus for the Treasury – £113.2 million in 2009/10 (Wilson, W., 2011, p 11) – despite the assets sold under the Right to Buy at substantially discounted prices. The high-rise, 'modernist' era did massive damage to council housing's image, as Labour's National Executive recognised in 1978:

> While these form only a part of the total public housing stock, there is no doubt that conditions on such estates cause considerable hardship to the tenants concerned, and can be exploited politically to foist a second-rate image onto public housing as a whole. (Labour Party National Executive, 1978, p 1)

Nonetheless, despite this representation problem and mounting local authority difficulties in managing their council houses, there was a good supply of decent homes available for low-cost renting. Commenting on the Right to Buy, Murie (2014, p 146) states: 'Privatisation would prove popular because what the state had built was popular'.

In 1997, with its quality housing and its assets stripped by the Right to Buy, a serious repair problem and an aura associated with 'Tower and Slab' (Urban, 2011), council housing was well on the way to the 'welfare' model familiar in the US. New Labour regarded council housing as 'Old Labour's' defunct product. Its strategy was to assimilate council housing and housing associations into a grouping labelled 'social housing', to promote transfer within this category, and to attempt to revamp the image of 'social' housing' by 'choice-based' lettings and a refurbishment programme based on the 'decent homes' idea. However, the image problem of local authority housing remains.

The patrician Tory element has almost disappeared and a 'welfare' approach now dominates Conservative thinking. Even at a time when ministers recognised a dearth in housing supply, they preferred to stimulate the private rented sector rather than relax controls on local authority borrowing to finance significant housing investment. These borrowing restrictions were a reason why local authorities were unable to replace houses sold under the 'one-for-one' replacement promise when the Right to Buy was 'reinvigorated'. The Conservative Party promotes a representation of council housing tenants as 'dependants' in need of 'over-parenting', a caricature supported by some newspapers. Frequent negative headlines appear, such as 'One in Five Council House Tenants Is on the Fiddle (and It Could Be Costing Taxpayers £13bn)' (*Daily Mail*, 2012a), 'My Big Fat Gypsy Council House' (*The Sun*, 2011) and 'Dole Queen Heather Frost Might Not Even Want Custom-Built Six-Bedroom Council' (*The Sun*, 2013). Recently, television has entered the 'poverty porn' arena via programmes – fictional or allegedly factual – such as *Shameless, Benefits Street, We All Pay for Your Benefits* and *The Scheme*. Savage et al (2015, p 335) note:

> On the social networking site Facebook there is a facility where you can send 'council estate' gifts to your friends. The most popular council estate gift is an image of young people in sportswear titled 'mob of chav scum': 824,000 people have sent this 'gift' to their friends on the site and this is followed by images such as 'piss-stained phone box' and 'rundown community centre'.

Such representations have done as much to harm the aura of council housing as Leonard Rossiter's Rupert Rigsby portrayal in the 1970s' sitcom *Rising Damp* did to damage private landlordism's image.

Further reading

Cowan, D. and McDermont, M. (2006) *Regulating Social Housing: Governing Decline*, Abingdon: Routledge.

Crossman, R. (1975) *The Diaries of a Cabinet Minister. Volume One: Minister of Housing 1964–66*, London: Hamish Hamilton and Jonathan Cape.

Dunleavy, P. (1981) *The Politics of Mass Housing in Britain: A Study of Corporate Power and Professional Influence in the Welfare State*, Oxford: Clarendon Press.

Glendinning, M. and Mulhesius, S. (1994) *Tower Block: Modern Public Housing in England, Scotland, Wales and Northern Ireland*, New Haven, CT: Yale University Press.

MacCrae, N. (1958) *A Nation of Council Tenantry*, London: Rented Homes Campaign.

Ridley, N. (1992) *'My Style of Government': The Thatcher Years*, London: Hutchinson.

Shapely, P. (2007b) *The Politics of Housing: Power, Consumer and Urban Culture*, Manchester: Manchester University Press.

SEVEN

Bending the 'Third Arm': politicians and housing associations

In the 1960s and 1970s, it became conventional to refer to housing associations as housing's 'third arm'. Neither private, for-profit, trading bodies, nor elected local authorities, associations were seen as suited to accommodating people with 'special needs' and operating in 'niche markets', especially reconditioning inner-city properties. Their independence from local electoral politics meant that they could assist controversial groups, such as ex-prisoners, and campaign on housing issues. Diversity in their volunteer management committees and the housing needs they met were regarded as great strengths. All the major parties supported housing associations but for different reasons. The Liberal Party viewed them as an element in the path to a participatory democracy. The Conservative Party perceived housing associations as an alternative to local authorities, whereas, in the 1970s, 'old' Labour looked to associations, with their growing radical dimension, as vehicles to 'socialise' private landlordism. New Labour regarded them as a 'social entrepreneur' substitute for the discredited council house sector. In 1974, housing associations owned 1.5% of the housing stock in England. This had increased to 10.1% by 2014, with much of this expansion occurring after 1988 as council house-building was restricted and stock transfer from local government was encouraged.

Hybrids

Czischke (2014, p 26) has defined housing associations as 'social purpose organisations, not owned by the State which operate on a non-profit basis'. They work between the state, communities and the market. Chevin (2013, p 62) has described them as 'social hearted and commercially minded'.

The Housing Act 1935 gave the generic term 'housing association' to organisations previously known under assorted labels, including 'housing trusts', 'housing societies' and 'public utility societies'. The Housing Act 1936 supplied a lengthy housing association definition, its essential features being an organisation for 'constructing, improving or managing or facilitating or encouraging housing for the working class', and with dividend rates controlled by the Treasury, they excluded profit-making for shareholder distribution. Associations were diverse in their legal status and objectives. Charitable almshouses, mainly for the elderly poor, dated back to 12th century and, at times, attracted politically controversy, as revealed in Anthony Trollope's *The Warden* (2004 [1855]). There were charitable trusts, such as Guinness and Peabody, and model dwelling companies wanting to demonstrate that they could supply decent homes for the poor with a return limited to 5% – historically deemed 'fair' (Piketty, 2014). Sometimes established as 'industrial housing companies', employers provided an assortment of dwellings, ranging from high-quality housing in Bournville, Saltaire and Port Sunlight, to the more basic accommodation supplied by colliery- and mill-owners, sometimes with a 'company store' monopoly. By the 1920s, the mine-owners held 180,000 houses, many via an umbrella organisation, the Industrial Housing Association, with the capital provided by the colliery companies and loans from the Public Works Loan Commissioners.

Although most employers resisted interference in their employees' domestic life, a few enthusiastically embraced surveillance, with, for example, the cotton firm Henry and Edward Ashworth declaring:

> We exercise control and superintendence over them for their moral and social improvement. The state and cleanliness of their rooms, their bedding and furniture are very minutely examined and the condition of their children, their income and habits of life, are carefully enquired into, and remarks thereon are entered in books. (Quoted in Factory Inquiry Commission, 1834, p 283)

This scrutiny contributed to unpopularity among the politically aware working class. As Mitchell (2010, p 84) comments:

> Provision of housing was a useful tool of the employers for exercising social control, as eviction was a powerful weapon. This was used most often to break strikes, and the dominance of tied houses in the Lanarkshire iron industry meant that it was almost impossible to develop trade unions, fight for decent wages and improve conditions of labour.

Housing cooperatives

Working-class people, often with Liberal Party connections, promoted housing cooperatives. As leader of the co-partnership housing movement, Henry Harvey Vivian, a carpenter and Liberal politician, set up a company to develop housing cooperatives, with shareholders, including tenants, and other investors in the venture. Fifty 'co-partnership' societies have been identified, the Ealing Tenants' Cooperative Society, formed in 1901, with tenants having eight seats on the Board of 11, being the best known. Garden cities can be added to the housing association inventory, for example, First Garden City Ltd, in which all its residents were shareholders, ran Letchworth. Housing's 'third arm' capacity for innovation was demonstrated by the building of a few complexes in the first garden cities based on Charlotte Perkin Gilman's ideas about abolishing women's domestic labour. These residences incorporated shared domestic, recreational and dining arrangements.

Housing the poor?

Housing association diversity contributed to endorsement across the political spectrum. The Conservatives liked their philanthropic dimension, whereas Labour was partial to their mutual, cooperative and non-profit component, albeit suspicious about the control involved in employer-provided houses, wary of the 'lady bountifuls' and sometimes accusing model dwelling companies of profiteering from housing need. To the Liberals, housing associations exemplified the diverse, 'associative' society that promoted character development.

Housing societies continued to develop up to the First World War – using 1911 Census returns, Spensley (1918) estimated that in Greater London, the trusts and companies owned 107,343 'rooms' – but associations had limitations as a response to the 'housing famine'. In 1914, they held less than 1% of the housing stock and their houses were concentrated in London, there being little provision in the North and Midlands. Moreover, the model dwelling companies failed in their attempt to demonstrate that the lowest-income groups could be housed with a 5% return to investors. Morris (2001, p 528) claims investors obtained a sound return, quoting Lord Stanley, echoing the Liberal Party view that any subsidy was a 'dole', as saying that 5% represented 'a fair and equal bargain between man and man for there was no sacrifice of independence on either side'.

Although, on occasion, the model dwelling companies received free land from aristocratic landowners, enabling them to house low-paid workers, some chose to provide artisan accommodation to 'add to the reputation of the neighbourhood' (Wohl, 1977, p 145). Even the charitable associations, with large endowments, attempting to obtain a 3.5% return on investment, struggled to house the poorest. Most properties built by charitable trusts and model dwelling companies were let to the middle and upper echelons of the working class, such as policemen, skilled and semi-skilled workers, and clerks. Charles Booth's (1969 [1902]) London survey revealed that 38.7% of London's population were 'poor', 'very poor' or 'lowest' but only 23.5% of 'philanthropic and semi-philanthropic' homes were inhabited by people in these categories. Perhaps housing low-income households was not the real intention. Stedman Jones (1992, p xx) maintains 'the separation of the respectable working class from the residuum had been a preoccupation of liberal theorists ever since the 1860s'. Part of the housing association rationale was to detach the 'respectable' worker from the influences of 'the semi-criminal class [who] … are the destructive class' (Royal Commission on the Housing of the Working Class, 1885, p 16).

The failure to house the poorest households generated internal politics within the housing association movement. Housing associations allowed middle-class women to enter the 'public' domain, albeit in the restricted 'domestic' domain. Octavia Hill built a considerable reputation for her 'female' expertise in 'housing management'. She claimed that refurbishing older property to minimum standards and good housing management were more appropriate responses to the needs of low-income groups than new-build. New-build advocates increasingly relied on 'filtering' theory to justify their activities (see Chapter Three).

Expensive inner-city land, plus a paternalistic approach, even to the 'labour aristocracy', produced Spartan accommodation in multi-storey buildings, with the tenants overseen by 'superintendents' or 'lady housing visitors'. Rules were strict – the main doors were locked at 11 pm and the gas lighting turned off. *Punch* satirised this 'over-parent' approach. Its 'Hints to Visiting and Relief Societies' advised:

> Having entered a poor person's dwelling, behave as if it were your own…. Make them tell you what they do with their rags; and how they are situated with regard to soap. Insist on being minutely informed how each of the family spends

every portion of his or her time…. Go home to your three courses and dessert. (*Punch*, 1844, p 108)

Housing association politics between the wars

In 1918, Christopher Addison – as befits a Liberal Party member, with its history of supporting 'voluntary action' – set up a committee to examine ways to channel finance to housing associations. In the event, financial assistance to housing associations under the Housing Act 1919 was less generous than to local government and, at first, associations were hampered by the need to use local authorities as intermediates in applying for central assistance. Ending this requirement in 1924 produced a flurry of housing association activity, with the formation of new associations such as Kensington Housing Trust in 1924 and, in 1928, Liverpool Improved Homes. Nevertheless, housing associations found it difficult to sustain a housing programme. For example, Manchester Housing Limited raised capital at 2.5% to build affordable homes for labourers but only managed to construct 52 houses. Associations received no mandatory rate contributions from local government, meaning higher rents.

Some Conservatives, concerned about the suburban council housing advance, were determined to halt its growth and the *Spectator* ran a sequence of articles warning against excessive local authority involvement in housing. In 1933, following a series of BBC radio broadcasts, Howard P. Marshall and Avice Trevelyan published *Slum*, in which they claimed that local authorities were 'exceedingly inefficient' and it was 'entirely wrong that housing and politics should be mixed together' (Marshall and Trevelyan, 1933, p 147). Their remedy was to establish a National Housing Corporation to supply accommodation via housing associations.

The Moyne Report

As 'general needs' subsidies to local authorities were ended, Hilton Young, the responsible minister, set up a committee chaired by Lord Moyne, a member of the Guinness Trust. Its remit included considering 'what, if any, further steps are necessary or desirable to promote the supply of houses for the working-classes, without public charge, through the agency of public utility societies or other bodies' (Moyne, 1933). Although searching for an alternative to local government to house the working classes, some Conservatives were also seeking a substitute for the slum landlord. Several Moyne Committee members had a low opinion of inner-city private landlords, regarding them as poor managers compared to Octavia Hill's 'lady housing visitors'. According to Lord Percy, a member of the Moyne Committee, the small property-owner had insufficient capital to develop his property and the 'evil could only be remedied by concentrating the management and development of large blocks of property in the hands of one agency' (quoted in Yelling, 1992, p 94). Percy's 'one agency' idea received support from Raymond Unwin, then President of the Royal Institute of British Architects, who suggested a National Board to be responsible for reconditioning and new-build. Unlike other 'Housing Corporation' ideas, intended to work through housing associations, Unwin's suggestion involved direct state housing supply, somewhat akin to the 2015 Conservative government's experiment in 'direct commissioning'. Unwin, Seebohm Rowntree and Lord Asquith formed a National Housing Committee to promote the National Board and the idea was taken up in the Labour Party's policy statement *Up with the Houses! Down with the Slums* (Labour Party, 1934).

Replacing local government?

It is possible to detect an attempted paradigm shift in the Moyne Committee's recommendations. Moyne concluded that in order to abate future commitments to slum clearance, local authorities should be granted compulsory powers to 'acquire, for reconditioning, working-class houses which are not in all respects fit for human habitation but can be made fit and to which a probable life of at least twenty years can be given' (Moyne, 1933, p 56).

Where an 'approved public utility society' existed, local authorities would acquire properties on behalf of the society, who would repair, improve and manage them. Moreover, in the absence of such a society, local government would be empowered to lease the houses to Housing Management Commissioners, 'with full discretion and independence in regard to the details of administration' (Moyne, 1933, p 56). To facilitate shifting housing societies' activity into older property rehabilitation, Moyne recommended setting up a Central Public Utility Council, with powers to promote and supervise 'approved' housing societies, and a central finance authority to make advances to societies. In addition, it anticipated that in urban areas containing working-class houses capable of improvement, many dwellings would be overcrowded and recommended that local authorities should be able to acquire overcrowded properties to sell on to housing associations.

Unsurprisingly, given the antagonism from the private landlord lobby, the committee specifically rebuffed the notion that its national agency should be involved in new-build. Moyne's recommendations marked a return to the 19th-century version of local authority involvement in housing, that is, slum acquisition – to which overcrowding homes were added – but no long-term involvement in ownership and management. This would be a housing association activity. Indeed, Moyne commented that, in future, local authorities might consider transfer or leasing their existing estates to housing associations. Overall, Moyne's recommendations anticipated stock transfer and an enhanced role for housing associations, to be implemented in the 1980s and 1990s.

The Moyne proposals met with staunch opposition from the 'big guns' in housing provision. Local government objected to the major cutback in its housing role but animosity also came from private developers resenting potential competition, albeit only in the inner cities. Hilton Young, the Health Minister, discarded Moyne's main recommendations. A note to the Treasury from the Ministry of Health explained why the civil servants objected to the Moyne proposals: 'Public Utility Societies have done excellent work.... But neither they, nor any other form of voluntary effort, provide a possible alternative to the powerful organisation of the local housing authorities for this or any other general housing purpose' (Ministry of Health, 1933).

Later, Sir Arthur Robinson (1933), Permanent Secretary to the Ministry of Health, voiced relief that his minister 'thought it right and possible to depart so far from Moyne'. He thought the contribution of housing associations to be 'a very small one' and 'ten years experience showed that they were neither efficient nor easy to deal with' and 'their members are not normally men of affairs'. To suggest 'that public utility societies should be put in a position to coerce local authorities was to suggest that the tail should swing the dinosaur'. He expressed concern about setting up a Central Public Utility Council because previous experience of such advisory bodies had proved 'singularly unfortunate in nearly every case'. According to Malpass (2001, p 233), associations had alienated support within the Ministry of Health by 'making persistent representations, complaining that they had been badly treated and pleading for further assistance'.

As Murie (2008, p 52) states, rejecting Moyne's strategy meant that 'housing associations were almost wholly dependent on local government if they wanted to look beyond charitable and other private sources of finance to fund their building'. Only a few local authorities

– notably, Birmingham with regard to improvement – worked through housing associations.

The North Eastern Housing Association was set up in County Durham in 1936 under measures taken to ameliorate the problems in 'special areas' experiencing high unemployment rates, and a similar organisation was established in Scotland (see Chapter Nine). Central government awarded grants to the North Eastern Housing Association, unavailable to local government, and 100% Treasury loans were on offer. By 1939, it had built 7,500 houses despite strong opposition from many local authorities in the area. A rationale for the North Eastern Housing Association was that authorities in depressed areas were unable to afford the rate contribution to council housing but many local authority councillors regarded it as a 'stalking horse' for reducing local authority involvement in housing supply (Malpass and Jones, 1996).

Cost-rent and co-ownership societies

In 1945, Bevan firmly rejected a 1944 Labour Party Conference proposal to set up a Housing Corporation to improve housing delivery and he resisted a scheme put forward by Douglas Jay, Atlee's Private Secretary, for a national housing agency to commission houses where local authorities were failing (Thomas-Symonds, 2014). After the Second World War, associations developed slowly in 'niche' areas such as providing accommodation for elderly people. However, the failure of the Rent Act 1957 prompted new Conservative thinking. In the early 1960s, an attempt was made to stimulate 'cost-rent' and 'co-ownership' schemes without direct subsidy but with loan capital available at a preferential rate. A 1963 White Paper, announcing a Housing Corporation, stated: 'Since the war there has been almost no building to let other than by public authorities. The result is a gap in housing provision; and this the Government intend to see filled' (MHLG, 1963, p 7). In Cabinet, Enoch Powell opposed establishing a Housing Corporation and reliance on the voluntary sector, arguing that 'A prospective 15,000 houses by 1967 are not worth the risk of this initiative proving a failure or the objections to creating a new state-guaranteed agency to do the job of private enterprise without profit' (Powell, 1963, paras 7, 8).

Housing Minister Sir Keith Joseph countered with the argument that Labour's policy on private landlord municipalisation was having a political impact, stating that 'We believe that the ever-increasing municipalisation is a bad thing; but we must provide our alternative'

(Joseph, 1963). Backed by Harold Macmillan, Joseph's view prevailed. Labour adopted the Housing Corporation idea and continued developing cost-rent and co-ownership societies.

'Cost-rent' societies were formed by developers and 'exchange professionals', such as solicitors and estate agents, who let the accommodation at cost price, without making a profit other than, of course, the fees charged by the 'exchange professionals' for their services. The idea underlying 'co-ownership societies' was that a sponsoring 'parent' society would develop and manage a housing scheme later to be owned collectively by the occupiers, who would appoint a management committee to oversee the managing agent's activities. Members would be both collective owners and individual tenants and if they left the scheme after a minimum period of residence, they became entitled to a premium reflecting the paid mortgage and any enhanced value.

Very few cost-rent homes were built because increases in interest rates in the 1960s made the rents too high and the Treasury resisted attempts to allow the cost-rent societies to claim the tax relief on mortgage interest available to owner-occupiers. Co-ownership societies had more impact because the co-owners were able to benefit from tax relief on mortgage interest, and many cost-rent schemes were later converted to co-ownership. However, the cooperative principles, imported from Scandinavia and alleged to have underpinned the UK initiative, appear to have had little influence. According to O'Hara (2012, p 6), 'Ministers were not interested ... in any attempt to embed co-operative societies in the British housing system'. Research by Clapham and Kintrea (1987, pp 157–8) led them to conclude that 'the management was often remote, unaccountable and inefficient', with 'a sense of residents' control almost totally absent'. Many co-owners 'failed to appreciate that they actually owned the houses themselves and management existed to serve them', regarding the tenure as akin to private renting. In the early 1980s, most co-ownership schemes were wound up, with the stock sold to their members.

'Genuine' cooperatives

To the cooperative enthusiast, Joseph's so-called 'co-ownership societies' were not authentic: cooperatives had to involve participation and a mutuality spirit. There are a number of variations on 'genuine' cooperatives but in par value co-ops – the purest form – members have only a nominal equity share, whereas in a co-ownership co-op, members can benefit from increases in property values.

'Genuine' cooperatives received a boost when Reg Freeson became Minister for Housing in 1974. Freeson had been involved in founding co-ops in London and wanted to develop the sector. He commissioned a Working Party on Housing Co-operatives and enabled common ownership co-ops to register with the Housing Corporation. Tenant management co-ops were encouraged and, later, short-life co-ops aimed at repairing rundown property could obtain resources from the Housing Corporation. The Working Party on Housing Co-operatives (DoE, 1975) recommended that a national organisation should be set up to act as a co-op promoter and a Co-operative Housing Agency was launched in 1976 under the Housing Corporation, with the intention that as co-operatives developed, they should become independent. Co-ops gained impetus but the Co-operative Housing Agency was closed in 1978 and par value co-op development lost momentum (Hands, 2015). The post-1979 Conservative governments and New Labour – despite its 'Third Way' mantra – showed little interest in promoting par value co-ops.

Consensus politics?

In the early 1970s, there appeared to be a consensus between the two main parties that greater housing association involvement in housing supply was desirable. The Conservatives were now desperate to find an alternative to local government to supply rented homes and the Housing Finance Act 1972 represented a step towards achieving this objective. Rent allowances made letting from a housing association more affordable to low-income groups. Labour saw merit in promoting housing associations as a mechanism for providing low-cost homes in Tory-controlled local authority areas, taking over accommodation from the private landlord, especially in 'stress areas', and as a more flexible delivery agent than local government. Anthony Crosland (1962) recommended more housing association involvement in housing supply but, at the time, associations had a somewhat conservative ethos, with Fée (2008) suggesting this as a reason why the Conservatives promoted their enhanced involvement.

Many Labour-controlled local authorities were suspicious of housing associations, regarding them as land competitors and 'a "fifth wheel to the local authority coach" or as an out-of-date and redundant form of housing provision' (Cullingworth, 1973, p 62). However, in the late 1960s, a different housing association breed started to emerge, often financed by Shelter, which had received large donations following the broadcast of *Cathy Come Home* in 1966.

Called the 'new philanthropists', these associations, more radical than traditional associations, were concerned with inner cities, opposed to the 'fee-grabbing' cost-rent and 'co-ownership societies' and had 'social movement' characteristics – 'not a mere housing sector, but a cause' (Young, 2001, p 89). Shelter, under Des Wilson's leadership, set the tone, combining service provision with vigorous political campaigning, much to the Charity Commissioners' distress (Wilson, D., 2011). Labour started to give associations extra encouragement, with the Housing Subsidies Act 1967 providing payments to housing associations, unavailable to local government, to acquire properties in 'stress areas'. *Widening the Choice: The Next Steps in Housing* (DoE, 1973), published by the Conservative government, set out proposals to lessen the 'polarisation' between homeownership and renting from a local authority via a strengthened Housing Corporation, and these proposals were incorporated into a Bill introduced into Parliament. The incoming Labour government adopted the Bill and it became the Housing Act 1974. The Act introduced new forms of assistance to housing associations. Housing Association Grant (HAG) – renamed Social Housing Grant (SHA) in 1996 – met any gap between the actual costs of a new scheme and the 'fair rents' set by rent officers, whereas Revenue Deficit Grant (RDG) dealt with any problems on housing association balance sheets. Only associations registered with the Housing Corporation, with its duty to supervise registered housing associations, could receive grants. Labour's reliance on housing associations was motivated, in part, by an attempt to boost housing production without the borrowing counting as public expenditure. The Housing Corporation Finance Company Limited was set up to borrow from the banks and to channel the funds via the Housing Corporation to housing associations, with – because it was a private company – its debts not counting as public spending. Unfortunately, the company lost money and had to be absorbed into the Housing Corporation, with its debts returning to 'public spending' (Barnett, 1982). Boosted by extra resources supplied to the Housing Corporation and good protection against insolvency, the housing association new-build programme accelerated, reaching 17,392 in 1977/78. Much housing association activity was focused on improving older property in 'stress areas': in 1978/79, 12,318 houses were rehabilitated.

Market politics

The election of a Conservative government in 1979, committed to culling quasi-autonomous non-governmental organisations ('quangos'), promoting homeownership, further cutting public expenditure, boosting public housing sales and introducing market principles into the public sector, promised testing times for housing associations. As the fourth-largest 'quango', the Housing Corporation was vulnerable to a cull, but it survived, albeit at the cost of staff reductions. Housing association properties were included in the Bill aimed at facilitating 'public' housing sales via the Right to Buy, but following intense lobbying in the House of Lords, charitable housing associations were excluded from the Housing Act 1980, much to the chagrin of the Housing Minister. Murie (2008, p 151) reports:

> John Stanley [the Housing Minister] had insisted that the dying and wounded were assembled in the House for the vote in order to win it. When told of the result he apparently said: 'Thank goodness for that', but he had evidently misunderstood because the vote was 286 against and 186 for. When this was pointed out to him it was said he went ballistic and was unapproachable for two hours.

The Thatcher government viewed housing associations as part of the 'public sector'. State assistance insulated them from market pressures and their borrowing contributed to public debt. In cash terms, spending by the Housing Corporation remained constant between 1982/83 and 1988/89 but higher costs produced a 33% fall in new completions despite housing association willingness – rapidly adapting to their new political masters – to become involved in schemes to stimulate homeownership. When Secretary of State for the Environment, Michael Heseltine promoted a number of low-cost homeownership initiatives, including an innovative scheme allowing people to identify a derelict property and renovate it with grants from the Housing Corporation. Shared ownership schemes – with owners sharing equity with a housing association and perhaps stair-casing to full ownership (Lund, 2017) – became an enduring feature of the Housing Corporation's housing programme.

The Housing Act 1988

The Housing Act 1988 marked a watershed in the history of housing associations and helped to change their ethos. Purkis (2010, p 9) comments:

There was for some a feeling akin to being floated on the stock exchange. Suits, smart cars and higher salaries appeared swiftly, and for bold spirits this was a time of pumping adrenalin as the sector found itself in pole position as the preferred developer of social housing.

The thinking underlying the Act was set out in *Housing: The Government's Proposals* (DoE, 1987). In future, housing associations would raise most of their capital finance from the private sector. All rents – local authority, private landlord and housing association – would float to market levels, with a more selective system of Housing Benefit protecting low-income households. Although the government did not use the term, a 'quasi-market' was to be created in rented accommodation, with Housing Benefit acting as form of voucher for use by a low-income tenant to choose between landlords. Higher rents would make loans from the private sector more attractive to the financial institutions. Thus, under a government intent on restricting public expenditure, associations obtained a major advantage over local authorities – because their debt was labelled 'private', they had greater access to capital. The price was exposure to risk, regarded by the Treasury as essential to the classification of housing associations as 'independent'. Associations would let their homes under the same legal regime as private landlords. They would compete for public grants by submitting a resource bid that achieved the desired government objectives with the lowest cost to the state. They would shoulder the financial consequences of their bids.

The new regime created divisions within the National Federation of Housing Associations (NFHA), with a faction enthusiastic about the new opportunities; indeed, some associations had pioneered private finance use before the 1988 Act and lobbied government for greater freedoms to tap private sector resources. Others were concerned that higher rents would be unaffordable to tenants. The government rejected pleas from the NFHA for a distinct housing association tenure with a tenant right to an 'affordable' rent.

After an early stumble due to a failure to anticipate committed schemes' costs, the new regime settled down. Helped by Section 106 agreements under the Town and Country Planning Act 1990, greater access to private finance, a reduction in land and building costs, and extra government resources granted as part of John Major's 'housing rescue package', new completions in the sector reached 30,849 in England in 1994. The cost was higher rents and a larger Housing

Benefit bill, with the proportion of tenants claiming the benefit rising from 53% to 69% between 1992 and 1997.

'Social' housing

The mounting Housing Benefit bill produced a policy change, with the move to market rents halted. The Housing Corporation started to try to influence rent levels by taking into account 'total government subsidy' – including Housing Benefit payments – when assessing bids. Later, *Our Future Homes: Opportunity, Choice, Responsibility* announced: 'We need to strike the right balance between getting more homes by keeping grant down and the risks of benefit dependency and the benefit costs of higher rent levels' (DoE and the Welsh Office, 1995, pp 10, 27). Linking housing associations to private landlords as part of the 'independent rented' sector went on the backburner; associations were now bonded to local authorities as 'social' rent suppliers, although 'social' rent was not defined. As a symbol that the Conservative Party had not totally abandoned the idea that housing association tenants should have a Right to Buy, a Right to Acquire was introduced in the Housing Act 1996. This gave housing association tenants a statutory right to acquire their homes at a discount on the open market value. However, ranging from £9,000 to £16,000, the markdowns were much lower than council housing discounts.

Stock transfer

As explained in Chapter Six, transfer under 'Tenant's Choice' was an abject failure and Housing Action Trusts were slow to develop. In contrast, voluntary stock transfer, an unanticipated outcome of Ridley's housing policy, was a success. Voluntary stock transfer was not new. In the early 1980s, Knowsley Council transferred 3,000 homes to Stockbridge Village Trust, Glasgow City Council set up a number of community-based associations to receive some of its stock and Oldham sold a proportion of its houses to private developers and housing associations for refurbishment and subsequent sales. However, a more robust stock transfer wave started in 1988 when Chiltern District Council transferred its entire 4,650 stock to the newly established Chiltern Hundreds Housing Association. Other local authorities, initially based in the South and Conservative-controlled, followed Chiltern's initiative. Such councils saw advantages in transfers because they had paid off most of the original stock loans and could use the capital receipts for local amenities. The ability to keep low-cost housing in their neighbourhood – housing association tenants did not have the Right to Buy – was also a factor in the decisions. Although there was no legal requirement for a tenant ballot on a transfer, a local authority had to 'consult' the tenants and obtain central government approval. As local authority restrictions on council house spending became tighter and compulsory competitive tendering for housing management services started, larger authorities became more interested in stock transfer. Central government was surprised and apprehensive about these voluntary transfers, suspecting that 'whole stock' transfers might lead to another local monopoly in rented housing for families and that 'transfers were effectively robbing the Treasury of revenue by putting rent surpluses beyond its reach' (Pawson, 2004, p 5). In 1993, a new regime was created to provide central government with greater control over the voluntary transfer process, with an annual programme limiting transfer size and a 'clawback' levy on the capital receipts flowing to local authorities.

The diversity and equality agenda

Diversity has been an important justification of housing associations as housing's 'third arm': they could meet special needs and involve, as decision-makers, people who may not be represented as elected local authority councillors. In the early 1980s, reports from academics and the Commission for Racial Equality highlighted racial discrimination in housing suppliers' activities, there were local anti-racist campaigns for improved access to housing and riots in 1981 and 1985. In this context, the Housing Corporation launched its Black and Minority Ethnic (BME) Housing Policy, directed to promoting BME associations to meet the housing requirements of minority communities, lever resources into disadvantaged neighbourhoods and encourage black leadership. The BME Housing Policy and subsequent initiatives helped to generate over 60 BME housing associations and is a good example of how housing's 'third arm' can demonstrate independence and innovation. However, the Housing Act 1988 required associations involved in development to have a secure asset base. Most minority ethnic associations, being relatively new, did not possess properties built at low cost to use as security on loans and were therefore at a disadvantage in the development process. The Housing Corporation encouraged minority ethnic associations to form partnerships with larger associations. BME National and Human Institute Project (2014, p 3) comment:

Some BME housing associations have thrived within group structures by taking advantage of the economies of scale offered, shared services and have realised internal transfer of housing.... Other BME housing associations were less fortunate in their choice of group and were subsequently wound down, their housing assimilated.

New Labour and 'social entrepreneurs'

New Labour was lukewarm on local government as a service provider; indeed, part of New Labour's identity was fashioned in response to alleged 'excesses' when the 'new urban left' and Militant Tendency – labelled the 'loony left' in some newspapers – controlled some local councils in the 1980s. Blair (1998, p 13) announced:

> The days of the all-purpose local authority that planned and delivered everything are gone. They are finished. Local authorities will still deliver some services but their distinctive leadership role will be to weave and knit together the contribution of the various local stakeholders.

Housing associations were a ready replacement for local government and, thus, in the housing association domain, power transfer from the Conservatives to New Labour was seamless. New Labour's 1997 manifesto (Labour Party, 1997) declared, 'We support a three-way partnership between the public, private and housing association sectors to promote good social housing', but with regard to new-build, the 'partnership' meant local authorities enabling housing associations.

The 2000 Green Paper *Quality and Choice: A Decent Home for All* stated that New Labour desired:

> a progressive shift in ownership so that the stock is more widely owned by a range of different organisations, including housing associations, local housing companies and tenant-led organisations, with tenants benefiting from a greater choice of housing providers and local authorities focusing more on their strategic housing responsibilities. (DETR, 2000a, p 17)

In 2002, Blair announced:

> Our vision is bold ... we can open up the possibility
> of entrepreneurial organisations – highly responsive to
> customers and with the freedom of the private sector – but
> which are driven by a commitment to public benefit rather
> than purely maximising profits to shareholders. (Blair, 2002)

Blair's approach embraced housing's 'third arm', with 'hybrid' housing associations neatly fitting into New Labour's 'Third Way' rhetoric. Housing associations were quick to emphasise their 'social' credentials through the 'Housing Plus' notion: strengthening skills and employability, as well as supplying housing. New Labour promoted stock transfer through a number of stratagems. A 'decent home' standard was set, with stock transfer as a mechanism for achieving the benchmark, and debt write-off and capital grants were offered in areas where the stock was in poor condition. All 'social' sector rents would be set by a common formula, so the possibility of a lower rent in the council sector disappeared.

Defending council housing

Stock transfer met with resistance, often from within the Labour Party. Such resistance was organised by 'Defend Council Housing'. Bradley (2013, p 3) views this campaign group as an attempt to sustain latent support for a 'general needs' rather than 'residual' view of council housing, 'under circumstances unfavourable for political mobilisation, thus preventing the extinction of excluded and denigrated beliefs'. 'Defend Council Housing' demanded more investment in council housing and argued that transfer would mean higher rents, lower security and unaccountable landlords. This confrontation brought the concession of Arms Length Management Organisations (see Chapter Six), but despite some victories for the anti-stock transfer campaigners, the initiative gained momentum, helped by a large resource advantage favouring a 'yes' vote in transfer ballot campaigns. Under New Labour, almost a million dwellings were removed from local authority ownership via transfer, and by 2010, there were no council houses in almost half the local authorities in England and Wales.

New Labour welcomed housing associations as stock transfer participants but it cut resources for new-build. Initially, this was the outcome of Gordon Brown's judgement as shadow Chancellor that adopting the Conservatives' spending proposals would protect New Labour against 'profligate' public spending charges. Brown's decision produced a decline in housing association new-build completions in

England from 22,629 in 1996 to 15,590 in 2003. Housing associations fared better in subsequent New Labour spending reviews but new-build resources remained scarce due to New Labour's decision to concentrate finance on improving the existing 'social' housing stock. By 2008, new housing completions by housing associations had reached 24,150, and during the 'credit crunch', finance was increased in an attempt to keep house-building buoyant when building for homeownership was in sharp decline. Thus, housing association new-build, 24,350 in 2010, represented about 26% of new-build, compared to housing associations' 9% share in 2003. As under John Major's government in the early 1990s, New Labour used housing associations to try to stabilise the construction industry.

The changing nature of housing associations

Mullins (2010, p 3) detects 'distinct divisions in the housing association sector relating to scale, types of activity and value base with certain types of associations paying much greater attention to third sector identity and links with other community based organisations'. A trend for the housing association houses to become more concentrated in the larger associations – mainly through 'agglomeration' (Pawson and Sosenko, 2012) – continued in the 2000s. The largest associations became 'big businesses', with portfolios stretching over the country. In 2015, the chief executives of the 100 largest housing associations obtained 'remuneration packages' – excluding employer pension contributions – averaging £182,780, with the Places for People Chief Executive receiving £481,507 (McCabe, 2015). The major associations formed a pressure group called 'g15' to promote their interests.

Commercial

The transforming nature of the major players in the housing association sector was reflected in the title of Morag McDermont's (2010) book *Governing Independence and Expertise: The Business of Housing Associations*. As they adopted a more business culture, some housing associations became eager to ensure that their activities remained classified as 'private' to maintain their advantage in access to private sector capital. When the 2008 Housing and Regeneration Bill was introduced into Parliament, with its provisions for greater housing association regulation, the National Housing Federation unsuccessfully lobbied the House of Lords, arguing that enhanced regulation would impede associations' ability to lever in private finance (Mullins, 2010) if it produced sector reclassification.

Allegations that, in becoming more commercial, housing associations had forgotten their roots, had lost diversity and had become consumed by 'profits' become more common. For example, in *A Better Deal for Nation Rent*, Elphicke and Mercer (2014) revealed that housing association 'profits' had increased from £203 million in 2009 to £1.93 billion in 2013. They claimed that these profits had been diverted to commercial activities rather than to additional 'social' homes. The commercial activities were justified by housing associations as necessary to generate future finance for 'social' housing but doubts remained as to whether this would happen: would associations be content to become long-term commercial institutions operating on a 'market' basis? Indeed, in 2014, the Policy Exchange suggested that a new category of housing associations should be created, called 'free housing associations', able to substitute government grants for government equity stakes, and because, unlike grants, these equity stakes would not count as public spending, more statutory restrictions on their activities could be removed. Such 'free housing associations' would determine their own rent policies, sell off expensive social homes and be allowed to determine their own allocation policies, that is, they would behave more like private landlords (Walker, 2014).

Social

In contrast, there are those who wanted to see housing associations return to their 1960s' spirit. Hazel Blears, a former Secretary of State for Communities and Local Government, speaking at the launch of a ResPublica report, *Acting on Localism: The Role of Housing Associations in Driving a Community Agenda*, said:

> At first I thought housing associations were supposed to be bottom-up community organisations, but as I watched this movement develop, it was actually heart-breaking to see all the energy and passion drained out of them.... This report is reinvigorating that social passion. (Blears, 2012, quoted in Duncan, 2013, p 2)

Labour's left, reflecting a traditional element in the party opposed to housing associations as local authority replacements, strongly criticised 'modern' housing associations. Historically, many housing associations were constituted as Industrial and Provident Associations, with membership based on a nominal £1 share and, in theory, this grass-roots membership determining the Board's composition. In fact, like building societies, the broad membership has almost no influence on policy, and housing associations were characterised as 'self-perpetuating oligarchies', with, post-2003, board members eligible to be paid. Tenant engagement varied across the sector but was normally low and some associations retained a paternalistic approach to their tenants. For example, Yarlington Housing Group, managing 9,000 homes, introduced 'Household Ambition Plans'. Included in the 'ambitions' that tenants would be expected to achieve were 'skills and qualifications so that you stand a better chance of finding the type of job you want', 'skills for life', including 'cookery, gardening or DIY', and 'thinking about what you eat, how much exercise you take and other things that affect your health, wellbeing and fitness' (Yarlington Housing Group, quoted in Johnson, 2013). Progress in meeting such ambitions would be taken into account in tenancy renewal decisions.

In a Parliamentary debate on 5 May 2011, Jeremy Corbyn, MP for Islington North, declared that he did not perceive any accountability in the majority of housing associations, and in his housing manifesto for the 2015 Labour Party leadership election, he said:

> There is a problem with housing associations. Initially set up to provide decent homes for people in need, many are developing into businesses that sell or rent at market levels. We need more democracy and accountability, and a return to their original purpose. (Corbyn, 2015)

Social cohesion

The diversity agenda set by the Housing Corporation in the 1980s receded under New Labour. The official report on the 2001 riots in Oldham, Burnley and Bradford set out the polarisation in the areas in terms of education, housing and social and cultural networks, talking of communities leading 'a series of parallel lives' (Home Office, 2001, p 9). 'Community cohesion' rather than equality became the framing concept, and within this construction, BME housing associations could be seen as promoting separation rather than integration. Beider (2012, p 49) comments:

> Community cohesion shaped public policy after its introduction in 2001.... Since its inception, the number of black led housing associations fell to a historic low, the

representative umbrella organisation, FBHO [Federation of Black Housing Organisations], closed and the Housing Corporation did not instigate a new black and ethnic minority strategy.

The Coalition government

The Liberal Democrats were sidelined in the Department for Communities and Local Government (DCLG), with Conservatives appointed to the three main portfolios. In an attempt to counter the housing production slump, New Labour had increased the resources available to housing associations, but in keeping with its austerity agenda, the Coalition government cut grants for new housing association homes. Within the reduced allocation, the government anticipated that between 2011 and 2015, 80,000 'affordable' homes could be provided at a total public cost of £1.8 billion via lower upfront grants accompanied by higher rents. 'Affordable' now meant up to 80% of market rent, and in addition to new homes being 'affordable', a proportion of re-let homes would be rented at up to 80% of market rent. This policy had the hallmarks of Ridley's 1988 move to market rents, with Housing Benefit 'taking the strain'.

The distinction between 'affordable' rent and 'social' rent, set somewhat lower and 'owned by local authorities and private registered providers for which guideline target rents are determined through the national rent regime' (DCLG, 2012e, p 5), was reinforced in the Homes and Communities Agency's (2014) 'Affordable Homes Programme 2015–18'. It stated:

> Social rent provision will only be supported in very limited circumstances. Government policy does not support the argument that only rents at or close to social rent levels are capable of meeting local needs – particularly when support for housing costs through Housing Benefit and Universal Credit is taken into account. (Homes and Communities Agency, 2014, para 92)

In addition, providers would be required to maximise the number of void conversions to the 'affordable rent' model and to show that they were selling off expensive properties to fund new homes – an initiative that led to some tenants discovering that their homes had been sold to private landlords, who were demanding higher rents (*Guardian*, 2016). On a more positive note for housing associations, in 2012, when the Treasury became concerned about a stagnating economy, the government announced its Affordable Homes Guarantees Programme to guarantee up to £10 billion of debt at low interest rates to help housing providers expand 'affordable' rented house supply.

The 2015 Conservative government

The 2015 Conservative Party manifesto's flagship housing proposal was to extend the council tenants' Right to Buy to housing association tenants – an idea put forward by Davis and Field (2012) and the Policy Exchange (2014). To some, despite a compensation offer, this was the decisive test of housing association independence. With a workable majority, the Conservative government would have had little difficulty in securing House of Commons approval but the House of Lords might have been troublesome. Forcing independent organisations to sell their assets is a bold move, and in 1980, the House of Lords had rejected a tenant Right to Buy for charitable housing associations' tenants. The issue was 'the rights of charitable housing associations to hold their assets in perpetuity' (Murie, 2008, p 151). Associations had champions in the House of Lords, notably, Baron Kerslake of Endcliffe, Chair of the Peabody Trust and formerly Chief Executive of the Homes and Communities Agency, Permanent Secretary to the DCLG and Civil Service Head. However, in 2015, circumstances were different to 1980. Under the Salisbury Convention, the House of Lords does not hinder measures included in party manifestos. The 1979 Conservative Party manifesto made no firm commitment to a Right to Buy for housing association tenants, stating only that 'As far as possible, we will extend these rights [the Right to Buy] to housing association tenants. At the very least, we shall give these associations the power to sell to their tenants' (Conservative Party, 1979).

The 2015 manifesto commitment was far more explicit. Nonetheless, the House of Lords, with no Conservative majority, was in a defiant mood. It fired a warning shot on its distaste for the extended Right to Buy by voting in favour of a crossbench amendment to the Charities Bill seeking to ensure that charities were not 'compelled to use or dispose of their assets in a way which is inconsistent with their charitable purposes'. In his speech to the Liberal Democrat Party Conference in September 2015, Tim Farron, the Liberal Democrat's new leader, indicated that Liberal Democrat peers were prepared to ditch the Salisbury Convention and vote against the compulsory sale of housing association properties (Farron, 2015).

Undermining resistance

Osborne and Cameron started to 'soften up' opposition from housing associations to selling their properties. Media stories appeared lamenting housing associations' weak performance in supplying houses. Osborne dismissed the housing association house-building record as 'not particularly impressive ... four out of five housing associations built no properties last year, so I wouldn't say they are proving to be the dynamic source of new housing in the country at the moment' (quoted in Brown, 2015a). In response to a parliamentary question, David Cameron said:

> I think it's vital though that we reform housing associations and make sure that they are more efficient. Frankly they are a part of the public sector that hasn't been through efficiencies, haven't improved their performance and I think it's about time that they did. (Quoted in *Independent*, 2015)

When Cameron made this statement, housing associations were not officially part of the public sector but his announcement implied that he was 'relaxed' about reclassification. It would add £60 billion to the public sector debt, but might also create problems for housing associations in raising finance.

Agreement

In September 2015, Greg Clark put forward a settlement, based on an offer from David Orr, Chief Executive of the National Housing Federation (NHF), that housing associations should sell homes voluntarily. Clark outlined two views on the future of housing associations. The 'bad cop' narrative was:

> I'll be completely candid, there are some who say that to achieve the transformation we need requires a fresh start – that the housing association sector has taken us so far but might not be the right partner for the future.... That a once insurgent movement has become staid – with development too low and executive salaries too high. That for the transformation in housing we seek we should look elsewhere. To councils through the devolution agenda, to private developers, to our own agencies in government and to new entities. (Clark, 2015, p 2)

The 'good cop' version was:

> this is a sector that has scored big successes over many years. That can be agile and adaptable to the changing opportunities and requirements of our nation. A sector that has always been respectful of the mandate of that successive governments have had.... A view that this is a sector which is a standing army of expertise, motivation and experience, capable of building hundreds of thousands of new homes that our country so desperately needs. (Clark, 2015, p 2)

Clark indicated that he was a 'good cop', claiming that a voluntary agreement by housing associations with the government to sell homes at discounts available to council house tenants would promote cordial government–housing association relationships.

A large majority of housing associations voted for the settlement – 86% of NHF members, covering 93% of all housing association rented homes. However, although the largest associations all voted to accept the agreement, only 55% of NHF affiliates voted 'yes' – 39% did not vote. Housing associations' gains were the possible avoidance of a naked threat, unspecified new regulatory 'freedoms' and some guarantee of full compensation for Right to Buy sale deficits. The Conservative government had backtracked on the *legal* Right to Buy, promised in the 2015 manifesto, but achieved all its other aims. It avoided a possibly damaging confrontation with the House of Lords and sidestepped the accusation of selling assets it did not own – a precedent that Labour might have applied to private renting. Moreover, it gained the chance to manage 'Right to Buy' implementation in line with the resources raised from selling high-value council houses and reduced the possibility that £60 billion would be added to the public debt. Speaking to the 2015 Conservative Party Conference, Cameron (2015a) described Greg Clark as 'brilliant'. In the event, based on 2008 New Labour housing regulations, the Office for National Statistics did reclassify housing associations as part of the public sector. The Office for Budget Responsibility (2015, p 1) declared: 'When implemented, we estimate that this will increase borrowing by £1.4 billion to £4.6 billion a year and add 3.1 to 3.4 per cent of GDP [gross domestic product] to public sector net debt'. However, the government immediately announced plans to implement deregulatory measures to take housing associations off the public sector balance sheet 'as quickly as possible' (Brown, 2015b). Such deregulation will need to be radical to ensure reclassification and has prompted concern that the protection of housing association tenants' interests will be undermined (Wilcox, 2016).

Conclusion

The apparent political party consensus on housing associations in the 1960s and 1970s masked different objectives. Labour, attracted by the more radical associations, viewed them as mechanisms to take over the private landlord sector and perhaps as vehicles to secure low-cost housing in Tory-controlled areas. The Conservatives regarded associations as means to eclipse council housing and as an embryo new private landlord sector. However, housing associations have been 'players' as well as 'pawns' (Johnston, 2004). Their 'expertise' and 'hybrid' nature allowed them to shape the regulatory regimes governing their activities (McDermont, 2010), 'new philanthropy' campaigning in the 1960s and 1970s focused attention on inner-city housing, and, for a time, BME housing associations gave minority ethnic groups a stronger voice in housing supply. The larger associations had a role in the change towards greater reliance on private finance and the NFHA eventually succeeded in stalling the move towards market rents when John Major's government rebranded housing associations as 'social' housing alongside local authorities, rather than part of the 'independent' sector bracketed with private landlords. Under New Labour, the housing association sector expanded but a large proportion of this growth came via stock transfer, and as part of its housing association–local authority housing convergence policy, New Labour kept a tight rein on housing association rents.

The large cuts in grants to housing associations initiated by the Coalition government pushed housing association new-let rents up to 80% of market rents and the sector appeared to become yet more commercially oriented. The Montague Report (DCLG, 2012c, p 10) declared that housing associations 'have the potential to become key players in the development of bespoke private rented housing' as 'a natural complement to HAs' [housing associations'] existing activities', and some associations set up subsidiaries to promote building for full market rent (Morrison, 2016). Although housing associations claimed that their commercial activities would cross-subsidise 'social' rent supply, the sector delivered only 9,590 'social' rented houses in 2014/15, compared to 38,950 in 2010/11.

Did the government–housing association 2015 deal guarantee housing associations a place in the political sun? The runes are mixed. The 2013 Budget announced that 'from 2015–16 social rents will rise by CPI [consumer price index] plus 1 per cent each year for 10 years' (HM Treasury, 2013) but the 2015 Summer Budget declared that there would be a rent reduction of 1% in 'social' rents for four years, substantially reducing resources available to housing associations. The 'Pay to Stay' scheme will make it more difficult for housing associations to create 'mixed communities' (see Lund, 2017), although, unlike local authorities, which must give the income from the move to market rents to the Treasury, housing associations retain a proportion of the additional resources. Section 106 agreements to secure affordable housing have been curtailed and the government has announced a start to direct central government housing commissioning. Housing associations were conspicuously absent from a lead role in regenerating council estates (Spurr, 2016). In its future housing programme, the Homes and Communities Agency (2016) eliminated housing for 'social' rent and directed associations towards shared ownership schemes. Grants of £4.7 billion were made available to associations, private builders and councils for the construction of 135,000 new shared ownership properties by 2020. In recognition that shared ownership had a low take-up, income eligibility conditions for participation in shared ownership schemes were increased to include all potential buyers with an income below £80,000 (£90,000 in London). A new scheme – Rent to Buy – gave grants for building homes to let at less than market rents for up to seven years to tenants saving to buy a home. Post-2018, government support will be firmly directed to 'affordable' homeownership, defined as up to £250,000 outside Greater London and £450,000 within the capital – somewhat remote from the housing associations' traditional goal of housing low-income households. Governments concerned about preserving a large accommodation pool available to low-income households at rents well below market levels require housing associations to deliver unless they use local government – an unlikely Conservative strategy despite Clark's inclusion of local authorities as potential suppliers in his 'bad cop' scenario. Governments interested in maximising the number of homes built for homeownership do not need housing associations, with their traditional 'social heart' – direct developer payments will be sufficient to pump-prime owner-occupation.

Nevertheless – ever Vicars of Bray – housing associations started to react to the government agenda via mergers, and in April 2016, three large associations – London and Quadrant, the Hyde Group and East Thames – announced their amalgamation, claiming that it would enable an extra 100,000 homes to be built over the next decade. Half would be for 'affordable' rent or sale and the rest left to the open market, with no mention of building for 'social' rent (Croucher, 2016). Moreover, on the same day as the merger announcement, the designate Deputy Chief Executive of the new organisation published *Knuckle Down*, in which she stated:

> We have been responsible and are partly to blame for the dependency culture we have created but in future we will be asking our residents to take more personal responsibility in respecting their homes and making an effort to help themselves. (Bailey, 2016)

The package was a total acceptance of the government's agenda. David Montague, designate Chief Executive, said:

> We have reached a tipping point in the sector: I think [more mergers] are inevitable. The big guys will merge with each other, the medium guys will merge with other medium-sized landlords and there will be some consolidation at the smaller end. I think in the future, you will see a smaller number of large organisations and not much in the middle. (Quoted in Apps, 2016)

Divisions in the 'housing association movement' – if this term 'movement' remains applicable – have become starker, with a precarious future for the smaller, more community-based associations.

Further reading

Malpass, P. (2001) 'The Uneven Development of "Social Rented Housing": Explaining the Historically Marginal Position of Housing Associations in Britain', *Housing Studies*, vol 16, no 2, pp 225–42.

McDermont, M. (2010) *Governing Independence and Expertise: The Business of Housing Associations*, Oregon, OR: Oxford and Portland.

Murie, A. (2008) *Moving Homes: The Housing Corporation 1964–2008*, London: Politicos.

O'Hara, G. (2012) *Governing Post-War Britain: The Paradoxes of Progress 1951–1973*, Basingstoke: Palgrave Macmillan.

Policy Exchange (2014) 'Freeing Housing Associations: Better Financing, More Homes'. Available at: http://www.policyexchange.org.uk/publications/category/item/freeing-housing-associations-better-financing-more-homes

Young, R. (2001) 'Housing Associations: The New Kid on the Block', in C. Jones and P. Robson (eds) *Health of Scottish Housing*, Aldershot: Ashgate, pp 89–109.

EIGHT

Homelessness politics

As Somerville (2013, pp 384–5) has argued:

> Homelessness is experienced by individuals (along any one of its dimensions) but it is also imagined, for example, by policy-makers, academics and the general public. Such imaginings (or ideological constructions) tend to take on a life of their own.

Homelessness 'imaginings' have a political dimension and homelessness definitions are linked to official statistics and causal notions to construct public messages about the problem's extent and nature, with the 'headline' statistics on 'rough sleepers', households accepted as homeless and households living in temporary accommodation being particularly salient. These messages carry implications for interpreting other social issues because homelessness is a compelling social inequality symbol. Thus, 'homelessness', under its various designations – 'masterless men', 'vagrancy', 'destitution', 'houseless poor', 'rootless', 'statutory homeless' and 'rough sleepers' – has had lasting political salience with its structural–agency constructions framing wider debates on the 'housing issue'.

The 'deserving' poor

The term 'homeless' was not used in the 19th century: its surrogates were 'destitution' – lacking the necessary means for subsistence, including shelter – and 'vagrancy' – 'without a settled way of living'. The remedy for destitution was the Poor Law, dating back to the 14th century and codified in 1601. The Elizabethan Poor Law was located in 'feudal ties' reinforced by mercantilist economic theory. Mercantilism emphasised the need for a favourable trade balance to secure the bullion necessary for the nation's defence and expansion. A wise sovereign should 'maintain all its objects (persons, things) in their rightful place' (Dean, 1991, p 30) and promote a large, productive population. The Elizabethan Poor Law placed a duty on parish churchwardens to appoint 'overseers of the poor' with the power to raise 'competent sums of money' by a compulsory rate. Local Poor Law operations were placed under the supervision of Justices of the Peace (JPs) – 'good and lawful men' – to guard the 'King's Peace'. Potentially, destitute people with an enduring connection to their locality – a 'settlement' – could benefit from the parish providing 'convenient houses of dwelling for the impotent poor' (An Act for the Relief of the Poor, quoted in Bruce, 1973, p 39) and the purchase of materials to set the 'potent' poor to work.

By the end of the 18th century, local Poor Law administration had produced a complex system varying from place to place. It operated as a social control mechanism, with 'workfare' or, on occasion, wage supplements for the able-bodied, plus accommodation for the 'impotent' poor, allegedly cementing 'squirearchy' and labourer relationships. Although local in administration, the Common Law – interpreted by JP assemblies establishing precedents at the Quarter Sessions and by further appeal to the King's Bench – governed the 'old' Poor Law. Under these 'noblesse oblige' procedures, it was claimed that a set of 'rights' to relief was established, including work provision at wages sufficient to pay rent and prevent 'destitution', based on obligations owed by Poor Law 'overseers' (Costello, 2014).

'Masterless' men

Parish assistance to prevent destitution was accompanied by 'laws of settlement' specifying which parish was responsible for relief. Numerous statutes were directed at 'outsiders'; a growing number of 'masterless men' who had taken to leaving their 'birth parishes' in search of work, adventure and freedom from feudal ties. Villages were said to be living 'in terror of the tramp' (Nichols, 2007), as the nursery rhyme 'Hark, hark, the dogs do bark, the beggars are coming to town' testifies, albeit that the Robin Hood legend suggests a warmer local reception. Their independence and tendency to live by their wits rather than by hard physical work was a cause for concern. Hence, the Vagrancy Act 1744 included in its vagrancy definition:

- those who travel with a bear or dancing bear;
- all persons concerned with performing interludes, tragedies, comedies, operas, plays, farces or other entertainments for the stage, not being authorised by law;
- minstrels and jugglers;
- those pretending to have skill in physiognomy, palmistry or fortune telling; and

- those using subtle crafts to deceive and impose, or playing or betting on unlawful games.

Some itinerants had a special vocabulary called 'canting' and were described as a 'fraternity', a 'company' and even a 'corporation' (Beier, 1987). They were 'rootless', and because they lacked parish ties – the 'settled way of living' that brought 'rights' to welfare – they were 'undeserving' and had to be ruthlessly suppressed. The 1547 Statute of Legal Settlement condemned 'foolish pity and mercy' for vagrants, declaring that sturdy beggars could be branded and made slaves for two years or for life on a second departure from a birth parish. The Vagrancy Act 1824 defined vagrancy as 'failure to maintain oneself' or as living as 'an unlicensed pedlar, a prostitute or a beggar'. Vagrants were divided into three groups according to their perceived character: 'idle and disorderly', 'rogues and vagabonds' and 'incorrigible rogues'. People 'sleeping out' were classified as 'idle and disorderly', but following a second offence, they became 'incorrigible rogues', punishable by imprisonment or a public flogging.

Paternalism versus 'rational' economics

Growing costs – between 1803 and 1833, poor rates in England and Wales increased by 62% – plus rural unrest prompted the Whigs, abetted by a Tory faction, to seek ways to reform the Poor Law. 'Rationalist' economics was influential in shaping the 'new' Poor Law. In his *An Introduction to the Principles of Morals and Legislation*, Jeremy Bentham (1970 [1781], p 229) defined happiness as the 'felicific calculus' of the factors reducing individual pain and enhancing individual pleasure, declaring that 'the greatest happiness of the greatest number – that is the measure of right and wrong'. Bentham (1798) applied his 'utilitarianism' to the Poor Law in *Pauper Management Improved*. He presented a plan to convert the 'dross of society into sterling'. Paupers would be sent to 'industry houses', run by a national joint-stock company and accommodating up to 5,000 people. Bentham claimed: 'Not one in a hundred is absolutely incapable of all employment. Not the motion of a finger – not a step – not a wink – not a whisper – but might be turned to account in the way of profit' (Bentham, 1798, quoted in Liberty Fund, 2013, p 3).

Adam Smith confined himself to condemning the settlement laws as a restriction on free labour movement. In *Principles of Political Economy and Taxation*, David Ricardo (1971 [1817]) argued that the Poor Law consumed resources available to pay wages, discouraged saving, encouraged idleness and therefore had to be abolished. Thomas Robert Malthus held the view that population increases in a geometrical ratio whereas the means of subsistence grows in an arithmetical ratio; hence, 'positive checks' on famine and plague were inevitable. He wanted to eradicate the Poor law because the security it offered encouraged early marriage and childbirth, diminished the worker's power to save by lowering the labour price, and weakened work incentives.

The Royal Commission into the Operation of the Poor Laws, 1832

The membership of a Royal Commission set up in 1832 by the Whigs included Nassau Senior, steeped in free market ideas, and Edwin Chadwick, Jeremy Bentham's secretary and friend. There were numerous opinions circulating about reform. The Tories, deriving their identity from loyalty to the Crown, had an interest in maintaining the 'King's Peace' through paternalistic local Poor Law operation, supervised by JPs, with their links to the Crown. This prompted them to defend the 'traditional' Poor Law, with its common law 'rights'. The Whigs, taking pride in their education in rational, Enlightenment thinking, were willing to apply the new political economy principles to Poor Law administration. A coterie of Tories was also interested in reform. Later to become known as 'Liberal Tories', the 'Noetics' – believers in the individual struggle for 'higher virtue' – had a strong representation on the Commission (Offer, 2006). Its report, published in 1834 (Checkland and Checkland, 1974), embodied an 'ideal male' notion as independent of state aid in maintaining himself and his family. The man who failed to match this standard was to be disciplined into 'higher virtue' by incarceration in a workhouse and, as a token of his loss of virtue, separation from his wife and children.

The 'new' Poor Law

The Poor Law Amendment Act 1834 incorporated many of the Royal Commission's recommendations, including the 'less eligibility' principle, that is, the situation of the able-bodied poor relief recipient 'on the whole shall not be made really or apparently as eligible as the independent labourer of the lowest class' (Checkland and Checkland, 1974, p 335). It included a clause denying a right of appeal to a JP if relief application was refused, thereby blocking channels that might reinforce a 'right to welfare'. Implementing the 1834 Act was troublesome, especially in the industrialising North, where some manufacturers regarded workhouses as expensive, and in places where industries were subject to trade cycles, it was pointless to force families into the workhouse during a downturn. The 'new' Poor Law had an important impact on the formation of the Chartist movement, which called the workhouses 'bastilles'.

By the 1870s, the workhouse system was well established but in the process of change. Workhouse resident classification was imprecise, there being, for example, no clear distinctions between the 'able-bodied', the sick, those with a mental disorder and the aged. Nonetheless, it appears that the number of 'able-bodied' men in the permanent wards was in decline – the working man's growing political influence produced a tendency to offer 'out-relief' or work creation programmes as workhouse alternatives. The County Asylums Act 1808 had made provision for the establishment of county asylums for the mentally ill but few had been set up until the Lunacy Act 1845 created the Lunacy Commission responsible for establishing asylums. Gradually, more mentally ill people were removed from the workhouse 'permanent' wards. They became the domains of elderly people, the sick – increasingly accommodated in separate 'infirmaries' – unmarried mothers and those with a mental disability.

Casual wards

In 1837, a regulation was introduced requiring food and a night's shelter to be given to any destitute person in case of 'sudden or urgent necessity'. Vagrancy, previously regarded primarily as a 'law and order' matter for the police and the courts – became, in part, a Poor Law authority responsibility. 'Causal wards' were added to the workhouse, wherein a 'work task' performance was rewarded with a meal and accommodation for the night. Workers 'on the tramp' would often move between workhouses; indeed, the 'tramp trail' received official recognition with 'way-tickets' issued for a particular route. Ticket-holders – the more 'respectable' wayfarers – were entitled to special treatment, such as exemption from work tasks, whereas the 'ticketless' were offered accommodation only in cases of 'severe distress'. Sleeping rough and nights in common lodging houses interspaced workhouse visits. Common lodging houses, known as 'dosshouses', accommodated a large number of casual workers: in the East End of London, for example, 8,500 beds were available, mainly used by dockworkers. The cheapest shelter was the 'two penny hangover', later described by George Orwell (2001 [1933], p 211) as:

> the lodgers sit in a row on a bench, there is a rope in front
> of them, and they lean on this as though leaning on a fence.
> A man, humorously called a valet, cuts the rope at five in
> the morning.

Common lodging houses were at the centre of Victorian concern about inner-city disorder and immorality. Their inhabitants were described as 'wandering hordes' (O' Neill, 2014) and the houses were regarded as dens of crime, depravation and vice – three of the prostitutes murdered by 'Jack the Ripper' lived in common lodging houses.

Royal Commission on the Poor Laws and Relief of Distress (1909)

In the early 20th century, the homelessness issue was contested between Charity Organisation Society and the Fabians Society 'experts'. The Fabians – championed by Sydney and Beatrice Webb – demanded the 'break-up' of the Poor Law, whereas the Charity Organisation Society – represented mainly by Helen and Bernard Bosanquet – wanted to retain its basic premises. Beatrice Webb and Helen Bosanquet were members of the Royal Commission on the Poor Laws and Relief of Distress, which issued two reports. The Majority Report, although recommending a number of reforms, wanted to preserve a Poor Law authority in the belief that there was an underlying factor in poverty causation – 'character' absence – which diminished the will to provide independently for contingences such as old age, unemployment and sickness. In contrast, the Minority Report called for a systematic 'Framework of Prevention', with the Poor Law divided into specialist domains such health, education, old age and the labour market. The Minority Report referred to the 'houseless poor', suggesting a particular housing problem distinct from the destitution, and subject to specific remedies from a specialised agency. With regard to homeless single men, the Minority Report concentrated on employment as the remedy. In a given year, 30,000 to 80,000 separate individuals made use of the casual wards but 'the army on the tramp' was far higher because many people avoided the casual wards altogether. It condemned the casual wards, stating that they were worse than prisons. Its remedy for 'the army on the tramp' was to establish 'farm colonies', where vagrants could acquire useful habits and skills to promote their employability. Other commentators were harsher. The report of the Vagrancy Committee (1906) recommended that the police should control the workhouse casual wards and 'way-ticket' distribution.

William Dawson believed that only 3% of 'the army on the tramp' was genuinely seeking work. The rest were 'loafers', who were being 'petted and coddled' by the authorities (Dawson, 1910, p 5). Harsh work camps were his solution. Indeed, there was a moral panic about vagrancy in the early 20th century, with 'sleeping out' prosecutions under the vagrancy legislation increasing from 5,500 a year in the late 1890s to 12,000 in 1907 (Rose, 2015).

Although the Poor Law Minority Report had little immediate impact on homelessness, its call for specialisation and prevention was reflected in the Mental Deficiency Act 1913, which made provision for 'mental defectives' to be detained in a state or certified institution or supervised in the community. The Act removed mentally disabled people from the workhouse, and by 1946, nearly 60,000 were detained in specialist institutions.

'Hidden from history': homelessness between the wars

Between the wars, homelessness was 'low' politics – so low that it was almost 'hidden from history'. After the 'respectable' unemployed working man with an insurance record had been largely disconnected from the workhouse test via paying 'extended' unemployment benefit, and then, in 1934, with the creation of the Unemployment Assistance Board, homelessness had little political salience. Workhouses were officially named 'poor law institutions' in 1913 and then 'public assistance institutions' in 1929, when mainstream local government assumed the Poor Law Guardians' role. They provided accommodation mainly for elderly people, single parents and those with physical or mental disabilities who had slipped through the specialist voluntary and statutory agencies' nets. Casual wards – often named 'Wayfarers' Reception Centres' – remained in demand from 'able-bodied' men 'without a settled way of living'. During the First World War, the number of people using the casual wards declined to 1,100, but by 1933, the 'number of casuals admitted' reached 15,900 – despite the government diverting some potential inmates into residential labour camps offering three months training in hard labour. Casual wards closed in the early 1920s had to be reopened. Surveys by the London County Council of men in lodging houses, night shelters and sleeping rough suggested that the 'number of casuals admitted' would have to be multiplied eightfold to estimate the number of people 'without a settled means of living'. As Krafchik (1983, p 195) points out, 'Statistics and other evidence suggest a positive correlation between unemployment and vagrancy.... Officials appear to have been unwilling to acknowledge this relationship'.

Provision for vagrants was local government's domain, monitored by the Ministry of Health. The Ministry for Labour and the Unemployment Assistance Board detached themselves from the issue, claiming to be responsible only for those 'normally in the labour market'. Deterrent principles continued, with a 1934 report on a casual wards stating:

> these people ought to be ashamed of themselves e.g. making the tramps spread margarine with their fingers, there being no cutlery, or turning them out without a bit of paper to wrap their crusts or in providing a single pot for night convenience. (Quoted in Krafchik, 1983, p 205)

However, the number of people prosecuted and imprisoned under the Vagrancy Act 1824 for 'wandering abroad and lodging in barns, etc., or in the open, without visible means of subsistence' was in steep decline – from an average of 8,954 per year between 1910 and 1914 to 263 in 1932 (House of Lords, 1933). In the late 1930s, the Ministry of Health attempted to encourage local authorities to rehabilitate vagrants, designating them as 'unemployable' rather than 'work-shy'. In 1944, with labour and soldiers in high demand, the number of 'casuals' in workhouses was only 200 (Krafchik, 1983, p 199).

The welfare state and homelessness

Under the National Assistance Act 1948, the National Assistance Board became responsible for cash payments to all people in need and for reception and resettlement centres, often located in the former workhouse 'casual wards'. 'Vagrancy' officially became a 'work' issue. Circular 136/46, issued in 1946, envisaged a system of 30 reception centres positioned around the country wherein 'rootless' men would be offered accommodation, 'casework' and referral to resettlement centres to change their work habits. Local authorities remained responsible for the other functions previously undertaken by public assistance committees and discharged these obligations through Welfare Committees. Thus, responsibility for the 'homeless' was divided between two agencies, with people now called 'rough sleepers' under National Assistance Board supervision and Welfare Committees responsible for 'family homelessness'.

Cathy Come Home

The National Assistance Act 1948 declared that it was 'An Act to terminate the existing poor law' but the poor law spirit did not expire. 'Part Three', as accommodation provided by Welfare Committees was called, mainly housed women with children and elderly people. Being the direct successor of the 19th-century 'less eligible' workhouse – with some accommodation being provided in former workhouses – the long-established negative attitudes towards its inhabitants persisted. If women and their partners could not provide the basics for their children in a full-employment welfare state, then this was likely to be caused by 'feckless' behaviour (Greve, 1971). Deterrence was applied, with only squalid accommodation, sometimes in communal dormitories or old caravans, on offer and it was common for a man to be separated from his wife and children: the man being told to look for lodgings in Salvation Army hostels and his wife and children housed in accommodation supplied by the Welfare Department. Audrey Harvey (1960) reported on the situation but her revelations had little impact. However, resistance from below was developing, with a group of fathers moving into a hostel with their partners and refusing to leave, prompting Kent County Council to change its rules (Lowe, 1986).

Cathy Come Home – a TV drama-documentary about Cathy's gradual decent from a secure, happy marriage into 'Part Three' accommodation and ending with her children being taken into care – had a powerful impact. *The Times* commented that it was 'A searing indictment of housing conditions', the *Observer* said that 'It isn't surprising that the BBC switchboard was jammed with calls. Jeremy Sandford's play … was angry, humane, wholly authentic.… He shows how press and TV can bring about direct social action' (press comments from *Warp*, 2013). 'Common-sense' understandings of homelessness started to change from personal, 'feckless' and 'agency' accounts to a 'structural' housing shortage explanation. Shelter, founded shortly before the broadcast of *Cathy Come Home*, was determined to anchor the structural explanation in the public psyche. Des Wilson (1970, p 18), Shelter's Director, claimed:

> The trouble is that the word 'homeless' has been officially linked with the word 'welfare'. Not only has the official number of homeless been falsified by definition, or lack of it, but the character of the homeless has also been falsified, and the authorities are able to infer that the homeless form

a small group that would inevitably end up in the cesspit of any society.

Wilson's aim 'was to relate homelessness to housing scarcity and not to welfare (in its administrative sense) and to get full recognition of the scale of the problem' (Wilson, 1970, p 9). He campaigned for a revised homelessness definition, including the 'invisible homeless': families in overcrowded accommodation and in physical danger because their property was unfit and lacking basic amenities, such as a lavatory and hot water. In 1969, Shelter launched its 'Face the Facts' campaign, arguing that the government's official 18,849 homelessness figure, based on the numbers in temporary accommodation, vastly underestimated the problem's scale. On Shelter's definition, it was 3 million (Shelter, 1969). Given the problem's scale, it was difficult to label homelessness as a 'personal problem'. As Wilson (1970, p 21) stated:

> A small and powerless group such as 18,849 officially homeless are hardly likely to command priority over the many other demands on the nation's resources. But if the homeless can be seen for who they are, and how many there are, numbering hundreds of thousands instead of hundreds, we might hope for better.

The Housing (Homeless Persons) Act 1977

The Labour government's (1964–70) reaction to *Cathy Come Home* was to accelerate the house-building programme, and in response to the London Squatters Campaign, housing homeless families in empty luxury flats and vacant houses, it issued a circular urging local authorities to make greater use of short-life properties by licensing them to tenants. However, the government denounced Shelter's homelessness definition, with David Ennals, Minister of Health and Social Security, declaring: 'I have seen references to 3 million homeless. This is ridiculous' (Ennals, 1969, quoted in Wilson, 1970, p 19). A response to the specific issues of homelessness management, highlighted in *Cathy Come Home*, was delayed.

The factual documentary *Johnny Go Home* (Yorkshire Television, 1975), about teenage runaways being forced into prostitution, raised the media profile of homelessness. Lobbying by the voluntary sector through the Joint Charities Group intensified and was successful in promoting a central government circular setting out a priority group list for rehousing and urging local authorities to shift responsibility for homelessness from Social Services Departments – the successors of Welfare Departments – to housing authorities. Many local authorities ignored this circular, prompting the Department of the Environment (DoE) to prepare a Bill on homelessness. Lack of government parliamentary time led to a call for a private member to sponsor the Bill and Stephen Ross, Liberal Party MP, responded. The 1977 Housing (Homeless Persons) Bill shifted the legal obligation to accommodate homeless people from social service authorities to housing authorities. It defined homelessness as the absence of a legal right to occupy a dwelling, and if a person was legally homeless, local authorities would have a duty to 'secure that accommodation becomes available for his occupation'. Many local authorities were unhappy about the Bill, fearing that they would not have the resources to implement it. Moreover, as the Bill passed through Parliament, concerns were expressed that, in the words of one MP, it was 'a charter for the rent dodger, scrounger and home-leaver' (Mr Rees-Davies, MP, quoted in Thompson, 1988, p 8). Thus, 'gatekeeping' clauses were inserted, such as 'intentionally' – if a person was in priority need but deemed 'intentionally' homeless, then the local authority only had obligations to supply accommodation for a limited period and to offer 'advice and assistance'. The Housing Homeless Persons Act 1977 was a compromise between: structural homelessness explanation promoters; local authorities, fearful that the legislation would overload their housing systems; politicians promoting 'fecklessness' as the cause of homelessness; and DoE civil servants, who acknowledged the need for reform. According to Crawson (2013, p 444), the DoE was more liberal in its approach to homelessness than other departments. Hugh Rossi, a former Conservative housing minister, who had tabled amendments to the Bill restricting local government obligations, accused DoE officials of 'reinstating everything taken out of the bill' in its Code of Guidance issued to local authorities on how to interpret the Act. Rossi was right. Hilton et al (2013, p 132) comments: 'The officials told the group [Joint Charities Group] that their "Code of Guidance" would reinstate everything taken out of the original Act in its passage in Parliament'. Thus, for example, the phrase in the Act giving local authorities the obligation to 'secure that accommodation becomes available to him' was interpreted in the Code of Guidance as an obligation to provide local authority or housing association accommodation. This interpretation survived until, in *R v London Borough of Brent ex parte Awua*, it was overturned by the House of Lords.

'Headline' homelessness

The duties placed on local government by the Housing (Homeless Persons) Act 1977 generated statistics on the number of households accepted as homeless and a households in temporary accommodation count. These became the 'headline' figures, with the definition adopted in the statistics regarded by the media as *the* homelessness definition. As 'homelessness' revealed in the official figures mounted and the issue climbed the political agenda, the homelessness definition annoyed and perplexed some politicians. Margaret Thatcher, recalling the late 1980s, said:

> The most disturbing political issue in housing at the time, however, was homelessness. It should immediately be said that the alarmingly large figures for the 'homeless' did not by definition reflect the number of people without roofs over their heads. Rather the published 'homelessness' figures described the number of people in certain statutorily determined 'priority groups' who were accepted for housing. In other words, far from being homeless they had homes provided by the local council. (Thatcher, 1993, p 603)

Later, John Prescott, Deputy Prime Minister in the Blair governments, commented:

> when I look at it, I see homeless people as people on the streets. I want to put this phrase into a proper context. Obviously, I want to get people out of B&Bs and temporary accommodation and into council homes, but then you have to question if this is still classed as homelessness. (Quoted in *Housing Today*, 2004)

Homelessness politics became more concerned with reducing the homelessness statistics than reducing homelessness.

'Structure' or 'agency'?

Political skirmishes between 'structural' explanations – placing the causes of homelessness in a housing shortage and allocation rules – and 'agency' explanations – locating causation in personal behaviour – reignited in the 1980s. In her first term of office, Thatcher received a paper on how the DoE intended to deal with homelessness. She felt let down by its contents, commenting 'This is the most disappointing housing document I have read during the lifetime of this government. It runs away from every problem it identifies ... and results in liaison with those who queue jump' (Thatcher, 1982).

Thatcher took no immediate action to reform the legislation but she started to promote homelessness explanations going with the grain of economic liberalism. Her objective was to isolate the homelessness issue from discourses on social and economic inequality. In declaring that 'there is no such thing as society', she used homelessness to illustrate her point, stating:

> too many children and people have been given to understand 'I have a problem, it is the Government's job to cope with it!' or 'I have a problem. I will go to get a grant to cope with it!' 'I am homeless, the Government must house me!' and so they are casting their problems on society and who is society? There is no such thing! (Thatcher, 1987)

Perverse incentives

In *Losing Ground*, Charles Murray (1984) claimed that poverty growth in the US was caused by 'perverse incentives' in the welfare system. In the 1950s, he asserted, poverty in the US declined rapidly, but in the mid-1960s, the decline stalled and poverty started to increase. Murray attributed this lost ground to the welfare reforms flowing from the 1960s' 'war on poverty', which made access to welfare payments and services effortless for female single parents, so it became easier for them to live without a male breadwinner. The reforms had created 'The Law of Unintended Rewards' – a system of 'perverse incentives' – in which undesirable behaviour was made more attractive by social transfers that rewarded such activities. Following her resignation as Prime Minister in 1990, Margaret Thatcher endorsed Murray's ideas (Thatcher, 1995, p 549) and the Thatcherite faction in John Major's Cabinet – Michael Portillo, John Redwood and Peter Lilley – promoted them.

Murray's thesis fitted well with public choice theory (Troutman et al, 1999) and the 'perverse incentives' idea provided the basis for a specific homelessness discourse targeted at female single parents. To a tune from *The Mikado*, Peter Lilley, then Secretary of State for Social Security, sang to the 1992 Conservative Party Conference:

I've got them on my list,

There's young ladies who get pregnant just to jump the housing queue,

And dads who won't support the kids of the ladies they have ... kissed,

And I haven't even mentioned all those scrounging Socialists,

I've got them on my list. (Lilley, 1992)

A Green Paper, *Access to Local Authority and Housing Association Tenancies* (DoE, 1994, p 4), asserted:

> by giving the local authority a greater responsibility towards those who can demonstrate 'homelessness' than towards anyone else in housing need, the current legislation creates a perverse incentive for people to have themselves accepted by a local authority as homeless.

Central–local relationships

There was a subplot in the 'perverse incentive' theme related to local government and national government relationships. The government suspected that Labour-controlled local authorities were lax in administering the gatekeeping clauses of the 1977 Act because rising homelessness figures not only embarrassed the Conservative government, but also increased local authority revenue because the formula on which the central government distributed grants to local authorities included a homelessness indictor. Warming to the 'perverse incentive' theme, the 1994 Green Paper claimed that 'it was wrong to put a substantial weight on a measure affected as much by authorities' administrative decisions as this puts authorities under inappropriate and perverse incentives' (DoE, 1994, p 7). The remedies to the 'perverse incentives' problem proposed in the Green Paper were a new homelessness definition as 'no accommodation of any sort available', housing any households accepted as homeless in the private landlord sector and allocating 'social tenancies' only via a waiting list, controlled by central regulations that downgraded homelessness as a reason for rehousing.

An erosion process

In the construction of the Housing Act 1996, the proposals in the Green Paper underwent an erosion process. By 1996, the emphasis on single-parent morality was beginning to generate 'perverse effects' for the Conservative Party. In his speech to the Conservative Party Conference, John Major (1993) claimed that it was 'time to return to core values, time to get back to basics ... to accepting responsibility for yourself and your family and not shuffling it off on other people and the state'. He made no reference to single parents' morality, but in the context of the comments on single parents coming from the Thatcherite camp, the slogan 'back to basics' was a signal for the media to turn the spotlight on Tory MPs' personal behaviour and morals. A series of sex scandals hit the headlines and the Conservative Party became associated with hypocrisy and sleaze. Moreover, the 'headline' homelessness figures based on the operations of the Housing (Homeless Persons) Act 1977 had started to decline. The Housing Act 1996 retained the 1977 homelessness definition, and although temporary accommodation could be provided for only two years, local authorities had the discretion to extend the stay. In addition, the clauses in the Act that specified the households to be given 'reasonable preference' in allocating social sector homes, although not specifically including homeless households, were sufficiently flexible to allow homeless households to be granted a high priority. Thus, in implementing the 1996 Act, local authorities had considerable discretion.

The Conservatives and rough sleeping

The 'priority need' clauses in the Housing (Homeless Persons) Act 1977 excluded the majority of the people experiencing the most visible form of homelessness – sleeping rough. Broadcast in 1971 by the BBC and written by Jeremy Sandford, *Edna, the Inebriate Woman* had far less political impact than *Cathy Come Home*. Although the main character was female, most of Edna's dialogue – including the oft-repeated 'I am not the vagrant' – came from the male rough sleepers quoted in *Down and Out in Britain* (Sandford, 1971). Despite its limited political impact, *Edna, the Inebriate Woman* was helpful in directing housing association attention to the single homelessness problem and promoting a less punitive approach to vagrancy. Under vagrancy legislation, rough sleeping only became an offence if it caused a nuisance.

The Housing Corporation launched its 'Hostels Initiative' in 1980, aimed at providing hostel accommodation via housing associations for the homeless and rootless. This initiative coincided with the closing of the largest hostels and resettlement centres. In the early 1980s, there was an increase in the number of young people sleeping on the streets. Thatcher believed that Housing Benefit availability was encouraging young people to leave home (Thatcher, 1993, p 603). Her response, based on the 'perverse incentives' argument, was to stop paying Housing Benefit to people under 18 and to reduce the amount paid to 18 to 25 year olds, but this did not mitigate the problem. Thatcher wanted 'young people back with their families, not in London living on benefits' (Thatcher, 1993, p 603) and refused to restore benefit cuts. However, 'street homeless' visibility, manifest in 'cardboard cities', had implications for perceptions of the Conservative Party's economic policies, tourism and leisure activities; indeed, in 1991, Sir George Young, then Minister for Housing and Planning, allegedly said that 'the homeless are what you step over when you come out of the opera' (*Economist*, 1991). Chris Patten, Secretary of State for the Environment towards the end of Thatcher's time in office, was sensitive to the Conservative image. A Rough Sleepers Initiative was started, costing £196 million over seven years, to contact rough sleepers in central London, allocate them to emergency hostel places and then offer more permanent, 'move on' accommodation. Nonetheless, Margaret Thatcher insisted:

> Crowds of drunken, dirty, often abusive and sometimes violent men must not be allowed to turn the central areas of the capital into no-go zones for ordinary citizens. The police must disperse them and prevent their coming back once it was clear that accommodation was available. (Thatcher, 1993, p 603)

John Major retained Margaret Thatcher's invective against rough sleepers, declaring that they were 'offensive eyesores' (Schoettler, 1994), but mindful that visible rough sleeping was an indication of 'the state of the nation', the Rough Sleepers Initiative was retained and enhanced, producing a gradual decline in rough-sleeper visibility.

New Labour and homelessness

Statutory homelessness

New Labour's 1997 election strategy was to concentrate on a few 'deliverable' manifesto pledges. Thus, although the manifesto was light on housing policies, it contained a specific pledge: 'to place a new duty on local authorities to protect those who are homeless through no fault of their own and are in priority need' (Labour Party, 1997, p 23). However, significant change to the Housing Act 1996 was delayed until New Labour's second term. The Homelessness Act 2002 imposed a duty on local authorities to develop a homelessness strategy, abolished the two-year limit on the provision of temporary housing and disallowed an assured short-hold tenancy offer in the private landlord sector unless this was acceptable to the homeless person. The 2002 Priority Need Order extended the groups designated as in priority need to cover those aged 16 and 17, care leavers aged 18 to 20, those vulnerable as a result of time spent in care, the armed forces, prison or custody, and those vulnerable because they had to leave home through violence or the threat of violence.

Prevention

New Labour's eligibility condition liberalisation increased the 'headline' figures on homelessness – by 2004, the number of homeless applicants in priority need had increased by 25% on the 1997 figure. In response, New Labour introduced a 'prevention' strategy. *Sustainable Communities: Settled Homes; Changing Lives, a Strategy for Tackling Homelessness* (ODPM, 2005, p 13) stated:

> We recognise that the provision of housing alone cannot solve homelessness. Underlying problems which led to homelessness in the first place have to be addressed in order to provide long-term solutions. Failure to address these root causes can lead to repeated episodes of homelessness.

The government defined homeless prevention as 'providing people with the ways and means to address their housing and other needs in order to avoid becoming homeless' (ODPM, 2005, p 15). It involved discussing 'housing options' with people approaching local authorities for help under the 1996 Act.

The policy was pushed forward by 'administrative stratagems' (Pawson, 2009), such as providing extra resources to local authorities to promote prevention, appointing prevention 'advisors' and setting new 'best value' performance indicators based on success in closing down the statutory homelessness route into secure accommodation. Assessed on its impact on reducing the 'headline' figure of statutory homelessness, the strategy was very successful, with the number of homeless applicants in priority need down to 42,390 in 2010, compared to 127,760 in 2005. The policy received minimal criticism, despite the closing down of the 1977 Act's route out of intolerable circumstances, such as substituting a 'panic room' for rehousing to prevent domestic abuse.

Rough sleeping

Rough sleeping was a fruitful domain for New Labour politics. It was a visible manifestation of the housing problem. As New Labour's 1997 manifesto stated: 'There is no more powerful symbol of Tory neglect in our society today than young people without homes living rough on the streets' (Labour Party, 1997). It could be overcome with limited resources, unlike the broader 'single homelessness' issue, covering rough sleepers plus those living in hostels, B&Bs and so-called sofa surfing (sleeping on other people's sofas). It was an arena for combining 'structure' and 'agency' explanations for maximum political impact, illustrating how 'tough love', with rights attached to obligations, would benefit both the individual and society.

Blair's Social Exclusion Unit's first report was on rough sleeping. It assembled evidence to demonstrate that the causes of sleeping rough were located in the rough sleepers' 'personal biographies': disturbed childhoods, institutionalisation, drug addiction and alcohol abuse (Social Exclusion Unit, 1998b). The remedy was located in 'joined-up' action addressing entrenched problems. Rough sleepers would be removed from the streets to some form of shelter to rupture the rough-sleeping 'street culture' and to facilitate 'help' via offers of treatment, occupation and work. Housing tended to be regarded as secondary to dealing with the rough sleepers' personal problems, with the idea of 'housing-readiness' influencing some programmes. Later, this idea was challenged by some voluntary sector organisations advocating 'Housing First', an idea developed in the US emphasising immediate housing with 'no preconditions of addressing wider social care and support needs' (Shelter, 2008, p 1).

Rights and responsibilities

Blair set out the 'common good' dimension to tackling rough sleeping in his foreword to the Social Exclusion Unit's report on rough sleeping. Sleeping rough was bad for those who slept rough 'as they are intensely vulnerable to crime, drugs and alcohol and at a high risk of illness and premature death'. It was also bad for the rest of society because 'many people feel intimidated by rough sleepers, beggars and street drinkers and rough sleeping can blight areas and endanger business and tourism' (Social Exclusion Unit, 1998b, p 7).

His rights/responsibilities agenda was reflected in the statement:

> Rough sleepers themselves have a responsibility to come in. Once we are satisfied that realistic alternatives are readily available we – and the public at large – are entitled to expect those working on the streets to seek to persuade people to take advantage of them. This includes the police. (DETR, 1999, p 10)

Local authorities were reminded of their powers under the vagrancy legislation, and in 2003, begging – often associated with rough sleeping and already an arrestable offence under the Vagrancy Act 1824 – became a recordable offence, that is, it had to be registered on national police records. The Home Office's (2003) anti-social behaviour action plan introduced targeted action to reduce begging in 30 areas. These measures were accompanied by the increasing privatisation of public spaces and enhanced street control by private security companies.

Although New Labour stressed 'agency' explanations to promote in the right-wing press, there was a sufficient 'structural' dimension to appeal to those with leftish inclinations. Help was on offer to rough sleepers and New Labour's 1997 manifesto had promised to use the capital receipts from the Right to Buy to build more homes. Measured in terms of reducing the visible rough-sleeping problem, New Labour's initiative was successful. The target, set in 1998, to reduce the number of rough sleepers by two thirds was met.

The Coalition government and homelessness

Under David Cameron's leadership, the Conservative Party, anxious to shed its 'nasty' party image, concentrated on 'rough sleeping': the most visible, and regarded by many on the Right as 'real', homelessness and a problem that could be reduced without large expenditure. Grant Shapps, to become Housing Minister, slept rough to attract attention to the problem, and in 2008, the Conservatives set up the Homelessness Foundation, with an advisory panel with the leading homelessness organisations represented. It condemned New Labour's rough-sleeper count as inaccurate and as omitting people in short-term accommodation such as hostels, B&Bs and sofa surfing. When the Homelessness Foundation was launched, Cameron said: 'I think that it is simply a disgrace that in the fifth biggest economy in the world that we have people homeless, people sleeping on the streets, sofa-surfers, people in hospitals' (quoted in Ryan, 2008).

Rough sleepers

The Conservatives' 2010 manifesto was a good intent declaration rather than a policy. It stated that 'We will implement a range of measures to address the problems of the homeless, including introducing more accurate street counts and ensuring a Minister in each relevant department has homelessness in their brief' (Conservative Party, 2010). A ministerial working group on homelessness was set up, and in 2011, *Vision to End Rough Sleeping: No Second Night Out Nationwide* (DCLG, 2011b) was published. It committed the government to working with the voluntary sector to reduce rough sleeping based on six principles, the dominant one being that 'new rough sleepers should be identified and helped off the streets immediately so that they do not fall into a dangerous rough sleeping lifestyle' (DCLG, 2011b, p 15).

As the post-2008 recession continued into 2012, there was a change in rough-sleeper characteristics, with the 2012 count revealing that 25% came from the Central European countries joining the European Union (EU) post-2004. Some local authorities started to work with the voluntary sector to 'reconnect' rough sleepers with their country of origin. The Polish charity Barka escorted rough sleepers back to Poland to join Barka's community-based social enterprises and supportive housing communities. In response to a parliamentary question, Baroness Hanham, Parliamentary Under Secretary of State, Communities and Local Government, declared:

> Local authorities and the Greater London Authority already work closely with the Home Office to tackle rough sleeping by destitute EU nationals across London. Where destitute EU nationals refuse to voluntarily depart with the help of the local authority, the Home Office will deploy its administrative removal powers. (House of Lords, 2013)

However, the rough-sleeper 'foreign' dimension masked other trends. As Fitzpatrick et al (2013, p 32) comment:

> while UK nationals now account for only just under half of the London total (46%), and this cohort has increased slightly less rapidly than overseas migrant rough sleepers in

recent years, the logged UK-origin rough sleeper total for 2012/13 was still up by 56% on the figure just two years earlier.

Under New Labour, only local authorities where there was a known, or suspected, rough-sleeping problem were required to provide a count. This meant that only 440 rough sleepers were counted. The Coalition government required that all areas across England had to provide counts or rough-sleeper number estimates. The first Coalition count in 2011 recorded 1,767 people sleeping rough but the 2015 count found 3,569 rough sleepers. In London, 36.4% of rough sleepers came from countries joining the EU between 2005 and 2007, with Romanians the largest category (DCLG, 2016a). However, there are problems involved in counting rough sleepers (see Lund, 2017) and such difficulties were a reason why the UK Statistics Authority (2015) declared that the rough-sleeper statistics were not fit for purpose.

Statutory homelessness

Statutory homelessness also increased under the Coalition government, with 60,940 households in accommodation arranged by local authorities under the homelessness legislation in late 2014, compared to 51,310 in 2010, with the number living in B&Bs more than doubling to 4,700. The Coalition government intensified the prevention strategy application, with the Department for Communities and Local Government (DCLG, 2015e) recording 209,300 prevention cases outside the statutory homelessness framework in 2013/14, compared to 140,900 in the New Labour government's last year. In 2014, more than three quarters of homeless cases were dealt with by prevention. The DCLG did not commission research into the impact of the policy.

Like New Labour, the Coalition government used every opportunity to emphasise the 'agency' elements in the causes of statutory homelessness. The smaller the problem, the greater the impact of 'agency' explanations, and in 2012, Iain Duncan Smith declared that the public would find the official definition of statutory homelessness 'strange' because it included the absence of a spare bedroom in the definition (*Daily Mail*, 2012b). In 'Making Every Contact Count: A Joint Approach to Preventing Homelessness' (DCLG, 2012f), 'Family breakdown was highlighted as a significant cause of homelessness, representing 18% of all acceptances in 2011/12 – almost 70% of these cases involved violence' (Wilson, 2013, p 4), and the document stated:

> But we know the answer does not just lie in homelessness services. For many people, becoming homeless is not the beginning of their problems; it comes at the end of a long line of crises, a long line of interactions with public and voluntary sector services, a long line of missed opportunities. We must change that. (DCLG, 2012f, p 1)

The Localism Act 2011 allowed local authorities to discharge their statutory homelessness duty by allocating households a tenancy in the private rented sector rather than in 'social' housing without having to secure agreement from the household. This was justified on the perverse incentive argument, used in justifying the Housing Act 1996, that is, 'the [current statutory arrangement] encourages some households to apply as homeless in order to secure reasonable preference and an effective guarantee of being offered social housing' (DCLG, 2010b, p 42). The cuts in Housing Benefit entitlement led to media reports that London councils were seeking accommodation outside the capital to use as temporary and permanent housing for households to whom they owed a statutory housing duty – a policy officially condemned by the government but, according to some commentators, covertly supported (Butler, P., 2012).

The 2015 Conservative government

All the political parties mentioned homelessness in their manifestos but with few robust ideas on how it might be reduced, indicating the symbolic value of homelessness as a political issue. The Labour Party (2015, p 46) said: 'all forms of homelessness are back on the rise, with rough sleeping having increased by 55 per cent. We are committed to reversing this trend by tackling the causes of homelessness and rough sleeping'. The Green Party (2015, p 43) declared its aim as 'ending rough sleeping completely' by giving public authorities a duty to prevent it. The Liberal Democrats (2015, p 100) promised 'a full review of the help single people get under homelessness legislation'. UKIP (2015, p 22), perhaps taking a lesson from Scotland in promoting national solidarity via homelessness assistance, said it was 'fully committed to maintaining a strong and supportive safety net for those who fall on hard times, whether through any fault of their own or not'. It promised to:

> establish a National Homeless Register to make it easier for those of no fixed abode to claim welfare entitlements; get access to medical and dental services; and enable support

services to identify those at risk of physical, psychological and sexual abuse. (UKIP, 2015, p 34)

The Conservative Party (2015, p 46) said 'We have also pioneered the use of social impact bonds and payment-by-results, and we will look to scale these up in the future, focusing on youth unemployment, mental health and homelessness'.

A report sponsored by the Joseph Rowntree Foundation and Shelter indicated that the 'bedroom tax', benefit sanctions and Housing Benefit cuts were fuelling England's rapidly worsening homelessness crisis and noted the rapidly rising evictions from private rented accommodation as a homelessness cause (Fitzpatrick et al, 2016). The 2015 Spending Review and Autumn Statement (HM Treasury, 2015a) promised to protect DCLG funding for targeted homelessness intervention and to provide an extra £40 million for services for domestic abuse victims. However, given the rapidly mounting homelessness headline statistics, action to reduce formally recorded homelessness can be anticipated.

Conclusion

The political salience of homelessness has varied over the last two hundred years. It had a high profile in the early 19th century: the outcome of Whig interest in 'rational political economics' and the Poor Law's increasing rate burden. However, the homelessness profile began to fade as the 'working man' was gradually removed from the Poor Law remit – first by a greater willingness to grant 'out-relief', then by work creation programmes and unemployment benefits. Homelessness in the 20th century became 'low' politics – about men 'without a settled way of living' and single women with children. It was only under special circumstances and for short periods, such as following the broadcast of *Cathy Come Home* and the sudden increase in rough sleeping in the early 1980s, that homelessness received high-level attention. Under the Coalition government, homelessness had a low profile. Although the rough-sleeper count increased in England between 2010 and 2015, the problem was less visible than in the 1980s and 1990s and politically obscured by the 'foreign nationals' issue. In 2014, Iain Duncan Smith, then Minister for Work and Pensions, claimed:

But actually what is happening progressively, more and more, is people mostly from southern and eastern Europe have actually ended up being Big Issue sellers and they claim, as self-employed, immediately, tax credits. So when we talk about benefits, they are not just out-of-work benefits, they are also in-work benefits that are being claimed. (Quoted in *Daily Express*, 2014)

The 'prevention' stratagem has had an impact on the 'headline' figure but officially recorded statutory homelessness was increasing, albeit that it remained well below its highpoint under New Labour in the mid-2000s. However, 'prevention' has been questioned by the UK Statistics Authority (2015, para 1.6), which declared that 'the statistics published in *Prevention and Relief* and *Rough Sleeping* cannot be designated as National Statistics' because they were not integrated with other statistics to produce a full picture of homelessness trend'.

Today, the 'policy networks' idea seems applicable to homelessness. In England, under the New Labour and the Coalition governments, there has been close contact between the central departments responsible for homelessness and the voluntary sector organisations that are relied on to implement policies and who, in turn, depend on central government resources to maintain their organisations. Together, they have developed a homelessness programme increasingly related to 'prevention' and 'personal' problems that lead to homelessness. Indeed, 'policy networks' cross political institution boundaries, with, for example, Northern Ireland, Wales and Scotland increasingly adopting the 'preventative' strategy developed in England, albeit in different legal contexts (see Chapter Nine). 'Housing First', with its emphasis on secure housing as a necessary condition for tackling the problems of homeless people with complex, multiple needs, has been adopted by a few organisations in the UK and is supported by research evidence (see, eg, Padgett et al, 2011; Bretherton and Pleace, 2015). However, 'Housing First' did not become a mainstream programme under the Coalition or Conservative governments, perhaps because such backing would help to shift homelessness from a 'personal' problem issue towards structural explanations.

Further reading

Crawson, N. (2013) 'Revisiting the 1977 Housing (Homeless Persons) Act: Westminster, Whitehall and the Homelessness Lobby', *Twentieth Century British History*, vol 24, no 3, pp 424–47.

Fitzpatrick, S., Pawson, H., Bramley, G., Wilcox, S. and Watts, B. (2016) 'The Homelessness Monitor: England, 2016'. Available at: http://www.crisis.org.uk/data/files/publications/Homelessness_Monitor_England_2016_FINAL_(V12).pdf

Pawson, H. (2009) 'Homelessness Policy in England: Promoting "Gatekeeping" or Effective Prevention?', in S. Fitzpatrick, D. Quilgars and N. Pleace (eds) *Homelessness in the UK: Problems and Solutions*, London: Chartered Institute of Housing, pp 90–104.

Somerville, P. (2013) 'Understanding Homelessness', *Housing, Theory and Society*, vol 30, no 4, pp 384–415.

Wilson, D. (2011) *Memoirs of a Minor Public Figure*, London: Quartet.

NINE

Devolution: where is the difference?

Before devolution in 1999, Scotland and Wales were constitutionally subject to the same housing regimes, but in Scotland, there were marked variations in housing outcomes when compared to England, the consequences of political struggles and 'the ways in which legislation was applied [that] reflected the activities of a distinctive Scottish bureaucracy which was a product of the wider Scottish civil society' (Murie, 2004, p 20). Northern Ireland had much more 'de jure' autonomy via Stormont, the Northern Ireland Parliament, until its suspension in 1972. Devolution released Scotland, Wales and Northern Ireland – when its Assembly was operational – from certain governance constraints imposed by Westminster. Each 'home nation' gained various degrees of legislative competence and discretion on how it spent its Westminster allocations on their devolved responsibilities, with the 'Barnett formula' determining Westminster 'block grants'. Devised in 1977 to distribute resources to the 'offices' in Scotland, Wales and Northern Ireland, the Barnett formula's rationale remains obscure but it appears to have been conceived partly to negate pressure from the Secretaries of State for Scotland, Wales and Northern Ireland in the 'horse-trading' for *extra* spending. Historic spending patterns dominate the distribution, so the higher housing spending in Scotland and Northern Ireland in the late 1970s had an impact. Every extra pound spent or cut in England on a devolved service is reflected in the amount distributed to Scotland, Wales and Northern Ireland, allocated according to relative population size.

According to Treasury calculations, in 2014/15, identifiable expenditure per head was £8,638 in England, £10,374 in Scotland, £9,904 in Wales and £11,106 in Northern Ireland (Keep, 2015b), giving some post-devolution administrations more scope than others to provide good services. Expenditure on 'Housing and Community Services' is imprecisely identified as a category within overall spending per head. In 2012/13, £132 was spent in England, £307 in Scotland, £224 in Wales and £477 in Northern Ireland (HM Treasury, 2014b), although such figures mask variations in social housing provision that do not feature fully in Treasury accounting.

Scotland

The official *Owners and Land and Heritages* (Comptroller-General of Inland Revenue for Scotland, 1874), followed by John Bateman's landownership enumeration (Bateman, 1883), revealed that the 1,758 largest landowners owned 92.8% of Scotland, compared to their 56.1% share in England. This concentration, plus recent highland clearance memories, made land a major issue. Henry George found a receptive audience on his first visit to Scotland in 1882 and his ideas were influential in forming the Highland Land League. The Highland Land League used rent strikes, riots and land occupations to highlight the crofters' problems – 'unfair' rents, no tenure security and the inability to secure compensation for crofter improvements when a holding was sold. The campaign was successful in that the Crofters' Holdings (Scotland) Act 1886 gave tenure security to crofters and set up the Crofters Commission to issue judgements on disputes between landlords and tenants. The Liberal Party's landownership platform contributed to its electoral success, there being only one general election from 1832 to 1918 in which the Liberals did not win a Scottish seat majority. In the early 20th century, Scotland's land politics had a particularly confrontational tone, with Labour's Tom Johnston, to become Secretary of State for Scotland in 1929, declaring in 1909:

> Show the people that our Old Nobility is not noble, that its lands are stolen lands – stolen either by force or fraud … do these things and you shatter the Romance that keeps the nation numb and spellbound whilst privilege picks its pockets. (Quoted in Wightman, 2013, p 3)

Housing conditions

Urbanisation in Scotland was highly concentrated. It developed via migration to the new industries from the highlands and Ireland and this movement continued well into the 20th century. Tenements were the main housing form for the working class, perhaps because the Scottish 'feu' land tenure system pushed up land acquisition costs by prevented short land leases. Most tenements were about three to five storeys high and distinctive because they were built with sandstone. Overcrowding levels were very high.

Slum clearance programmes in Edinburgh and Glasgow depleted the accommodation available to the working class. Glasgow's City Improvement Trust, set up by a special Act of Parliament in 1866 and with powers to build houses, displaced 25,375 people but only supplied 1,646 new dwellings. Its housing supply powers were strongly opposed by the Glasgow Landlords' Association because the Trust could secure finance at a lower rate than available to landlords (Fraser and Maver, 1996). Edinburgh demolished 2,721 houses, with only 340 new houses provided. Commenting on the Edinburgh clearance, started in the late 1860s, Smith (1994, p 1) states:

> it probably helped to perpetuate slum conditions, as filtered-down houses became more crowded and dilapidated in their turn. Edinburgh's officials came to the same realization in the 1890s, which led them to accept the need for municipal re-housing projects as the essential complement to slum clearance.

Little was done to improve housing conditions in the late 19th and early 20th centuries, perhaps due to the complacency of the Royal Commission on the Housing of the Working Classes (1885), which, on limited evidence, found that housing defects in Scotland's cities were lower than in London (Rodger, 1989). However, in 1917, the Royal Commission on Housing in Scotland revealed the problem's extent and nature. The Commission had to rely on a special investigation to quantify the issue: 283,654 people lived in overcrowded conditions, 25,908 houses needed repair and 57,764 dwellings should be demolished (Royal Commission on Housing in Scotland, 1917). Witness descriptions of living conditions supplemented these statistics. In Glasgow, for example, the Anderston high tenements were described as:

> The sunk flat houses even in a hot dry summer remain damp and unwholesome. The stairs down to these houses are almost invariably dark and dirty, the passages pitch dark on the brightest day, so that only by feeling along the walls can one discover the doors.... In all these closes the stairs are filthy and evil-smelling, water-closets constantly choked and foul water running down the stairs.... One street is known as 'The Coffin Close,' so bad is its repute. (Royal Commission on Housing in Scotland, 1917, p 4)

Antipathy towards private landlords was, in part, a legacy of hostility to 'the landed interest' in Ireland and the Scottish highlands that the migrants brought into Scotland's urban areas. It was also a reaction to the 'factors' – landlord's agents – who made aggressive use of the Scottish 'right of hypothec' to claim furniture and a workman's tools if rent was not paid. Scotland's distinct legal system, retained in the union, meant that lets were on contracts renewed each year and early agreements were necessary to retain a tenancy. Resentment erupted in the 1915 Glasgow rent strike (see Chapter Four). The 'Red Clydesiders' demanded municipal housing, and municipal housing is what they got. Glasgow, housing about 23% of Scotland's population in 1931, was at the hub of housing politics.

Council housing

The 1917 Royal Commission on Housing in Scotland was in no doubt that rectifying Scotland's housing problem required state action. It stated:

> The local authorities must be placed under a unmistakable obligation to maintain a continuous and systematic survey of their housing accommodation [and] – failing provision by any other agencies – to undertake themselves with financial assistance from the state – the necessary building schemes. (Royal Commission on Housing in Scotland, 1917, p 6)

Most houses built in Scotland between the wars were council houses. Building Glasgow's first council house programme produced tensions between Glasgow and Westminster, with Glasgow Corporation constantly protesting about central interference in its 'municipal mission' (Morgan, 1989). As in England, there were differences in local enthusiasm for council housing, with, for example, Glasgow far more eager to build than Edinburgh (O'Carroll, 1996), where a very high proportion of councillors were private landlords. Indeed, Edinburgh, controlled by the 'Progressives' – an assortment of non-socialist councillors concerned to oppose 'socialism' and keep the rates down – pursued an active council house sales policy between the wars.

Scottish Conservative MPs showed more interest in council housing than their English counterparts. Walter Elliot, MP for Kelvingrove in Glasgow and then Under-Secretary of State for Scotland, tried to promote council housing using a visit by Stanley Baldwin to Glasgow to extract an extra subsidy promise for steel houses, prefabricated by local firms, to become known as 'tin cans'. Baldwin's promise annoyed Neville Chamberlain, Minister for Health, who on a visit to Dundee, extolled homeownership's virtues and spoke 'not at all playfully of the need of his Department to be "exceedingly watchful" that the Scottish Office got no more out of this government than its due share' (Begg, 1996, p 33).

Although Cohen (no date) has detected a developing religious fissure in Glasgow in the 1930s with the rise of the Scottish Protestant League, other commentators have attributed the low sectarian profile in Scotland's housing policies – compared to its impact in Northern Ireland – to the non-sectarian dispersal of Glasgow inner-city inhabitants into new council estates. Bruce, Glendinning and Rosie (2004, p 95) comment:

> The Catholic and Labour-dominated council had no reason to separate Catholics and Protestants in the shift of population. In Belfast and Londonderry, on the other hand, control over housing allocation was a key pillar of Unionist power: housing segregation maintained predicable electoral outcomes.

The Scottish Special Housing Association

In 1937, the Scottish Special Housing Association was formed to build homes in 'distressed' areas. Wary of 'Greeks bearing gifts', many Labour politicians did not welcome the association. In Glasgow, the council was anxious to protect its direct labour organisation, which, by the late 1930s, had build 66% of Glasgow's council houses.

During the Second World War, the Scottish Housing Advisory Committee was set up to plan housing production when the war was over. It identified a 500,000 housing deficit, with all potential suppliers required to meet this need. Alongside local government, the Scottish Special Housing Association would be a significant player, with its house production expanded and its expertise in non-traditional building methods, such as steel and concrete, utilised. The Housing (Scotland) Act 1944 extended the Scottish Special Housing Association's remit to the whole of Scotland. 'Independent' housing associations were to be offered the same access to material licences as local authorities. However, with Bevan, a staunch local authority supporter, the responsible minister, local authorities were allocated the commanding role in post-Second World War housing construction, much to the satisfaction of Scottish Labour councillors. Subsequent Conservative governments showed more enthusiasm for housing associations, and by 1972, the Scottish Special Housing Association had built 46,000 'general needs' homes.

The 'Scottish dimension'

Rose (1982, p 103) has claimed that 'In every political sense the territorial ministries are much more part of Whitehall than they are part of Scotland, Wales or Northern Ireland', but Glendinning and Muthesius (1994, p 177) identified a distinct Scottish dimension to post-war housing politics:

> The great power of senior Scottish Office officials enabled them to evolve consistent Departmental policies almost independent of the views of individual Ministers' ... arising from an informal alliance between Administrators and powerful local authorities both committed to high output and low rents.

Although united on the need for high output, the Scottish Office and Glasgow Corporation disagreed on where to build the houses. Robert Bruce's 1945 scheme (see Chapter One) was strongly supported by Glasgow Corporation, partially because it retained the financial base thought necessary to support Glasgow's shipbuilding industry. The Scottish Office backed a different plan produced by the Clyde Valley Regional Advisory Committee (1946), advised by Sir Patrick Abercrombie, involving housing Glasgow's 'overspill' population in new towns and containing Glasgow's growth by a green belt. Keating (1988, p 20) claims 'This philosophy proved anathema to the corporation (city council) of Glasgow and, when, in 1947 the first new town was duly designated at East Kilbride, it was in the teeth of opposition from the city'. Later, Glasgow reluctantly accepted new town construction but the conflicting planning visions created uncertainty. Glasgow Corporation's objective to retain its population was boosted in the mid-1950s when difficulties in finding 'overspill' areas forced the Scottish Office to be more tolerant of high-rises.

Throughout the 1950s and 1960s, the Scottish Office constantly reminded Whitehall that housing conditions in Scotland were dire and it adopted a more collectivist approach than Westminster. For example, in the early 1950s, it wanted powers for local authorities to acquire not just slums, but properties up to the standard of 'good and tenantable repair'. This alarmed English officials, who opposed the proposals, stating that 'we do not want local authorities to become landlords of more than the minimum possible number of houses' (Ministry of Housing and Local Government, quoted in Yelling, 1995, p 58). However, the officials in the Scottish Office had some success in promoting a new town in Cumbernauld at a time when Conservative Party policy at Westminster was against more new towns. According to Keating and Carter (1987, p 395):

> Winning over the Treasury was no easy task. It regarded the whole business of Scottish housing finance with the greatest suspicion in view of the persistently low levels of rents and what it saw as the disastrous financial basis of the existing new towns at Kilbride and Glenrothes.

The Secretary of State for Scotland, advised by his officials:

> conjured up the nationalist bogey, suggesting that the Scottish Nationalists might gain political advantage by pointing to the contrast with London's eight new towns; and played on Treasury suspicion of Glasgow, saying that if the Corporation were allowed to build the project itself rather than having a new town, it might locate its 'worst' citizens out there. (Keating and Carter, 1987, p 396)

When England moved towards local authority housing only for slum clearance, in Scotland, there was no question of abandoning 'general needs' building – 'despite MHLG [Ministry of Housing and Local Government] grumbles about the resulting "awkward variance" and Treasury exasperation at Scotland's "hopelessly uneconomic" public housing finance' (Glendinning and Muthesius, 1994, p 177).

Throughout the 1960s, Glasgow maintained its ambition to retain population in its city boundaries. Dick Mabon, Minister of State for Scotland during 1967–70, commented:

> There was this prejudice 'We are not going to allow our city to run down to three-quarters of a million!'. And, although they half-heartedly agreed to overspill arrangements, the Glasgow councillors really didn't have it in their hearts to carry them out. (Mabon, 1997, p 55)

The Treasury found Glasgow's attitude irksome and promoted population dispersal in an attempt to undermine the city's power. The Scottish Special Housing Association was used a vehicle to promote 'overspill' development outside Glasgow's boundaries, which, as in the 1930s, was controversial because it usurped local government's housing role. It also charged higher rents and differential rent schemes, prompting rent strikes in the early 1950s. It was also under pressure from the UK Treasury to restrict access to its houses from middle-income households.

Gibb (1989, p 161) notes that in the 1957–69 slum clearance/redevelopment phase:

> the engine of destruction ran at full throttle, resulting in population displacement, social disruption, and the isolation of residual, aged and unskilled groups. The whole process of urgency deciding scale, scale providing speed, and speed and scale spawning huge problems for the future, was one which local and national politicians alike, with few exceptions, were unable to grasp.

A new industrial investment dearth, the decline in Glasgow's traditional industries and the dispersal policies promoted by the Scottish Office produced a 22% decline in Glasgow's population between 1971 and 1981. By the late 1970s, council housing had become a central element in Scotland's politics. Forty of Scotland's 71 constituencies had a council tenant majority, with Glasgow Garscadden, Donald Dewar's seat, containing 96% (Hassan and Shaw, 2012).

Homeownership

Before the First World War, the homeownership rate in Scotland was approximately the same as in England, but by 1971, only 29% of Scottish householders were homeowners, compared to 50.5% in England. The low owner-occupation rate in Scotland can be explained, in part, by the restricted opportunities to become a homeowner. The poor-quality tenements in the private landlord stock did not tempt tenants to buy their inner-city homes and Scotland did not experience Southern England's 1930s' suburban boom. Cheap council housing had an impact. Checkland (1976, p 92) claims that under Labour control post-1933, the Glasgow Corporation 'has been increasingly a social service run by the Labour Party centred on public sector housing at low rents'. Rodger and El Qaddo (1989, p 208) note that 'by the 1950s the erosion of council rents meant they were less than half the pre-war levels in real terms'. These low rents produced 'a heavily subsidised "good deal" for many middle income Scots' (Maclennan, 2001, p 154) – indicating how low-cost rental can overcome a 'homeownership ideology' (Murie and Williams, 2015). When Labour was contemplating a UK scheme to expand council houses sales, *Scottish*

Housing: A Consultative Document (Scottish Development Department, 1977) identified the low owner-occupation rate in Scotland and supported council house sales as a way to bring Scotland closer to the European average.

Scotland's tenure structure changed significantly under the Thatcher/Major governments. In 1996, 59.2% of Scottish householders were owner-occupiers, 29.7% rented from the public sector, 4.4% were housing association tenants and 6.8% rented from private landlords. The Right to Buy, under the Tenants Rights Etc (Scotland) Act 1980, was the dominant factor in this tenure transformation. After a slow start compared to England, Right to Buy sales accelerated and exceeded the English rate. Owner-occupation was also encouraged through 'Gro-Grants', providing eligible developers with the minimum funding needed to meet the difference between construction costs and market value in designated urban and rural areas. By 2001, no Scottish parliamentary constituency had a council tenant majority, with 37.2% being the highest proportion.

Housing associations

In 1972, when 25% of Scottish households still had an outside lavatory, a group of Govan tenants campaigned for indoor lavatories in tenements, and, helped by a housing association buying their properties, they were successful (Young, 2013). Following this tenant-led campaign, community-based housing associations – with substantial resident representation on management committees – were developed in the 1970s as vehicles to deliver older home improvement. As council capital programmes were squeezed in the 1980s, the community-based model was used for a number of small-scale council house stock transfers to housing associations and cooperatives.

Scottish Homes was set up in 1988 by amalgamating the Housing Corporation for Scotland with the Scottish Special Housing Association, creating a large quasi-autonomous non-governmental organisation ('quango'), which, to the satisfaction of the Scottish Office, allowed Scotland to break free from the English Housing Corporation, regarded as dominating the small Housing Corporation for Scotland (Robertson, 2001). Initially, a significant proportion of Scottish Homes' resources were directed to four 'Urban Partnership Areas' in Castlemilk, Whitfield, Ferguslie Park and Wester Hailes, and the quango embarked upon an energetic stock transfer programme with the intention of transferring its entire stock of 74,000 homes. Under the Major government, housing associations fared well in comparison to England.

The Scottish government

Margaret Thatcher, having praised her radical political agenda in England, remarked that 'There was no Tartan Thatcherite revolution' (Thatcher, 1993, p 618). MacWhirter (2009, p 2) claims:

> Margaret Thatcher still occupies a prominent place in Scottish political demonology. Gordon Brown may have invited her for tea, but there are precious few homes in Scotland that would take her in, even now. No prime minister in history, Labour or Conservative, has generated such hostility for so long from so many in Scotland. Almost from the moment that Thatcher entered No 10 in 1979, the Scottish Tories went into a tailspin from which they never recovered. They were wiped out in the 1997 general election.

Housing was devolved to the Scottish Parliament in 1999. However, as Gibb (2014, p 29) states, 'housing policy is better conceived as a hybrid of devolved and reserved powers'. Housing Benefit, as an aspect of social security, was reserved for Westminster, as were the bulk of taxation powers, mortgage market regulation and the overall fiscal framework determining the resources that the Scottish government could use and producing 'spillover effects' that the Scottish, and other devolved governments, had to manage.

According to some commentators, the use of proportional representation to elect the Scottish Parliament was aimed at producing a more inclusive and cooperative, and less adversarial, form of politics (Hazell, 2000), to which might be added the aim of preventing a Scottish National Party (SNP) majority. The first two elections in 1999 and 2003 resulted in New Labour-dominated coalitions with the Liberal Democrats. In 2007, the SNP formed a one-party minority government, with confidence and supply support from the Scottish Green Party and Scottish Conservatives. It quickly renamed the Scottish Executive the Scottish Government. On winning an overall majority in 2011, the SNP assumed full control.

'Social' housing

Those who, in 1999, expected a return to council housing as a main housing policy instrument were to be disappointed. Scottish Homes, accused of being 'an interventionist body with a privatising public purpose' and 'out of kilter with Scottish political opinion' (Robertson, 2001, p 131), was absorbed into Communities Scotland, an executive agency directly accountable to ministers. This was part of variable initiatives across the devolved administrations to reduce the 'democratic deficit' arising from unaccountable quangos (Birrell, 2008). New Labour robustly promoted stock transfer in Scotland, with Arms Length Management Organisations not being an option. However, anticipating significant opposition, New Labour offered incentives. The transfers would be to smaller, community-based associations. The Treasury agreed it would absorb any outstanding debt on the council stock transferred, leaving only any 'dowry' that might be required to ensure the new landlord had the necessary funds to undertake the required improvements to be financed by the local authority involved. Scotland went further than England by introducing the Scottish Secure Tenancy in the Housing (Scotland) Act 2001, applying to both local authority and registered social landlord tenants. In 2003, Glasgow's housing stock was transferred to Glasgow Housing Association, a not-for-profit company, with its Board consisting of tenants, councillors and independent representatives. The majority of tenants supported the transfer, which was facilitated by the Scottish Executive not charging for early debt redemption, unlike the Birmingham transfer, which received a 'no' vote from tenants and would have involved a £208 million penalty for early debt redemption. New Labour also promised there would be a further transfer to smaller, community-based associations. Under SNP control, stock transfer declined. Wilcox et al (2010, p 9) commented 'While Scotland more forcefully promoted stock transfers following devolution, that stance has now softened'. In Scotland, 19% of the local authority stock had been transferred to housing associations by 2010, compared to 24% in England.

The Scottish Government did not pursue the 'affordable' homes (up to 80% of market rents) policy adopted in England. In 2013/14, grants to associations under the Scottish 'Affordable Homes' Programme were, on average, 50% of a new housing association home's construction costs, and although housing association output declined, local authorities made a significant contribution to new social housing. Almost a quarter of Scotland's housing belongs to housing associations or local government, compared to 17% in England. This helps to explain why the gap between the proportion of children in poverty (below 60% of median income) before and after housing costs is 6% in Scotland, compared to 11% in England (DWP, 2015).

The Right to Buy

The Right to Buy was Margaret Thatcher's flagship housing policy, and a symbolic, if lukewarm, break with Thatcherism was made when the Labour–Liberal Democrat administration introduced a 'modernised' Right to Buy in 2001, applying it to all new social housing tenants, with the qualifying period extended from two to five years and discounts subject to a £15,000 maximum. The Housing (Scotland) Act 2010, passed by an SNP administration, abolished the Right to Buy for new tenants. However, despite these gestures applying to new tenants, the Right to Buy was more buoyant in Scotland compared to England because in Scotland, existing tenants were not subject to the limitations on discounts imposed in England in the mid-2000s. Average discounts in Scotland were 57% in 2008, compared to 28% in England (Wilcox et al, 2015) and the Treasury did not appropriate the lion's share of capital receipts. The Right to Buy depleted the Scottish 'social' housing stock, although the higher level of new 'social' housing completions than in England and Wales mitigated the sales impact.

In 2012, the Scottish Government issued a consultation paper, 'The Future of the Right to Buy in Scotland: A Consultation' (Scottish Government, 2012). The responses to the consultation showed that 92% of housing associations in Scotland and 81% of local authorities supported abolition, along with four out of five tenant groups. The Housing Scotland Act 2014 made provision for the Right to Buy in Scotland to end in 2016.

Owner-occupation and private landlords

The Right to Buy helped to push owner-occupation in Scotland up to 65.4% in 2007. Between 2002 and 2007, house prices increased faster in Scotland than in the UK, but post-2008, the change was about the UK average, leaving prices in Scotland above Wales, Northern Ireland and four of the English regions. Restrictions on mortgage availability post-2008 meant that the owner-occupied sector had declined to 58% by 2014, with the private landlord sector increasing from 9.6% in 2007 to 14.8% in 2014. Under the Antisocial Behaviour etc (Scotland) Act 2004, almost all private landlords had to apply for registration with their local authority as 'fit and proper persons' in order to let property, and in 2012, landlords were required to issue tenants with an information pack.

In 2013, the Scottish Government released a strategy paper on the private rented sector (Scottish Government, 2013) followed by two consultation documents, which included the possibility of greater security for tenants and raising the rent control issue. Rent control was supported by the Living Rent Campaign, arguing that local councils should be able to implement specific local measures if housing costs were more than one third of a tenant's income. The landlord interest, represented by the Scottish Association of Landlords, campaigned against rent controls. The Private Housing (Tenancies) (Scotland) Act 2016 limited rent increases to one per year, with three months' notice, and gave local authorities powers to control rents in rent pressure areas.

Homelessness

Homelessness has come to symbolise a distinctive Scottish standpoint on social policy that, at least in rhetoric, emphasises egalitarianism, social inclusion, collectivism, social justice and 'social citizenship' (Mooney and Scott, 2012). Homelessness policy became a way to express solidarity in a Scottish identity. This 'rights-based' approach has not always characterised the Scottish attitude. Initially, the application of the Housing (Homeless Persons) Act 1977 to Scotland was opposed by Scottish local authorities and the Scottish Office (Gibson, no date). Nonetheless, a distinctive Scottish approach started to emerge in the 1990s when the punitive approach applied in England by the Housing Act 1996 was resisted in Scotland (Keating, 2010).

The Homelessness (Scotland) Act 2003 made provision for the distinction between priority and non-priority need to be gradually phased, so that, by the end of 2012, all unintentionally homeless people would be entitled to 'settled' accommodation, not an 'assured short-hold' dominant in the private landlord sector. Under the new legislation, the number of applications for assistance assessed as 'in priority need' increased and there was a rapid rise in the number of households in temporary accommodation – up from 4,060 in 2002 to 10,815 in 2010 (Scottish Government, 2010). The percentage of new 'social' landlord lets to homeless people increased from 26.8% in 2004/05 to 44.5% in 2010/11, prompting some concern about the system acting 'against "hard working families" who wish to remain in their local area close to their existing kin networks' (McKee and Phillips, 2012, p 230).

In response to the 'homelessness route' becoming dominant in access to social housing, Scotland adopted the English 'prevention' strategy. In 2009, new guidance was issued to local authorities on homelessness prevention endorsing the housing options approach. There was a decline in homelessness post-2012, attributed by the Scottish Government (2014, p 1) to 'the impact of housing options/homelessness prevention strategies adopted by most local authorities over the past few years rather than to changes in the underlying drivers of homelessness'. Spurr (2014) reported that Glasgow Council was under investigation by the Scottish Housing Regulator over its homelessness provision after 235 of 391 homeless people had been turned away in six months.

Land

As Chenevix-Trench and Philip (2001, p 9) comment, land issues remain 'central to the Scottish psyche'. Landownership was widely discussed in the devolution debate, and the Land Reform Act 2003 introduced new rights of public access to land and inland water, provided a right to 'first refusal' to local community groups when land was up for sale, and provided an absolute right to buy for crofting communities. This forced sale to crofting communities, equivalent to compulsory purchase, was controversial, with accusations made of a 'Zimbabwean land grab' (Mitchell, 2014, p 259). However, take-up of the rights under the 2003 Act was limited (Warren and McKee, 2011).

After the publication of *The Land of Scotland and the Common Good* (Land Reform Review Group, 2014), the SNP re-examined the land issue. First Minister Nicola Sturgeon told the Scottish Parliament that 'Scotland's land must be an asset that benefits the many, not the few' (quoted in Hetherington, 2015, p 22). A consultation document was issued (Scottish Government, 2015a) followed by the publication of the Land Reform (Scotland) Bill. It contained a number of provisions to make landownership and use in Scotland more transparent and to create an enhanced right for community bodies to buy land, rural and urban, to further sustainable development.

Land release for new homes has been less controversial in Scotland than in England, although, in 2015, the Scottish Government set up a planning system review to recommend ways to remove unnecessary blockages in the decision-making process. There was no Scottish equivalent of the English 'localism' agenda, and in Scotland, there has been continued reliance on undiluted 'Section 75 agreements', similar to 'Section 106' agreements in England, to capture development gain. Compared to England, Scotland's house-building record since devolution has been sound, consistently producing at least 25% more houses per head of population (Scottish Government, 2015b).

Housing and the independence debate

Housing policy – apart from the 'bedroom tax' – had a low profile in the debates leading to the 2014 referendum on independence for Scotland. The Scottish Government's 670-page White Paper on the referendum devoted only just over two pages to housing, focusing on the social housing sector, Housing Benefit and energy efficiency (Scottish Government, 2013). The 'bedroom tax' affected an estimated 80,000 families in Scotland and carried the symbolism that the Conservatives still governed Scotland – 90% of Scottish MPs had voted against the tax. The Scottish Government used its powers to mitigate the tax's impact via discretionary payments and the SNP promised its abolition in an independent Scotland.

As decision day on independence for Scotland drew closer and a public opinion poll indicated a 'yes' majority, a joint statement was published by Better Together, organising the 'no' campaign, and co-signed by the three main UK party leaders. This gave a commitment to grant Scotland increased powers over domestic taxes and parts of the social security system and suggested that the Barnett formula would continue in the event of a 'no' vote.

Wales

Enthusiasm for devolution was lower in Wales, with 50.3% of the voters favouring devolution in the 1997 referendum, compared to 74% in Scotland and 71% in Northern Ireland. When established in 1999, the National Assembly for Wales was not granted primary legislative powers, although it could change secondary legislation. The Government of Wales Act 2006 made provision for the National Assembly for Wales to initiate a Legislative Competence Order (LCO), thereby reducing dependence on finding an appropriate Westminster Bill to attach a Welsh dimension. The Executive of the National Assembly for Wales became the Welsh Government. In early 2010, the National Assembly for Wales voted for a referendum on further law-making powers, and following a positive referendum result, the Assembly assumed new powers in 2011, enabling it to make laws in all 20 areas devolved to Wales, including housing. The Wales Act 2014 devolved land stamp duty, business rates and landfill tax to Wales and provided for a referendum in Wales on whether income tax elements should be devolved.

Prior to devolution, housing policy in Wales was similar to policy in England, albeit discharged initially through the Welsh Board of Health and later by the Welsh Office. Historically, the land issue had a Welsh dimension. The Welsh Land, Commercial and Labour League was formed in 1886 to provide a voice for farmers and labourers facing rent increases. A special Welsh feature was the added tithe payment to the Church of England paid in the rent, bitterly opposed by Welsh non-conformists. Although mainly legal in its protest, there were occasional unlawful outbreaks, such as demolishing enclosure fences. Lloyd George had connections with the League, which was successful in obtaining a Royal Commission on Land in Wales and Monmouthshire, reporting in 1896. The Royal Commission claimed that the landlord–tenant relationship in Wales was satisfactory and later agitation around the land issue was absorbed into Lloyd George's 'People's Budget' dispute with the House of Lords.

Wales has a higher homeownership rate than England. In some Welsh coalfields, there was a working–class owner-occupation tradition, with 'building clubs' formed to raise money to enable coalminers to buy houses. In explaining the Welsh homeownership rate, Thompson (2004) adds the lack of industrial capital to provide an adequate supply of rented accommodation and active encouragement from industrialists, who believed that homeownership would promote responsible citizenship and were sometimes willing to offer loans. Sir Henry Tyler, chairman of the Rhymney Iron Company, claimed in 1906 that workers who owned their own houses 'become conservatives, and good supporters of general good government, rather than of one or the other political party' (quoted in Thompson, 2004, pp 254–5).

Post-1900, there were Welsh versions of UK initiatives. For example, in 1911, H. Stanley Jevons, Professor of Economics at University College Cardiff, became Managing Director of a company set up to establish a garden suburb designed by Raymond Unwin and involving a workers' cooperative, but it was unfortunately forced into liquidation. Preservation of rural Wales featured predominantly between the wars, with the Campaign for the Protection of Rural Wales set up in 1928. Clough Williams-Ellis argued for preserving rural Wales, stating that 'I want to see Wales keeping her own honest Welsh traditions and not becoming an imitation of England' (Williams-Ellis, 1930, p 72). After the Second World War, two new towns were designated – Cwmbran (in 1949) and Newtown (in 1967) – but only one green belt, located between Cardiff and Newport. The Welsh language has had a role in housing politics, with the purchase of second homes in rural Wales seen as a threat to opportunities for local people and as eroding the Welsh language.

Post-1945, Wales has been a Labour stronghold, with Labour gaining 58.3% of the vote in 1945, rising to 60.7% in 1966. Labour's low point was in 1983, with a 37.3% vote share, but this had increased to 54.7% in 1997. Before devolution, houses in Wales were older than in the other parts of the UK and this was reflected in the poorer housing stock condition (Bourton and Leather, 2000), with Wales having a higher proportion of low-income households living in poorer-quality housing than England or Scotland.

The National Assembly for Wales

Until 2010, the housing policies adopted in Wales were similar to England, with 'Welsh' often incorporated into each new initiative's title. The Welsh Government promoted stock transfer – without, as in England, an Arms Length Management Organisation. Initially, stock transfer, despite being promoted on a mutual community housing model – the houses were owned by a cooperative of which all tenants were members – and by the Treasury absorbing debt, had limited success. Post-2007, the policy gained momentum, and by 2010, the housing association stock had increased to 9.9% – similar to the English percentage. However a 'no vote' sequence in the Vale of Glamorgan, Flintshire and Caerphilly stalled the programme. In 2010, only 26% of the 'social' housing stock in Wales met the Welsh Housing Quality Standard, albeit a somewhat more exacting standard than in England (Welsh Audit Office, 2012). The initial slow pace of stock transfer is a reason for this but Fitzpatrick et al (2013, p 4) also point out that 'Wales also has a far less favourable financial devolution settlement, compared to Scotland, particularly in respect of council housing finances where it continues to make payments (£68 million in 2012/13) of rental "surpluses" to HM Treasury'.

Homelessness

Local authority homelessness acceptances followed the same trajectory as in England, reaching a high point of 10,071 in 2004 before declining to 5,100 in 2010. In contrast to England, where homelessness acceptances increased post-2010, the Welsh figure remained constant and the number of households living in temporary accommodation declined. In 2014, the prevention strategy became more prominent when the Welsh government introduced the first Welsh housing legislation into the Welsh Assembly. The Housing (Wales) Act 2014 placed a stronger duty on local authorities to prevent homelessness and allowed them to use suitable accommodation in the private sector to house homeless people. 'Priority need' categories were retained, except that ex-prisoners were excluded, but local authorities had duties to prevent and relieve homelessness with regard to households not in 'priority need' categories. Moreover, the legislation extended the 'threatened with homelessness' definition from 28 to 56 days, giving local authorities a longer time to engage in prevention. Local authorities were expected to have a comprehensive range of interventions listed in the statutory guidance.

Sustainability

The National Assembly for Wales adopted a more enthusiastic approach to sustainability than in England, with all new houses required to reach an energy-efficiency level, applied in England only to social housing providers. The Welsh Government announced its intension to make sprinklers compulsory and to impose additional carbon reduction measures. The Welsh sustainability agenda attracted criticism from the Conservatives. In 2013, Eric Pickles, then Secretary of State for Communities and Local Government, stated:

> Let us look at Labour's record on housing there [Wales]. Labour has failed to boost house-building starts by a mere 1% as compared to 19% in England. Labour in Wales hit the housing market with extra red tape, adding £13,000 to the cost of building a new home in comparison with England. (Pickles, 2013)

Pickles' 'red tape' comment was based on complaints from Redrow South Wales, a building firm, that future carbon emission reduction requirements would deter house-building in Wales. The Welsh Government responded by requiring an 8% cut in carbon emissions from 2014, rather than the planned 40%, and postponing the requirement to install sprinklers in new homes.

The Right to Buy/private landlords

Post-2010, the National Assembly for Wales has adopted a different direction to Westminster on the Right to Buy, with discounts restricted to £8,000, local authorities allowed to suspend the Right to Buy in specified circumstances and Labour announcing its intention to abolish the Right to Buy.

The National Assembly for Wales has been more proactive than Westminster in its approach to the private landlord sector and the Housing (Wales) Act 2014 established the compulsory registration of private landlords and lettings agencies. It also allowed councils to charge twice the rate of council tax on long-term empty homes, part of a positive approach to empty homes started in 2012 with a £20 million investment that had brought 4,371 empty homes into use by the end of 2014. However, since devolution, the house-building record in Wales has been disappointing, with the number of new houses completed per head of population being consistently lower than in England (Scottish Government, 2015a).

Northern Ireland

Land politics were forged in Ireland. The *Return of Owners of Land* (Local Government Board, Ireland, 1876) revealed that 6,500 landlords – British or Protestant Anglo-Irish – owned over 90% of Irish land, with an average of 27,000 acres each. The tenants numbered half a million and were overwhelmingly Catholic. Post-1879, bad harvests devastated the relative small farmer prosperity that followed the 1845–50 famine and produced a 'land war' led by Charles Stewart Parnell and his Irish National Land League. Close connections with nationalist struggles made land a sensitive issue. In the early 19th century, the Anglo-Irish Protestant landowners let their land to 'middlemen', who would then sublet it to Catholic smallholders. Henry George was influential in highlighting the 'land issue', although his solution to the problem was different to Parnell, who advocated the break-up of the landed estates into smallholdings rather than a single land tax. In 1881, Gladstone's Liberal government, alarmed by the growth in Irish nationalism, passed a Land Act granting 'fair rents', fixity of tenure and freedom of sale, supervised by an Irish Land Commission. It also allowed public loans of up to 75% of the purchase price to tenant farmers if the owner was willing to sell. This rural tenant population's 'special treatment' produced demands for assistance to urban renters.

Council housing

The first subsidised state housing was built under various Labourers Acts applying to Ireland in the late 19th and early 20th centuries. The measures 'arose from the need to appease the Irish Party in lieu of dealing with the thornier question of self-government', and 'by 1914 a total of nearly 50,000 cottages had been built for agricultural labourers, mostly with subsidy from the Imperial Exchequer' (Fraser, 1996, pp 41, 21). Henry George had directed attention to the landlord's power in urban areas, stating 'if he wished to introduce an Irish peasant to some of the worst sights attributable to landlordism, he would take him to see Dublin, Cork, and Belfast' (George, 1883). The Town Tenants (Ireland) Act 1906 gave rights to urban tenants to retain the value of their improvements. The Housing of the Working Classes (Ireland) Act 1908, known as the Clancy Act after its promoter John Joseph Clancy, an Irish Nationalist, gave limited subsidies to facilitate building council houses in urban areas.

Although Ireland pioneered subsidised council housing, Stormont disliked the idea. In the interwar years, council housing building per 1,000 population was far lower than in England and Wales (Murie et al, 1971). Stormont relied on small subsidies to the private sector – 'such a simple scheme.... Ordinary people could build themselves a nice house, and get a subsidy for it. It had no politics in it and it cost very little money' (Brett, 1986, p 18) – but private sector building was also lower than in England and Wales. Part of the explanation for this housing dearth can be located in the sounder quality of Belfast's housing – industrialisation was late in Belfast and much of its housing was built to 'by-law' standards – but the absence of class politics in a political system based on religion was a contributory factor.

The investment dearth in new housing between the wars, population growth concentrated in specific areas and the Second World War 'blitz' produced a serious housing problem. In 1946, it was agreed that there should be parity in services and taxation between Northern Ireland and Britain. However, recognising the poor local authority performance in building houses between the wars, the Northern Ireland Housing Trust was set up under the Housing Act (Northern Ireland) 1945 – 'hotly opposed by the Unionist old guard' (Brett, 1986, p 26) – tasked with providing housing accommodation for workers in coordination with local authorities.

The Northern Ireland Housing Executive

In 1971, 66 local authorities, three new town commissioners and the Northern Ireland Housing Trust discharged Northern Ireland's housing function. The owner-occupied sector formed 46.6% of the stock, 34.8% was 'state' housing, 18.8% was privately rented and a very small proportion rented from housing associations. Between 1949 and 1967, new house completions per 1,000 in Northern Ireland were below the Great Britain average: 3.5 per 1,000 in Northern Ireland, compared to 5 per 1,000 in Great Britain (McPeake, 2014).

Following the civil rights marches – the first in 1968 as a protest against housing allocations – and the subsequent intensification of violence, the Westminster government set up the Cameron Commission to inquire into the unrest. The Commission commented:

> In both fields – work and housing – political intervention and discrimination against Catholics was alleged to be operative.... We are not only strongly of opinion that these complaints must be placed very high in the list of deeply felt and justified grievances and that their remedy, both by any necessary legislative or administrative action – if fairly carried out, and seen to be so carried out – would be a major step towards healing the communal divisions which lie so close to the root of these disorders. (Cameron, 1969, paras 129–130)

In 1969, Home Secretary James Callaghan reported reaction to an appointed Northern Ireland Housing Executive:

> Amongst the flurry of suggestions that I put to them that afternoon the one that caused the greatest consternation was that there should be a single authority for the allocation and building of housing. They regarded the idea with near horror on political and administrative grounds for, of course, it went to the heart of political patronage. (Quoted in Brett, 1986, p 10)

An appointed Northern Ireland Housing Executive was set up in 1971. The Executive became responsible for over 150,000 homes transferred from local government and other agencies.

The Northern Ireland Housing Executive was a 'depoliticised', comprehensive housing authority set up to remove discrimination in housing allocation and to improve overall housing conditions. A 1974 House Condition Survey found that Northern Ireland 'had the worst housing conditions in Britain and amongst the worst in Europe' (Northern Ireland Housing Executive, 2011, p 19). House-building per 1,000 population in Northern Ireland had 'achieved parity by the mid-1990s' (Paris, 2001, p 15) and was well above the Great Britain average from the late 1990s (McPeake, 2014). Connolly and Knox (1991) claim that the territorial 'housing policy network' operating in Northern Ireland – the Housing Executive, the Department of the Environment, Northern Ireland Office and local government – was successful in arguing the special case for housing expenditure in Northern Ireland and even managed to resist Thatcher's 'tenants' choice' and Housing Action Trusts. By 2011 – measured by the presence of health and safety 'hazards' – Davison et al (2012) found that the relatively new condition of the Northern Ireland housing stock produced standards higher than in England and Wales. The unitary points system for allocating housing helped to promote the Northern Ireland Executive's reputation for neutrality in housing policy. Murtagh (2001, p 84) comments:

> Avoidance of any engagement with even the language of conflict, or sectarianism, became an important organisational value in distancing the Housing Executive from the pre-reform period of bias and discrimination.... When the organisation tentatively strayed into this area ... it was to underscore the structural complexity of the task and the limits on a social housing agency to address the problems.

The Northern Ireland Assembly

The Northern Ireland Assembly, elected by proportional representation, was established under the 1998 'Belfast' or 'Good Friday' Agreement. It was allowed legislative competence across the social policy domain, including housing, and the Northern Ireland Housing Executive became accountable to the Northern Ireland Assembly via a division of the Northern Ireland Executive – the Department for Social Development. The Assembly was suspended three times, the longest period being from 14 October 2002 until 7 May 2007. On suspension, the Assembly's powers reverted to the Northern Ireland Office.

Given the Northern Ireland Housing Executive's dominance in housing since 1971, the long suspension of the Northern Ireland Assembly and the power sharing built into the devolution agreements, it is not surprising that housing policy in Northern Ireland has been described as 'technocratic' (Muir, 2012). Indeed, in Northern Ireland, the need for new social housing is assessed on the 'Net Stock Model' (NSM), which takes into account both demographic change and the ability of the private sector to meet the household formation arising from this change. Social housing is intended to meet any deficit, and in Northern Ireland, social housing production relative to population has been higher than in England, Scotland and Wales.

Overall, policy has tended to reflect English policy modified in relationship to Northern Ireland's 'civic dynamics' and the difficulties involved in securing agreement between the political parties, up to five, represented on the Executive. Power sharing has tended to produce the 'lowest common denominator' (McLaughlin, 2005; Birrell and Gray, 2011). Thus, for example, stock transfer from the Northern Ireland Housing Executive was not promoted due to 'the potential problems of community ownership in the context of communal conflict' (Birrell, 2009, p 67), the absence of large existing associations to take the stock and the lack of political consensus on the policy. The stock transfer restraint contributed to housing associations owning only 3.3% of the Northern Ireland stock, compared to 10% in England, although, in the late 1990s, housing associations, assisted by grants and land transfer from the Northern Ireland Housing Executive, became responsible for new social housing.

In 2002, the average Northern Ireland house price was 35% less than the UK average; by 2007, it was 2% more (Pawson and Wilcox, 2013) – the 'peace dividend', the close connection to the 'Celtic Tiger' Irish economy and the credit boom all contributing to the bubble. The bubble burst in 2008, and by 2011, the average house price was down to £141,331 – 42% less than the UK average. New private completions fell from 16,930 in 2006 to 6,430 in 2012, boosted by only 400 extra houses built by housing associations. A price boom impact was an increase in private landlordism, a tendency that continued into the bust as Buy to Let landlords snapped up 'bargains'. In 2002, 6.6% of the stock was rented privately; in 2015, the figure was 21% and its importance was recognised by the introduction of a private landlord registration scheme (Brown, 2016).

Muir (2012) has attempted to assess the impact of devolution on social housing since the restoration of the Northern Ireland Assembly in 2007. Based on policy analysis and interviews with five policymakers, Muir concluded that politicians were more sensitive to 'civic dynamics' and political interests than the 'technocrats' working in the system. She stated:

> the 2007–11 Assembly and Executive electoral term marked a transitional phase between a technocratic past, in which bureaucrats were in control, and policy ownership of the social housing policy field by newly powerful elected politicians. This gradual transition may be why the very

active Northern Ireland policy networks, complete with impressive links to other parts of the UK, were unable to move forward cherished policy goals such as a housing strategy, developer contributions, and – in a wider policy arena – the 'Cohesion, Sharing and Integration' strategy. (Muir, 2012, p 18)

In 2013, Nelson McCausland, Democratic Unionist Party member and Minister for Social Development, made an announcement on the conclusions drawn from a fundamental review of the Northern Ireland Housing Executive (Northern Ireland Assembly, 2012). McCausland set out plans to split the Northern Ireland Housing Executive into landlord and strategic functions, with strategic issues staying within the department and landlord functions moving to the housing association sector. The Department for Social Development, supported by a regional housing body, would take responsibility for overall housing strategy, policy, legislation and funding, plus regulation and inspection. By transferring the organisation's 90,000 homes to housing associations, the Department hoped to attract private investment into the stock (see Chapter Seven). However, despite questions surrounding its role, the Northern Ireland Housing Executive had built a formidable reputation in Northern Ireland as a force for good and had considerable political support. By May 2016, no firm decisions on its future had been made.

Mixed estates

Faced by the multiple problems involved in managing housing in the context of violence, the Northern Ireland Housing Executive did not attempt to engineer mixed estates: segregation according to religion grew between 1971 and 1991 but did not increase between 1991 and 2001. In 2004, the *Belfast Telegraph* stated:

> Across the whole of Northern Ireland, 92.5% of all 100,000 public homes are segregated.... Belfast city was always pretty bad, but this is the worst ever, and may be the worst in Western Europe. Polarisation is greater than it ever was – it's a really tragic commentary on the state of the society. (Quoted in Byrne et al, 2006, p 13)

In 2006, the Northern Ireland Housing Executive set up the Shared Future Housing Programme. Although some politicians were demanding new social housing provision based on religious divisions, future new-build schemes would have a better balance of people from different religious backgrounds and grants and advisors would enable community organisations to celebrate diversity and bring together people in existing areas. Creating balanced communities has been difficult, with the *Irish News* reporting:

> Republicans have used Irish flags to mark out a new social housing estate as their territory in a mirror image of the actions of loyalist paramilitaries. Sinn Féin has condemned the erection of tricolours outside a social housing development on the outskirts of north Belfast and called for their immediate removal. The fresh attempt by republicans to claim the site at the Mill Road in Newtownabbey comes just days after loyalists were criticised for staking their claim on a similar shared housing development in Carryduff, Co Down, by erecting flags on 'every lamp post'. (*Irish News*, 2015)

Planning

Under devolution, physical planning became the responsibility of the Planning Service, an Executive within the Department of the Environment. The Department of Regional Development (DRD) had a strategic planning position and was responsible for the implementation of the Regional Development Strategy. These mechanisms remained when direct rule was operating but were subject to Westminster rather than Assembly control. Northern Ireland has extensive green belt areas, with the Belfast green belt, called the 'stop-line', introduced in 1964 by Stormont. Nevertheless, physical planning was not a significant restraint on housing development. 'Local government played no direct role in planning' (Paris et al, 2003, p 167); the 26 local government authorities acted as pressure groups via consultation.

The Planning Act Northern Ireland 2011 made provision for the restoration of planning powers to local government in 2015, with the number of authorities reduced to 11. However, these powers were constrained, with local authorities required to act with 'community partners' in compiling a community plan, and were accompanied by guidance similar to that contained in England's 2012 National Planning Policy Framework. 'The Strategic Planning Policy Statement for Northern Ireland' (Department of the Environment, Northern Ireland, 2015, para 3.8) stated:

Under the SPPS [Strategic Planning Policy Statement], the guiding principle for planning authorities in determining planning applications is that sustainable development should be permitted, having regard to the development plan and all other material considerations, unless the proposed development will cause demonstrable harm to interests of acknowledged importance.

Welfare reform

'Welfare reform' implementation in Northern Ireland, in particular, the 'bedroom tax', was troublesome. Social security was formally a devolved matter, as it had been from 1922 to 1972, and significant change meant special Northern Ireland legislation. However, adherence to UK benefit parity was a condition of Westminster financial support (Parry, 2007). The Coalition government's 'welfare reform' package had a greater impact in Northern Ireland than in Scotland, Wales or any English region, 'costing an estimated £630 a year for every working-age adult – even without implementing the bedroom tax' (Wilcox et al, 2014, p 17). Moreover, a shortage of smaller homes and community divisions made it more difficult for households to downsize.

The 'spare room subsidy' removal was included in a Northern Ireland welfare reform Bill but the Bill was shelved, allegedly because Sinn Fein President, Gerry Adams, opposed to the austerity agenda in the Republic of Ireland, could not be seen to be enforcing cuts in the North (Reidy, 2014). The initial inability of the Northern Ireland Assembly to agree a budget, with £114 million Westminster grant reductions for not implementing the 'bedroom tax', produced a crisis. Sinn Fein blocked welfare reform and the issue featured strongly in the 2015 general election campaign.

The Democratic Unionist Party opposed the 'bedroom tax' in the Westminster Parliament and called for its abolition in its 2015 manifesto (Democratic Unionist Party, 2015). Nolan (2014, p 71) has suggested that the fissure between the wealthy and the poor, rather than the differences between the two main factions – Catholics and Protestants – has historically been of restricted concern in Northern Ireland, but the 'bedroom tax' sparked disquiet across the Northern Ireland parties. The impasse on welfare reform continued after the election, derailing Northern Ireland finances. Sinn Fein continued to resist welfare reform and, with the SDLP (Social Democratic Labour Party) and Green Party, made a 'petition of concern', blocking welfare reform because it did not receive the required cross–community support. However, the issue became entangled with the role of Sinn Fein in the power-sharing executive, with allegations that some of its members remained involved in the Irish Republican Army. A settlement was made on 17 November 2015 involving Northern Ireland acceptance of welfare reform elements in return for the devolution of Corporation Tax, an assortment of extra resources and a commitment of £585 million of Northern Irish government funding that effectively ended the 'bedroom tax' and considerably reduced the impact of other 'welfare reforms' in the pipeline (Northern Ireland Executive, 2015).

Conclusion

Birrell (2009, p 94) placed devolved housing policy in his 'incremental change and low level differences' category, as opposed to his 'innovations, flagship policies and distinctiveness' grouping. In Wales and in Scotland, these 'low level differences' tended to reflect internal 'old' and 'new' divisions within the Labour Party on issues related to 'privatisation', such as stock transfer and the Right to Buy. In Scotland, some differences seemed symbolic, for example, placing limitations on the Right to Buy for new tenants but retaining large discounts for existing tenants. Commenting on the early years of devolution in Northern Ireland, Paris, Gray and Muir (2003, p 174) maintain:

> The big and overwhelming political issue in Northern Ireland remained its constitutional status. The system of checks and balances within the Assembly and Executive provided for interesting debates and disagreements. It is hard to disagree with Murray's (2002) contention, however, that what was happening was more like a large council allocating moneys from central government within fairly narrowly defined parameters.

Thus, it was tempting to conclude that devolved housing policy had brought increased regional national policy ownership, not driven by politics. Indeed, Mullins and Murie (2006, p 10) concluded their devolution discussion by stating that 'It seems unlikely that devolution will exert a sufficiently strong influence to overwhelm the nationalizing, unifying and converging forces of national economic management, global markets and "housing developers" approaches to design and marketing'. However, the 2000s was a singular time for housing policy. New Labour – proud to be without ideology and with the motto 'what works counts' – was in control at Westminster as well as in Wales and Scotland, whereas in Northern Ireland, sectarian politics still dominated the agenda.

The Conservative-led Coalition government was more ideological than New Labour. Discounts on the Right to Buy were extended in England, private landlordism was encouraged and 'affordable' rents – up to 80% of the market rent – were introduced. Justified by the need for 'austerity' in public finances, UK-wide reductions in Housing Benefit entitlements were set in motion. All the devolved governments opposed the Housing Benefit cuts, and the 'bedroom tax', with its disproportionate impact on Scotland, Wales and Northern Ireland, became a symbol of Westminster dominance. Although following some English policies such as Help to Buy and the extra Land Stamp Duty on second homes, the SNP managed to enhance Scottish identity by opposition to austerity. It also endorsed different policy directions to England, such as land reform, ending the Right to Buy, stronger private landlord regulation and promoting council housing. These positions – reminiscent of 'old' Labour – contributed to the party trouncing Labour in Scotland in the 2015 general election. Welsh politicians attempted to replicate the Scottish approach, albeit with less fervour and less political success. Resistance to the 'bedroom tax' in Northern Ireland produced a noteworthy victory over the Westminster government and perhaps a distant signal that attention was starting to turn to economic divisions: Birrell and Gray (2016, p 329) identify 'even a political consensus in Northern Ireland about the need to reduce the impact of austerity measures'. Nonetheless, although policy divergence has emerged, the wider economic context has produced continuities, such as the growth in private landlordism, in all four 'home nations'.

Free from Liberal Democrat restraint, the 2015 Conservative government has augmented the Coalition government's policies – a Right to Buy for housing association tenants, restrictions on access to 'social' housing, concentrating new housing construction on homeownership, more Housing Benefit cuts and so on – thereby widening the English divergence from Scotland, Wales and Northern Ireland. Indeed, McKee, Muir and Moore (2016, p 1) refer to England as an 'outlier' in housing policy terms.

Further reading

Birrell, D. (2009) *The Impact of Devolution on Social Policy*, Bristol: The Policy Press.

Cameron, Lord (1969) *Disturbances in Northern Ireland: Report of the Commission under the Chairmanship of Lord Cameron*, Cmd 532, Belfast: HMSO.

Gibb, K. (2014) 'Housing Policy in Scotland Since Devolution: Divergence, Crisis, Integration and Opportunity', *Journal of Poverty and Social Justice*, vol 23, no 1, pp 29–42.

Glendinning, M. (ed) (1997) *Rebuilding Scotland: The Postwar Vision 1945–1975*, East Linton: The Tuckwell Press, pp 50–61.

Maclennan, D. and O'Sullivan, A. (2013) 'Localism, Devolution and Housing Policies', *Housing Studies*, vol 28, no 4, pp 599–615.

Mooney, G. and Scott, J. (2012) *Social Justice and Social Policy in Scotland*, Bristol: The Policy Press.

Muir, J. (2012) 'Policy Difference and Policy Ownership under UK Devolution: Social Housing Policy in Northern Ireland', Institute of Spatial and Environmental Planning, Queen's University Belfast Working Paper No 5.

O'Carroll, A. (1996) 'Historical Perspectives on Tenure Development in Two Scottish Cities', in H. Currie and A. Murie (eds) *Housing in Scotland*, Coventry: Chartered Institute of Housing, pp 16–30.

Wightman, A. (2013) *The Poor Had No Lawyers: Who Owns Scotland (and How They Got It)*, Edinburgh: Birlinn.

TEN

Conclusion: power, planning and protest

Power

Public choice theorists claim that politicians seek election to obtain personal power, kudos and material advantage. The 'career politician' – living *off* politics rather than *for* politics (King, 2015) and operating through media spin, focus groups and close attention to the 'median voter' in marginal seats – has given this allegation more credibility but it is a calumny when applied to politicians with convictions, such as Aneurin Bevan and Margaret Thatcher. Nevertheless, on franchise extension, all politicians, ideological or pragmatic, had to cultivate popular support to acquire and retain state power.

Housing our masters

Franchise enlargement in the latter part of the 19th century formally incorporated the male householder into the 'body politic'. The Liberal politician Robert Lowe told the House of Commons: 'it will be absolutely necessary that you should prevail on our future masters to learn their letters' (Lowe, 1867). This remark entered educational folklore as 'we must educate our masters', and in a wider social reform context, Sydney Webb declared:

> If you allow the tramway conductor to vote he will not forever be satisfied with exercising the vote over such matters as the appointment of the Ambassador to Paris ... he will seek to obtain some kind of control as a voter over the conditions under which he lives. (Quoted in Gilbert, 1966, p 25)

'Housing our masters' became a pressing electoral concern, especially following the widespread agitation on the housing issue in the 1880s. However, although prepared to allow local authorities to construct housing in inner cities on the claim that the market did not function in such areas because workers had to live near their workplaces, both the Liberals and the Conservatives were unwilling to subsidise working-class housing. All the housing initiatives prior to 1919 were circumscribed by a 'no loss' requirement, albeit that this condition was overlooked by the 'Progressives' when in control of the London County Council.

The electoral impact of the universal franchise awarded in 1918 (women received the vote on equal terms to men in 1928) was tempered between the wars by Labour's need to establish electoral credibility in relation to the Liberal Party and internal Liberal and Labour divisions. Nevertheless, the Conservatives, in power for most of the interwar period but alert to Labour's potential electoral appeal, reinstated subsidies for local authority house construction after a short hiatus and provided state support to encourage working-class owner-occupation. Tenant agitation and ballot box considerations toned down their ambition to allow landlords to charge market rents.

The 'numbers game'

In the 1945 general election, Labour received 49.7% of the votes and the Conservatives received 36.2%, with Rubinstein (2006, p 81) attributing Labour's victory to 'the fact that the social class system had by 1945 created a working class in Britain united enough to vote together and sufficiently self-confident to vote Labour'. In 1951, Labour's share was 48.8% and the Conservative share 48% but the vote distribution produced a Conservative government. Commenting on Bevan's housing record, Thomas-Symonds (2014, p 161) states that 'the voters were not satisfied with the rate of progress ... and their verdict was far more important than the verdict of history'. Hugh Dalton, who became responsible for housing in 1950, called Bevan 'a tremendous Tory' (quoted in Timmins, 1996, p 145) for insisting that local authorities should build a high proportion of three-bedroomed houses with two lavatories. Post-1951, housing production escalated, impelled by a formidable 'numbers game' between Labour and the Conservatives. Gimson (2013, p 1) comments that 'Macmillan kept his and his team's eyes firmly fixed on the numbers.... Totals were displayed in the department along the lines of a cricket scoreboard'. Timmins (1996, p 234) observes:

> Crossman's 1965 Housing White Paper had by then [1966] turned the 400,000 target into one of 500,000 per year by 1970 – a commitment which Howard (1990) records as

'even more recklessly characterised by Wilson in the 1966 election as "not a lightly given pledge – it is a promise"'.

Labour's 1975 White Paper on public expenditure (Treasury, 1975, p 71) declared 'To achieve a much larger programme of new housing and acquisition of new dwellings increased expenditure is needed to bear a major part of the cost of capital'.

Between 1951 and 1979, new housing construction in the UK averaged 324,000 per year, with 48% in the 'social' sector, demonstrating that the state can deliver. Despite 'numbers game' consequences in housing form, new-build plus renovating older houses produced significant improvements in housing conditions. For example, the percentage of households without a fixed bath declined from 37.6% in 1951 to 1.9% in 1981. Thus, although housing distribution was not primarily according to need – hence the 'wobbly pillar in the welfare state' accusation (Torgersen, 1987) – a high housing production level was a constant 'classic' welfare state characteristic.

In the late 1970s, housing politics started to turn towards consumerism and choice rather than supply. The Labour government's post-1976 economic problems produced a sharp drop in housing output – from 322,000 in 1976 to 251,000 in 1979 – with local authority housing taking the biggest hit. In making the public expenditure cuts producing the decline, Denis Healey, Labour's Chancellor, argued: 'the truth of the matter is that in asking for an increased social wage those who are doing so are not speaking for their members in giving [it] a higher priority than personal expenditure' (quoted in Clark, 2001, p 18). That is, workers wanted more personal rather than more collective consumption.

Reduced housing production continued into the 1980s, when new house construction declined to 217,000 per annum, and to 189,000 in the 1990s, rising to 191,000 in the 2000s against a rapid increase in population. There was a fall in the new 'social' sector home percentage, down to 24% in the 1980s, 18% in the 1990s and 14% in the 2000s. Housing associationsous did not replace local authorities as a large-scale housing producer mainly due to a sharp fall in government 'social' housing investment. As Bentley (2016, p 5) states: 'the supply of housing has only ever been sufficient when private sector output was topped up by public investment'. Falling supply was accompanied by housing recommodification. Dewilde and De Decker (2016, p 123) note:

The 1980s heralded a qualitatively new and more pervasive era of commodification as housing itself became a fictitious commodity when it was taken over by finance ... meaning that profit-making increasingly occurs through financial channels rather than through trade and commodity production.

Class

In part, the switch from supply to consumerism reflected ongoing changes in the class structure. Class was paramount in voting behaviour during the mid-20th century, with one commentator going so far as to state that 'Class is the basis of British party politics; all else is embellishment and detail' (Pulzer, 1967, p 5). However, in the 1960s, the class structure started to change, and under Weberian social class accounts – emphasising 'life chances' associated with varied 'market situations' rather than owning the means of production – the 'housing classes' idea became influential. Rex and Moore (1969) identified a number of 'housing classes' engaged in struggles over resource distribution via positions in the housing market and bureaucratic regulation of public-sector housing allocation. Cleavages related to consumption rather than relationships to production were distinguished, with Saunders (1990) specifying owner-occupation–renting as the key division. Scott (2007, p 4) claims that the new working-class suburban areas were important in this class realignment, stating: 'Yet there is a strong consensus among both the early studies and more recent critiques that new residential communities were in the vanguard of changes in working-class social relations and that these changes were strongly linked to post-war affluence'.

Changes in the class structure were accompanied by partisan and class dealignment in voting behaviour. In the 1951 general election, the Labour and Conservative parties were supported by 97.1% of the electorate; by 2015, this had declined to 69%. In the 1950s and 1960s, four fifths of middle-class voters opted for the Conservatives and two thirds of the working class voted Labour (Wright et al, 2000, p 84). In 2015, 44% of middle-class voters chose the Conservative Party and 35% of the working class voted Labour (Cowley and Kavanagh, 2016, p 381).

In 2015, Savage et al claimed that because social stratification had altered so fundamentally, a new classification was necessary based on adding 'social' and 'cultural' capital to 'economic' capital. Their taxonomy had seven categories: the elite; the established middle class;

the technical middle class; new affluent workers; the traditional working class; emergent service workers; and the precariat (Savage et al, 2015). Class and tenure were strongly associated, with the elite, concentrated in London and the Home Counties, having a 97% homeownership rate and 80% of the precariat – characterised by frequent movement from unemployment into low-paid jobs – living in rented accommodation.

Choice

These class structure changes had an impact on, and were influenced by, housing politics. Choice is central to neoliberal thinking (Friedman and Friedman, 1980) and Margaret Thatcher promoted the idea. She claimed that 'Choice is the essence of ethics: if there were no choice, there would be no ethics, no good, no evil; good and evil have meaning only insofar as man is free to choose' (Thatcher, 1977, p 1).

The Right to Buy was justified, in part, on the choice argument. Owner-occupation in the UK increased from 55.4% in 1979 to 67.3% in 1997, but without Right to Buy sales, in 1997, the figure would have been 59.8%. The Right to Buy was accompanied by 'tenants choice', state help to private landlords via tax breaks and the attempt to create a 'quasi-market' in rented accommodation (Gibb, 2015). New Labour followed the choice agenda, endorsing private landlordism, stock transfer from local government to housing associations and 'choice-based lettings'; indeed, an article summarising New Labour's approach had the title 'The Inexorable Rise of the Rational Consumer?'(Marsh, 2004). Homeownership was promoted as the ideal preference.

The electoral price for sustaining homeownership was that politicians had to nurture ever-increasing house prices. Failure risked political penalty. House prices supplied drab or cheerful backdrops to election campaigns. The territorial imbalances in house price change helped John Major in the 1992 general election (Pattie et al, 1995). By 1997, house prices had declined by £4,480 in cash terms (Deverell-Smith Ltd, 2015), and although there was a greater swing to New Labour among homeowners who thought house prices were in decline (Dorling et al, 1999), this was an insignificant factor in the 1997 general election outcome because, as the election approached, overall prices were increasing. New Labour won the 2001 and 2005 general elections against a rising house price backdrop but lost in 2010 following a price slump. Keegan (2012) recounts a meeting that Gordon Brown held with his staff to review housing policy. One adviser said that there was a serious housing crisis and an urgent need to build more 'social' housing, to which another trusted aide responded, 'If we did that it would hit house prices and lose the election'. Criticised for his Help to Buy boost to the housing market, George Osborne allegedly told the Cabinet: 'Hopefully we will get a little housing boom and everyone will be happy as property values go up' (quoted in Grice, 2013). House prices increased by 8% in 2015. This 'onwards and upwards' house price political drug is manifest in demand- rather than supply-side stimulants. The various market-support packages such as Help to Buy totalled £43 billion in 2015, whereas affordable housing investment was only £18 billion (Wilcox et al, 2016). This bias is related to the UK banking business. As Ryan-Collins (2016) observes, the main activity that UK banks engage in is domestic mortgage lending, not lending to business. Being 'too big to fail', their financial difficulties post-2008 had to be tackled by reviving house prices, a mission accomplished, notably, in London, by Help to Buy and Funding for Lending. Once unleashed, a housing market feeding frenzy has its own momentum – until the next fall, hopefully for the politicians involved, between elections, thereby allowing time for an engineered recovery. Commodified housing not only boosts banks, asset-based welfare and electoral support, it also has a major role in national finance – in 2014/15, Stamp Duty Land Tax alone raised £10.7 billion and was predicted to rise to £17.8 billion in 2020/21 (Statistics Portal, 2016). Moreover, local government finance is increasingly dependent on property, and by 2020, increases in local revenue will come only from residential and business rate expansion. Indeed, there is a case for arguing that housing is now a cornerstone rather than a 'wobbly pillar' in the welfare state (Malpass, 2008; Walks, 2016).

The Conservative manifesto promise to extend the Right to Buy to housing association tenants was unpopular with electorate as a whole. Only 28% thought that it was a good idea (Clarke et al, 2015), and perhaps aware that a private tenant backlash might develop, the Conservatives did not highlight the policy in its national campaign, although they may have targeted local leaflets on housing association tenants in marginal seats. It is difficult to assess Right to Buy's impact on housing association tenants. The Ipsos Mori poll analysis, reflecting a general tendency to lump all housing association and local authority tenants into a single category that ignores tenure politics, did not divide 'social' tenants into those living in the housing association and local authority sectors – by 2015, the split was ten housing association tenants to seven local authority tenants. In the 2015 election, the 3% 'social' tenant swing to Labour was small – far lower than the 10% swing among private renters (Ipsos Mori, 2015c), perhaps indicating that housing association tenants voted for a potential substantial windfall.

However, United Kingdom Independence party (UKIP) had strong support in some 'social' housing areas and a survey of 7,000 housing associations tenants (Sheffield Hallam University, 2016) found that two thirds were not interested in exploring the new Right to Buy and only a small proportion of those interested could afford to buy their homes. Associations will receive compensation for 'Right to Buy' discounts but the Conservative policy bearing is towards new housing association rentals at 80% of market value, shared ownership and 20% discounts on owner-occupied 'Starter Homes' – a long way from the association movement's historic mission to supply low-cost rented properties.

'Generation rent'

In 1988, when security and tenure was ended and market rents were introduced for new tenants, private landlords operated in niche markets and the sector had slipped under the political radar. However, by 2015, the term 'generation rent' was well established in the political lexicon, with Walker (2016, p 128, emphasis in original) expressing generation rent's grievances:

> A renter effectively pays not once but three times: first in rent, second as an unpaid caretaker of an inflating asset and third with the freedoms they forfeit. With the silent passing of every standing order, their roles, their status – their *class* becomes more and more entrenched, and the possibility of escape reduced.

Housing became the number one voter concern in the capital. There was a 3.4% swing to Labour from the Conservatives in London in the 2015 general election, producing four Labour gains from the Conservatives, a respectable catch given the party's poor performance elsewhere. Nationwide swings to Labour of 12% by people aged 18–24, 6% among those aged 25–34, 4% by those aged 35–44 and 10% among private renters (Ipsos Mori, 2015c) indicate a possible 'generation rent' impact. Unhappily for Labour, turnout was the inverse of support: 43% (aged 18–24), 54% (aged 25–35), 64% (aged 35–44) and 51% by private renters. Labour's new leader, Jeremy Corbyn, appointed Gloria De Piero to the shadow cabinet with responsibility for young people and voter registration.

Both Labour and Conservative London mayoral candidates placed housing at the top of their priority lists, with Labour's Sadiq Khan (2016, p 6) declaring that 'My first priority will be tackling the housing crisis' and the Conservative candidate, Zac Goldsmith, stating that 'Housing is the most important issue facing London' (Goldsmith, 2016b, p 1). Khan won the 2016 London mayoral election, obtaining 44.23% of the vote on the first round, compared to Goldsmith's 35.03% share, roughly comparable to the London shares in the 2015 general election, but Khan's share increased to 56.8% compared to Goldsmith's 43.2% after the distribution of second preferences in the second round.

The Conservative-led Coalition government shielded pensioners from the austerity agenda. In the housing domain, pensioners were unaffected by the 'bedroom tax' and there was no suggestion of penalties for underoccupation in the owner-occupied sector despite 61% of those who owned their house outright underoccupying their homes (DCLG, 2015f). There was an 8% swing against Labour among the over 65s, with a 78% turnout (Ipsos Mori, 2015c).

Private landlordism

Aware that private landlordism was the Achilles heel in the Conservatives' 'property-owning democracy' vision and private landlordism's salience in the 2016 London mayoral election, Chancellor George Osborne introduced measures aimed at curbing its growth – reducing tax breaks and introducing an extra Land Stamp Duty levy on house transactions. However, the impact of these measures on mitigating private landlordism's resurgence appears limited. The amount projected to be raised from the extra Land Stamp Duty levy – £825 million in 2019/20 (HM Treasury, 2015b) – indicates only a modest reduction in property acquisition by landlords, which, over time, will be fuelled by the sale of higher-value council houses and the transfer of houses bought by housing association tenants. More than three quarters of private renters want to buy and only 8% of private renters with children choose to rent privately (DCLG, 2011c).

The 'English Housing Survey 2014–15' revealed that the growth in private landlordism had stalled, with a slightly lower proportion of households renting privately in 2014/15 than in 2013/14 (DCLG, 2016b). Other figures showed an increase from 19.8% in 2014 to 20.2% in 2015 (DCLG, 2016c). In the Coalition government's term in office, the number of households renting privately in England increased by 469,600. At least 25% of MPs, mainly Conservative, gain an income from renting (*Guardian*, 2015b), £9 billion was paid to landlords per year in Housing Benefit and 33% of privately let homes are below the 'decent' standard. With rents rising at 8.5% per annum in 2015, growing tenant organisation (Walker and Jeraj, 2016) and UK landlord equity at £818 billion (Dorling, 2014b), private landlordism is a volatile political issue.

'Governmentality': inclusion

Social constructionism's main contribution to understanding power resides in the 'governmentality' idea, which focuses on the ways that governments attempt to produce citizens best suited to acquiesce to their policies. Faced by the electoral requirement to 'house our masters' but unwilling to subsidise working-class housing, the 'new' Liberals concentrated on offering political inclusion via 'character' development. Thomas Hill Green (1836–82), tutor at Balliol College and active member of the Liberal Party, provided the stratagem's philosophical rationale. He argued that 'When we speak of freedom as something to be so highly prized, we mean the positive power or capacity of doing or enjoying something worth doing, and that, too, something we do or enjoy in common with others' (Green, 1881, p 9).

Thus, *full* inclusion in the 'body politic' required accomplishment through 'higher' education and civic participation via self-help organisations such as Friendly Societies, whose membership included three quarters of manual workers at the end of the 19th century. In 1903, the Association to Promote the Higher Education of Working Men was set up (renamed the 'Workers Educational Association' in 1905), to which the 'artisan' trade unions subscribed, and the 'new' Liberals endorsed building societies, housing associations and housing cooperatives. Taxing 'unearned' increments arising from community-produced increases in land values added a radical dimension to 'new' Liberalism but this resource was for community use not for subsidies to individuals. The approach was summarised by Hobhouse when he declared that 'The man who, without further aid than the universally available shares in the social inheritance which is to fall to him as a citizen, pays his way through life, is to be justly regarded as self-supporting' (Hobhouse, 1974 [1911], p 24).

To solidify the inclusion aura, the enfranchised working-class male householder was contrasted with the disenfranchised male 'residuum' and the 'universal' disenfranchised female. The 'residuum' lacked 'character' and required 'over-parenting', and the female's domain was domestic not political. Helen Bosanquet (1906) set out the rationale for women's domestic role in *The Family*. She claimed that men were 'incapable of the more domestic duties incident on rearing children' and it was 'largely this incapacity which gives him the power both of concentration and width of view' (Bosanquet, 1906, pp 272–3).

In contrast, women had a duty to ensure that their husbands and children were 'well cared for, both physically and morally and it is generally agreed that this duty can be properly fulfilled only by personal attention' (Bosanquet, 1906, p 279). Women's domestic orientation was considered as suitable to deal with issues such as education, poor relief and housing; hence, single women received the right to vote in the Municipal Franchise Act 1869 on the same terms as men and the Local Government Act 1894 extended this right to some married women. Octavia Hill's housing management techniques were lauded because of her female expertise in household matters.

'Governmentality': exclusion

The Conservatives adopted 'governability' through the character development stratagem between the wars, applying it via the 'property-owning democracy' idea, associated with a 'home', not a house. They targeted this ideal at the middle class and the 'respectable' working man, expecting the notion would trickle down the working class. This emphasis on owner-occupiers' superior citizenship continued beyond the Second World War and the contrast with the 'featherbedded', 'dependent' council tenant became more strident under Margaret Thatcher's leadership. Blair's approach was more restrained but his first speech as Prime Minister – on the 'underclass' and rights bonded to obligations – was delivered at a local authority estate (Blair, 1997a). Moreover, New Labour made strong links between rough sleeping and dysfunctional personal biographies (Social Exclusion Unit, 1998b) and attempted to link statutory homelessness to dysfunctional families by focusing on 'repeat' homelessness (see Lund, 2017). The Coalition government introduced initiatives, such as giving local authorities powers to set time limits to tenancies and 'Pay to Stay', to further residualise the local authority housing sector. Although the Liberal Democrats in the Coalition supported an enhanced role for local government in new-build, the Conservatives baulked at the idea and even a specific promise from the Prime Minister of a one-to-one replacement for houses sold under the 'reinvigorated' Right to Buy was set aside.

The outlook for local authority housing in England under the 2015 Conservative government looks bleak. The 2016 Housing Act requires local authorities to make a payment to the Treasury based on assumptions about selling higher-value council homes. These levies are supposed to leave sufficient finance for local authorities to replace the sold stock but this will only be possible if funds are available after housing associations have been compensated for their 'Right to Buy' discount losses, calculated to cost £1.5 billion per year (Savills, 2015). The Local Government Association (2016) has estimated that up to 2020, 88,000 council houses will be lost and only 8,000 replaced. Making tenants with modest household incomes pay market rents under the new mandatory 'Pay to Stay' scheme will push tenants to leave the sector or buy their homes under the Right to Buy, and limits on tenant security will further 'residualise' the sector. It is also possible that housing associations – under the new 'freedoms' necessary for their debt to be classified as private – will not have to offer nomination rights to local authorities, leaving local authorities with the responsibility for housing the more troublesome tenants. Section 106 agreements to create 'mixed' communities have been downgraded and regenerating a hundred council estates may result in displacing existing tenants and a reduction in council house availability.

These changes are linked to 'governability'. Cameron (2015) promised to turn 'generation rent' into 'generation buy'. 'Respectable' homeowners can be contrasted to yet more 'residualised' local authority tenants, vulnerable to stigma and associated behaviour controls along the lines suggested in Centre for Social Justice's (2008) report *Breakthrough Britain: Housing Poverty, from Social Breakdown to Social Mobility*. Council tenants are possible subjects for the Behavioural Insights Team – also known as the 'Nudge Unit' – originally located in the Cabinet Office but now a social purpose company, partly owned by Cabinet Office employees. The pitch echoes the past when the 'irresponsible' 'social' tenant, in need of 'over-parenting', was contrasted with the 'responsible' homeowner. It has connections to changes in the poverty definition. In July 2015, the new Conservative government announced that it would scrap the child poverty definition in the Child Poverty Act 2010 (60% of equivalised median income) and replace it with a new measure. Iain Duncan Smith, then Secretary of State for Work and Pensions, said:

> New legislation to replace the Child Poverty Act 2010 will use:
>
> - the proportion of children living in workless household as well as long-term workless households
> - the educational attainment of all pupils and the most disadvantaged pupils at age 16
>
> The government will also develop a range of other measures and indicators of root causes of poverty, including family

breakdown, debt and addiction, setting these out in a children's life chances strategy. (Duncan Smith, 2015)

The 2016 Welfare Reform and Work Act effectively repealed the 2010 Child Poverty Act, renaming it the 'Life Chances Act'. It abolished the income thresholds, reporting duties and requirements for national and local child poverty strategies in the 2010 Act and introduced new reporting requirements on 'life chances' as measured by the number of workless households and by educational attainment (Hussain, 2016). The Conservatives, aided by media 'disgust discourses' and 'poverty porn', have constructed a disturbing council house tenant image. The 2015 Conservative government's attitude to council tenants was revealed in the evidence to the House of Commons Select Committee on Communities and Local Government given by the National Tenants Organisations, representing four tenant organisations. It stated that they had made numerous requests for information and meetings with ministers and civil servants but:

> Sadly, we have not received any responses to any of these inquiries, apart from a brief meeting with a DCLG [Department for Communities and Local Government] officer who was only partially briefed on the Government's changes. This all means that the Government is not currently in communication with social housing tenants in England, the people who are most affected by the most fundamental changes to our sector since the 1980s. (National Tenants Organisations, 2015, paras 26–28).

None of the 17 members of the advisory panel appointed to oversee the regeneration of a hundred council estates was a tenant.

Planning

The 'new' Liberalism and Fabian socialism shared a belief in organic theory. Society was constantly evolving towards a higher, more rational, order. It followed that knowing the 'facts', accompanied by inductive reasoning, would produce a logical answer to the problem under examination, which, being rational, would go with the organic evolutionary grain. The Fabians were more dogmatic about 'rational' planning than the 'new' Liberals, with Sydney Webb asserting that government must become 'more and more the business of elaborately trained experts, and less and less the immediate outcome of popular feeling' (Webb, 1908, quoted Greenleaf, 1983, pp 359–60). To the Fabians, 'Good government was essentially a matter of applying the appropriate expertise, based on scientific research and professional training' (Leach, 2015, p 111).

Planning was to be the antidote to the market, and the idea that trained experts, with professional knowledge unknown to the layperson, should guide activity was not restricted to architectural expertise. It also included social 'experts', with their alleged ability to identify social problems and produce 'rational' – thereby undisputable – solutions based on statistical evidence. The Fabians' model was Edwin Chadwick, described by Sidney Webb in 1899 as 'the great sanitary reformer and public servant' (MacKenzie, 2008, p 97). Policy analysis was analysis *for*, not analysis *of*, policy with the term 'housing' used as a verb in the discourse. Whereas electoral pressure influenced housing *supply*, housing *form* and *distribution* were governed by 'expertise', generating 'slum' clearance, 'needs'-based allocation schemes, green belts, garden cities, new towns, suburban cottage estates without embellishment built sometimes on 'Radburn' traffic-free principles, high-rises and deck-access flats, and so on. Ward (1976, p 4) claims 'The moment that housing, a universal human activity, becomes defined as a problem, a housing problems industry is born, with an army of experts, bureaucrats and researchers, whose existence is a guarantee that the problem won't go away'.

In *Seeing It Like a State*, Scott (1998, pp 93, 95) labels planning as 'high modernism', stating:

> The troubling features of high modernism derive, for the most part, from its claim to speak about the improvement of the human condition with the authority of scientific knowledge and the tendency to disallow other competing sources of judgement.... High modernist ideology tends to devalue and banish politics.

Under the Thatcher/Major governments, social engineering receded, but when New Labour obtained political power, it reappeared, albeit in modified form.

What works is what counts

New Labour stressed its pragmatic approach, with Tony Blair's foreword to New Labour's 1997 manifesto declaring:

> We will be a radical government. New Labour is a party of ideas and ideals but not of outdated ideology. What counts is what works. The objectives are radical. The means will be modern. Britain will be better with new Labour. (Blair, 1997b)

New Labour relied on academic knowledge to demonstrate what works. It attached evaluation projects to all its area initiatives, and in 2006, the National Housing and Planning Advice Unit, with substantial academic representation, was set up to obtain intelligence on the housing market. Such academic policy process participation generated controversy within the 'housing studies' domain that focused on involvement in urban renewal when a series of reports by the Centre for Urban and Regional Studies at Birmingham University, led by Brendan Nevin, identified 'low-demand' housing areas along the M62 corridor. New Labour set up the Housing Market Renewal Pathfinder Programme in 2003 to reshape demand by demolition and new-build, and some academics involved in detecting 'low demand' were engaged in the programme's implementation. This academic participation provoked criticism, with Allen (2009, p 53) claiming that the housing researchers' knowledge was not superior to 'that what exists in the heads of people that live in houses'. Housing 'experts' were being used to promote government policies, thereby violating the understandings that ordinary working-class people have of their housing situation.

Planning politics

The Town and Country Planning Act 1947 appropriated development rights for community use. Ownership no longer conferred the right to develop land. Planning permission from local planning authorities, subject to appeal to the relevant central minister, was required. The Act promised a Fabian utopia: 'rational' plans for an entire area's well-being would be devised against which individual planning applications could be judged. The reality was different. The recently revealed local plan dearth suggests that each application has been subject to local pressure group interests rather than a 'common good' concern. The Act created 'planning politics', setting rural against urban authorities – institutionalised by Duncan Sandys' 1955 green belt circular – and organised 'insiders' against unorganised 'outsiders'. Significantly, the Conservatives, although dismantling much of the 1940s' planning legislation, such as betterment taxation and new towns, retained local controls on new development.

New Labour attempted to address the planning constraint issue by creating a regional tier to planning decisions, but in the countdown to the 2010 general election, both the Conservatives and the Liberal Democrats robustly opposed New Labour's mechanisms to stimulate land release. They claimed that their objections were against the imposition of regional targets on local government but there were significant electoral rewards to harvest from opposing housing development. In 2010, more than half of current homeowners said that they would oppose new housing being built in their area (National Housing Planning and Advice Unit, 2010) and this was likely to underestimate opposition as when a planning application is submitted, those strongly opposed can influence the people with more moderate attitudes. Only 5% of the public thought that letting developers build more homes was an answer to the housing problem (DCLG, 2011c).

Soon after the 2010 general election, the Coalition government abolished New Labour's regional targets, substituting local determinations of housing requirements, but with a stagnating economy, it introduced new 'top-down' mechanisms to cajole local authorities into releasing land. This U-turn on planning control was short-lived. As the 2015 general election approached, the Conservatives adopted a more robust greenfield and green belt protection stance, whereas the Liberal Democrats embraced land release. The Liberal Democrats lost many seats to the Conservatives across 'Middle England', indicating that the Conservatives' 'greenfield protection' position compared to the Liberal Democrats abandonment of 'community politics' for 'responsible government' – reflected in a willingness to promote new development – had an impact. Opposition to new development has declined since 2010 (DCLG, 2015g). Nonetheless, an Ipsos Mori (2015b) examination of attitudes to development commissioned by Shelter revealed that those most likely to be actively opposed to new development in their areas were older/retired outright property-owners with a tendency to support the UKIP and read the *Express*, known for its celebration of house price increases. The Conservative anti-development stance in the 2015 general election may have helped it recover UKIP support and the Liberal Democrats, whose 2015 manifesto adopted a strong pro-development stance.

The brownfield promise

The 2015 Conservative government's answer to the land problem is to concentrate new development on brownfield 'housing zones'. It introduced a number of measures to boost development on brownfield sites, including legislation to make planning approval in principle automatic for brownfield areas and extra state aid to promote building Starter Homes on such sites. However, brownfield development has limitations as an answer to the housing question. According to research by the University of the West of England, carried out on behalf of the Campaign for the Protection of Rural England, there is sufficient brownfield land for 960,000 homes in England. This is only about a four-year supply at housing requirement estimates as currently calculated (Sinnett et al, 2014), and many sites, perhaps 40%, may be unprofitable to develop (Hudson, 2015). Although new brownfield sites become available, the existing supply is diminishing at an accelerating rate and site availability does not coincide with housing demand. The DCLG's impact assessment of the National Planning Policy Framework (DCLG, 2012g, p 42) commented:

> Internal analysis based on Homes and Communities Agency data shows, for example, that 88 (or 27 per cent of) local councils currently have less than five years of brownfield land suitable for housing based on current build [100,000 per year] and density levels.

It also noted that national targets on brownfield land use:

> had negative outcomes, resulting in imbalances in housing provision for example between blocks of flats and family homes with gardens. The brownfield target was also seen to drive up land prices in certain areas and would increasingly limit the supply of new housing as stocks of brownfield land are used up, which would harm first time buyers. (DCLG, 2012g, p 42)

In 2014/15, brownfield new-build dwelling density was 37 per hectare, compared to 27 for non-previously developed land (DCLG, 2016d), indicating how high density is related to brownfield site use. Commenting on London brownfield land availability, Quod and Shelter (2016, p 7) state that 'if brownfield is our only option it is highly unlikely that London will be able to build enough new homes quickly enough'. Moreover, as the *Economist* (2013) has noted:

> First, no one really wants to live on the typical brownfield site. The Barking Riverside site was formerly occupied by a collection of power stations which shut down in the late 1970s and 1980s. It is still bleak. Enormous electricity pylons stretch as far as the eye can see, running from a nearby substation. On the opposite side of the riverbank sits a sewage treatment plant. Further up the river is an oil depot.

According to Evans and Unsworth (2011), flats built at high densities were not what people wanted: new high-rise occupants in Leeds wished to move away from the city centre.

Greenfield sites and green belts

'Generation rent' may recoil at its only homeownership prospect being high-density 'hutches' on brownfield sites. If it does, there is an alternative route made possible by the National Planning Policy Framework (DCLG, 2012a), which, if used, provides a mechanism to cajole local authorities into releasing 'greenfield' and green belt land. After the 2015 general election, there were early signs that the Treasury intended to apply this instrument. *Fixing the Foundations: Creating a More Prosperous Nation* (HM Treasury, 2015c, p 11) – the so-called 'productivity plan' – announced tougher action 'to ensure that local authorities are using their powers to get local plans in place and make homes available for local people, intervening to arrange for local plans to be written where necessary'. It also stated that it would strengthen the duties of neighbouring authorities to cooperate in preparing local plans, a reflection that cities – Osborne's 'powerhouse' mechanism for generating growth outside London – were becoming frustrated by their containment. Birmingham, for example, was experiencing similar problems to the major cities in the 1950s and 1960s. Wilding (2015) comments:

> According to the council, the city needs to build 89,000 homes between now and 2031, of which 34,000 need to be affordable. But there simply aren't enough sites available within the city boundary. The proposed solution involves a two-pronged approach: releasing green belt land for

development and asking neighbouring authorities to help with the overspill.

Cheshire East, coveted by Manchester in the 1950s and, in 2015, a major commuter area for the 'Northern Powerhouse', was under considerable pressure to release green belt land having had its local plan rejected by the Planning Inspectorate as 'unduly pessimistic' and with a 'serious mismatch between the economic strategy and the housing strategy' (Infrastructure Intelligence, 2015, p 1).

Local plan preparation is an important element in land release, and in October 2015, the Prime Minister announced that councils 'must produce local plans for new homes in their area by 2017 – or the government will ensure, in consultation with local people, those plans are produced for them' (Prime Minister's Office, 2015, p 1). This statement, together with a proposal that areas without an up-to-date development plan would lose the New Homes Bonus, indicated that the government would like early local resolutions to land release conflicts rather than having to rely on 'planning by appeal' to the Secretary of State for Communities and Local Government. It wanted to avoid new 'turf wars' – perhaps prompted by a Liberal Democrat return to community politics to restore its fortunes, as well as backbench Conservative pressure – in the countdown to the 2020 general election. In his 'Spending Review and Autumn Statement' (HM Treasury, 2015a), Osborne announced that the government would be receptive to 'Starter Homes' development on brownfield areas within green belts, and a consultation paper (DCLG, 2015h, p 20) declared:

> We propose to change policy to support the regeneration of previously developed brownfield sites in the Green Belt by allowing them to be developed in the same way as other brownfield land, providing this contributes to the delivery of starter homes, and subject to local consultation.

Moreover, the emphasis on economic growth, as reflected in the business and residential rates, as the main funder of local services will encourage land release (see Chapter Three). In April 2016, the Campaign to Protect Rural England (2016, p 1) claimed that 'More than a quarter of a million houses [are] now planned for green belt land'.

Protest

Marx and Engels believed that the state could not be a mechanism for improving working-class conditions but there is evidence that pressure on and through the state can have an impact. In the late 19th century, Henry Mayers Hyndman's Social Democratic Federation used housing as an arena for protest against capitalism and its agitation ensured that housing remained high on the political agenda throughout the 1880s. In 1915, locally based protest on rents, backed by some industrial trade unions and the Independent Labour Party, influenced the introduction of rent control, and 'bottom-up' pressure had an impact on housing policy between the wars. Lloyd George skilfully used the Bolshevik threat to cajole the Conservatives into accepting subsidised council housing and Wheatley's 1923 agreement with the unions – a sustained house-building programme backed by government assistance to local authorities in return for modifying restrictive practices – survived its planned 10-year lifespan, albeit with cutbacks in housing quality. Resistance from council tenants curbed differential rent schemes and local agitation reined in the Conservative Party's attempt to revive private landlordism by abolishing rent controls.

The notion of a 'post-war consensus' on social policy is somewhat exaggerated, with a 'compromised settlement' being a more appropriate term, especially in the housing domain. After the Second World War, the strong industrial trade union influence in the Labour Party, Conservative apprehensiveness about trade union power and fluctuations between Labour and Conservative governments made 'protest from below' less urgent. Indeed, Richard Crossman observed in 1952 that 'the planned Welfare State is really the adaptation of capitalism to the demands of modern trade unionism' (quoted in Bedarida, 1990, p 198). In the late 1970s, around 58% of workers were trade union members and collective bargaining set 82% of workforce wages (Hayes and Novitz, 2014). In 1979, 29.2% of households in England rented from a local authority, the private rented sector housed 11.4% of households and 2% of households rented from a housing association. House prices were 2.8 times average earnings and the percentage of income spent on housing costs and rents across all housing tenure types – gross of Housing Benefit and including mortgage interest payments, rents, water charges, buildings insurance premiums for owner-occupiers, and ground rents and service charges – was 8% (Belfield et al, 2015).

By the 1980s, the decline in private landlordism had reduced the salience of tenant protest, and despite dramatic private landlord sector growth and the changing nature of its tenants, 'bottom-up' dissent, although growing, remained muted and fragmented. Direct local authority tenant campaigns became more important as neoliberalism's market pursuit intensified, and such pressure – often backed by Unison – had some success in stalling moves to switch local authority housing from local government to 'alternative' landlords via 'tenants choice', Housing Action Trusts and stock transfer programmes. However, as Cole and Furbey (1994) explain, even when a third of households were local authority tenants, there were barriers to their power as 'urban social movements'. There were internal economic and social divisions, as revealed in differential rent conflicts and allocation controversies. Rent-striking tenants were more vulnerable than striking industrial workers. Moreover, 'hidden injuries of class ... and the toll which they extract in the form of fatalism, resignation, distrust of neighbours, alienation from organisations and lack of confidence should not be understated' (Cole and Furbey, 1994, p 158).

Commenting on the 2014 situation, Bradley (2014, pp 4, 5) states that 'In the United Kingdom the assault on social housing is far advanced.... Although new protest and direct action occasionally shatters its quiescence, the tenants' movement in the UK appears to have been stunned by the scale of this assault'. The neoliberal agenda prevailed. By 2012, 26% of workers were union members and collective bargaining covered only 23% of workers' wages (Hayes and Novitz, 2014). In 2015, the local government's housing stock portion in England was 7.0%, private landlords held 20.2% and housing associations held 10.1%. The percentage of income spent on housing costs and rents across all housing tenure types was 16% in 2013, with rental costs (housing association, local authority and private landlords) leaping from 8% in 1979 to 27% of household income in 2013 (Belfield et al, 2015). Dissent from the least privileged housing sectors had become far less potent than local and national campaigns – orchestrated by the Campaign to Protect Rural England and the National Trust – to block development.

The 'wicked' politics of housing

Housing has been labelled a 'wicked' problem (Adams, 2011; Taylor, 2015): complex, open-ended and intractable. 'It is a really big issue', said Martin Wolf (2015) in the *Financial Times*, 'that is, of course, why no politician dares touch it'. Cohen (2013) put the matter more bluntly:

> We are in a housing crisis that extends from the homeless on the street well into the middle class. We have couples deciding not to have children because they do not have the

space to house them. We have people paying extortionate rents, and the lowest rate of new home construction in almost a century. Yet ministers just sit there like gouty old men in the 19th hole.

There is no shortage of 'rational' answers to the housing question. The long list includes a review of green belts to allow building on their least attractive and lowest amenity parts (Cheshire, 2013; Broadway Malyan, 2015), and rent control in the private landlord sector (Bentley, 2015). Excluding local government housing investment from the public debt definition (Chartered Institute of Housing, 2010) has also been advocated, as has taxing property and land values to check house prices and secure more resources for housing investment (Barker, 2014; Jones, 2015). However, as Crookston (2015, p 1) has commented, 'the current housing agenda in Britain is characterised by a spectacular and jarring disassociation between a lot of analysis of serious problems, and an apparent inability to entertain or adopt credible solutions'. The disassociation is political.

The 'housing issue' is less fiendish in Scotland. A sturdy Scottish national identity, well tapped by the Scottish National Party (SNP) aware of traditional 'old' Labour antipathy to landowners and private landlords, has generated policies to mitigate the housing problem. Despite a degree of policy 'tokenism' – limiting private landlord rent increases to one per year is hardly different to England – Scotland, both in its policy narrative and action, seems a very different place to England with regard to housing policy. Indeed, the Scottish Conservative and Unionist Party (2016) manifesto rejected a Right to Buy for housing association tenants, endorsed a 50,000 a year affordable housing target and proposed rent control in the private landlord sector in return for grants.

Since devolution, relative to population size, new housing supply has increased at a faster rate in Scotland than in England. Between 2004 and 2014, 31 private sector houses per 1,000 people were completed in Scotland compared to 23 in England, and from 2008 to 2014, seven times more social houses were built relative to population than in England (*Economist*, 2015, p 1). Moreover, the 2016 SNP manifesto for the 2016 Scottish Parliament election promised that 'we will invest £3 billion to build at least 50,000 affordable homes over the next five years and 35,000 of these homes will be in the social rented sector' (Scottish National Party, 2016, p 23). Adjusted for population size, this was equivalent to building 350,000 houses in England for 'social' rent by 2020. Maclennan and O'Sullivan (2013, p 609) have noted that 'Between 2007 and 2011 a Scottish National Party minority government began to sketch out a new municipalism for social housing provision in Scotland', and this municipal orientation has accelerated. Local authorities in Scotland – with higher grants, free from Housing Revenue Account caps, and with the knowledge that with Right to Buy ending, they can keep what they build – has had a growing role in housing delivery, building four times more homes than in England between 2013 and 2015.

Scottish voters are somewhat more 'left-wing' than voters in England and Wales, with 43.8% of Scottish people wanting tax and spending to rise, compared to 36.4% of voters in England and Wales (British Social Attitudes, 2015), but a Scottish identity underpins attitudes to 'tax and spend'. In the 2016 Scottish parliamentary election, Scottish Labour moved to the left of the Scottish National Party, advocating higher taxation to fund public services and a land value tax, and outbidding the Scottish National Party by 10,000 in its new 'affordable' housing commitment (Scottish Labour Party, 2016). It did not improve Labour's electoral appeal. Although the Scottish Nationalist Party did not obtain an overall majority in the 2016 Scottish Parliament election, Labour lost 13 seats. The Conservatives gained 16 seats and became the second-largest party in the Scottish Parliament.

Despite the political complexity surrounding housing policy in Northern Ireland since 2000, 91 new homes per 1,000 population have been built in Northern Ireland, compared to 40 per 1,000 population in England, although the 'Troubles' associated with Northern Ireland's underlying divisions have promoted public sector housing investment.

The Conservative Party had its best general election result in Wales for 30 years, increasing its vote share by 1% and gaining three seats. It targeted the National Assembly for Wales as an example of Labour's ineptitude in delivering services, in particular, health care and housing, raising issues about Labour's approach to housing in Wales, with its emphasis on sustainability, ending the Right to Buy and regulating private landlords. The Welsh Government's record in new housing construction has been disappointing – 35 per 1,000 population since 2000 and only 1.9 per 1,000 population each year since 2010 – with the Conservative Party blaming this Welsh housing dearth on the obsessive Welsh approach to sustainable development. After the 2016 Welsh Assembly election, Labour – with 29 seats – remained the largest single party, followed by Plaid Cymru (12 seats), Welsh Conservatives (11 seats), UKIP (seven seats) and the Welsh Liberal Democrats (one seat).

Housing's political 'wickedness' is historically embedded. Urban containment started in the 1930s and the planning machinery for its continuance was set down in the Town and Country Planning Act 1947. Remarking on the post-war planning system's impact, Sir Peter Hall stated: 'The ruralites, especially the well-heeled ones, were the clear gainers: planning, by establishing a polite English version of apartheid, simply preserved the status quo and thus their comfortable lifestyle' (quoted in Miles, 2012).

Meen, Gibb, Leishman and Nygaard (2016, p 310) comment:

> There are trade-offs between groups; the fact that all options are unpalatable to the electorate constrains the willingness of politicians to make fundamental changes. Housing falls into the too difficult category; instead, policies tinker around the edges or are partial without taking into account the wider consequences of the actions. Even the most radical politicians have been constrained by the history of past policies.

In the 2015 general election, the Liberal Democrats' vote haemorrhaged to the Conservatives in wealthier, more suburban, seats and to Labour in poorer, more ethnically diverse, urban areas, with the voters in suburban England – in middle-class seats with falling unemployment and rising incomes – swinging from Labour. Political parties drop their electoral bombs on the marginal constituencies, seeking out the median voter. 'Generation rent' tends not vote: in 2014, the proportion of private renters registered to vote was 31% lower than outright owners and 26% below that of mortgage-holders (Uberoi, 2016). 'Generation own' retains is marginal seat salience, is sensitive to house price decline, regards housing wealth as 'deserved' (Smith et al, 2006), dislikes new development and votes.

The dormant class dimension in politics was revealed in the 23 June 2016 referendum on whether to remain in or leave the European Union. Marginal seat targeting is irrelevant in referenda: all votes matter to the outcome. In the nationwide ballot, people living in the more deprived areas of England and Wales voted for exit and voter turnout in such areas was high. They blamed their deteriorating incomes – Hills et al (2016, p 280) record a real 11% reduction for men and 9% for women in the weekly earnings of social tenants in full-time employment between 2006/08 and 2013 – on immigration. According to an exit poll (Ashcroft, 2016), 64% of social classes D–E and over two thirds of social tenants voted to leave the European Union. One commentator observed 'In this Brexit vote, the poor turned on an elite who ignored them' (Jack, 2016). In a *Spectator* article Brendon O'Neill claimed '77 per cent of local authorities in which lots of people earn a low wage (of less than £23,000) voted Leave, compared with only 35 per cent of areas with decent pay packets'. Describing the result as a 'Peasants Revolt', he asserted, 'Class was the deciding factor in the vote' and the working class 'have a strong sense of being ruled over by institutions that fundamentally loathe them, or at least consider them to be in dire need of moral and social correction' (O'Neill, 2016, pp 1-2). The 'precariat' hit back.

In her first speech as Prime Minister, Theresa May, aware that rival politicians could harness this discontent, invoked 'One Nation Conservatism'. She claimed the 'Union' meant not only 'the precious bond between England, Scotland, Wales and Northern Ireland' but a union 'between all of our citizens, every one of us, whoever we are and wherever we're from'. Her speech was interspersed with phrases such as 'fighting against the burning injustice that, if you're born poor, you will die on average 9 years earlier than others' and 'if you're a white, working-class boy, you're less likely than anybody else in Britain to go to university' (May, 2016, p 1).

'One Nation Conservatism' has a long history of invocation by Conservative politicians. The phrase is usually attributed to Disraeli but he never used the term 'One Nation'. In *Sybil* (Disraeli, 1998 [1845]), a novel but containing thinly disguised narrative on Disraeli's political approach, he spoke of two nations – the rich and the poor. His aim was not to reduce the divide but to make the 'two nation' division more acceptable via a more imaginative rhetorical emphasis on the obligations of the rich (Hurd and Young, 2013). Indeed, despite the Irish famine tragedy, Disraeli organised opposition to Peel's reform of the Corn Laws that were aimed at making food cheaper for the poor.

Margaret Thatcher, on becoming Prime Minister, declared 'Where there is discord, may we bring harmony' (Thatcher, 1979a). David Cameron, in his first speech on remaining Prime Minister after the 2015 General Election, said 'I want my party, and I hope a government I would like to lead, to reclaim a mantle that we should never have lost – the mantle of One Nation, one United Kingdom' (Cameron, 2015b). In concluding his 2015 Summer Budget statement George Osborne (2015a) declared 'The Budget today puts security first....The national security of a Britain that defends itself and its values. A plan for working people. One purpose. One policy. One nation'.

Despite the departure from the front bench of many of the Conservative elite who had governed the United Kingdom for six years – David Cameron, George Osborne, Oliver Letwin, Michael

Gove – May's first cabinet, on Willetts' (1992) wet/dry Conservative barometer, had a parched aura. As examples, David Davis, Secretary of State for Exiting the European Union, regards all houses let at below market rents as subsidised (Davis and Field, 2012). Liam Fox, Secretary of State for International Relations, has strongly opposed Green Belt development in his North Somerset constituency (Fox, 2015) and views unchecked migration as the cause of the housing problem (Planning Resource, 2016). Sajid Javid, the new Secretary of State for Communities and Local Government staunchly opposed new residential development in his constituency (*Bromsgrove Standard*, 2016) and Gavin Barwell, the new Minister for Housing and Planning, also joined the long list of ministers who have objected to new housing in their constituencies. *Inside Croydon* (2016) commented:

> How, too, will Barwell reconcile his position as housing minister and the need to deliver tens of thousands of new homes with some of his local campaigning, after he spent the past year as a constituency MP stirring up the people of Shirley to oppose the building of new homes?

The only reference to housing in May's speech on becoming Prime Minister – 'You have your own home, but you worry about paying a mortgage' – related to owner-occupation. A 2016 House of Lords Select Committee on Economic Affairs report remarked 'The government is primarily focused on building for home ownership, neglecting housing for affordable and social rent', adding 'The government's aim is not to stop house prices rising, rather their priority is to encourage home ownership without cost to existing owners' (House of Lords Select Committee on Economic Affairs, 2016, pp 3 and 29). A signal of a new approach would be to relax rules on local authority borrowing to allow more council houses to be built but it appears that May will continue to construct what Harloe (1995, p 36) called market capitalism's 'outer defence' around homeownership. In England and Wales, housing's contemporary 'wickedness' remains entrenched in its politics.

References

Aalbers, M.B. (2012) 'European Mortgage Markets: Before and After the Financial Crisis', in M.B. Aalbers (ed) *Subprime Cities: The Political Economy of Housing Markets*, Chichester: Wiley Blackwell, pp 120–50.

Abercrombie, L.P. (1948) 'A Great City', lecture given at Wilson Hall, University of Melbourne.

Abercrombie, L.P. (1959) *Town and Country Planning*, Oxford: Oxford University Press.

Adams, D. (2011) 'The "Wicked" Problem of Planning for Housing Development', *Housing Studies*, vol 26, no 2, pp 951–60.

Addison, P. (2013) *Churchill on the Home Front 1900–1955*, London: Faber and Faber.

Alexander, A. (2009) *Britain's New Towns: Garden Cities to Sustainable Communities*, Abingdon: Routledge.

Allen, C. (2008) *Housing Market Renewal and Social Class*, Abingdon: Routledge.

Allen, C. (2009) 'The Fallacy of "Housing Studies": Philosophical Problems of Knowledge and Understanding in Housing Research', *Housing Theory and Society*, vol 26, no 1, pp 53–79.

Allen, C. (2016) 'Getting "Out There" and Impacting: The Problem of Housing and Urban Research and its Anarchist Alternative', *Housing Theory and Society*, published online, 3 March. Available at: http://www.tandfonline.com/action/showAxaArticles?journalCode=shou20

Amati, M. (ed) (2008) *Urban Green Belts in the Twenty-first Century*, Aldershot: Ashgate.

Ansell, B. (2013) 'The Political Economy of Ownership: Housing Markets and the Welfare State'. Available at: http://users.ox.ac.uk/~polf0487/papers/Ansell%20Political%20Economy%20of%20Ownership%20Jan%202013.pdf

Apps, P. (2013) 'Lib Dems Accuse Tories of Blocking 25,000 Homes', *Inside Housing*, 15 July.

Apps, P. (2015a) '30,000 Council Homes Sold Since Right to Buy Discounts Raised', *Inside Housing*, 25 June.

Apps, P. (2015b) 'Full Data Released: Right to Buy to Let', *Inside Housing*, 21 August.

Apps, P. (2016) 'Montague: Merger Marks Sector "Tipping Point"', *Inside Housing*, 6 April.

Archer, T. (1865) *The Paupers, the Thief and the Convict: Sketches of Some of Their Homes, Haunts and Habits*, London: Groombridge and Sons.

Armstrong, A. (2016) 'Commentary: UK Housing Market: Problems and Policies', *National Institute Economic Review*, no 235, February, pp 5–8.

Ashcroft, Lord (2013) 'Marginal Territory: The Seats That Will Decide the Next Election'. Available at: http://lordashcroftpolls.com/2013/03/marginal-territory-the-seats-that-will-decide-the-next-election/

Ashcroft, Lord (2016) 'How the United Kingdom voted on Thursday'. Available at: http://lordashcroftpolls.com/wp-content/uploads/2016/06/How-the-UK-voted-Full-tables-1.pdf

Bailey, E. (2016) 'Knuckle Down', *Inside Housing*, 6 April.

Ball, M. and Sunderland, D. (2006) *An Economic History of London 1800–1914*, Abingdon: Routledge.

Bank of England (2015) 'News Release: Financial Policy Committee Statement from Its Policy Meeting, 23 September 2015'. Available at: http://www.bankofengland.co.uk/publications/Pages/news/2015/022.aspx

Bank of England (2016) 'Underwriting Standards for Buy-to-Let Mortgage Contracts'. Available at: http://www.bankofengland.co.uk/pra/Pages/publications/cp/2016/cp1116.aspx

Barker, K. (2004) *Delivering Stability: Securing Our Future Housing Needs; Final Report, Recommendations*, London: HM Treasury. Available at: http://webarchive.nationalarchives.gov.uk/+/http://www.hm-treasury.gov.uk/consultations_and_legislation/barker/consult_barker_index.cfm

Barker, K. (2014) *Housing: Where's the Plan?* London: London Publishing Partnership.

Barlow, A. (Chair) (1940) *Royal Commission on the Distribution of the Industrial Population*, Cmd. 6153, London: HMSO.

Barnes, H. (1926) *Housing: The Facts and the Future*, London: Ernest Benn.

Barnes M (1971) Rent Assessment Committees (Hearings) HC Deb 22 June 1971 vol. 819 cc1387-96. Available at: http://hansard.millbanksystems.com/commons/1971/jun/22/rent-assessment-committees-hearings#column_1388

Barnett, J. (1982) *Inside the Treasury*, London: Andre Deutch.

Barnett, M.J. (1969) *The Politics of Legislation: The Rent Act of 1957*, London: Weidenfeld and Nicolson.

Bateman, J. (1883) *The Great Landowners of Great Britain and Ireland – A List of All Owners of Three Thousand Acres and Upwards*, London: Harrison and Sons.

BBC News (2014) 'Child Poverty Definition Change "Put on Hold"', 27 February. Available at: http://www.bbc.co.uk/news/uk-politics-26362035

BBC News (2016) 'Brexit would hit house prices, says Osborne', 21 May. Available at: http://www.bbc.co.uk/news/business-36344425

Beckett, A. (2015) *Promised You a Miracle: Why 1980–82 Made Modern Britain*, London: Allen Lane.

Bedarida, F. (1990) *A Social History of England 1851–1990*, London: Routledge.

Begg, T. (1996) *Housing Policy in Scotland*, Edinburgh: John Donald Publishers Ltd.

Beider, H. (2012) *Race, Housing and Community: Perspectives on Policy and Practice*, Chichester: Wiley-Blackwell.

Beier, A.L. (1987) *Masterless Men: The Vagrancy Problem in England 1560–1640*, London: Methuen.

Belfield, C., Chandler, D. and Joyce, R. (2015) *Housing: Trends in Prices, Costs and Tenure*, London: Institute of Fiscal Studies.

Belfield, C., Cribb, J., Hood, A. and Joyce, R. (2016) *Living Standards, Poverty and Inequality in the UK: 2016*. Available at: http://www.ifs.org.uk/publications/8371

Bellamy, J. and Magdoff, F. (2009) *The Great Financial Crisis: Causes and Consequences*, New York, NY: Monthly Review Press.

Bengtsson, B. (2012) 'Housing Politics and Political Science', in D.F. Clapham, W.A.V. Clark and K. Gibb (eds) *The Sage Handbook of Housing Studies*, London: Sage, pp 206–29.

Bengtsson, B. (2015) 'Between Structure and Thatcher: Towards a Research Agenda for Theory-Informed Actor-Related Analysis of Housing Politics', *Housing Studies*, vol 30, no 5, pp 677–93.

Bentham, J. (1798) 'Pauper Management Improved'. Available at: http://studymore.org.uk/xben.htm

Bentham, J. (1970 [1781]) *An Introduction to the Principles of Morals and Legislation*, London: Athlone Press.

Bentley, D. (2015) *The Future of Private Renting: Shaping a Fairer Market for Tenants and Taxpayers*, London: Civitas.

Bentley, D. (2016) *The Housing Question: Overcoming the Shortage of Homes*, London: Civitas.

Besant, A. (1989) 'Industry under Socialism', in G.B. Shaw (ed) *Fabian Essays in Socialism*, London: Fabian Society, pp 136–54.

Bevan, A. (1945) 'House of Commons Debates', vol 414, cols 1222/1223, October.

Bevan, A. (1946) 'Speech to the Labour Party Conference at Scarborough'. Available at: http://www.britishpathe.com/video/bevan-speaks-on-housing-at-labour-conference/query/262807

Beveridge, W. (1942) *Report of the Inter-Departmental Committee on Social Insurance and Allied Services*, London: HMSO.

Beveridge, W. (1943) *Pillars of Security*, London: George Allen and Unwin.

Birrell, D. (2008) 'Devolution and Quangos in the United Kingdom: The Implementation of Principles and Policies for Rationalisation and Democratisation', *Policy Studies*, vol 29, no 1, pp 35–49.

Birrell, D. (2009) *The Impact of Devolution on Social Policy*, Bristol: The Policy Press.

Birrell, D. (2012) 'Intergovernmental Relations and Political Parties in Northern Ireland', *British Journal of Politics and International Relations*, vol 14, pp 270–84.

Birrell, D. and Gray, A.M. (2011) 'Governance and Social policy in Northern Ireland 2007–2010: Consensus and Eithne Mcloughlin's Lowest Common Denominator Thesis', *Social Policy and Society*, vol 11, no 1, pp 15–25.

Birrell, D. and Gray, A.M. (2016) 'Social Policy, the Devolved Administrations in the UK Coalition Government', in H. Bochel and M. Powell (eds) *The Coalition Government and Social Policy: Restructuring the Welfare State*, Bristol: The Policy Press, pp 325–46.

Blair, T. (1997a) 'Speech by Prime Minister', Aylesbury Estate, 2 June.

Blair, T. (1997b) 'Foreword to the 1997 Labour Party Manifesto'. Available at: http://www.politicsresources.net/area/uk/man/lab97.htm

Blair, T. (1998) *Leading the Way: A New Vision for Local Government*, London: Institute for Public Policy Research.

Blair, T. (2002) 'Foreword to *Social Enterprise: A Strategy for Success*'. Available at: http://www.faf-gmbh.de/www/media/socialenterpriseastrategyforsucess.pdf

Blair, T. (2010) *A Journey*, London: Hutchinson.

Blaug, M. (ed) (1992) *Henry George (1839–1897)*, Aldershot: Edward Elgar.

BME National and Human Institute Project (2014) 'Deep Roots, Diverse Communities, Dedicated Service: The Legacy, Value and Future Potential of Black and Minority Ethnic Housing Organisations in England'. Available at: http://www.google.co.uk/url?url=http://www.housingnet.co.uk/download_pdf/725&rct=j&frm=1&q=&esrc=s&sa=U&ved=0ahUKEwiy6rHru4bMAhWJtxQKHf2FB-kQFggUMAA&usg=AFQjCNHdPnv36yVcG94XeA93QFQSnr5LxQ

Booth, C. (1969 [1902]) *The Life and Labour of the People of London* (vol 3), London: Macmillan.

Bosanquet, H. (1902) *The Strength of the People: A Study in Social Economics*, London: Macmillan.

Bosanquet, H. (1906) *The Family*, London: Macmillan.

Bourton, W. and Leather, P. (2000) 'Housing Stock Condition and Renewal', in R. Smith, T. Stirling and P. Williams (eds) *Housing in Wales: The Policy Agenda in an Era of Devolution*, London: Chartered Institute of Housing, pp 50–62.

Boyle, D. (2013) *Broke: Who Killed the Middle Classes?* London: Fourth Estate.

Boys Smith, N. and Morton, A. (2013) *Create Streets: Not Just Multi-Storey Estates*, London: Policy Exchange.

Brabrook, W.J. (2009 [1906]) *Building Societies*, Charleston, SC: BiblioBazaar.

Bradley, Q. (2013) 'Universal Claims: Welfare Housing Reform in UK Cities and the Resilience of a Right to Housing', paper presented to the RGS–IBG Annual International Conference 'New Geographical Frontiers', 28–30 August, London.

Bradley, Q. (2014) *The Tenants' Movement: Resident Involvement, Community Action and the Contentious Politics of Housing*, Abingdon: Routledge.

Brand, J. (1992) *Parliamentary Parties: Policy and Power*, Oxford: Clarendon Press.

Branson, N. and Heinemann, M. (1973) *Britain in the Nineteen Thirties*, St Albans: Panther.

Bretherton, J. and Pleace, N. (2015) *Housing First in England: An Evaluation of Nine Services*, York: Centre for Housing Policy, University of York.

Brett, C. (1986) *Housing in a Divided Community*, London: Institute of Public Administration.

Bridgen, P. and Lowe, R. (1998) *Welfare Policy under the Conservatives 1951–1964. A Guide to Documents in the Public Record Office*, Kew: Public Record Office.

Briggs, A. (1952) *History of Birmingham Volume 11*, Oxford: Oxford University Press.

Briggs, A. (1968) *Victorian Cities*, London: Pelican.

British Institute of Public Opinion Polls (1945) 'Documentation'. Available at: http://www.esds.ac.uk/doc/2044/mrdoc/pdf/guide.pdf

British Social Attitudes (2013) 'British Social Attitudes 29'. Available at: http://www.bsa.natcen.ac.uk/media/38852/bsa29_full_report.pdf

British Social Attitudes (2015) 'British Social Attitudes 31'. Available at: http://www.bsa.natcen.ac.uk/latest-report/british-social-attitudes-31/key-findings/britain-2014.aspx

Broadway Malyan (2015) 'Fifty Shades of Green Belt Report'. Available at: http://issuu.com/broadwaymalyan/docs/50_shades_of_green_belt_report

Brock, L.G. (Chair) (1933) *The Report of the Departmental Committee on Sterilisation*, London: HMSO.

Brodie, M. (2004) *The Politics of the Poor: The East End of London 1885–1914*, Oxford: Oxford University Press.

Broich, J. (2013) *London: Water and the Making of the Modern City*, Pittsburgh, PA: University of Pittsburgh Press.

Bromsgrove Standard (2016) 'MP Sajid Javid slams Redditch Council's plans to build 2,800 homes in Bromsgrove's green belt', 22 March. Available at: http://bromsgrovestandard.co.uk/news/mp-sajid-javid-slams-redditch-councils-plans-build-2800-homes-bromsgroves-green-belt/

Brown, C. (2015a) 'Osborne Slams Associations' Housebuilding Record', *Inside Housing*, 9 September.

Brown, C. (2015b) 'Clegg: I Halted Rent Cut Five Years Ago', *Inside Housing*, 23 October.

Brown, C. (2016) 'CIH NI Calls for PRS Licensing', *Inside Housing*, 5 February.

Brownfield Briefing (2015) 'Pathfinders to Chaos'. Available at: https://brownfieldbriefing.com/36453/pathfinders-to-chaos

Bruce, M. (1973) *The Rise of the Welfare State: English Social Policy 1601–1971*, London: Weidenfeld and Nicolson.

Bruce, R. (1945) *First Planning Report to the Highways and Planning Committee of the Corporation of the City of Glasgow*, Glasgow: Corporation of the City of Glasgow.

Bruce, S., Glendinning, T. and Rosie, M. (2004) *Sectarianism in Scotland*, Edinburgh: Edinburgh University Press.

Brundage, A. (1988) *England's 'Prussian Minister': Edwin Chadwick and the Politics of Government Growth, 1832–1854*, Pennsylvania, PA: Pennsylvania University Press.

Bruton, M. and Nicholson, D.J. (1986) *Local Planning in Practice*, Abingdon: Routledge.

Buchanan, J.M. (2003) 'Public Choice: Politics without Romance', *Policy*, Spring. Available at: http://www.montana.edu/hfretwell/documents/332/buchananpublicchoice.pdf

Burnett, J. (1978) *A Social History of Housing 1815–1970*, Newton Abbot: David and Charles.

Butler, D. and Kavanagh, D. (1980) *The British General Election of 1979*, Basingstoke: Macmillan.

Butler, E. (2012) *Public Choice: A Primer*, London: Institute of Economic Affairs.

Butler, P. (2012) 'Homelessness and Welfare Politics: The Strange Tale of Andy Gale', *Guardian*, 13 December. Available at: http://www.theguardian.com/society/patrick-butler-cuts-blog/2012/dec/13/housing-homelessness-politics-strange-tale-andy-gale

Butler, P. (2014) 'Council Spending Cuts: The North Loses Out to the South'. Available at: http://www.theguardian.com/society/patrick-butler-cuts-blog/2013/jan/11/council-cuts-north-loses-out-to-the-south-newcastle

Butler, R.A.B. (Lord) (1971) *The Art of the Possible*, London: Hamilton.

Byrne, J., Hansson, U. and Bell, J. (2006) *Shared Living: Mixed Residential Communities in Northern Ireland*, Belfast: Institute for Conflict Research.

Cabinet (1926) 'Standing Committee on Expenditure', CP (54) 26. Available at: http://filestore.nationalarchives.gov.uk/pdfs/large/cab-24-178.pdf

Cabinet (1931) 'Rent Restriction. Conclusions of a Meeting of the Cabinet Held at 10, Downing Street, S.W.1., on Wednesday, December 9th, 1931', CP 305 (31). Available at: http://filestore.nationalarchives.gov.uk/pdfs/large/cab-24-225.pdf

Cabinet (1932) 'Housing Policy. Conclusions of a Meeting of the Cabinet Held at 10 Downing Street, S.W.1, on November 23rd, 1932', CP 286 (32). Available at: http://filestore.nationalarchives.gov.uk/pdfs/large/cab-24-234.pdf

Cabinet (1934) 'Housing Policy: Memorandum of the Ministry of Health', CP 208 (34). Available at: http://filestore.nationalarchives.gov.uk/pdfs/large/cab-24-250.pdf

Cabinet (1953) 'The Rents of Council Houses', CP (53) 219. Available at: http://filestore.nationalarchives.gov.uk/pdfs/large/cab-129-62.pdf

Cabinet (1955) 'Conclusions of a Meeting of the Cabinet Held at 10 Downing Street, S.W.1, on Tuesday, 7th June, 1955, at 11 a.m.', CM (55) 12. Available at: http://filestore.nationalarchives.gov.uk/pdfs/large/cab-128-29.pdf

Cabinet Office (2013) 'What We Do'. Available at: https://www.gov.uk/government/organisations/cabinet-office/about

Cabinet Office (2014) 'Queen's Speech'. Available at: https://www.gov.uk/government/speeches/queens-speech-2014

Cabinet Office (2016) 'Government Announces New Clause to Be Inserted into Grant Agreements'. Available at: https://www.gov.uk/government/news/government-announces-new-clause-to-be-inserted-into-grant-agreements

Cadwalladr, C. (2013) 'When We Pay Rent to Our Mps, We Have a Problem', *Guardian*, 17 July.

Cameron, D. (2006) 'We'll Build More Homes. and They Will Be Beautiful: People Must Be Given a Bigger Say. The Current System Is Bananas', *Independent*, 26 March.

Cameron, D. (2011a) 'London Riots: Prime Minister's Statement in Full', *Telegraph*, 9 August.

Cameron, D. (2011b) 'PM Statement on Violence in England', 10 August. Available at: https://www.gov.uk/government/speeches/pm-statement-on-violence-in-england

Cameron, D. (2015a) 'Speech to Conservative Party Conference: Full Text', 7 October. Available at: http://www.mirror.co.uk/news/uk-news/david-camerons-full-speech-conservative-6589711

Cameron, D. (2015b), 'David Cameron's Victory Speech: Full Text', *Independent*, 9 May. Available at: http://www.independent.co.uk/news/uk/politics/generalelection/david-camerons-victory-speech-the-full-text-of-the-speech-delivered-on-downing-street-10236230.html

Cameron, D. (2016) *Estate Regeneration: Article by David Cameron*, London: Prime Minister's Office. Available at: https://www.gov.uk/government/speeches/estate-regeneration-article-by-david-cameron

Cameron, Lord (1969) *Disturbances in Northern Ireland: Report of the Commission under the Chairmanship of Lord Cameron*, Cmd 532, Belfast: HMSO.

Campaign to Protect Rural England (2011) 'What We Want to See in the National Planning Policy Framework: A Summary by the Campaign to Protect Rural England'. Available at: www.cpre.org.uk/resources/housing-and-planning/planning/.../1390

Campaign to Protect Rural England (2016) 'More Than a Quarter of a Million Houses Now Planned for Green Belt Land'. Available at: http://www.cpre.org.uk/media-centre/latest-news-releases/item/4278-more-than-a-quarter-of-a-million-houses-now-planned-for-green-belt-land

Campbell, J. (1993) *Edward Heath: A Biography*, London: Jonathan Cape.

Cannadine, D. (1990) *The Decline and Fall of the British Aristocracy*, Yale, CT: Yale University Press.

Cao, D. (2014) 'How a Grassroots Campaign Saved a Suburb: Raised Voices and Special Chemistry: The Politics of Walkley's Resistance'. Available at: https://walkleyhistory.wordpress.com/2013/01/18/how-a-grassroots-campaign-saved-a-suburb/

Castells, M. (1977) *The Urban Question*, London: Edward Arnold.

Castells, M. (1983) *The City and the Grassroots*, Berkeley, CA: University of California Press.

Castles, F. (1998) 'The Really Big Trade-Off: Home Ownership and the Welfare State in the New World and the Old', *Acta Politica*, vol 33, no 1, pp 5–19.

Centre for Social Justice (2006) *Interim Report on the State of the Nation*, London: Centre for Social Justice.

Centre for Social Justice (2008) *Breakthrough Britain: Housing Poverty, from Social Breakdown to Social Mobility*, London: Centre for Social Justice.

Chadwick, E. (1842) *Report on the Sanitary Condition of the Labouring Population of Great Britain*, London: HMSO.

Chartered Institute of Housing (2010) *Briefing Paper on Borrowing Rules and Council Housing: The Case for Harmonising the UK with the Rest of the EU*, London: Chartered Institute of Housing. Available at: http://www.cih.org/resources/policy/Consultation%20responses/BorrowingRulesandCouncilHousing-Apr10.pdf

Chartered Institute of Housing, the National Housing Federation and Shelter (2011) 'Housing Report No 1'. Available at: http://england.shelter.org.uk/__data/assets/pdf_file/0011/387992/The_Housing_Report_October_2011.pdf

Checkland, S.G. (1976) *The Upas Tree: Glasgow 1875–1975*, Glasgow: Glasgow University Press.

Checkland, S.G. and Checkland, E.O. (eds) (1974) *The Poor Law Report of 1834*, Harmondsworth: Penguin.

Chenevix-Trench, H. and Philip, L.J. (2001) 'Community and Conservation Land Ownership in Highland Scotland: A Common Focus in a Changing Context', *Scottish Geographical Journal*, vol 117, no 2, pp 139–56.

Cheshire, P. (2013) 'Turning Houses into Gold: The Failure of British Planning', *CentrePiece*, Spring. Available at: http://cep.lse.ac.uk/pubs/download/cp417.pdf

Chesney, K. (1970) *The Victorian Underworld*, Devon: Readers Union Limited.

Chevin, D. (2013) *Social Hearted, Commercially Minded: A Report on Tomorrow's Housing Associations*, London: The Smith Institute.

Churchill, W. (1909) 'Speech Given at the King's Theatre', Edinburgh, 17 July.

Clapham, D. (2006) 'Housing Policy and the Discourse of Globalization', *International Journal of Housing Policy*, vol 6, no 1, pp 55–76.

Clapham, D. (2012) 'Social Policy Approaches to Housing Research', in D.F. Clapham, W.A.V. Clark and K. Gibb (eds) *The Sage Handbook of Housing Studies*, London: Sage, pp 163–73.

Clapham, D.F. and Kintrea, K. (1987) 'Importing Housing Policy: Housing Co-operatives in Britain and Scandinavia', *Housing Studies*, vol 2, no 3, pp 157–69.

Clapham, D.F., Clark W.A.V. and Gibb, K. (eds) (2012) *The Sage Handbook of Housing Studies*, London: Sage.

Clark, G. (2015) 'Speech to the National Housing Federation, 23 September', *Inside Housing*, 24 September. Available at: http://www.insidehousing.co.uk/policy/politics/central-government/greg-clark-speech-to-nhf-conference-full-transcript/7011930.article

Clark, T. (2001) *The Limits of Social Democracy? Tax and Spend under Labour, 1974–79*, London: Institute for Fiscal Studies.

Clarke, H.D., Kellner, P., Stewart, M., Twyman, J. and Whiteley, P. (2015) *Austerity and Political Choice in Britain*, London: AIAA.

Clarke, S. and Ginsburg, N. (1975) 'The Political Economy of Housing', in (eds)*Political Economy and the Housing Question*, London: Conference of Socialist Economists.

Clyde Valley Regional Advisory Committee (1946) *Clyde Valley Regional Plan 1946*, London: HMSO.

Cockburn, C. (1977) *Local State: Management of Cities and People*, London: Pluto Press.

Cohen, G. (no date) '"Happy Hunting Ground of the Crank?" The Independent Labour Party and Local Labour Politics in Glasgow and Norwich 1932–45'. Available at: http://www.academia.edu/1511307/Happy_Hunting_Ground_of_the_Crank_The_Independent_Labour_Party_and_Local_Labour_Politics_in_Glasgow_and_Norwich_1932-45

Cohen, N. (2013) 'A Coalition of the Complacent', *Spectator*, 7 January. Available at: http://blogs.spectator.co.uk/nick-cohen/2013/01/a-coalition-of-the-complacent/

Cole, I. and Furbey, R. (1994) *The Eclipse of Council Housing*, London: Routledge.

Coleman, A. (1986) *Utopia on Trial*, London: Hilary Shipman.

Coles, A. (1989) 'Satisfying Preference', *Housing Review*, vol 38, no 4, pp 1–3.

Commission on Civil Society and Democratic Engagement (2014) *Impact of the Lobbying Act on Civil Society and Democratic Engagement*, London: Commission on Civil Society and Democratic Engagement.

Comptroller-General of Inland Revenue for Scotland (1874) *Owners and Land and Heritages*, Edinburgh: Comptroller-General of Inland Revenue for Scotland.

Connolly, M. and Knox, C. (1991) 'Policy Differences within the United Kingdom: The Case of Housing Policy in Northern Ireland 1979–89', *Public Administration*, vol 69, autumn, pp 303–24.

Conservative Party (1951) *Conservative Party Manifesto*, London: Conservative Party.

Conservative Party (1964) *Conservative Party Manifesto: Prosperity with a Purpose*, London: Conservative Party. Available at: http://www.conservative-party.net/manifestos/1964/1964-conservative-manifesto.shtml

Conservative Party (1970) *1970 Conservative Party General Election Manifesto: A Better Tomorrow*, London: Conservative Party.

Conservative Party (1974a) *February 1974 Conservative Party General Election Manifesto: Firm Action for a Fair Britain*, London: Conservative Party.

Conservative Party (1974b) *October 1974 Conservative Party General Election Manifesto: Putting Britain First*, London: Conservative Party.

Conservative Party (1979) *Conservative Party General Election Manifesto*, London: Conservative Party.

Conservative Party (1989) *The Campaign Guide, 1989*, London: Thatcher Foundation. Available at: http://www.margaretthatcher.org/document/110802

Conservative Party (2010) *Invitation to Join the Government of Britain: Conservative Party Manifesto*, London: Conservative Party.

Conservative Party (2015) *The Conservative Party Manifesto 2015*, London: Conservative Party.

Conservative Party Archives (1949) 'National Federation of Property Owners to Woolton', CCO/ 3/2/122, 5 October.

Corbyn, J. (2015) 'Tackling the Housing Crisis'. Available at: https://d3n8a8pro7vhmx.cloudfront.net/jeremyforlabour/pages/106/attachments/original/1438782182/housing.pdf?1438782182

Costello, K. (2014) '"More Equitable than the Judgement of the Justices of the Peace": The King's Bench and the Poor Laws 1630–1800', *The Journal of Legal History*, vol 35, no 1, pp 3–26.

Council of Mortgage Lenders (2013) 'Helping the Bank of Mum and Dad'. Available at: https://www.cml.org.uk/news/news-and-views/533/

Country Land and Business Association (2016) 'About the CLA'. Available at: https://www.cla.org.uk/about-cla

Cowan, D. and McDermont, M. (2006) *Regulating Social Housing: Governing Decline*, Abingdon: Routledge.

Cowley, P. and Kavanagh, D. (2016) *The British General Election of 2015*, Basingstoke: Palgrave Macmillan.

Cox, A. (1984) *Adversary Politics and Land: The Conflict Over Land and Property Policy in Post-War Britain*, Cambridge: Cambridge University Press.

Craig, P. (1986) 'The House That Jerry Built? Building Societies, the State and the Politics of Owner-Occupation', *Housing Studies*, vol 1, no 2, pp 87–108.

Crawson, N. (2013) 'Revisiting the 1977 Housing (Homeless Persons) Act: Westminster, Whitehall and the Homelessness Lobby', *Twentieth Century British History*, vol 24, no 3, pp 424–47.

Crisp, R., Pearson, S. and Gore, T. (2015) 'Rethinking the Impact of Regeneration on Poverty: A (Partial) Defence of a "Failed" Policy', *Journal of Poverty and Social Justice*, vol 23, no 3, pp 167–87.

Crook, T. and Kemp, P.A. (2011) *Transforming Private Landlords: Housing, Markets and Public Policy*, Chichester: Wiley-Blackwell.

Crookston, M. (2004) *Garden Suburbs of Tomorrow: A New Future for Cottage Estates*, Abingdon: Routledge.

Crookston, M. (2015) 'Meeting the Housing Challenge: British Experience, European Lessons', *Built Environment*, vol 41, no 2, pp 1–5.

Crosby, T.L. (2014) *The Unknown Lloyd George: A Statesman in Conflict*, London: I.B. Tauris.

Crosland, C.A.R (1962) *The Conservative Enemy: A Programme of Radical Reform for the 1960s*, London: Cape.

Crossman, R. (1965) 'Speech in the Second Reading of the Housing Subsidies Bill', 15 December.

Crossman, R. (1975) *The Diaries of a Cabinet Minister. Volume One: Minister of Housing 1964–66*, London: Hamish Hamilton and Jonathan Cape.

Crouch, C. and Wolf, M. (1970) 'Inequality in Housing', in P. Townsend and N. Bosanquet (eds) *Labour and Inequality: Sixteen Fabian Essays*, Dorking: David Neil and Co, pp 26–46.

Croucher, S. (2016) 'Three Housing Associations in £30bn Merger Talks to Create Giant UK House-Builder', *International Business Times*, 6 April. Available at: http://www.ibtimes.co.uk/three-housing-associations-30bn-merger-talks-create-giant-uk-housebuilder-1553471

Cullingworth, J.B. (1973) *Problems of an Urban Society Volume 2: The Social Context of Planning*, London: George Allen and Unwin.

Currell, S. (2010) 'Breeding Better Babies in the Eugenic Garden City', *Modernist Cultures*, vol 5, no 3, pp 267–90.

Czischke, D. (2014) *Social Housing Organisations in England and The Netherlands: Between the State, Market and Community*, Delft: TUDelft.

Daily Express (2014) 'Tory Minister Attacks EU Over European Migrants Selling the Big Issue to Claim Benefits', 5 June.

Daily Mail (2012a) 'One in Five Council House Tenants Is on the Fiddle (and It Could Be Costing Taxpayers £13bn)', 23 January.

Daily Mail (2012b) 'If Your Children Share a Room You May Be Classed as Homeless! IDS in Row with Charity Shelter', 24 January.

Daily Mail (2013) 'The judicial review system is not a promotional tool for countless Left-wing campaigners', 5 September.

Daily Mail (2014) 'Landlords Face Buy-Let-Tax Probe, Second-Home-Owners Face Investigation, Concern Grows Undeclared Profits', July.

Daily Mail (2015) 'Housing Fat Cats' Hypocrisy: Furious Backlash at PM's Right-to-Buy Revolution ... from Housing Chiefs with Lavish Homes and Six-Figure Salaries', 14 April.

Daily Mirror (2013) 'Great Tory Housing Shame: Third of Ex-Council Homes Now Owned by Rich Landlords'. Available at: http://www.mirror.co.uk/news/uk-news/right-to-buy-housing-shame-third-ex-council-1743338

Darling, A. (2011) *Back from the Brink: 1000 Days at Number 11*, London: Atlantic Books.

Daunton, M.J. (1983) *House and Home in the Victorian City: Working-Class Housing 1850–1914*, London: Edward Arnold.

Daunton, M.J. (1987) *A Property Owning Democracy? Housing in Britain*, London: Faber and Faber.

Davies, A. (2013) '"Right to Buy": The Development of a Conservative Housing Policy, 1950–1980', *Contemporary British History*, vol 27, no 4, pp 421–44.

Davis, D. and Field, F. (2012) *Right to Buy 2*, London: Institute for Public Policy Research.

Davis, J. (2008) 'Macmillan's Martyr: The Pilgrim Case, the "Land Grab" and the Tory Housing Drive, 1951–9', *Planning Perspectives*, vol 23, no 2, pp 125-146.

Davison, M., Nicol, S., Roys, M., Garrett, H., Beaumont, A. and Turner, C. (2012) *The Cost of Poor Housing in Northern Ireland*, London: IHS BRE Press.

Dawson, W.H. (1910) *The Vagrancy Problem: The Case for Measures of Restraint for Tramps, Loafers and Unemployables with a Study of Continental Detention Colonies and Labour Houses*, London: King and Son.

DCLG (Department for Communities and Local Government) (2007) 'Homes for the Future: More Affordable, More Sustainable', cm7191. Available at: https://www.gov.uk/government/uploads/system/uploads/attachment_data/file/243191/7191.pdf

DCLG (2010a) 'Private Landlord Survey 2010'. Available at: https://www.gov.uk/government/statistics/private-landlords-survey-2010

DCLG (2010b) 'Local Decisions: A Fairer Future for Social Housing'. Available at: https://www.gov.uk/government/uploads/system/uploads/attachment_data/file/8512/1775577.pdf

DCLG (2011a) 'The Draft Planning Policy Framework'. Available at: https://www.gov.uk/government/consultations/draft-national-planning-policy-framework

DCLG (2011b) 'Vision to End Rough Sleeping: No Second Night Out Nationwide'. Available at: https://www.gov.uk/government/publications/vision-to-end-rough-sleeping--2

DCLG (2011c) 'Public Attitudes to Housing in England: Report Based on the Results from the British Social Attitudes Survey'. Available at: https://www.gov.uk/government/publications/public-attitudes-to-housing-in-england-results-from-the-british-social-attitudes-survey

DCLG (2012a) 'National Planning Policy Framework'. Available at: https://www.gov.uk/government/uploads/system/uploads/attachment_data/file/6077/2116950.pdf

DCLG (2012b) 'Tracking Economic and Child Income Deprivation at Neighbourhood Level in England, 1999–2009'. Available at: https://www.gov.uk/government/statistics/tracking-economic-and-child-income-deprivation-at-neighbourhood-level-in-england-1999-to-2009

DCLG (2012c) 'A Review of the Barriers to Institutional Investment in Private Rented Homes', (Montague Report). Available at: http://socialwelfare.bl.uk/subject-areas/services-activity/housing-homelessness/departmentforcommunitiesandlocalgovernment/1356572204242.pdf

DCLG (2012d) 'Plan to Boost Housebuilding, Jobs and the Economy'. Available at: http://www.communities.gov.uk/news/corporate/2211918

DCLG (2012e) 'Definitions of General Housing Terms'. Available at: https://www.gov.uk/definitions-of-general-housing-terms

DCLG (2012f) 'Making Every Contact Count: A Joint Approach to Preventing Homelessness'. Available at: https://www.gov.uk/government/publications/making-every-contact-count-a-joint-approach-to-preventing-homelessness

DCLG (2012g) 'National Planning Policy Framework: Impact Assessment'. Available at: https://www.gov.uk/government/uploads/system/uploads/attachment_data/file/11804/2172846.pdf

DCLG (2013a) 'Government Response to the Riots, Communities and Victims Panel's Final Report'. Available at: https://www.gov.uk/government/uploads/system/uploads/attachment_data/file/211617/Govt_Response_to_the_Riots_-_Final_Report.pdf

DCLG (2013b) 'English Housing Survey Headline Report 2011–12'. Available at: https://www.gov.uk/government/uploads/system/uploads/attachment_data/file/211288/EHS_Headline_Report_2011-2012.pdf

DCLG (2014) 'Locally-led Garden Cities'. Available at: https://www.gov.uk/government/uploads/system/uploads/attachment_data/file/303324/20140414_Locally-led_Garden_Cities_final_signed.pdf

DCLG (2015a) 'Land Value Estimates for Policy Appraisal'. Available at: https://www.gov.uk/government/publications/land-value-estimates-for-policy-appraisal

DCLG (2015b) 'Selective Licensing in the Private Rented Sector: A Guide for Local Authorities'. Available at: https://www.gov.uk/government/uploads/system/uploads/attachment_data/file/418551/150327_Guidance_on_selective_licensing_applications_FINAL_updated_isbn.pdf

DCLG (2015c) 'Tackling Rogue Landlords and Improving the Private Rental Sector: A Technical Discussion Paper'. Available at: https://www.gov.uk/government/consultations/tackling-rogue-landlords-and-improving-the-private-rental-sector

DCLG (2015d) 'Extending Mandatory Licensing of Houses in Multiple Occupation (Hmos) and Related Reforms: A Technical Discussion Document'. Available at: https://www.gov.uk/government/uploads/system/uploads/attachment_data/file/474408/151106_HMO_discussion_Doc_FINAL_for_publication.pdf

DCLG (2015e) 'Live Tables on Homelessness'. Available at: https://www.gov.uk/government/statistical-data-sets/live-tables-on-homelessness

DCLG (2015f) 'English Housing Survey Headline Report 2013–14'. Available at: https://www.gov.uk/government/uploads/system/uploads/attachment_data/file/406740/English_Housing_Survey_Headline_Report_2013-14.pdf

DCLG (2015g) 'Public Attitudes to House Building: Findings from the 2014 British Social Attitudes Survey'. Available at: https://www.gov.uk/government/uploads/system/uploads/attachment_data/file/412347/British_Social_Attitudes_Survey_2014_report.pdf

DCLG (2015h) 'Consultation on Proposed Changes to National Planning Policy'. Available at: https://www.gov.uk/government/uploads/system/uploads/attachment_data/file/488276/151207_Consultation_document.pdf

DCLG (2016a) 'Rough Sleeping Statistics: Autumn 2015, England'. Available at: https://www.gov.uk/government/uploads/system/uploads/attachment_data/file/503015/Rough_Sleeping_Autumn_2015_statistical_release.pdf

DCLG (2016b) 'English Housing Survey 2014–15: Headline Report'. Available at: https://www.gov.uk/government/statistics/english-housing-survey-2014-to-2015-headline-report

DCLG (2016c) 'Dwelling Stock Estimates, England 2015'. Available at: https://www.gov.uk/government/uploads/system/uploads/attachment_data/file/519475/Dwelling_Stock_Estimates_2015_England.pdf

DCLG (2016d) 'Land Use Change Statistics in England: 2014–15'. Available at: https://www.gov.uk/government/statistics/land-use-change-statistics-2014-to-2015

Dean, M. (1991) *The Constitution of Poverty: Towards a Genealogy of Liberal Governance*, Abingdon: Routledge.

Dean, M. (2013) *Democracy under Attack: How the Media Distort Policy and Politics*, Bristol: The Policy Press.

Democratic Unionist Party (2015) 'DUP Westminster Election Manifesto 2015'. Available at: http://dev.mydup.com/images/uploads/publications/DUP_Manifesto_2015_LR.pdf

Denham, A. and Garnett, M. (2001) *Keith Joseph*, Chesham: Acumen.

Denning, Lord (1976) 'Liverpool City Council versus Irwin'. Available at: https://en.wikipedia.org/wiki/Liverpool_City_Council_v_Irwin

Dennis, N. (1972) *People and Planning: The Sociology of Housing in Sunderland*, London: Faber and Faber.

Department of Energy and Climate Change (2015) 'Domestic Green Deal and Energy Company Obligation in Great Britain: Headline report'. Available at: https://www.gov.uk/government/uploads/system/uploads/attachment_data/file/477288/Headline_Release_-_GD___ECO_in_GB_19_Nov_Final.pdf

Department of the Environment, Northern Ireland (2015) 'The Strategic Planning Policy Statement for Northern Ireland: Planning for Sustainable Development'. Available at: http://offlinehbpl.hbpl.co.uk/NewsAttachments/RLP/final_spps_september_2015.pdf

DETR (Department for the Environment, Transport and the Regions) (1999) *Rough Sleeping: The Government's Strategy: Coming in Out of the Cold*, London: DETR.

DETR (2000a) *Quality and Choice: A Decent Home for All: The Housing Green Paper*, London: DETR.

DETR (2000b) *National Framework for Tenant Participation Compacts*, London: DETR.

Deverell-Smith Ltd (2015) 'The Politics of Property'. Available at: http://www.deverellsmith.com/wp-content/uploads/2015/03/Deverell-Smith-The-Politics-of-Property-1974-2015.pdf

Dewilde, C. and De Decker, P. (2016) 'Changing Inequalities in Housing Outcomes across Western Europe', *Housing, Theory and Society*, vol 33, no 2, pp 121–61.

Dewsnup, D. (1907) *The Housing Problem in England*, Manchester: Manchester University Press.

Dickens, C. (1993 [1852]) *Bleak House*, London: Wordsworth.

Dickens, C. (1996 [1857]) *Little Dorit*, London: Wordsworth.

Dictionary.com (2016) 'Housing'. Available at: http://www.dictionary.com/browse/housing

Disraeli, B. (1872) 'Speech at the Free Trade Hall, Manchester', 2 April.

Disraeli, B. (1998 [1895]) *Sybil, Or the Two Nations*, Oxford: Oxford University Press.

DoE (Department of the Environment) (1971) *Fair Deal for Housing*, Cmnd 4728, London: HMSO.

DoE (1973) *Widening the Choice: The Next Steps in Housing*, Cmnd 5280, London: HMSO.

DoE (1975) *Report of the Working Party on Housing Co-ops*, London: HMSO.

DoE (1977a) *Policy for the Inner Cities*, Cmnd 6845, London: HMSO.

DoE (1977b) *Inner Area Studies: Liverpool, Birmingham and Lambeth, Summaries of Consultants' Final Reports*, London: HMSO.

DoE (1985) *Home Improvement – A New Approach*, Cmnd 9513, London: HMSO.

DoE (1987) *Housing: The Government's Proposals*, Cm 212, London: HMSO.

DoE (1994) *Access to Local Authority and Housing Association Tenancies*, London: Department for the Environment.

DoE and the Welsh Office (1995) *Our Future Homes: Opportunity, Choice, Responsibility*, Cm 2901, HMSO: London.

Doling, J. and Davies, M. (1984) *Public Control of Privately Rented Housing*, Aldershot: Gower.

Doling, J. and Elsinga, M. (eds) (2006) *Home Ownership. Getting in, Getting from, Getting Out*, Delft: DUP Science.

Donnison, D. (1967) *The Government of Housing*, London: Penguin.

Dorling, D. (2014a) *Inequality and the 1%*, London: Verso.

Dorling, D. (2014b) *All That Is Solid; the Great Housing Disaster*, London: Allen Lane.

Dorling, D., Pattie, C.J. and Johnston, R.J. (1999) *Voting and the Housing Market: The Impact of New Labour*, London: Council of Mortgage Lenders.

Dudley, Earl (Chair) (1944) *Design and Dwellings: Report of the Sub-committee on the Design of Dwellings of the Central Housing Advisory Committee*, London: HMSO.

Duncan, P. (2013) 'Acting on Localism: A Bigger Role for Housing Associations in Driving the Community Agenda'. Available at: http://www.socialregeneration.com/app/assets/files/news/eastmidspresentationfinal.pdf

Duncan Smith, I. (2015) 'Government to Strengthen Child Poverty Measure'. Available at: https://www.gov.uk/government/news/government-to-strengthen-child-poverty-measure

Duncombe, J. (1835) *The Dens of London Exposed*, London: J. Duncombe.

Dunleavy, P. (1981) *The Politics of Mass Housing in Britain: A Study of Corporate Power and Professional Influence in the Welfare State*, Oxford: Clarendon Press.

Dunleavy, P. (1991) *Democracy, Bureaucracy and Public Choice: Economic Approaches in Political Science: Economic Explanations in Political Science*, Abingdon: Routledge.

DWP (Department for Work and Pensions) (2013a) 'Benefit Expenditure Tables'. Available at: https://www.gov.uk/government/statistics/benefit-expenditure-and-caseload-tables-2013

DWP (2013b) 'Public Perceptions of the Benefit Cap and Pre-Implementation Impacts'. Available at: https://www.gov.uk/government/uploads/system/uploads/attachment_data/file/212132/dwp-benefit-cap-report.pdf

DWP (2014) 'Evaluation of the Removal of the Spare Room Subsidy: Interim Report'. Available at: https://www.gov.uk/government/uploads/system/uploads/attachment_data/file/329948/rr882-evaluation-of-removal-of-the-spare-room-subsidy

DWP (2015) 'Households Below Average Income'. Available at: https://www.gov.uk/government/statistics/households-below-average-income-19941995-to-20132014

Early, F. (2001) 'Mortgage Equity Withdrawal', *Housing Finance*, no 51, Council of Mortgage Lenders, London.

Economist (1991) 'By George: Housing Policy', 9 November.

Economist (2013) 'Housing and Planning: The Brownfields Delusion', 2 May.

Economist (2015) 'Everyman's Castle: Why Building Houses Is Easier North of the Border', *Economist*, 4 April.

Edwards, C. and Imrie, R. (2015) *The Short Guide to Urban Policy*, Bristol: The Policy Press.

Electoral Commission (2011) 'Great Britain's Electoral Registers 2011'. Available at: http://www.electoralcommission.org.uk/__data/assets/pdf_file/0007/145366/Great-Britains-electoral-registers-2011.pdf

Elphicke, N. and Mercer, C. (2014) *A Better Deal for Nation Rent*, Surrey: Million Homes and Million Lives. Available at: http://www.millionhomes.org/downloads/better-deal.pdf

Elson, M.J. (1986) *Green Belts: Conflict Mediation in the Urban Fringe*, London: Heinemann.

Engels, F. (1997 [1872]) *The Housing Question*, Moscow: Progress Publishers.

Englander, D. (1983) *Landlord and Tenant in Urban Britain 1838–1918*, Oxford: Clarendon Press.

Estates Gazette (1953) no 164.

Evans, A. and Unsworth, R. (2011) 'Housing Densities and Consumer Choice', *Urban Studies*, vol 49, no 6, pp 1163–77.

Evans, S. (2009) 'The Not So Odd Couple: Margaret Thatcher and One Nation Conservatism', *Contemporary British History*, vol 23, no 1, p 109.

Factory Inquiry Commission (1834) *Supplementary Report of the Central Board*, London: HMSO.

Farron, T. (2015) 'Tim Farron's Conference Speech in Full'. Available at: http://www.politics.co.uk/comment-analysis/2015/09/23/tim-farron-s-lib-dem-conference-speech-in-full

Federation of Master Builders (2016) 'About the FNB'. Available at: http://www.fmb.org.uk/about-the-fmb/

Fée, D. (2008) 'The Privatization of Council Housing in Britain: The Strange Death of Public Sector Housing in Britain', in S. Body-Gendrot , J. Carré and R. Garbaye (eds) *A City of One's Own: Blurring the Boundaries Between Private and Public*, Aldershot: Ashgate, pp 41–56.

Field, W.H. (1997) 'Policy and the British Voter: Council Housing, Social Change, and Party Preference in the 1980s', *Electoral Studies*, vol 16, no 2, pp 195–202.

Field Consulting (2016) 'Field Consulting'. Available at: https://www.linkedin.com/company/field-consulting-uk

Fielding, S. (1992) 'The People Want? The Meaning of the 1945 General Election', *The Historical Journal*, vol 35, no 3, pp 623–39.

Financial Conduct Authority (2015) 'Getting a Mortgage'. Available at: http://www.fca.org.uk/consumers/financial-services-products/mortgages/mortgage-market-review.

Financial Times (2013) 'Cameron's Interest in Garden Cities Wilts', 30 December.

Financial Times (2015) 'George Osborne Hands Local Councils Control of Business Rates', 5 October.

Financial Times (2016) 'Social Housing £1bn Boost Comes with Brexit Warning', 24 April.

Finlayson, G.B.A.M. (1994) *Citizenship and Social Welfare in Britain 1830–1990*, Edinburgh: Edinburgh University Press.

Fircher, F. and Gottweis, H. (2012) *The Argumentative Turn Revisited*, Durham: Duke University Press.

Fishman, R. (1989) *Bourgeois Utopias: The Rise and Fall of Suburbia*, New York, NY: Basic Books.

Fishman, W.J. (1988) *East End 1888*, London: George Duckworth and Co.

Fitzpatrick, S., Pawson, H., Bramley, G. and Wilcox, S., with Watts, B. (2013) *The Homelessness Monitor: England 2013*, London: Crisis.

Fitzpatrick, S., Pawson, H., Bramley, G., Wilcox, S. and Watts, B. (2016) 'The Homelessness Monitor: England, 2016'. Available at: http://www.crisis.org.uk/data/files/publications/Homelessness_Monitor_England_2016_FINAL_(V12).pdf

FitzRoy, A.W.F. (Chair) (1904) *Inter-Departmental Committee on Physical Deterioration, Reports and Appendix*, Cd 2175, Cd2210, Cd 2186, London: HMSO.

Flint, J. (2000) 'The Responsible Tenant: Housing Governance and the Politics of Behaviour', *Housing Studies*, vol 19, no 6, pp 893–910.

Foot, M. (1975) *Aneurin Bevan: 1945–60, Vol 2*, London: Paladin.

Forrest, R. and Murie, A. (1988) *Selling the Welfare State: The Privatisation of Public Housing*, Abingdon: Routledge.

Forward (1915) 5 June.

Foucault, M. (1977) *Discipline and Punish: The Birth of the Prison*, London: Allen Lane.

Fox, L. (2015) 'Building Applications in North Somerset: 2015 Update'. Available at: http://www.liamfox.co.uk/campaigns/building-applications-north-somerset-june-2015-update

Francis, H.A. (Chair) (1971) *Committee on the Rent Acts*, Cmnd 4609, London: HMSO.

Francis, M. (1997) *Ideas and Policies under Labour 1945–1951: Building a New Britain*, Manchester: Manchester University Press.

Francis, M. (2012) '"A Crusade to Enfranchise the Many": Thatcherism and the "Property-Owning Democracy"', *Twentieth Century British History*, vol 23, no 2, pp 275–97.

Fraser, D. (1993) *The Evolution of the British Welfare State* (3rd edn), Basingstoke: Palgrave Macmillan.

Fraser, M. (1996) *John Bull's Other Homes: State Housing and British Policy in Ireland*, Liverpool: Liverpool University Press.

Fraser, W.H and Maver, I. (eds) (1996) *Glasgow, Volume 11, 1830 to 1912*, Manchester: Manchester University Press.

Friedman, M. and Friedman, R. (1980) *Free to Choose: A Personal Statement*, London: Pelican.

Friedrich, C.J. (1937) *Constitutional Government and Politics*, New York, NY: Harper and Brothers.

Gardiner, J. (2010) *The Thirties: An Intimate History*, London: Harper Press.

Garside, P. (1988) '"Unhealthy Areas": Town Panning, Eugenics and the Slums, 1890–1945', *Planning Perspectives*, vol 3, no 2, pp 24–46.

Gaskell, M. (1990) 'Introduction', in M. Gaskell (ed) *Slums*, Leicester: Leicester University Press, pp 1–15.

Gauldie, E. (1974) *Cruel Habitations: A History of Working-Class Housing 1780–1918*, London: Allen and Unwin.

Geddes, E. (Chair) (1922) *First Interim Report of the Committee on National Expenditure*, Cmd 1581, London: HMSO.

George, H. (1883) 'The Great Question', *Irish World*, 27 January, pp 1–7.

George, H. (1979 [1879]) *Progress and Poverty*, London: Hogarth Press.

Gibb, A. (1989) 'Policy and Politics in Scottish Housing since 1945', in R. Rodger (ed) *Scottish Housing in the Twentieth Century*, Leicester: Leicester University Press, pp 155–85.

Gibb, K. (2014) 'Housing Policy in Scotland Since Devolution: Divergence, Crisis, Integration and Opportunity', *Journal of Poverty and Social Justice*, vol 23, no 1, pp 29–42.

Gibb, K. (2015) 'The Social Housing Quasi-Market: Discussion Paper No 4', Centre for Public Policy for Regions. Available at: http://www.gla.ac.uk/media/media_4283_en.pdf

Gibbon, G. and Bell, R.W. (1939) *History of the London County Council 1889–1939*, London: Macmillan.

Gibson, H. (no date) 'How Scotland Got the Housing (Homeless Persons) Act'. Available at: https://www.era.lib.ed.ac.uk/bitstream/handle/1842/9029/1979_4_How%20Scotland%20got%20the%20Housing%20(Homeless%20Persons)%20Act.pdf?sequence=1

Gilbert, B.B. (1966) *The Evolution of National Insurance in Great Britain: The Origins of the Welfare State*, London: M. Joseph.

Gilbert, B.B. (1970) *British Social Policy 1914–1939*, London: B.T. Batsford Ltd.

Gilmour, I. (1969) *The Body Politic*, London: Hutchinson.

Gimson, A. (2013) 'How Macmillan Built 300,000 Houses a Year'. Available at: http://www.conservativehome.com/thetorydiary/2013/10/how-macmillan-built-300000-houses-a-year.html

Glendinning, M. (ed) (1997) *Rebuilding Scotland: The Postwar Vision 1945–1975*, East Linton: The Tuckwell Press, pp 50–61.

Glendinning, M. and Mulhesius, S. (1994) *Tower Block: Modern Public Housing in England, Scotland, Wales and Northern Ireland*, New Haven, CT: Yale University Press.

Goldsmith, Z. (2016a) 'London's Green Spaces Are Safer with Me, Not Sadiq Kkan', *Daily Telegraph*, 5 March. Available at: http://www.telegraph.co.uk/news/politics/zac-goldsmith/12180728/Londons-green-spaces-are-safer-with-me-not-Sadiq-Khan.html

Goldsmith, Z. (2016b) 'Zac – My Plans to Build a Better London'. Available at: https://backzac2016.com/backzacnews/2016/3/zac-my-plans-to-build-a-better-london

Gov.uk (2010) 'Eric Pickles Puts Stop to Flawed Regional Strategies'. Available at: https://www.gov.uk/government/news/eric-pickles-puts-stop-to-flawed-regional-strategies-today

Gower Davies, J. (1972) *The Evangelist Bureaucrat: Study of a Planning Exercise in Newcastle-upon-Tyne*, London: Tavistock.

Grayson, J. (1996) *Opening the Window: Revealing the Hidden History of Tenants Organisations*, London: Tenant Participation Advisory Service.

Green, T.H. (1881) *Liberal Legislation and Freedom of Contract*, London: Simpkin Marshall.

Greenleaf, W.H. (1983) *The British Political Tradition Volume Two: The Ideological Heritage*, London: Methuen.

Green Party (2015) *For the Common Good: General Election Manifesto 2015*, London: Green Party.

Greve, J. (1971) *Homelessness in London*, London: Chatto and Windus.

Grice, A. (2013) 'Inside Westminster: George Osborne's Housing Boom Will Echo into the Future', *Independent*, 9 October.

Griffin, H. (1893) 'Weekly Property as an Investment', *Transactions of the Surveyors' Institute*, no 26.

Griffith, M. (2012) *We Must Fix It: Delivering Reform of the Building Sector to Meet the UK's Housing and Economic Challenges*, London: Institute for Public Policy Research.

Griffith-Boscawen, A. (1925) *Memories*, London: John Murray.

Griffiths, J.A.G (1966) *Central Departments and Local Authorities*, London: George Allen and Unwin.

Guardian (1973) 'Interview with Sir Keith Joseph', 12 November.

Guardian (2013) 'Forget Buy-to-Let, the Latest Gravy Train Is Rent-to-Rent', 29 June.

Guardian (2015a) 'Lynton Crosby: The Man Who Really Won the Election for the Tories', 8 May.

Guardian (2015b) 'Number of MPs Who Earn from Renting Out Property Rises by a Third', 6 May.

Guardian (2015c) 'How Cameron Adviser Helped Thwart Plan to Aid Young Black People after 1985 Riots', 30 December.

Guardian (2016) 'Charity's Flat Sale Leaves Residents Facing Eviction', 6 February.

Halcrow, M. (1989) *Keith Joseph: A Single Mind*, Basingstoke: Macmillan.

Hall, P., Gracey, H., Drewett, R. and Thomas, R. (1973) *The Containment of Urban England, Volume One: Urban and Metropolitan Growth Processes or Megalopolis Denied*, London: George Allen and Unwin.

Hamlin, C. (1995) 'Could You Starve to Death in England in 1839? The Chadwick-Farr Controversy and the Loss of the "Social" in Public Health', *American Journal of Public Health*, vol 85, no 6, pp 856–66.

Hancock, L. and Mooney, G. (2013) '"Welfare ghettos" and the "Broken Society": Territorial Stigmatization in the Contemporary UK', *Housing, Theory and Society*, vol 30, no 1, pp 46–64.

Hands, J. (2015) *Housing Co-operatives*, London: Castleton Publishers.

Harari, D. (2015) 'Regional and Local Economic Growth Statistics, House of Commons Library Briefing Paper Number 05795'. Available at: http://researchbriefings.parliament.uk/ResearchBriefing/Summary/SN05795#fullreport

Harloe, M. (1995) *The People's Home: Social Rented Housing in Europe and America*, Oxford: Blackwell.

Harris, J. (1993) *The Penguin Social History of Britain: Private Lives, Public Spirit: Britain 1870–1914*, London: Penguin.

Harris, R. (2012) '"Ragged Urchins Play on Marquetry Floors": The Discourse of *Filtering* Is Reconstructed, 1920s–1950s', *Housing Policy Debate*, vol 22, no 3, pp 463–84.

Harvey, A. (1960) *Casualties of the Welfare State*, London: Fabian Society.

Harvey, A. (2013) 'Zero-Carbon Home "Dithering" Is Threatening UK Housing Industry', *Guardian*, 18 February.

Harwood, E. and Powers, A. (eds) (2008) *Housing the Twentieth Century Nation*, London: Twentieth Century Society.

Hassan, G. and Shaw, E. (2012) *The Strange Death of Labour Scotland*, Edinburgh: Edinburgh University Press.

Hay, C., Lister, M. and Marsh, D. (eds) (2006) *The State: Theories and Issues*, Basingstoke: Palgrave Macmillan.

Hayes, L. and Novitz, T. (2014) *Trade Unions and Economic Inequality*, London: Institute of Employment Rights.

Hazell, R. (ed) (2000) *The State and the Nations: The First Year of Devolution in the United Kingdom*, London: Academic Imprint.

Heffer, S. (2013) *High Minds: The Victorians and the Birth of Modern Britain*, London: Random House.

Heseltine, Lord (2012) *No Stone Unturned: In Pursuit of Growth*, London: Department for Business, Education and Skills. Available at: https://www.gov.uk/government/uploads/system/uploads/attachment_data/file/34648/12-1213-no-stone-unturned-in-pursuit-of-growth.pdf

Heseltine, M. (1990) *Where There's A Will*, London: Arrow Books.

Heseltine, M. (2000) *Life in the Jungle: My Autobiography*, London: Hodder and Stroughton.

Hetherington, P. (2015) *Whose Land Is Our Land? The Use and Abuse of Britain's Forgotten Acres*, Bristol: The Policy Press.

Hilber, C.A.L. (2015) *UK Housing and Planning Policies: The Evidence from Economic Research*, London: London school of Economics and Political Science.

Hill, O. (1883) 'Improvements, Now Practicable, Common Sense and the Dwellings of the Poor', *Nineteenth Century*, vol 14, pp 925–33.

Hills, J. (1991) *Unravelling Housing Finance: Subsidies, Benefits and Taxation*, Oxford: Clarendon.

Hills, J. (2014) *Good Times, Bad Times: The Welfare Myth of Them and Us*, Bristol: The Policy Press.

Hills, J., Cunliffe, J. and Obolenskaya, P. (2016) 'The changing structure of UK inequality since the crisis', in R. Lupton, T. Burchardt, J. Hills, K. Stewart and P. Vizard (eds) *Social Policy in a Cold Climate: Policies and their Consequences since the Crisis*, Bristol: Policy Press.

Hilton, M., McKay, J., Crowson, N. and Mouhot, J. (2013) *The Politics of Expertise: How NEOs Shaped Modern Britain*, Oxford: Oxford University Press.

Hilton Young, E. (1934) 'Cabinet Minutes', PRO CAB 24/7 CP 12(34) CP 46(34).

Himmelfarb, G. (1984) *The Idea of Poverty: England in the Early Industrial Age*, London: Faber and Faber.

Hirschman, A.O. (1970) *Exit, Voice and Loyalty: Responses to Decline in Firms, Organizations and States*, Harvard, MA: Harvard University Press.

HM Government (2010) 'The Coalition: Our Programme for Government'. Available at: https://www.gov.uk/government/uploads/system/uploads/attachment_data/file/78977/coalition_programme_for_government.pdf

HM Government (2011) 'Laying the Foundations: A Housing Strategy for England'. Available at: https://www.gov.uk/government/uploads/system/uploads/attachment_data/file/7532/2033676.pdf

HM Revenue and Customs, (2014) 'UK Stamp Tax Statistics 2013/14'. Available at: https://www.gov.uk/government/uploads/system/uploads/attachment_data/file/358908/AnnualStampTaxes-Release-Sep14.pdf

HM Treasury (2005) *Britain Meeting the Global Challenge: Enterprise, Fairness and Responsibility, Pre-Budget Report, December 2005*, London: HM Treasury.

HM Treasury (2013) 'Investing in Britain's Future', Cm 8669. Available at: https://www.gov.uk/government/uploads/system/uploads/attachment_data/file/209279/PU1524_IUK_new_template.pdf

HM Treasury (2014a) 'Autumn Statement'. Available at: https://www.gov.uk/government/uploads/system/uploads/attachment_data/file/382327/44695_Accessible.pdf

HM Treasury (2014b) 'Public Expenditure: Statistical Analyses 2014'. Available at: https://www.gov.uk/government/statistics/public-expenditure-statistical-analyses-2014

HM Treasury (2015a) 'Spending Review and Autumn Statement 2015'. Available at: https://www.gov.uk/government/publications/spending-review-and-autumn-statement-2015-documents/spending-review-and-autumn-statement-2015

HM Treasury (2015b) 'Spending Review and Autumn Statement 2015: Policy Costings'. Available at: https://www.gov.uk/government/uploads/system/uploads/attachment_data/file/480565/SRAS2015_policy_costings_amended_page_25.pdf

HM Treasury (2015c) 'Fixing the Foundations: Creating a More Prosperous Nation', Cm 9098, July. Available at: https://www.gov.uk/government/uploads/system/uploads/attachment_data/file/443898/Productivity_Plan_web.pdf

HM Treasury (2016) 'National Infrastructure Commission: Consultation', Cm 9182. Available at: https://www.gov.uk/government/uploads/system/uploads/attachment_data/file/489952/National_infrastructure_commission_jan_16_web_final.pdf

HM Treasury and Greater Manchester Combined Authority (2014) 'Greater Manchester Agreement: Devolution to the Greater Manchester Combined Authority and Transition to a Directly Elected Mayor'. Available at: https://www.gov.uk/government/uploads/system/uploads/attachment_data/file/369858/Greater_Manchester_Agreement_i.pdf

Hoath, D.C. (1981) *Council Housing*, London: Sweet and Maxwell.

Hobhouse, H. (1994) 'Public Housing in Poplar: The Inter-war Years', *Survey of London*, vols 43 and 44: Poplar, Blackwall and Isle of Dogs, pp 23–37. Available at: http://www.british-history.ac.uk/report.aspx?compid=46467

Hobhouse, L.T (1974 [1911]) *Liberalism*, New York: Galaxy Books.

Hobson, D. (1999) *The National Wealth: Who Gets What in Britain*, London: Harper/Collins.

Hodson, C.B.S. (1923) 'Eugenics and National Health', *Journal of the Royal Society for the Promotion of Health*, July, p 248.

Holmans, A.E. (2005) *Historical Statistics of Housing in Britain*, Department of Land Economy, Cambridge: University of Cambridge.

Home Builders Federation (2015) 'What We Do'. Available at: http://www.hbf.co.uk/

Homelet (2015) *Homelet Rental Index*. Available at:https://homelet.co.uk/assets/documents/HL3729-May-2015-HomeLet-Rental-Index-08.06.15.pdf

Home Office (2001) 'Building Cohesive Communities: Report of the Ministerial Group on Public Order and Community Cohesion'. Available at: http://resources.cohesioninstitute.org.uk/Publications/Documents/Document/DownloadDocumentsFile.aspx?recordId=94&file=PDFversionhttp://resources.cohesioninstitute.org.uk/Publications/Documents/Document/Default.aspx?recordId=94

Home Office (2003) *Together Tackling Anti-Social Behaviour: Action Plan*, London: Home Office.

Homes and Communities Agency (2014) 'Affordable Homes Programme 2015–18'. Available at: https://www.gov.uk/government/collections/affordable-homes-programme-2015-to-2018-guidance-and-allocations

Homes and Communities Agency (2016) 'Shared Ownership and Affordable Homes Programme 2016 to 2021: Prospectus'. Available at: https://www.gov.uk/government/uploads/system/uploads/attachment_data/file/517678/SO_and_AHP_prospectus_13_04_16.pdf

House of Commons Communities and Local Government Committee (2013) 'The Private Rented Sector: First Report of Session 2013–14'. Available at: http://www.publications.parliament.uk/pa/cm201314/cmselect/cmcomloc/50/50ii.pdf

House of Lords (1933) 'Sleeping Out (Convictions)', HD Deb 29 June.

House of Lords (2013) 'Homelessness: Rough Sleepers', *Hansard*, 13 April. Available at: http://www.theyworkforyou.com/wrans/?id=2013-04-10a.306.0

House of Lords Select Committee on Economic Affairs (2016) *First Report of Session 2016–17: Building more Homes*, HL Paper 20. Available at: http://www.publications.parliament.uk/pa/ld201617/ldselect/ldeconaf/20/20.pdf

Housing Today (2004) 'Prescott to Rethink ODPM Definition of Homelessness', 26 November.

Howard, A. (1990) *Crossman: The Pursuit of Power*, London: Jonathan Cape.

Howard, E. (1898) *To-morrow: A Peaceful Path to Real Reform*, London: Swan Sonnenschein & Co.

Howard, E. (1902) *Garden Cities of Tomorrow*, London: Faber.

Howarth, T.E.B. (1985) *Prospect and Reality: Great Britain 1945–55*, London: Collins.

Howe, G. (1994) *Conflict of Loyalty*, London: Pan Books.

Howe, G. and Jones, C. (1956) *Houses to Let*, London: Bow Group.

Hudson, N. (2015) *Land for New Homes*, London: Savills.

Hulne, C. (2009) 'Cleaning Up the House', *Guardian*, 27 January.

Hunt, T. (2004) *Building Jerusalem: The Rise and Fall of the Victorian City*, London: Weidenfeld and Nicolson.

Hurd, D and Young, E. (2013) *Disraeli or The Two Lives*, London: Phoenix.

Hussain, I. (2016) 'When will the key provisions of the Welfare Reform and Work Act come into force?'. Available at: http://www.cpag.org.uk/content/when-will-key-provisions-welfare-reform-and-work-act-come-force

Hylton, S. (2010) *Manchester: A History*, Chicago, IL: Phillimore and Sons.

IMLA (Intermediary Mortgage Lenders Association) (2014) 'Reshaping Housing Tenure in the UK: The Role of Buy-to-Let', May. Available at: http://www.imla.org.uk/perch/resources/imla-reshaping-housing-tenure-in-the-uk-the-role-of-buy-to-let-may-2014.pdf

Independent (2013a) 'Exclusive: Private Landlords Evading at Least £550 Million Tax on Rental Income', 30 October.

Independent (2013b) 'Economic Focus: Does Anyone Think Help to Buy Is a Good Idea?', 1 October.

Independent (2015) 'PMQs: Read Jeremy Corbyn's Six Opening Questions – and David Cameron's Predictable Answers', 17 September.

Independent (2016) 'The Coalition Legacy is Being Squandered', 26 February.

Infrastructure Intelligence (2015) 'Cheshire East – Vital Lessons for the Northern Powerhouse'. Available at: http://www.infrastructure-intelligence.com/article/may-2015/cheshire-east-vital-lessons-northern-powerhouse

Inside Croydon (2016), 'Promotion to Housing Minister could have Barwell bricking it', 17 July. Available at: https://insidecroydon.com/2016/07/17/promotion-to-housing-minister-could-have-barwell-bricking-it/

Inside Housing (2012) 'Grant Shapps in HMR "Luftwaffe" Attack', 20 April.

Inside Housing (2013) 'Land Banking Developers to Lose Planning Permission, Says Boles', 11 November.

Inside Housing (2014) 'Tory "Concerns" Over Boles Planning Rhetoric', 2 January.

Inside Housing (2015) 'Pickles Blocks 9,200 Homes in Build Up to Election', 10 April.

Inside Housing (2016) 'Cloud overhanging development plans', 1 July.

Institute of Economic Affairs (2013) 'What We Do'. Available at: http://www.iea.org.uk/about/what-we-do

Ipsos Mori (2013) 'Political Monitor May 2013'. Available at: http://www.ipsos-mori.com/researchpublications/researcharchive/3176/Ipsos-MORI-Political-Monitor-May-2013.aspx

Ipsos Mori (2015a) '2015 Political Monitor'. Available at: https://www.ipsos-mori.com/Assets/Docs/April15_2_Pol%20Monitor%20charts_FINAL_Tue_050515_v1_1,010.pdf

Ipsos Mori (2015b) 'Economist/Ipsos MORI April 2015 Issues Index'. Available at: https://www.ipsos-mori.com/researchpublications/researcharchive/3566/EconomistIpsos-MORI-April-2015-Issues-Index.aspx

Ipsos Mori (2015c) 'How Britain Voted in 2015'. Available at: https://www.ipsos-mori.com/researchpublications/researcharchive/3575/How-Britain-voted-in-2015.aspx?view=wide

Irish News (2015) 'Tricolours Appear Beside North Belfast Housing Development', 28 October. Available at: http://www.irishnews.com/news/2015/10/28/news/irish-tricolours-appear-beside-north-belfast-housing-development-306751/

Jacobs, K. and Manzi, T. (2016) '"The Party's Over": Critical Junctures, Crises and the Politics of Housing Policy', *Housing Studies*, published online, 18 April. Available at: http://www.tandfonline.com/action/showAxaArticles?journalCode=chos20

Jack, I (2016) 'In *Guardian* this Brexit vote, the poor turned on an elite who ignored them', 25th June.

Jasper, J.M. (2014) *Protest: A Cultural Introduction to Social Movements*, Cambridge: Polity.

Jenkin, P (1983) 'Green Belts', HC Deb 26 October 1983 vol 47 cc276-8 276.

Jenkins, S. (2006) *Thatcher & Sons: A Revolution in Three Acts*, London: Allen Lane.

Jenkins, S. (2011) 'Call This Planning Reform? It's a Recipe for Civil War', *Guardian*, 13 December.

Jennings, J.H. (1971) 'Geographical Implications of the Municipal Housing Programme in England and Wales 1919–1939, *Urban Studies*, vol 82, no 2, pp 121–38.

John, P. (1998) *Analysing Public Policy*, London: Printer.

Johnson, A. (2013) 'Social Housing Residents Told to Sign "Ambition" Plan as Part of Tenancies', *Independent*, 26 April.

Johnson, B. (2014) 'Cleggton Keynes in England's Rolling Hills? No Thanks, Nick', *Telegraph*, 19 January.

Johnston, A. (2004) *English Housing Associations, 1965–96: Players More Than Pawns Through 30 Years of Government Funding*, Oxford: Oxford University Press.

Johnston, R.J. (1987) 'A Note on Housing Tenure and Voting in Britain, 1983', *Housing Studies*, vol 2, no 2, pp 114–15.

Jones, B., Kavanagh, D., Moran, M. and Norton, P. (1994) *Politics UK*, Hemel Hempstead: Harvester Wheatsheaf.

Jones, C. (2010) 'The Right to Buy', in P. Malpass and R. Rowlands (eds) *Housing, Markets and Policy*, Abingdon: Routledge, pp 59–75.

Jones, H. (2000) '"This is Magnificent!": 300,000 Houses a Year and the Tory Revival after 1945', *Contemporary British History*, vol 14, no 1 pp 99–121.

Jones, T. (1969) *Whitehall Diary Volume 1*, London: Oxford University Press.

Jones, O. (2015) 'Why Labour Must Become the Party of Home Ownership', *Guardian*, 25 September.

Joseph, K. (1963) 'White Paper on Housing', C(63)80, PRO: CAB129/113, 10 May. Available at: http://discovery.nationalarchives.gov.uk/details/r/D7659703

Joseph, K. (1964) 'Land Values: Memorandum by the Minister of Housing and Local Government and Minister for Welsh Affairs', CP (64) 145, 17 July. Available at: http://filestore.nationalarchives.gov.uk/pdfs/small/cab-129-118-c-127.pdf

Joseph, K. (1976) *Stranded in the Middle Ground*, London: Centre for Policy Studies.

Just Space (2014) *Staying Put: The Anti- Gentrification Handbook for Council Tenants in London*, London: Calverts Co-operative.

Keating, M. (1988) *The City That Refused To Die, Glasgow: The Politics of Urban Regeneration*, Aberdeen: Aberdeen University Press.

Keating, M. (2010) *The Government of Scotland: Public Policy Making after Devolution*, Edinburgh: Edinburgh University Press.

Keating, M. and Carter, C. (1987) 'Policy-Making and the Scottish Office: The Designation of Cumbernauld New Town', *Public Administration*, vol 65, Winter, pp 391–405.

Keegan, W. (2012) *'Saving the World': Gordon Brown Reconsidered*, London: Searching Finance Ltd.

Keep, M. (2015) 'The Barnett Formula', House of Commons Briefing Paper, Number 7386. Available at: http://researchbriefings.files.parliament.uk/documents/CBP-7386/CBP-7386.pdf

Kemeny, J. (1992) *Housing and Social Theory*, London: Routledge.

Kemp, P.A. (1982) 'Housing Landlordism in Late Nineteenth-Century Britain', *Environment and Planning*, vol 14, no 11, pp 1437–47.

Kemp, P.A. (2009) 'The Transformation of Private Renting', in P. Malpass and A. Murie (eds) *Housing, Markets and Policy*, Abingdon: Routledge, pp 122–43.

Kemp, P.A. (2015) 'Private Renting After the Global Financial Crisis', *Housing Studies*, vol 30, no 4, pp 601–20.

Khan, S. (2016) *Sadiq Khan for London: A Manifesto for all Londoners*, London: London Labour Party.

King, A. (2015) *Who Governs Britain?* London: Pelican.

Kingman, D. (2013) *Why BTL equals 'Big Tax Let-off': How the UK Tax System Hands Buy-to-Let Landlords an Unfair Advantage*, London: Intergenerational Foundation.

KPMG (2014) *Building the Homes We Need: A Programme for the 2015 Government*, London: KPMG.

Krafchik, M. (1983) 'Unemployment and Vagrancy in the 1930s: Deterrence, Rehabilitation and the Depression', *Journal of Social Policy*, vol 12, no 2, pp 195–214.

Kwarteng, K. (2015) *Thatcher's Trial: Six Months That Defined a Leader*, London: Bloomsbury.

Kynaston, D. (2007) *Austerity Britain 1945–1951*, London: Bloomsbury.

Kynaston, D. (2009) *Family Britain 1951–1957*, London: Bloomsbury.

Kynaston, D. (2014) *Modernity Britain: Book Two: The Shake of the Dice*, London: Bloomsbury.

Labour Party (1934) *Up with the Houses! Down with the Slums*, London: Labour Party.

Labour Party (1945) 'Labour Party Election Manifesto: Let Us Face the Future'. Available at: http://www.politicsresources.net/area/uk/man/lab45.htm

Labour Party (1951) *Campaign Quotations: A Political Reference Book Telling Who Said What, Where and When*, London: Labour Party.

Labour Party (1959) 'Labour Party Manifesto: Britain Belongs To You'. Available at: http://www.politicsresources.net/area/uk/man/lab59.htm

Labour Party (1964) 'Labour Party Manifesto: The New Britain'. Available at: http://www.politicsresources.net/area/uk/man/lab64.htm

Labour Party (1983) 'A New Hope for Britain'. Available at: http://www.politicsresources.net/area/uk/man/lab83.htm

Labour Party (1997) *New Labour Because Britain Deserves Better*, London: Labour Party.

Labour Party (2010) *Labour Party Manifesto 2010: A Future Fair For All*, London: Labour Party.

Labour Party (2015) *Britain Can Be Better: Labour Party Manifesto, 2015*, London: Labour Party.

Labour Party National Executive (1978) *A New Deal for Council Housing; Interim Proposals*, London: Labour Party.

Lambert, R. (2015) 'If the Chancellor Wants to Wipe Out Buy to Let, Why Doesn't He Just Say So?'. Available at: http://www.landlords.org.uk/news-campaigns/news/if-the-chancellor-wants-wipe-out-buy-let-why-doesnt-he-just-say-so

Land Reform Review Group (2014) *The Land of Scotland and the Common Good*, Edinburgh: Land Reform Review Group Secretariat.

Langford, D.A. (1982) *Direct Labour Organisations in the Construction Industry*, Aldershot: Gower.

Larsen, D. (no date) 'The First Intelligence Prime Minister: David Lloyd George (1916–1922)'. Available at: https://www.gov.uk/government/uploads/system/uploads/attachment_data/file/80179/Lloyd-George-as-PM.pdf

Lasswell, H.D. (1951) 'The Policy Orientation', in D. Lerner and H.D. Lasswell (eds) *The Policy Sciences: Recent Developments in Scope and Method*, Stanford, CA: Stanford University Press.

Lawrence, P.E. (1951) 'Henry George's British Mission', *American Quarterly*, vol 3, no 3, pp 232–43.

Laws, D. (2016) *Coalition: The Inside Story of the Conservative–Liberal Democrat Coalition Government*, London: Biteback Publications.

Leach, R. (2015) *Political Ideology in Britain*, Basingstoke: Palgrave.

Le Corbusier (1964 [1933]) *The Radiant City*, London: Faber and Faber.

Lee, N. (2007) 'Creating a 'Property-Owning Democracy': The Conservative Party and Popular Capitalism, 1918–1951', MA Dissertation, University of Durham, UK.

Lees, L. and Leys, P. (2008) 'Introduction to the Special Issue, Gentrification as Public Policy', *Urban Studies*, vol 45, no 12, pp 2379–84.

Legacy, C., Davison, G. and Liu, E. (2016) 'Delivering Social Housing: Examining the Nexus between Social Housing and Democratic Planning', *Housing, Theory and Society*, published online, 26 February. Available at: http://www.tandfonline.com/action/showAxaArticles?journalCode=shou20

Le Grand, J. (2003) *Motivation, Agency and Public Policy: Of Knights and Knaves, Pawns and Queens*, Oxford: Oxford University Press.

Lewis, B. (2014) 'Housing Minister Brandon Lewis Blasts Award Winning Garden City as Urban Sprawl', *Independent*, 12 September.

Lewis, B. (2015) 'Written Statement to Parliament: Planning Update'. Available at: https://www.gov.uk/government/speeches/planning-update.

Lewis, P. (2014) *Everyman's Castle: The Story of Our Cottages, Country Houses, Terraces, Flats, Semis and Bungalows*, London: Frances Lincoln Limited.

Liberal Democrats (2010) 'Liberal Democrat Manifesto 2010'. Available at: http://www.politicsresources.net/area/uk/ge10/man/parties/libdem_manifesto_2010.pdf

Liberal Democrats (2015) *Manifesto 2015: Stronger Economy, Fairer Society, Opportunity for All*, London: Liberal Democrats.

Liberty Fund (2013) 'Pauper Management Improved'. Available at: http://oll.libertyfund.org/?option=com_staticxt&staticfile=show.php%3Ftitle=2208&chapter=207476&layout=html&Itemid=27

Lilley, P. (1992) 'I Have a Little List', speech to the Conservative Party Conference, October.

Lindenthal, D. and Eichholtz. P. (2012) 'House Prices and Market Institutions: The Dutch Experience', in A. Bardhan, R.H. Edelstein and C.A. Kroll (eds) *Global Housing Markets: Crises, Policies, and Institutions*, Hoboken, NJ: John Wiley, pp 135–56.

Lipsey, D. (2013) *In the Corridors of Power*, London: Biteback.

Liverpool Victoria Insurance (2014) 'Shrinking Family Home Drives a Surge in Overcrowding'. Available at: http://www.lv.com/about-us/press/article/shrinking-family-home-overcrowding

Lloyd, J. (2013) *Whose Home? Understanding Landlords and Their Effect on Public Policy*, London: The Strategic Society Centre.

Lloyd George, D. (1909) 'Speech at Edinburgh Castle', Limehouse, London, 30 July. Available at: http://www.parliament.uk/about/living-heritage/evolutionofparliament/houseoflords/parliamentacts/collections/limehouse/

Lloyd George, D. (1919) 'Minutes of a Meeting of the War Cabinet Held at 10, Downing Street, S.W., on Monday, March 3, 1919, at 11.30 A.M.', War Cabinet 539. Available at: http://filestore.nationalarchives.gov.uk/pdfs/large/cab-23-9.pdf

Local Government Association (2016) '80,000 Council Homes Could Be Lost by 2020'. Available at: http://www.local.gov.uk/web/guest/media-releases/-/journal_content/56/10180/7668062/NEWS

Local Government Board, Ireland (1876) *Land Owners in Ireland: Return of Owners of Land of One Acre and Upwards in the Several Counties, Counties of Cities, and Counties of Towns in Ireland*, Ireland: HMSO.

Londonist (2016) 'London Tenants Pay More Than 50% Income in Rent'. Available at: http://londonist.com/2013/01/london-tenants-pay-more-than-50-income-in-rent

London Assembly Housing Committee (2015) 'Knock It Down or Do It Up? The Challenge of Estate Regeneration'. Available at: https://www.london.gov.uk/sites/default/files/gla_migrate_files_destination/KnockItDownOrDoItUp_0.pdf

London Evening Standard (2015) '*Evening Standard* Comment: Housing Is the Big Election Issue for London', 27 April.

Lowe, R. (1867) *Hansard 3*, 188, 15 July, col. 549.

Lowe, S. (1986) *Urban Social Movements: The City after Castells*, Basingstoke: Macmillan Education.

Lund, B. (2011) *Understanding Housing Policy* (2nd edn), Bristol: The Policy Press.

Lund, B. (2017) *Understanding Housing Policy* (3rd edn), Bristol: The Policy Press.

Lupton, R. (2013) *Labour's Record on Neighbourhood Renewal in England*, London: Centre for the Analysis of Social Exclusion, London School of Economics.

Lupton, R. and Fitzgerald, A. (2015) *The Coalition's Record on Area Regeneration and Neighbourhood Renewal 2010–2015*, London: Centre for the Analysis of Social Exclusion, London School of Economics.

Lyons, M. (Chair) (2014) 'The Lyons Housing Review: Mobilising across the Nation to Build the Homes Our Children Need'. Available at: http://www.lgcplus.com/Journals/2014/10/16/n/z/i/Lyons-Housing-Review.pdf

Mabon, J.D. (1997) 'Rebuilding Scotland: The Role of Government', in M. Glendinning (ed) *Rebuilding Scotland: The Postwar Vision 1945–1975*, East Linton: The Tuckwell Press, pp 50–61.

MacCrae, N. (1958) *A Nation of Council Tenantry*, London: Rented Homes Campaign.

MacKenzie, N. (2008) *The Letters of Sidney and Beatrice Webb Volume 2 1892–1911*, Cambridge: Cambridge University Press.

MacKenzie, N. and MacKenzie, J. (1984) *The Diary of Beatrice Webb Volume Three 1905–1924: The Power to Alter Things*, London: Virago.

Maclennan, D. (2001) 'Owner Occupation: New Patterns, Policies and Parliament', in C. Jones and P. Robson (eds) *Health of Scottish Housing*, Aldershot: Ashgate, pp 148–80.

Maclennan, D. (2012) 'Understanding Housing Markets: Real Progress or Stalled Agendas?', in D.F. Clapham, W.A.V. Clark and K. Gibb (eds) *The Sage Handbook of Housing Studies*, London: Sage, pp 5–26.

Maclennan, D. and O'Sullivan, A. (2013) 'Localism, Devolution and Housing Policies', *Housing Studies*, vol 28, no 4, pp 599–615.

Macleod, I. (1973 [1954]) 'Sanitas Sanitatum: "The Condition of the People"', in I. Fisher (ed) *Ian Macleod*, London: Andre Deutsch Ltd, p 330.

Macmillan, H. (1952) 'House of Commons Debates', vol 496, Col 723.

Macmillan, H. (1969) *The Tides of Fortune*, London: Macmillan.

Macmillan, H. (2004) *The Macmillan Diaries: The Cabinet Years 1950–1957* (ed P. Catterall), London: Pan Macmillan.

Macmillan, M. (2016) *History's People: Personalities and the Past*, London: Profile Books.

MacWhirter, I. (2009) 'That Bloody Woman', *New Statesman*, 26 February.

Maier, E. (2014) 'More Than a Numbers Game', *Inside Housing*, 24 November.

Major, J. (1993) '*Speech to the Conservative Party Conference at Blackpool*'. Available at: http://www.britishpoliticalspeech.org/speech-archive.htm?speech=139

Mallock, W.H. (1882) 'The Functions of Wealth', *Contemporary Review*, February, vol 41, pp 195–220.

Malpass, P. (1992) 'Investment Strategies', in C. Grant (ed) *Built to Last? Reflections on British Housing Policy*, London: Roof.

Malpass, P. (2001) 'The Uneven Development of "Social Rented Housing": Explaining the Historically Marginal Position of Housing Associations in Britain', *Housing Studies*, vol 16, no 2, pp 225–42.

Malpass, P. (2003a) 'Wartime Planning for Post-War Housing in Britain: The Whitehall Debate, 1941–5', *Planning Perspectives*, vol 18, pp 177–96.

Malpass, P. (2003b) 'Private Enterprise in Eclipse? A Reassessment of British Housing Policy in the 1940s', *Housing Studies*, vol 18, no 5, pp 645–59.

Malpass, P. (2008) 'Housing and the New Welfare State: Wobbly Pillar or Cornerstone?', *Housing Studies*, vol 23, no 1, pp 1–19.

Malpass, P. and Jones, C. (1996) 'The "Fourth Experiment"? The Ministry of Health, the Commissioner for Special Areas and the North Eastern Housing Association', *Planning Perspectives*, vol 11, no 3, pp 303–21.

Manchester Evening News (1957) 8 April.

Marr, A. (2009) *The Making of Modern Britain: From Queen Victoria to V.E. Day*, London: Pan.

Marsh, A. (2004) 'The Inexorable Rise of the Rational Consumer? The Blair Government and the Reshaping of Social Housing', *European Journal of Housing Policy*, vol 4, no 2, pp 185–208.

Marsh, A. and Riseborough, M. (1998) 'Expanding Private Renting: Flexibility at a Price?', in A. Marsh and D. Mullins (eds) *Housing and Public Policy: Citizenship, Choice and Control*, Buckingham: Open University Press, pp 99–123.

Marsh, L.G. and Olsen, J.P. (1984) 'The New Institutionalism: Organisational Factors in Political Life', *American Political Science Review*, no 78, pp 738–49.

Marshall, H. and Trevelyan, A. (1933) *Slum*, London: Heinemann.

Masterman, C.F.G. (1909) *The Condition of England*, London: Methuen.

May, G., Sir (Chair) (1931) *Report of the Committee on National Expenditure*, Cmd 3920, London: HMSO.

May, T. (2016) 'Statement from the new Prime Minister Theresa May', Prime Minister's Office. Available at: https://www.gov.uk/government/speeches/statement-from-the-new-prime-minister-theresa-may

Mayne, A. (1993) *The Imagined Slum: Newspaper Representation in Three Cities, 1870–1914*, Leicester: Leicester University Press.

Mayor of London (2012) *Private Renting*, London: Mayor of London.

Mazumder, P.M.H. (1992) *Eugenics, Human Genetics and Human Failings: The Eugenics Society, its Sources and its Critics in Britain*, Abingdon: Routledge.

McCabe, J. (2015) 'Chief Executive Pay Revealed', *Inside Housing*, 11 September.

McDermont, M. (2010) *Governing Independence and Expertise: The Business of Housing Associations*, Oregon, OR: Oxford and Portland.

McKee, K. and Phillips, D. (2012) 'Social Housing and Homelessness Policies: Reconciling Social Justice', in G. Mooney and J. Scott (eds) *Social Justice and Social Policy in Scotland*, Bristol: The Policy Press, pp 223–35.

McKee, K., Muir, J. and Moore, T. (2016) 'Housing Policy in the UK: The Importance of Spatial Nuance', *Housing Studies*. Available at: http://www.tandfonline.com/action/showAxaArticles?journalCode=chos20

McKie, R. (1971) *Housing and the Whitehall Bulldozer*, London: Institute of Economic Affairs.

McLaughlin, E. (2005) 'Governance and Social Policy in Northern Ireland (1999–2002): The Devolution Years and Postscript', in M. Powell, L. Bauld and J. Clarke (eds) *Social Policy Review 17: Analysis and Debate in Social Policy 2005*, Bristol: The Policy Press, pp 107–21.

McPeake, J. (2014) 'The Changing Face of Housing Need in Northern Ireland'. Available at: http://www.qub.ac.uk/schools/SchoolofPlanningArchitectureandCivilEngineering/Planning/FileStore/Filetoupload,481422,en.pdf

Mearns, A. (1883) *The Bitter Cry of Outcast London: An Inquiry into the Condition of the Abject Poor*, London: James Clarke and Co.

Meen, G., Gibb, K., Leishman, C. and Nygaard, C. (2016) *Housing Economics: A Historical Approach*, Basingstoke: Palgrave Macmillan.

Melling, J. (1983) *Rent Strikes*, Edinburgh: Polygon Books.

Merrett, S., with Gray, F. (1982) *Owner-Occupation in Britain*, Abingdon: Routledge and Kegan Paul.

MHLG (Ministry of Housing and Local Government) (1953) *Housing: The Next Step*, Cmd 8996, London: HMSO.

MHLG (1955) *Green Belts: Circular 42/55*, London: HMSO.

MHLG (1958) *Flats and Houses*, London: HMSO.

MHLG (1963) *Housing*, Cmnd 2050, London: HMSO.

MHLG (1965) *The Housing Programme 1965–70*, Cmnd 2838, London: HMSO.

MHLG (1968) *Old Houses into New Homes*, Cmnd 3602, London: HMSO.

Midwinter, E. (1985) 'The Politics of Council House Finance', in D. McCrone (ed) *The Scottish Government Yearbook 1985*, Edinburgh: Edinburgh University, pp 134–51.

Miles, C. (2012) 'Planning – The "Polite English Version of Apartheid"'. Available at: http://www.24dash.com/blogs/colin_wiles/2012/03/03/Planning-the-polite-English-version-of-apartheid/

Milner Holland, E. (Chair) (1965) *Report of the Committee on Housing in Greater London*, Cmnd 2605, London: HMSO.

Ministry of Health (1931) *Report of the Inter-Departmental Committee on the Rent Restrictions Acts* (The Marley Committee), Cmd 3911, London: HMSO.

Ministry of Health (1933) 'Housing Authorities', Circular 1331 (England and Wales), Cab 87(33). Available at: http://filestore.nationalarchives.gov.uk/pdfs/small/cab-24-239-CP-87-5.pdf

Mishra, R. (1981) *Society and Social Policy: Theory and Practice of Welfare*, Basingstoke: Palgrave Macmillan.

Mitchell, I.R. (2010) *Clydeside: Red, Orange and Green*, Edinburgh: Luath Press.

Mitchell, J. (2014) *The Scottish Question*, Oxford: Oxford University Press.

Mooney, G. and Scott, J. (2012) 'Devolution, Social Justice and Social Policy: The Scottish Context', in G. Mooney and J. Scott (eds) *Social Justice and Social Policy in Scotland*, Bristol: The Policy Press, pp 1–24.

Mooney, G., McCall, V. and Paton, K. (2015) 'Exploring the Use of Large Sporting Events in the Post-Crash, Post-Welfare City: A "Legacy" of Increasing Insecurity?', *Local Economy*, vol 30, no 8, pp 910–24.

Moore, C. (2013) *Margaret Thatcher: The Authorized Biography Volume One: Not for Turning*, London: Allen Lane.

Moore, C. (2015) *Margaret Thatcher: The Authorized Biography Volume Two: Everything She Wants*, London: Allen Lane.

Moore, R. (1980) *Reconditioning the Slums: The Development and Role of Housing Rehabilitation*, London: Polytechnic of Central London.

Morgan, K. (2002) 'The Conservative Party and Mass Housing 1918–39', in S. Ball and I. Holliday (eds) *Mass Conservatism: The Conservatives and the Public since the 1880s*, London: Frank Cass, pp 58-78.

Morgan, K. (2005) 'The Problem of the Epoch? Labour and Housing, 1918–51', *Twentieth Century British History*, vol 16, no 3, pp 227–55.

Morgan, K. and Morgan, J. (1980) *Portrait of a Progressive: The Political Career of Christopher, Viscount Addison*, Oxford: Clarendon Press.

Morgan, K.G. (1971) *The Age of Lloyd George: The Liberal Party and British Politics*, London: Allen and Unwin.

Morgan, M. and Cruickshank, H. (2014) 'Quantifying the Extent of Space Shortages: English Dwellings', *Building Research & Information*, vol 42, no 6, pp 710–24.

Morgan, N.J. (1989) '"8 Cottages for Glasgow Citizens": Innovation in Municipal House-Building in Glasgow in the Inter-War Years', in R. Rodger (ed) *Scottish Housing in the Twentieth Century*, Leicester: Leicester University Press, pp 125–44.

Morris, S. (2001) 'Market Solutions for Social Problems: Working-Class Housing in Nineteenth Century London', *Economic History Review*, vol LIV, no 3, pp 525–45.

Morris, W. (1885) *Manifesto of the Socialist League*, London: Socialist League Office.

Morrison, N. (2016) 'Institutional Logics and Organisational Hybridity: English Housing Associations' Diversification into the Private Rented Sector', *Housing Studies*, published online, 21 March. Available at: http://www.tandfonline.com/doi/abs/10.1080/02673037.2016.11 50428?journalCode=chos20

Morton, A. (2012) *Why Aren't We Building Enough Attractive Homes? Myths, Misunderstandings and Solutions*, London: Policy Exchange.

Morton, A. (2016) 'How to deliver a One Nation housing policy', Conservative Home, 21 July. Available at: http://www. conservativehome.com/thetorydiary/2016/07/delivering-a-one-nation-housing-policy.html

Mount, F. (2012) *The New Few or a Very British Oligarchy: Power and Inequality in Britain Now*, London: Simon and Schuster.

Moyne, W.E. (Chair) (1933) *Report of the Departmental Committee on Housing*, cmd 4397, London: HMSO.

Muir, J. (2012) 'Policy Difference and Policy Ownership under UK Devolution: Social Housing Policy in Northern Ireland', Institute of Spatial and Environmental Planning, Queen's University Belfast Working Paper no 5. Available at: https://www.qub.ac.uk/research-centres/TheInstituteofSpatialandEnvironmentalPlanning/Impact/WorkingPapers/FileStore/Filetoupload,432509,en.pdf

Mullins, D. (2010) 'Housing associations', Third Sector Research Centre Working Paper 16. Available at: http://www.birmingham.ac.uk/generic/tsrc/documents/tsrc/working-papers/working-paper-16.pdf

Mullins, D. and Murie, A. (eds) (2006) *Housing Policy in the UK*, Basingstoke: Palgrave Macmillan.

Murie, A. (2004) 'Scottish Housing: The Context', in D. Sim (ed) *Housing and Public Policy in Post-Devolution Scotland*, Coventry: Chartered Institute of Housing, pp 16–32.

Murie, A. (2008) *Moving Homes: The Housing Corporation 1964–2008*, London: Politicos.

Murie, A. (2014) 'The Housing Legacy of Thatcherism', in S. Farrall and C. Hay (eds) *The Legacy of Thatcherism: Assessing and Exploring Thatcherite Social and Economic Policies*, Oxford: Oxford University Press, pp 143–66.

Murie, A. (2016) *The Right to Buy? Selling off Public and Social Housing*, Bristol: Policy Press.

Murie, A. and Williams, P. (2015) 'A Presumption in Favour of Home Ownership? Reconsidering Housing Tenure Strategies', *Housing Studies*, vol 30, no 5, pp 656–76.

Murie, A., Birrell, W.D., Hillyard, P.A.R. and Roche, D. (1971) 'Housing Policy between the Wars: Northern Ireland, England and Wales', *Social Policy and Administration*, vol 5, no 4, pp 263–79.

Murray, C. (1984) *Losing Ground*, New York, NY: Basic Books.

Murray, C. (1992) *The Emerging British Underclass*, London: Institute of Economic Affairs.

Murray, G. (2002) 'As I See It', *Derry Journal*, 26 March, p 22.

Murtagh, B. (2001) 'Social Conflict and Housing Policy', in C. Paris (ed) *Housing in Northern Ireland – And Comparisons with the Republic of Ireland*, London: Chartered Institute of Ireland, pp 79–93.

National Audit Office (2014) 'Departmental Overview: The Performance of the Department for Communities and Local Government 2013–14'. Available at: https://www.nao.org.uk/wp-content/uploads/2014/10/Departmental-overview-communities-and-local-government.pdf

National Housing Federation (2013) 'About Us'. Available at: http://www.housing.org.uk/about_us.aspx

National Housing Planning and Advice Unit (2010) 'Public Attitudes to Housing 2010'. Available at: http://webarchive.nationalarchives.gov.uk/20120919132719/http://www.communities.gov.uk/documents/507390/nhpau/pdf/16127041.pdf

National Landlords Association (2015) 'Landlord Support for Labour and Lib Dems Halves Since 2010 Election'. Available at: http://www.landlords.org.uk/news-campaigns/news/landlord-support-labour-and-lib-dems-halves-2010-election

National Tenants Organisations (2015) 'Written Evidence to House of Commons Select Committee, Communities and Local Government, The Housing Association Sector and Right to Buy'. Available at: http://data.parliament.uk/writtenevidence/committeeevidence.svc/evidencedocument/communities-and-local-government-committee/the-housing-association-sector-and-the-right-to-buy/written/24138.html

Nationwide (2015) 'House Price Index'. Available at: http://www.nationwide.co.uk/~/media/MainSite/documents/about/house-price-index/Dec-Q4-2015.pdf

Newman, O. (1973) *Defensible Space*, London: Architectural Press.

New Policy Institute (2015) 'A Nation of Renters: How England Moved from Secure Family Homes Towards Rundown Rentals'. Available at: https://www.citizensadvice.org.uk/Global/CitizensAdvice/Housing%20Publications/A%20nation%20of%20renters.pdf

Newton, J. (1994) *All in One Place: The British Housing Story 1973–1993*, London: Catholic Housing Aid Society.

Nichols, J. (2007) *The Art of Poverty: Irony and Ideal in Sixteenth-Century Beggar Imagery*, Manchester: Manchester University Press.

Niskanen, W.A. (1973) *Bureaucracy: Servant or Master?* London: Institute of Economic Affairs.

Nolan, P. (2014) *Northern Ireland Peace Monitoring Report: Number Three*, Belfast: Community Relations Council.

North Tyneside Community Development Project (1978) *North Shields: Working Class Politics and Housing 1900–1977*, Newcastle-upon-Tyne: Benwell Community Project.

Northern Ireland Assembly (2012) 'Written Statement to the Assembly by Social Development Minister Nelson McCausland', Northern Ireland Executive Press Release 9/1/2013, Northern Ireland Assembly, Belfast.

Northern Ireland Housing Executive (2011) 'More than Bricks: Forty Years of the Housing Executive'. Available at: http://www.nihe.gov.uk/more_than_bricks.pdf

Northern Ireland Housing Executive (2015) 'A Fresh Start: The Stormont Agreement and Implementation Plan'. Available at: http://www.northernireland.gov.uk/a-fresh-start-stormont-agreement.pdf

Oakeshott, M. and Henry, R. (2013) 'Nimby Revolt Hits David Cameron in His Own Back Yard', *Sunday Times*, 10 November.

Observer (2016) 'Britain's Housing Crisis', 1 May.

O'Carroll, A. (1996) 'The Influence of Local Authorities on the Growth of Owner Occupation: Edinburgh and Glasgow 1914–1939', *Planning Perspectives*, vol 11, no 1, pp 55–72.

O'Carroll, A. (1996) 'Historical Perspectives on Tenure Development in Two Scottish Cities', in H. Currie and A. Murie (eds) *Housing in Scotland*, Coventry: Chartered Institute of Housing, pp 16–30.

ODPM (Office of the Deputy Prime Minister) (2003) *Exploitation of the Right to Buy Scheme by Companies*, London: ODPM.

ODPM (2005) *Sustainable Communities: Settled Homes; Changing Lives, a Strategy for Tackling Homelessness*, London: ODPM.

Offe, C. (1984) *Contradictions of the Welfare State*, London: Hutchinson.

Offer, A. (1981) *Property and Politics 1870–1914: Landownership, Law, Ideology and Urban Development in England*, Cambridge: Cambridge University Press.

Offer, J. (2006) *An Intellectual History of British Social Policy: Idealism versus Non-Idealism*, Bristol: The Policy Press.

Office for Budget Responsibility (2015) 'Economic and Fiscal Outlook – November 2015'. Available at: http://budgetresponsibility.org.uk/docs/dlm_uploads/PressNotice_EFO_November2015.pdf

Office for National Statistics (2012) '2011 Census, Population and Household Estimates for England and Wales'. Available at: http://www.ons.gov.uk/peoplepopulationandcommunity/populationandmigration/populationestimates/bulletins/2011censu populationandhouseholdestimatesforenglandandwales/2012-07-16

Office for National Statistics (2013) 'A Century of Home Ownership and Renting in England and Wales'. Available at: http://webarchive.nationalarchives.gov.uk/20160105160709/http://www.ons.gov.uk/ons/rel/census/2011-census-analysis/a-century-of-home-ownership-and-renting-in-england-and-wales/short-story-on-housing.html

Office for National Statistics (2015) '*House Price Index, June 2015*'. Available at: http://www.ons.gov.uk/ons/rel/hpi/house-price-index/june-2015/stb-june-2015.html

O'Hara, G. (2012) *Governing Post-War Britain: The Paradoxes of Progress 1951–1973*, Basingstoke: Palgrave Macmillan.

O'Neill, B. (2016) 'Brexit voters are not thick, not racist: just poor', *Spectator*, 2 July.

O'Neill, J. (2014) *The Secret World of the Victorian Lodging House*, Barnsley: Pen and Sword.

Orbach, L. (1977) *Homes for Heroes*, London: Seely Service.

Ortalo-Magné, F. and Prat, A. (2007) 'The Political Economy of Housing Supply: Homeowners, Workers, and Voters'. Available at: http://core.ac.uk/download/files/67/93423.pdf

Orwell, G. (1937) *The Road to Wigan Pier*, London: Penguin.

Orwell, G. (2001 [1933]) *Down and Out in Paris and London*, London: Penguin.

Osborne, G. (2011) '2011 Budget: A Strong Stable Economy, Growth and Fairness'. Available at: http://webarchive.nationalarchives.gov.uk/20130129110402/http:/www.hm-treasury.gov.uk/2011budget.htm

Osborne, G. (2014) 'Chancellor George Osborne's Autumn Statement 2014 Speech', 3 December. Available at: https://www.gov.uk/government/speeches/chancellor-george-osbornes-autumn-statement-2014-speech

Osborne, G. (2015a) 'Chancellor George Osborne's Summer Budget 2015 Speech'. Available at: https://www.gov.uk/government/speeches/chancellor-george-osbornes-summer-budget-2015-speech

Osborne, G. (2015b) 'Chancellor George Osborne's Spending Review and Autumn Statement 2015 speech'. Available at: https://www.gov.uk/government/speeches/chancellor-george-osbornes-spending-review-and-autumn-statement-2015-speech

Oxford Dictionaries (2016), 'Rachmanism', http://www.oxforddictionaries.com/definition/english/rachmanism?q=Rachmanism

Oxford English Dictionary (2013) 'Politics'. Available at: http://www.oxforddictionaries.com/definition/english/politics

Packer, I. (1996) 'The Conservatives and the Ideology of Landownership 1910–1914', in M. Francis and I. Zweiniger-Bargielowska (eds) *The Conservatives and British Society 1880–1990*, Cardiff: University of Wales, pp 39–57.

Packer, I. (2001) *Lloyd George, Liberalism and the Land: The Land Issue and Party Politics in England, 1906–1914*, Suffolk: Boydell Press.

Padgett, D.K., Stanhope, V., Henwood, B.F. and Stefancic, A. (2011) 'Substance Use Outcomes in "Housing First" and "Treatment First" Consumers After One Year', *Community Mental Health Journal*, vol 47, no 3, pp 227–32.

Pahl, R.E. (1975) *Whose City?* Harmondsworth: Penguin.

Paris, C. (ed) (2001) *Housing in Northern Ireland – And Comparisons with the Republic of Ireland*, London and Coventry: Chartered Institute of Housing.

Paris, C. and Muir, J. (2002) 'After Housing Policy: Housing and the UK General Election 2001', *Housing Studies*, vol 17, no 1, pp 151–64.

Paris, C., Gray, P. and Muir, J. (2003) 'Devolving Housing Policy and Practice in Northern Ireland 1998–2002', *Housing Studies*, vol 18, no 2, pp 159–75.

Parry, R. (2007) 'Social Security under Devolution in the United Kingdom'. Available at: http://www.socialpolicy.ed.ac.uk/__data/assets/pdf_file/0016/10168/Parry_05_SocialSecurityunderDevolution.pdf

Parsons, T. (1951) *The Social System*, Abingdon: Routledge.

Passmore, M. (2015) 'The Responses of Labour-Controlled London Local Authorities to Major Changes in Housing Policy, 1971–1983'. Available at: http://www.history.ac.uk/history-online/theses/thesis/in-progress/responses-london-labour-controlled-local-authorities-major-changes-housing

Pattie, C., Dorling, D. and Johnston, R. (1995) 'A Debt-Owing Democracy: The Political Impact of Housing Market Recession at the British General Election of 1992', *Urban Studies*, vol 32, no 8, pp 1293–315.

Pautz, H. (2012) *Think-Tanks, Social Democracy and Social Policy*, Basingstoke: Palgrave.

Pawley, M. (1978) *Home Ownership*, London: Architectural Press.

Pawson, H. (2004) 'Reviewing Stock Transfer', paper to Housing Studies Association Spring Conference, Sheffield Hallam University, 15–16 April.

Pawson, H. (2009) 'Homelessness Policy in England: Promoting "Gatekeeping" or Effective Prevention?', in S. Fitzpatrick, D. Quilgars and N. Pleace (eds) *Homelessness in the UK: Problems and Solutions*, London: Chartered Institute of Housing, pp 90–104.

Pawson, H. and Sosenko, F. (2012) 'The Supply-Side Modernisation of Social Housing in England: Analysing Mechanics, Trends and Consequences', *Housing Studies*, vol 27, no 6, pp 783–804.

Pawson, H. and Wilcox, S. (2013) '*UK Housing Review2013*'. Available at: http://www.york.ac.uk/res/ukhr/ukhr13/index.htm

Payne, S. (2015) *Towards 'Zero Carbon' Housing Futures*, Sheffield: University of Sheffield.

Pennington, M. (2000) *Planning and the Political Market: Public Choice and the Politics of Government Failure*, London: Athlone Press.

Pennington, M. (2002) *Liberating the Land: The Case for Private Land Use Planning*, London: Institute of Economic Affairs.

Pickles, E. (2013) 'Pickles Attacks Labour's Housing Record in Wales'. Available at: http://conservativehome.blogs.com/localgovernment/2013/05/pickles-attacks-labours-housing-record-in-wales.html

Pickles, E. and Lewis, B. (2014) 'Councils Must Protect Our Precious Green Belt Land'. Available at: https://www.gov.uk/government/news/councils-must-protect-our-precious-green-belt-land

Piketty, T. (2014) *Capital in the Twenty-First Century*, Cambridge, MA: The Belknap Press of Harvard University.

Planning Resource (2016) 'Brexit MP in warning over immigration's impact on the housing crisis'. Available at: http://www.planningresource.co.uk/article/1397355/brexit-mp-warning-immigrations-impact-housing-crisis

Policy Exchange (2013a) 'About Us'. Available at: http://www.policyexchange.org.uk/about-us

Policy Exchange (2013b) *Taxing Issues? Reducing Housing Demand or Increasing Housing Supply*, London: Policy Exchange. Available at: http://www.policyexchange.org.uk/publications/category/item/taxing-issues-reducing-housing-demand-or-increasing-housing-supply

Policy Exchange (2014) 'Freeing Housing Associations: Better Financing, More Homes'. Available at: http://www.policyexchange.org.uk/publications/category/item/freeing-housing-associations-better-financing-more-homes

Porritt, J. and Winner, D. (1988) *The Coming of the Greens*, London: Fontana/Collins.

Poulantzas, N. (1973) *Political Power and Social Classes*, London: New Left Books.

Powell, E. (1963) 'White Paper on Housing Policy: Memorandum by the Minister for Health', C 63(84). Available at: http://filestore.nationalarchives.gov.uk/pdfs/small/cab-129-113-c-84.pdf

Powell, J. (2010) *The New Machiavelli: How to Wield Power in the Modern World*, London: Bodley Head.

PricewaterhouseCoopers (2016) 'UK should avoid severe recession or house price crash despite growth downgrades following Brexit vote'. Available at: http://pwc.blogs.com/press_room/2016/07/uk-should-avoid-severe-recession-or-house-price-crash-despite-growth-downgrades-following-brexit-vot.html

Prideaux, S. (2005) *Not So New Labour: A Sociological Critique of New Labour's Policy and Practice*, Bristol: The Policy Press.

Prime Minister's Office (2015) 'Prime Minister: Councils Must Deliver Local Plans for New Homes by 2017', press release, 12 October. Available at: https://www.gov.uk/government/news/prime-minister-councils-must-deliver-local-plans-for-new-homes-by-2017

Pringle, J.C. (1929) 'Slums and Eugenics. Review *The Slum Problem* by B.S. Townroe', *Eugenics Review*, vol 20, no 4, pp 273–74. Available at: http://europepmc.org/backend/ptpmcrender.fcgi?accid=PMC2984786&blobtype=pdf

Pulzer, P.G.J. (1967) *Political Representation and Elections: Parties and Voting in Great Britain*, New York, NY: Praeger.

Punch (1844) 'Hints to Visiting and Relief Societies', no VII, p 108.

Purkis, A. (2010) *Housing Associations in England and the Future of Voluntary Sector Organisation*, London: Baring Foundation.

Quod and London First (2015) '*Green Belt: A Place for Londoners*'. Available at: http://londonfirst.co.uk/wp-content/uploads/2015/02/Green-Belt-Report-February-2015.pdf

Quod and Shelter (2016) 'When Brownfield Isn't Enough, Strategic Options for London's Growth'. Available at: http://england.shelter.org.uk/__data/assets/pdf_file/0003/1239330/2016_02_29_When_Brownfield_isnt_enough.pdf

Raison, T. (1990) *The Tories and the Welfare State: A History of Conservative Social Policy Since the Second World War*, London: St Martin's Press.

Ramsden, J. (1978) *The Age of Balfour and Baldwin 1902–1940*, London: Longman.

Ravetz, A. (1986) *The Governance of Space: Town Planning in Modern Society*, London: Faber and Faber.

Rebanks, J. (2015) *The Shepherd's Life: A Tale of the Lake District*, London: Allen Lane.

Redbrick (2014) 'We All Agree Something Must Be Done About Rent'. Available at: https://redbrickblog.wordpress.com/2014/01/

Redcliffe-Maud, Lord (1969) *Royal Commission on Local Government in England 1966–1969*, Cmnd 4010, London: HMSO.

Reidy, P. (2014) 'Locked in Deadlock', *Inside Housing*, 22 November.

Resolution Foundation (2016) 'Resolution Foundation'. Available at: http://www.resolutionfoundation.org/us/about/

Rex, J. and Moore, R. (1969) *Race, Community and Conflict: Study of Sparkbrook*, Oxford: Oxford University Press.

Rhodes, R.A.W. (2006) 'Policy Network Analysis', in M. Moran, M. Rein and R.E. Goodin (eds) *The Oxford Handbook of Public Policy*, Oxford: Oxford University Press, pp 425–47.

RIBA (Royal Institute of British Architects) (2011) *The Case for Space: The Size of England's New Homes*, London: Royal Institute of British Architects.

Ricardo, D. (1971 [1817]) *Principles of Political Economy and Taxation*, Harmondsworth: Penguin.

Richards, J. (1953) *Architectural Review*, vol 114, July, pp 28–35.

Richardson, J.J. (2000) 'Government, Interest Groups and Policy Change', *Political Studies*, vol 48, no 5, pp 1006–25.

Ridley, N. (1988) 'Commons Debates', 2 November, col 1157.

Ridley, N. (1992) *'My Style of Government': The Thatcher Years*, London: Hutchinson.

Ridley, Viscount (Chair) (1945) *Report of the Inter-departmental Committee on Rent Control*, Cmd 6621, London: HMSO.

Roberts, A. (1999) *Salisbury: Victorian Titan*, London: Phoenix.

Roberts, R. (1973) *The Classic Slum: Salford Life in the First Quarter of the Century*, Harmondsworth: Penguin.

Robertson, D. (2001) 'Scottish Homes: A Legacy', in C. Jones and P. Robson (eds) *Health of Scottish Housing*, Aldershot: Ashgate, pp 110–33.

Robertson, E.T. (1884) *The State and the Slums*, London: Liberty and Property Defence League.

Robinson, A., Sir (1933) 'Speech to Moyne Committee Conference', PRO HLG 29/213, 4 November.

Rodger, R. (1989) 'Crisis and Confrontation in Scottish Housing 1880–1914', in R. Rodger (ed) *Scottish Housing in the Twentieth Century*, Leicester: Leicester University Press, pp 25–53.

Rodger, R. and El Qaddo, H. (1989) 'The Scottish Special Housing Association and the Implementation of Housing Policy 1937–87', in R. Rodger (ed) *Scottish Housing in the Twentieth Century*, Leicester: Leicester University Press, pp 184–213.

Ronald, R. (2008) *The Ideology of Home Ownership: Homeowner Societies and the Role of Housing*, London: AIAA.

Ronald, R. (2015) *The Revival of Private Landlordism in the UK and the Mobilization of Housing Wealth*, Birmingham: Centre on Housing Assets and Savings Management. Available at: policy/CHASM/briefing-papers/2015/bp11-2015-private-landlordism.pdf

Rose, L. (2015) *'Rogues and Vagabonds': Vagrant Underworld in Britain 1815–1985*, Abingdon: Routledge.

Rose, R. (1982) *The Territorial Dimension in Government: Understanding the United Kingdom*, Chatham, NJ: Chatham House Publications.

Ross, T. (2015) *Why the Tories Won: The Inside Story of the 2015 Election*, London: Biteback.

Royal Commission on Housing in Scotland (1917) *Report of the Royal Commission on the Housing of the Industrial Population of Scotland Rural and Urban*, Cd 8734, Edinburgh: HMSO.

Royal Commission on the Housing of the Working Classes (1885) *Reports, with Minutes of Evidence*, London: HMSO.

Royal Commission on the Poor Laws and Relief of Distress (1909) *Minority Report of the Royal Commission on the Poor Laws and Relief of Distress*, Cd 4499, London: HMSO.

Rubinstein, D. (2006) *The Labour Party and British Society 1880–2005*, Brighton: Sussex Academic Press.

Ruddick, G. (2015) 'Revealed: Housebuilders Sitting on 600,000 Plots of Land', *Guardian*, 30 December.

Rugg, J. and Rhodes, D. (2008) *Review of Private Sector Rented Housing*, York: Centre for Housing Policy, University of York.

Russell, M. and Sciara, M. (2008) 'The Policy Impact of Defeats in the House of Lords', *British Journal of Politics and International Relations*, vol 10, no 4, pp 571–89.

Ryan, R. (2008) 'Tories Launch New Group to Tackle Homelessness', *Guardian*, 15 May.

Ryan-Collins, J. (2016) 'UK Housing: Fixing the "Doom Loop" between Land Value, Inadequate Supply and Insecure Financing'. Available at: http://blog.politics.ox.ac.uk/11946-2/

Sandbrook, D. (2012) *Seasons in the Sun: The Battle for Britain 1974–1979*, London: Allen Lane.

Sandford, J. (1971) *Down and Out in Britain*, London: New English Library.

Saunders, P. (1990) *A Nation of Home Owners*, Abingdon: Routledge.

Saunders, P. (2016) *Restoring a Nation of Home Owners: What went Wrong with Home Ownership in Britain, and How to Start Putting it Right*, London: Civitas. Available at: http://www.civitas.org.uk/content/files/Restoring-a-Nation-of-Home-Owners.pdf

Savage, M., Cunningham, N., Devine, F., Friedman, S., Laurison, D., Mckenzie, L., Miles, A., Snee, H. and Wakeling, P. (2015) *Social Class in the 21st Century*, London: Pelican.

Save Britain's Heritage (2011) 'Reviving Britain's Terraces: Life After Pathfinder'. Available at: http://www.savebritainsheritage.org/campaigns/item/144/Reviving-Britains-Terraces-Life-after-Pathfinder

Savills (2014a) 'London's Overseas Buyers Have Been Overstated', July. Available at: http://www.savills.co.uk/_news/article/55328/177606-0/7/2014/london-s-overseas-buyers-have-been-overstated--says-savills

Savills (2014b) 'CIL – Is It Delivering?', November. Available at: http://pdf.euro.savills.co.uk/uk/residential---other/spotlight-cil.pdf

Savills (2015) 'Spotlight Beyond the Election: What Next for Planning?', Spring. Available at: http://pdf.euro.savills.co.uk/residential---other/spotlight-beyond-the-election.pdf

Scarman, Lord (1981) *The Brixton Disorders, April 10–12, 1981: Inquiry Report*, London: Stationery Office.

Schifferes, S. (1976) 'Council Tenants and Housing Policy in the 1930s: The Contradictions of State Intervention', in M. Edwards, F. Gray, S. Merrett and J. Swann (eds) *Housing and Class in Britain*, London: Conference of Socialist Economists.

Schmidt, M. (2003) 'How, Where and When Does Discourse Matter in Small States' Welfare State Adjustment?', *New Political Economy*, vol 8, no 1, pp 127–46.

Schoettler, C. (1994) '200 in London Protest Major's Labeling of Beggars as "Offensive Eyesores"', *London Bureau of the Sun*, 30 May. Available at: http://articles.baltimoresun.com/1994-05-30/news/1994150011_1_john-major-homeless-in-london-trafalgar-square

Scott, J.C. (1998) *Seeing It Like a State*, Yale, CT: Yale University Press.

Scott, L. (Chair) (1942) *Report of the Committee on Land Utilisation in Rural Areas*, Cmd 6378, London: HMSO.

Scott, P. (2007) *'Embourgeoisement' Before Affluence? Suburbanisation and the Social Filtering of Working-Class Communities in Interwar Britain*, Henley: University of Henley. Available at: http://www.henley.ac.uk/web/FILES/management/041.pdf

Scott, P. (2013) *The Making of the Modern British Home: The Suburban Semi and Family Life between the Wars*, Oxford: Oxford University Press.

Scottish Conservative and Unionist Party (2016) 'A Strong Opposition – a Strong Scotland'. Available at: http://www.scottishconservatives.com/wordpress/wp-content/uploads/2016/04/Scottish-Conservative-Manifesto_2016-DIGITAL-SINGLE-PAGES.pdf

Scottish Development Department (1977) *Scottish Housing: A Consultative Document*, Cmd 6852, Edinburgh: Stationery Office.

Scottish Government (2010) 'Operation of the Homeless Persons Legislation in Scotland 2009/10'. Available at: http://www.scotland.gov.uk/Publications/2010/08/31093245/26

Scottish Government (2012) 'The Future of the Right to Buy in Scotland: A Consultation'. Available at: http://www.scotland.gov.uk/Resource/0039/00394388.pdf

Scottish Government (2013) *Scotland's Future: Your Guide to an Independent Scotland*, Edinburgh: Scottish Government.

Scottish Government (2014) 'Operation of the Homeless Persons Legislation in Scotland, 2013–14'. Available at: http://www.gov.scot/Publications/2014/06/3967

Scottish Government (2015a) *A Consultation on the Future of Land Reform in Scotland*, Edinburgh: Scottish Government.

Scottish Government (2015b) 'Housing Statistics for Scotland: Quarterly Update March 2015'. Available at: http://www.gov.scot/Publications/2015/03/4194/3

Scottish Labour Party (2016) 'Invest in Scotland's Future: Both Votes Labour'. Available at: http://www.scottishlabour.org.uk/page/-/images/Manifesto%202016/Scottish%20Labour%20Manifesto%202016.pdf

Scottish National Party (2016) 'Re-Elect: SNP Manifesto 2016'. Available at: http://www.snp.org/manifesto

Searle, G.R. (1976) *Eugenics and Politics in Britain*, Leyden, Netherlands: Noordhoff International.

Secretary of State for Business, Innovation & Skills (2010) *Local Growth: Realising Every Place's Potential*, Cm7961, London: Stationery Office.

Secretary of State for the Environment (1996) *Household Growth: Where Shall We Live?*, Cm 3271, London: Stationery Office.

Secretary of State for the Environment and Secretary of State for Wales (1977) *Housing Policy: A Consultative Document*, London: HMSO.

Secretary of State for Work and Pensions (2012) *Measuring Child Poverty: A Consultation on Better Measures of Child Poverty*, Cm 8483, London: The Stationery Office Limited.

Seely, A. (2013) *Inheritance Tax*, Standard Note SN93, London: House of Commons.

Shaftesbury, Lord (1883) 'The Mischief of State Aid', *The Nineteenth Century*, vol 14, pp 934–9.

Shapely, P. (2007a) 'Council Wars: Manchester's Overspill Battles', in B.M. Doyle (ed) *Urban Politics and Space in the Nineteenth and Twentieth Centuries: Regional Perspectives*, Newcastle: Cambridge Scholars Publishing, pp 99–115.

Shapely, P. (2007b) *The Politics of Housing: Power, Consumer and Urban Culture*, Manchester: Manchester University Press.

Shapely, P. (2014) *People and Planning: Report of the Skeffington Committee on Public Participation in Planning with an Introduction by Peter Shapely*, Abingdon: Routledge.

Shapps, G. (2011) 'House of Commons Debates', 24 November, c30-1WS.

Sharp, D. and Rendel, S. (2008) *Connell Ward and Lucas: Modernist Architecture in England*, London: Frances Lincoln.

Sharp, T. (1932) *Town and Countryside: Some Aspects of Urban and Rural Development*, Oxford: Oxford University Press.

Shaw, G.B. (1892) 'Widower's Houses: A Play'. Available at: http://archive.org/stream/widowershouspl00shawuoft/widowershouspl00shawuoft_djvu.txt

Shaw, G.B. (1908) *The Commonsense of Municipal Trading*, London: Fabian Society.

Sheffield Hallam University (2016) 'Tenants Unable To Join Right to Buy Scheme'. Available at: http://www.shu.ac.uk/mediacentre/tenants-unable-join-right-buy-scheme

Shelter (1969) *Face the Facts*, London: Shelter.

Shelter (1973) *Slum Clearance*, London: Shelter.

Shelter (2008) 'Good Practice: Briefing Housing First'. Available at: http://england.shelter.org.uk/professional_resources/policy_and_research/policy_library/policy_library_folder/housing_first_-_a_good_practice_briefing

Shelter (2015a) 'Housing in the Marginals: How Is England's Housing Shortage Affecting Political Battlegrounds?', March. Available at: http://england.shelter.org.uk/__data/assets/pdf_file/0003/1094277/2015_Housing_in_the_marginalsv2.pdf

Shelter (2015b) 'Addressing Our Housing Shortage: Engaging the Silent Majority'. Available at: http://england.shelter.org.uk/professional_resources/policy_and_research/policy_library/policy_library_folder/report_engaging_the_silent_majority

Simmie, J. (1993) *Planning at the Crossroads*, London: UCL Press.

Simmonds, A.G.V. (2002) 'Raising Rachman: The Origins of the Rent Act, 1957', *The Historical Journal*, vol 45, no 4, pp 843–68.

Sinnett, D., Carmichael, L., Williams, K. and Miner, P. (2014) 'From Wasted Space to Living Spaces: The Availability of Brownfield Land for Housing Development in England'. Available at: http://eprints.uwe.ac.uk/24995/

Skeffington, A. (1969) *People and Planning: Report of the Skeffington Committee on Public Participation in Planning*, London: HMSO.

Skelton, N. (1924) *Constructive Conservatism*, London: William Blackwood and Sons.

Smith, J.E. (1993) *The Idea Brokers: Think Tanks and the Rise of the New Policy Elite*, New York, NY: Free Press.

Smith, P.G. (1994) 'Slum Clearance as an Instrument of Sanitary Reform: The Flawed Vision of Edinburgh's First Slum Clearance Scheme', *Planning Perspectives*, vol 9, no 1, pp 1–27.

Smith, S.J. (1987) 'Residential Segregation: A Geography of English Racism?', in P. Jackson (ed) *Race and Racism: Essays in Social Geography*, London: Allen and Unwin, pp 22–41.

Smith, S.J., Cook, N. and Searle, B.A. (2006) 'From Canny Consumer to Care-Full Citizen: Towards a Nation of Home Stewardship?'. Available at: http://www.consume.bbk.ac.uk/working_papers/SmithBohWkgPapSept06.pdf

Smith Institute (2016) 'About the Smith Institute'. Available at: https://thesmithinstitute.wordpress.com/about/

Smyth, J. and Robertson, D. (2013) 'Local Elites and Social Control: Building Council Houses in Stirling between the Wars', *Urban History*, vol 40, no 2, pp 336–54., 2013

Snowden, C (2012) *Sock Puppets: How the Government Lobbies Itself and Why*, London: Institute for Economic Affairs.

Social Exclusion Unit (1998a) *Bringing Britain Together: A National Strategy for Neighbourhood Renewal*, London: Cabinet Office.

Social Exclusion Unit (1998b) *Rough Sleeping*, Cm 4008, London: The Stationery Office.

Social Market Foundation (2016) 'Our Work'. Available at: http://www.smf.co.uk/

Somerville, P. (2013) 'Understanding Homelessness', *Housing, Theory and Society*, vol 30, no 4, pp 384–415.

Somerville, P. (2016) 'Coalition Housing Policy in England', in H. Bochel and M. Powell (eds) *The Coalition Government and Social Policy: Restructuring the Welfare State*, Bristol: Policy Press, pp 151–78.

Speight, G. (2000) *Who Bought the Inter-War Semi? The Socio-Economic Characteristics of New-House Buyers in the 1930s*, Discussion Papers in Economic and Social History, Oxford: Oxford University Press.

Spensley, J.C. (1918) 'Urban Housing Problems', *Journal of the Royal Statistical Society*, vol LXXXI, Part 2, pp 162–228.

Spurr, H. (2014) 'Turning Homeless Away', *Inside Housing*, 18 March.

Spurr, H. (2016) 'Orr Calls for Associations to Lead Regen', *Inside Housing*, 18 January.

Standing, G. (2014) *The Precariat: The New Dangerous Class*, London: Bloomsbury Academic.

Stannage, T. (1980) *Baldwin Thwarts the Opposition*, London: Croom Helm.

Statistics Portal (2016) 'Forecasted Stamp Duty Land Tax Income in the United Kingdom (UK) from 2015/2016 to 2020/2021 (in Billion GBP)'. Available at: http://www.statista.com/statistics/375122/stamp-duty-land-tax-income-forecast-united-kingdom-uk/

Stedman Jones, G. (1992) *Outcast London: A Study in the Relationship between Classes in Victorian Society*, London: Penguin.

Stephens, M. (2003) 'Globalisation and Housing Finance Systems in Advanced and Transition Economies', *Urban Studies*, vol 40, part 5.6, pp 1011–26.

Stephens, M. (2016) 'Evolving Devolution', in S. Wilcox, J. Perry, M. Stephens and P. Williams (eds) *UK Housing Review 2016*, Coventry: Chartered Institute of Housing, pp 31–42.

Stothart, C. (2015) 'Right to Buy Extension Not Part of ONS Review of Housing Associations', *Social Housing*, 30 September.

Swenarton, M. (1981) *Homes Fit for Heroes*, Aldershot: Ashgate.

Swenarton, M. (2008) *Building the New Jerusalem: Architecture, Housing and Politics 1900–1930*, Bracknell: BRE Press.

Tallon, A. (2013) *Urban Regeneration in the UK, Second Edition*, Abingdon: Routledge.

Taylor, E.J. (2013) 'Do House Values Influence Resistance to Development? A Spatial Analysis of Planning Objection and Appeals in Melbourne', *Urban Policy and Research*, vol 31, no 1, pp 5–26.

Taylor, M. (2015) 'Housing is the Nation's Most Urgent and Complex Challenge. Yet We're Paralysed', *Guardian*, 15 August.

Telegraph (2011) 'The Horrors Hidden in the Draft National Planning Policy Framework', 19 September.

Telegraph (2014) 'Nick Boles Told to Apologise for "Costing Tories Seats"', 6 May.

Tenants' History (2013) 'The Birth of the Council Tenants Movement: A Study of the 1934 Leeds Rent Strike'. Available at: http://tenantshistory.leedstenants.org.uk/rentstrike/1934.html

Thatcher, M. (1950) 'General Election Pamphlet', Thatcher Foundation. Available at: http://www.margaretthatcher.org/document/100859

Thatcher, M. (1965) HC 3R [Rent Bill] Hansard, House of Commons 715/1181-85.

Thatcher, M. (1966) HC S 2R [Land Commission Bill], House of Commons. Available at: http://www.margaretthatcher.org/document/101442

Thatcher, M. (1977) 'Speech to Zurich Economic Society: "The New Renaissance"', Thatcher Foundation. Available at: http://www.margaretthatcher.org/document/103336

Thatcher, M. (1979a) 'Note from the Prime Minister to the Chancellor of the Exchequer', Cabinet Papers, 24 June.

Thatcher, M. (1979b) 'Remarks on becoming Prime Minister (St Francis's prayer)', Thatcher Foundation. Available at: http://www.margaretthatcher.org/document/104078

Thatcher, M. (1982) 'Comments on Department of the Environment Review of the 1977 Housing (Homeless Persons) Act', Thatcher Foundation. Available at: http://7f11a30961219bd1a71e-b9527bc5dce0df4456f4c5548db2e5c2.r10.cf1.rackcdn.com/820208%20hsltn%20let%20PREM19-0795%20f25.pdf

Thatcher, M. (1987) 'Interview with Douglas Keay', *Woman's Own*, 31 October.

Thatcher, M. (1993) *The Downing Street Years*, London: HarperCollins.

Thatcher, M. (1995) *The Path to Power*, London: HarperCollins.

Thatcher, M. (2002) *Statecraft*, London: HarperCollins.

Theakston, K. (1993) 'Evelyn Sharp', *Contemporary Record*, vol 7, no 1, pp 32–148.

The Star (1888) 'The Premier's Rookeries Fall', 1 October.

The Sun (2011) 'My Big Fat Gypsy House', 7 February.

The Sun (2012) 'Council House Boot for the Rich', 19 May.

The Sun (2013) 'Dole Queen Heather Frost Might Not Even Want Custom-Built Six-Bedroom Council Mansion', 20 February.

Thomas-Symonds, N. (2014) *Nye: The Political Life of Aneurin Bevan*, London: I.B. Tauris.

Thompson, L. (1988) *An Act of Compromise*, London: Shelter.

Thompson, S. (2004) 'Conservative Bloom on Socialism's Compost Heap: Working-Class Home Ownership in South Wales, c. 1890–1939', in R.R. Davies and R.A. Jenkins (eds) *From Medieval to Modern Wales: Historical Essays in Honour of Kenneth O. Morgan and Ralph A. Griffiths*, Cardiff: University of Wales.

Tichelar, M. (2003) 'The Labour Party, Agricultural Policy and the Retreat from Rural Land Nationalisation During the Second World War'. Available at: http://www.bahs.org.uk/AGHR/ARTICLES/51n2a6.pdf

Tiesdell, S. (2001) 'A Forgotten Policy? A Perspective on the Evolution and Transformation of Housing Action Trust Policy, 1987–99', *European Journal of Housing Policy*, vol 1, no 3, pp 357–83.

Timmins, N. (1996) *The Five Giants: A Biography of the Welfare State*, London: HarperCollins.

Torgersen, U. (1987) 'Housing: The Wobbly Pillar under the Welfare State', in B. Turner, J. Kemeny and L. Lundqvist (eds) *Between State and Market: Housing in the Post-Industrial Era*, Stockholm: Almqvist and Wiksell, pp 116–26.

Touche Ross (1994) *Westminster City Council, Audit of Accounts 1987/88 and Subsequent Years: Designated Sales; Note of the Appointed Auditors Provisional Findings and Views*, London: Touche Ross.

Townroe, B.S. (1927) 'The Dutch System', *Spectator*, 3 December.

Townroe, B.S. (1928) *The Slum Problem*, London: Longman Green.

Townroe, B.S. (1936) *Britain Rebuilding: The Slum and Overcrowding Campaigns*, London: Frederick Muller Ltd.

Treasury (1975) *Public Expenditure*, London: HMSO.

Treasury (1979) *Public Expenditure*, Cmnd 7439, London: HMSO.

Trollope, A. (2004 [1855]) *The Warden*, London: Penguin Classics.

Troutman, W.H., Jackson, J.D. and Elelund, R.B. (1999) 'Public Policy, Perverse Incentives, and the Homeless Problem', *Public Choice*, vol 98, nos 1/2, pp 195–212.

Tsubaki, T. (1993) 'Post-War Reconstruction and the Questions of Popular Housing Provision, 1939–1951: The Debates and Implementation of Policy, with Particular Reference to Coventry and Portsmouth'. Available at: http://wrap.warwick.ac.uk/34728/1/WRAP_THESIS_Tsubaki_1993.pdf

Tucker, J. (1966) *Honourable Estates*, London: Victor Gollancz.

Tudor Walters, J. (Chair) (1918) *Building Construction in Connection with the Provision of Dwellings for the Working Classes*, Cmd 9191, London: HMSO.

Tullock, G. (2006) *The Vote Motive*, London: Institute for Economic Affairs.

Turner, J.F.C. (1976) *Housing by People: Towards Autonomy in Building Environments*, London: Marion Boyars.

Uberoi, E. (2016) 'Political Disengagement in the UK: Who Is Disengaged?', House of Commons Briefing Paper, no CBP7501. Available at: http://researchbriefings.files.parliament.uk/documents/CBP-7501/CBP-7501.pdf

UKIP (United Kingdom Independence Party) (2015) *Believe in Britain: UKIP Manifesto 2015*, London: UKIP.

UK Statistics Authority (2015) 'Statistics on Homelessness and Rough Sleeping in England (Produced by the Department for Communities and Local Government): Assessment of Compliance with the Code of Practice for Official Statistics Assessment Report 320'. Available at: https://www.statisticsauthority.gov.uk/wp-content/uploads/2015/12/images-assessmentreport320statisticsonhomelessnessandroughsleepinginenglan_tcm97-45078.pdf

United Nations (1997) 'Framework Convention on Climate Change'. Available at: http://unfccc.int/kyoto_protocol/items/3145.php

Urban, F. (2011) *Tower and Slab: Histories of Global Mass Housing*, Abingdon: Routledge.

Urban Task Force (1999) *Towards an Urban Renaissance*, London: Stationery Office.

Uthwatt, A.A. (Chair) (1942) *Report Expert Committee on Compensation and Betterment*, London: HMSO.

Vagrancy Committee (1906) *Proposed Vagrancy Bill. Report of the Departmental Committee on Vagrancy*, Cd.2852, London: HMSO.

Vaughan, J. (2009) 'The First Labour Government and the Civil Service'. Available at: https://kclpure.kcl.ac.uk/portal/files/2932326/440474.pdf

Voigt, W. (1989) 'The Garden City as Eugenic Utopia', *Planning Perspectives*, vol 3, no 3, pp 295–312.

Wachel, H.M. (1986) *The Money Mandarins: The Making of a Supranational Economic Order*, New York, NY: Pantheon.

Wachter, S.M., Cho, M. and Tcha, M.J. (2014) *The Global Financial Crisis and Housing: A New Policy Paradigm*, London: Edward Elgar.

Wacquant, L. (2007) 'Territorial Stigmatisation in the Age of Advanced Marginality', *Thesis Eleven*, vol 91, no 1, pp 66–77.

Wales, R., Sir (2013) 'Evidence to the Select Committee on Communities and Local Government', Monday 25 March, Question 323. Available at: http://www.publications.parliament.uk/pa/cm201213/cmselect/cmcomloc/uc953-v/uc953v.pdf

Walker, C. (2014) *Freeing Housing Associations: Better Financing, More Homes*, London: Policy Exchange.

Walker, P. (1977) *The Ascent of Britain*, London: Sidwick and Jackson.

Walker, P. (1991) *Staying Power*, London: Bloomsbury.

Walker, R. (2016) 'The Inequality Machine', in R. Walker and S. Jeraj (eds) *The Rent Trap: How We Fell Into It and How We Get Out Of It*, London: Pluto Press, pp 113–33.

Walker, R. and Jeraj, S. (2016) *The Rent Trap: How We Fell Into It and How We Get Out Of It*, London: Pluto Press.

Walks, A. (2016) 'Homeownership, Asset-based Welfare and the Neighbourhood Segregation of Wealth', published online, 14 April. Available at: http://www.tandfonline.com/action/showAxaArticles?journalCode=chos20

Ward, C. (1976) 'Preface', in J.F.C. Turner (ed) *Housing by People: Towards Autonomy in Building Environments*, London: Marion Boyars, pp 4–10.

Ward, S.V. (2004) *Planning and Urban Change*, London: Sage.

Warp (2013) 'Press Comments on Cathy'. Available at: http://www.jeremysandford.org.uk/jsarchive/warp-press-comment-on-cathy.html

Warren, C. and McKee, A. (2011) 'The Scottish Revolution? Evaluating the Impacts of Post-Devolution Land Reform', *Scottish Geographical Journal*, vol 127, no 1, pp 17–39.

Watson, M. (2008) 'Constituting Monetary Conservatives via the "Savings Habit": New Labour and the British Housing Market Bubble', *Comparative European Politics*, vol 6, no 3, pp 285–304. Available at: http://dx.doi.org/ 10.1057/cep.2008.12

Weiler, P. (2000) 'The Rise and Fall of the Conservatives' "Grand Design for Housing", 1951–64', *Contemporary British History*, vol 14, no 1, pp 122–50.

Wells, H.G. (1905) *A Modern Utopia*, London: Chapman and Hall.

Welsh Audit Office (2012) 'Progress in Meeting the Welsh Housing Quality Standard'. Available at: https://www.audit.wales/system/files/publications/Progress_in_delivering_the_Welsh_Housing_Quality_Standard_English_2012.pdf

Wemyss, Lord (1884) 'Hansard', third series, CCLXXXIV, 1700–1703.

Wheatley, J. (1914) *A Reply to the Critics of £8 Cottages*, Glasgow: Civic Press.

White, R.W. (1992) *Rude Awakenings: What the Homeless Crisis Tells Us*, San Francisco, CA: ICS Press.

Whitehead, C. (1980) 'Fiscal Aspects of Housing', in C. Sandford, C. Pond and R. Walker (eds) *Taxation and Social Policy*, London: Heinemann, pp 68–73.

Wightman, A. (2013) *The Poor Had No Lawyers: Who Owns Scotland (and How They Got It)*, Edinburgh: Birlinn.

Wilcox, S. (2016) 'Pushing the Social Sector to the Margins', in S. Wilcox, J. Perry, M. Stephens and P. Williams (eds) *UK Housing Review 2016*, Coventry: Chartered Institute of Housing, pp 14–20.

Wilcox, S., Fitzpatrick, S., Stephens, M., Pleace, N., Wallace, A. and Rhodes, D. (2010) *The Impact of Devolution: Housing and Homelessness*, York: Joseph Rowntree Foundation.

Wilcox, S., Perry, J. and Williams, P. (2014) *UK Housing Review: 2014 Briefing Paper*, London: Chartered Institute of Housing.

Wilcox, S., Perry, J. and Williams, P. (2015) *UK Housing Review: 2015 Briefing Paper*, London: Chartered Institute of Housing.

Wilcox, S. Perry, J., Stephens, M. and Williams, P. (2016) *UK Housing Review 2016*, London: Chartered Institute of Housing.

Wilding, M. (2015) 'Battle for Birmingham', *Inside Housing*, 13 August.

Willetts, D. (1992) *Modern Conservatism*, London: Penguin.

Williams, N.J., Sewel, J.B. and Twine, F.E. (1987) 'Council House Sales and the Electorate: Voting Behaviour and Ideological Implications', *Housing Studies*, vol 4, no 2, pp 274–82.

Williams-Ellis, C. (1930) 'Wales and the Octopus', in *Welsh Housing and Development Year Book, No 1*, Cardiff: Welsh Housing and Development Association, pp 71–3.

Williams-Ellis, C. (ed) (1937) *Britain and the Beast*, London: J.M. Dent and Sons.

Williams-Ellis, C. (1996 [1928]) *England and the Octopus*, London: Council for the Protection of Rural England.

Williamson, P. (1999) *Stanley Baldwin: Conservative Leadership and National Values*, Cambridge: Cambridge University Press.

Wilson, D. (1970) *I Know It Was the Place's Fault*, London: Oliphants.

Wilson, D. (2011) *Memoirs of a Minor Public Figure*, London: Quartet.

Wilson, W. (2011) *The Reform of Housing Revenue Account Subsidy*, Standard Note: SN/SP/4341, London: House of Commons.

Wilson, W. (2013) *Homelessness in England*, SN/SP/1164, London: House of Commons.

Wilson, W. (2014) *The Fair Rent Regime*, SN/SP/638, London: House of Commons.

Wintour, P. (2012) 'We Need to Build Houses on a Third More Land, Says Planning Minister', *Guardian*, 27 November.

Wohl, A.S. (1977) *The Eternal Slum: Housing and Social Policy in Victorian London*, London: Edward Arnold.

Wohl, A.S. (1983) *Endangered Lives: Public Health in Victorian Britain*, London: Methuen.

Wolf, M. (2015) 'The Solution to England's Housing Crisis Lies in the Green Belt', *Financial Times*, 5 February.

Woolton, Lord (1952) 'Woolton, "A Property Owning Democracy"', Public Records Office: CAB129/53, C(52)207, 20 June.

Work Foundation (2012) *People of Place: Urban Policy in an Age of Austerity*, Lancaster: Work Foundation.

Wright, O. (2016) 'Developers Accused of Profiting by Restricting Supply of New Homes', *Independent*, 2 March.

Wright, T. (ed) (2000) with Clements, R., Gay, O., Seaton, P.S., Weston, A.S., Winetrobe, B.K. and Wood, E. *The British Political Process*, London: Routledge.

Yelling, J.A. (1992) *Slums and Redevelopment: Policy and Practice in England, 1918–45, with Particular Reference to London*, London: UCL Press.

Yelling, J.A. (1995) 'Public Policy, Urban Renewal and Property Ownership, 1945–55', *Urban History*, vol 22, pp 48–62.

Yorkshire Television (1975) *Johnny Go Home*, Leeds: Yorkshire Television.

Young, H. (1989) *One of Us: Life of Margaret Thatcher*, London: Macmillan.

Young, K. (1970) *Sir Alec Douglas-Home*, London: Littlehampton Book Services Ltd.

Young, P. and Willmott, P. (1957) *Family and Kinship in East London*, London: Penguin.

Young, R. (2001) 'Housing Associations: The New Kid on the Block', in C. Jones and P. Robson (eds) *Health of Scottish Housing*, Aldershot, Ashgate, pp 89–109.

Young, R. (2013) *Annie's Loo: The Govan Origins of Scotland's Community Based Housing Associations*, Glendaruel: Argyll Publications.

Index